# Developments in British Politics 6

17630

*Developments* titles available from Palgrave

Laura Cram, Desmond Dinan and Neill Nugent (eds)
DEVELOPMENTS IN THE EUROPEAN UNION

Patrick Dunleavy, Andrew Gamble, Richard Heffernan, Ian Holliday and
Gillian Peele (eds)
DEVELOPMENTS IN BRITISH POLITICS 6
Revised Edition

Alain Guyomarch, Howard Machin, Peter A. Hall and Jack Hayward (eds)
DEVELOPMENTS IN FRENCH POLITICS 2

Gillian Peele, Christopher Bailey, Bruce Cain and B. Guy Peters (eds)
DEVELOPMENTS IN AMERICAN POLITICS 4

Paul Heywood, Erik Jones and Martin Rhodes (eds)
DEVELOPMENTS IN WEST EUROPEAN POLITICS 2

Gordon Smith, William E. Paterson and Stephen Padgett (eds)
DEVELOPMENTS IN GERMAN POLITICS 2

Stephen White, Judy Batt and Paul Lewis (eds)
DEVELOPMENTS IN CENTRAL AND EAST
EUROPEAN POLITICS 2

Stephen White, Alex Pravda and Zvi Gitelman (eds)
DEVELOPMENTS IN RUSSIAN POLITICS 5

*Of related interest*

Ian Holliday, Andrew Gamble and Geraint Parry (eds)
FUNDAMENTALS IN BRITISH POLITICS

If you have any comments or suggestions regarding the
above or other possible *Developments* title, please write to
Steven Kennedy, Palgrave, Houndmills, Basingstoke RG21 6XS, UK
or e-mail s.kennedy@palgrave.com

# Developments in British Politics 6

## Revised edition

**Edited by**

**Patrick Dunleavy**

**Andrew Gamble**

**Richard Heffernan**

**Ian Holliday**

**and**

**Gillian Peele**

palgrave

Revised edition published 2002 by
PALGRAVE
Houndmills, Basingstoke, Hampshire RG21 6XS and
175 Fifth Avenue, New York, N.Y. 10010
Companies and representatives throughout the world

PALGRAVE is the new global academic imprint of
St. Martin's Press LLC Scholarly and Reference Division and
Palgrave Publishers Ltd (formerly Macmillan Press Ltd).

ISBN 0–333–97389–5

This book is printed on paper suitable for recycling and made from
fully managed and sustained forest sources.

A catalogue record for this book is available from the British Library.

Library of Congress Cataloging-in-Publication Data
Developments in British politics 6 / edited by Patrick Dunleavy . . . [et al.].—Rev. ed.
    p. cm.
  Includes bibliographical references and index.
  ISBN 0–333–97389–5 (pbk.)
  1. Great Britain—Politics and government—1979–1997. 2. Great Britain–Politics and
  government—1997– I. Title: Developments in British politics six. II. Dunleavy, Patrick.
  JN231 .D494 2002
  941.085'9—dc21                                                        2002017003

Copy-edited and typeset by Povey–Edmondson
Tavistock and Rochdale, England

10  9  8  7  6  5  4  3  2  1
11  10  09  08  07  06  05  04  03  02

Printed and bound in Great Britain by
Creative Print & Design (Wales), Ebbw Vale

# Contents

# List of Figures, Tables and Boxes

## Figures

## Tables

## Boxes

# Preface

This revised edition of *Developments in British Politics 6* has been updated to take account of political events since initial publication in April 2000. The introduction has been substantially recast to cover the key reforms that have swept British politics in recent years and the 2001 general election. Chapter 8 on Elections and Party Politics is an entirely new chapter providing full coverage of the 2001 general election and analysing the impacts of political and electoral change, particularly the emergence of multiple electoral systems in Britain, on the British party system and on politics in general. Chapter 6 on Executives and Administrations has been substantially revised in light of changes in the core executive since 2000, particularly in Downing Street and to the Cabinet System. Other chapters have been reworked and updated, principally to remove out-of-date material but without including substantial new material. A more fundamental reassessment of developments since 2000 will be provided in *Developments in British Politics 7*, which is already in preparation for publication in the mid-term of the second Blair government.

We would like to thank our contributors once again for their efforts to make sense of the major reforms sweeping the British polity, and for placing those reforms in the context of wider political science debates. As ever, we would also like to pay particular thanks to our publisher, Steven Kennedy, for his customary insight, drive and good-natured encouragement. With this revised edition we welcome Richard Heffernan to the editorial team.

*Patrick Dunleavy*
*Andrew Gamble*
*Richard Heffernan*
*Ian Holliday*
*Gillian Peele*

---

This revised edition supersedes the original web update material to *Developments in British Politics 6*. Any further update material in the light of developments after this revised edition went to press will be posted at the same address:
< http://www.palgrave.com/politics/dunleavy > .

---

# Acknowledgements

The editors and publishers thank the following for permission to reproduce copyright material: Sage, for Table 14.1, from G. Esping Andersen (ed.), *Welfare States in Transition: National adaptations in global economics* (1996); Policy Press, for Table 14.2, from T. Burchardt and J. Hills, 'Public Expenditure and the Public/Private Mix', in M. Powell (ed.), *New Labour, New Welfare State* (1999); The National Assembly for Wales, for Box 7.1, from *Record of Proceedings* of the debate on 21 July 1999.

# Notes on the Contributors

**Pete Alcock** is Professor of Social Policy and Administration at the University of Birmingham and Head of the Department of Social Policy and Social Work. He is the author of *Social Policy in Britain* and *Understanding Poverty* and co-editor of *The Student's Companion to Social Policy*, as well as number of other books and articles.

**Philip Cowley** is Lecturer in the Department of Politics at the University of Hull. One of life's deputies, he is Deputy Director of the Centre for Legislative Studies and Deputy Editor of the *Journal of Legislative Studies*. His publications include *Conscience and Parliament* (ed.) and over 30 articles and chapters.

**Patrick Dunleavy** is Professor of Government at the London School of Economics. Educated at Corpus Christi College, Oxford, and Nuffield College, Oxford, he worked at the Open University before moving to the LSE in 1979. He has published *Democracy, Bureaucracy and Public Choice* (1991) and many other books and papers.

**Steven Fielding** is Senior Lecturer in the School of English, Sociology, Politics and Contemporary History, University of Salford. His recent publications include *Labour: Decline and Renewal* (1999), *The Labour Party: 'Socialism' and Society since 1951* and *'England Arise!' The Labour Party and Popular Politics in 1940s Britain*.

**Elizabeth Frazer** is Official Fellow and Tutor in Politics, New College, Oxford, and lecturer in Politics, Faculty of Social Studies, University of Oxford. She is author of *The Problems of Communitarian Politics: Unity and Conflict*. Recent work also includes articles on political education. Her current research is focused on normative models of 'public life'.

**Andrew Gamble** is Professor of Politics and Director of the Political Economy Research Centre, University of Sheffield. His books include *Politics and Fate*, and *After Empire: British Politics at the Beginning of the Twenty-first Century*. He is co-editor of *Fundamentals in British Politics* and *The New Social Democracy*.

**Richard Heffernan** is Lecturer in Government and Politics at The Open University. His publications include *New Labour and Thatcherism: Political Change in Britain*, *The Labour Party: A Centenary History* and *Defeat from the Jaws of Victory: Inside Kinnock's Labour Party*.

**Simon Hix** is Reader in European Union Politics and Policy at the London School of Economics and Political Science. His publications include *The Political System of the European Union* and (with C. Lord) *Political Parties in the European Union*.

**Ian Holliday** is Professor of Policy Studies at the City University of Hong Kong. His recent publications include *The British Cabinet System* (co-authored), *Fundamentals in British Politics* (co-edited) and journal articles on British politics and policy. He co-edits the journal *Party Politics*.

**Andrew Jordan** lectures in environmental politics in the School of Environmental Sciences at the University of East Anglia. He has published extensively on issues surrounding the long-term impact of the EU on the traditional style, structures and procedures of British environmental policy. He co-edits the journals *Environment and Planning C (Government and Policy)* and *Global Environmental Change*, and is a contributing author of the 2001 Intergovernmental Panel on Climate Change (IPCC) report.

**Helen Margetts** is Professor of Political Science at the School of Public Policy, University College London. She is the author of *Information Technology in Government: Britain and America* and has written many journal articles on electoral systems, government information and communication technologies and administrative reform.

**Gillian Peele** is Fellow and Tutor in Politics at Lady Margaret Hall, Oxford. She is the author of *Governing the UK*, and an editor of *Developments in American Politics 3*. She is currently working on a study of the Conservative Party since 1979.

**Jon Pierre** is Professor of Political Science at the University of Gothenburg, Sweden. He previously held a chair in politics at the University of Strathclyde. His recent publications include *Governance, Politics and the State* (with Guy Peters), *Debating Governance: Authority, Steering and Networks* (ed.) and *Partnerships in Urban Governance: European and American Experiences* (ed.).

**Margaret Scammell** is Lecturer in Media and Communications, Department of Social Psychology, London School of Economics. Recent books include *Designer Politics*, *On Message: Communicating the Campaign*, and *Media, Journalism and Democracy* (edited).

**Joanna Spear** is a Senior Lecturer in War Studies at King's College London. Her research interests include US and British foreign policy, the international defence trade and arms control and disarmament. Her publications include *Carter and Arms Sales* and *The Changing Labour Party* (edited with Martin J. Smith).

**Gerry Stoker** is Professor of Politics at the University of Manchester. His most recent publications are (ed.) *The New Management of British Local Governance* and (ed.) *The New Politics of British Local Governance*.

**Colin Thain** is Professor of Comparative Public Policy at the University of Ulster. He is co-author of *The Treasury and Whitehall* and author of forthcoming books on comparative budgeting in the G7 and UK economic policy.

**Paul Webb** is Professor of Politics at the University of Sussex. Associate Editor of *Party Politics*, he is the author of *The Modern British Party System*, *Trade Unions and the British Electorate* and numerous chapters and articles on British and comparative party politics. He is currently co-editing two comparative volumes on parties in democratic societies for Oxford University Press.

# Chapter 1

# Introduction: Into Labour's Second Term

PATRICK DUNLEAVY, ANDREW GAMBLE,
RICHARD HEFFERNAN, IAN HOLLIDAY AND GILLIAN PEELE

The outcome of the June 2001 General Election was never in doubt, its most remarkable feature that it was as near a mirror image of the 1997 result as could be imagined. The re-election of the Labour government with another landslide Commons majority was long a forgone conclusion. Throughout the 1997 Parliament, one or two perhaps rogue autumn 2000 polls aside, the Labour Party never ceded a commanding opinion poll lead, and therefore duly secured, for the first time in its 101-year history, a second term for a Labour government. The parties' share of the vote was more or less identical as in 1997, the swing between parties essentially non-existent, and this was sufficient to grant Labour a House of Commons majority of 166, the second largest Commons majority since 1945, Labour's 179 1997 majority being the largest.

Of those voting, a plurality (nowhere near an absolute majority) of electors (and only 25 per cent of the total electorate) endorsed Labour, sufficient in terms of Commons seats to provide the government with, in Tony Blair's words, a renewed mandate and an instruction to deliver on its pledges. However, the election also saw a precipitous drop in turnout, down from 71.4 per cent to 59.4, a unprecedented fall of 12 per cent and an all-time low in modern electioneering. Although the electoral base fashioned by New Labour has propelled the party into government two elections running, fewer electors, firm Labour partisans aside, perhaps voted Labour in 2001 with any deep sense of enthusiasm. Less than ever before felt sufficiently enthused to register a vote, and the same can perhaps be said for Conservative voters as the Conservative Party drifted ever rightwards in search of a non-European Britain and ever lower levels of taxation and public expenditure. A fall in turnout of the magnitude witnessed in 2001 may reflect a rise in voter hostility, ignorance or simply plain indifference to the political process. Alternatively, it may simply reflect the fact that electors were demotivated to vote by an electoral contest when its result, a Labour victory, was never in doubt.

Yet, if the 2001 election was a non-event, a groundhog day rerun of 1997, many argue that the same cannot be said for the political transformations

1

currently being enacted in Britain. At the beginning of the twenty-first century there are sharply differing views as to where British politics is heading, and what impacts these political changes may have upon the traditional form of the Westminster model of government, one hitherto predicated on the majoritarian political system and centralized government that underpins the unitary British state. One argument is that British politics is much as it has always been; change happens very slowly and incrementally, and in a context which is heavily determined by the legacies of the past. A second argument, and one with which the editors of this book have more sympathy, is that the combined impact of major structural changes are steadily transforming the substance and style of British politics. The immediate origin of these changes can be traced to events and decisions taken since the Labour government took office in 1997, but they have much deeper historical roots. How far these changes will go and whether they will be fully implemented remains to be seen, and it is with the shape of this emerging polity that this book is concerned.

## At the heart of Europe?

The first major structural change involves the UK's relationship with Europe, expressed most sharply in the issue of whether Britain should or should not join the European currency union. The UK, like Denmark and Sweden, met the conditions of membership, but chose not to enter in the first phase. This was, however, only the latest in a series of episodes that have characterized Britain's uneasy relationship with the EU ever since the first steps to European integration were taken in the 1950s. Gradually the UK has engaged with Europe, and has accepted (usually with a time lag) every major step towards closer integration. But the single currency dramatizes once again the crucial issue of sovereignty and how prepared Britain should be to merge or pool its decision-making capacities with the rest of Europe in the pursuit of its national interest. This issue has in the past split both major parties. In the 1960s, 1970s and early 1980s, it caused most problems for Labour: the party fought the 1983 General Election on a pledge to take Britain out of the EU. Since the late 1980s, however, the Conservatives have been most deeply divided on the merits of closer integration.

The issue is whether the British national interest is best served by specific measures of cooperation like currency union or whether such measures mean an irreversible and unacceptable loss of control over areas of policy judged crucial for the well being of the British people. The difficulty for the opponents of further integration is whether it is possible to oppose closer involvement without advocating withdrawal from the EU altogether. So long as Britain remains within the EU the pressures for closer integration will be powerful and hard to resist, because of the clear benefits that can be shown to flow from them. Since joining the EU in 1973 Britain has been part of a multi-level polity that has had important effects on the way in which British political institutions operate. While cutting itself adrift from the EU and re-establishing itself as an 'independent' power is still possible, the decision on whether to join the euro will be a key moment, a fundamental strategic choice for the British state with far-reaching consequences for the British political system.

As British public opinion, inflamed to some extent by the tabloid newspapers, has moved in an anti-European direction, the Blair government has adopted a 'wait and see' stance on joining the euro. Being committed to a referendum on entry likely to be held some time in the 2001 Parliament, perhaps in 2002 or 2003, the government will have then to make a decision. At the moment, ministers support joining 'when the time is right', adopting a 'when, rather than if' attitude, but having declared in favour of entry provided certain economic tests are met and it is in Britain's 'national interest' to join, the government has yet to decide whether it is ready to declare totally in favour in practice, even if certain ministers are prepared to do so.

Standing behind the debate about the euro is the larger issue of how the EU is likely to develop in the years to come, and a key concern for the Blair government, as indeed for each of its predecessors since the late 1950s, is how it can best influence European developments to Britain's advantage. As a result, Labour Europeans, the vast majority of the parliamentary party, maintain that unless Britain becomes part of the euro zone a historic chance to shape the EU in Britain's national interest (and the opportunity to exert international influence through Europe) will once again be lost. While Blair is widely perceived to favour entry to the euro (yet stopping short from making an unequivocal declaration), the degree of enthusiasm within the Labour government, demonstrated by Chancellor Gordon Brown's studied caution, what he describes as 'pro-Euro realism', has been so far pragmatic in character. This reflects not only a measured approach to a vexing subject, but also the belief that monetary union may probably be inevitable and that Britain will have to join for economic and geo-political reasons, provided its macroeconomic stability is enhanced and that entry is politically beneficial, or at the very least not harmful, to the Labour government.

It has long been acknowledged that being on the inside European track offers the fullest opportunities for British influence in Europe, and, indeed, in the world. Labour believes that in Blair it has a statesman who can help set the European agenda in the post-Kohl/Mitterrand era. In addition, Blair is himself eager to position Britain as a bridge between Europe and the US (whatever Europe may think), forging a new Euro-Atlantic unity in the post-Cold War world, something that has clearly been evidenced in Labour's strong backing for the US and the war on terrorism following the destruction of the World Trade Centre and the attack on the Pentagon on 11 September 2001.

## A new constitutional settlement?

The second structural change is the programme of constitutional reform launched by the Labour government in 1997. The immediate spur for this programme was the reaction by the opposition parties to the way in which the country was governed between 1979 and 1997, but its antecedents also lay in failed attempts to reform the British constitution – including the House of Lords, the electoral system, devolution and freedom of information – which litter the twentieth century. Labour's programme has been the most radical and the most comprehensive since the beginning of the century, but it has also been beset with many problems and inconsistencies. The government has continued the trend towards centralization of power in Downing Street, at the same time as it has devolved power. The constitutional agenda makes sense only if there is change in ethos and a political culture that is much more tolerant of political diversity and pluralism. As one of the two main parties of the Westminster state, Labour has found it extremely difficult to embrace pluralism and to tolerate diversity, and has gone to extraordinary lengths to keep tight central party control over the new assemblies and leaders it has created. If the new forms of multi-level governance survive, however, this can only be a transitional phase; structures have been put in place which will deliver a more diverse and at times conflictual polity. Scotland, Wales and Northern Ireland will increasingly diverge from the Westminster model, and may use their position to challenge Westminster. Labour's current pre-eminence in the Scottish and Welsh assemblies masks the extent to which they could one day come into conflict with the Westminster Parliament, and even now the SNP and Plaid Cymru are powerful oppositional forces in Scotland and in Wales. The larger question of the UK's place in Europe, discussed above, is also being given different answers in the constituent parts of the UK, and could make EU politics and policy yet harder to manage from Westminster.

One notable feature of the constitutional reform agenda is that the experience of formulating and legislating complex schemes of constitutional change has shown how difficult it is for the government to control the way its initiatives develop once they 'go live'. Elections to the Scottish Parliament and the Welsh Assembly produced results that saw Labour in a much less assured position than had been anticipated. It is now forced to govern in coalition in Scotland, and as a minority in Wales. The introduction of a directly elected mayor in London proved politically embarrassing as Ken Livingstone, elected as an independent having been denied the Labour nomination thanks to a Millbank fix, proceeded to vigorously challenge the government's support for part-privatisation of the London underground. Of course, these developments in the core arrangements of the British political system do not sit altogether easily with New Labour's emphasis on internal party discipline and the prime minister's preference for highly personalized control within the government. However, once let out of the bottle, constitutional reform may prove a genie that can not be put back. The implication of devolved assemblies, of more powerful mayors, and of a bill of rights may be a greater pluralism within the state, the enhancement of checks and balances on the executive and a tolerance of diversity. Time alone will tell if this is so.

## Which way for British parties?

The third structural change is a radical ongoing reform of the party system, and the possibility of a fundamental political realignment. This, too, has not emerged overnight. The party system was severely shaken in the 1970s and 1980s and both major parties have been significantly changed, in terms of their organization, their ethos, their ideology and their policies. At the same time there has been a substantial growth of third parties, and this remains a key feature of the current party system, however disguised it may be by the lack of proportionality between seats and votes in the electoral system.

Both main parties have undergone a dramatic reshaping of their ideology and their interest coalitions in the last twenty years, and this alone makes a return to the old two-party system impossible. The old foundaions of Conservative support and ideology during the twentieth century – Empire, Property, the Union and the Constitution – have all been either weakened or undermined altogether. Thatcherism accelerated this process of eliminating the old institutional bases of Conservatism by means of its market fundamentalism and its success in destroying the institutional bases of Labourism in British politics. Ironically, it opened the way for the radical modernizing leadership of new Labour which has redrawn the ideological map of British politics to the Conservatives' disadvantage. The defining feature of Blair-led Labour has been its willingness to accommodate to the political and economic world within which it finds itself, its 'third way' agenda reflecting the pursuit of social reforms by empowering and liberalizing the market, championing wealth creation, promoting privatization, boosting business and encouraging entrepreneurship. In contrast, after 1945, building on a collectivist political worldview developed in the 1930s and 1940s, Labour's economic policy reflected an ideational framework in which the role of the state was to manipulate the market, controlling, directing and taming it through the social democratic, quasi-corporatist state. While the state retains considerable responsibilities for economic regulation and management, its involvement in the working of the market has been considerably reduced over the past twenty-five years. Contemporary mainstream politics having moved significantly away from the policy agenda associated with the post-war social democratic era, Labour, in economic policy terms, has moved to its right, abandoning old-style Labour statism and collectivism, thus colonizing political terrain previously occupied by the Conservative Party.

The ideological formula that stands at the heart of what is sometimes called the 'new Labour project' is both pragmatic and broad. The pragmatic element emphasizes means not ends, enabling Labour to accept the implications not just of markets but of the new global economy. By drawing on a number of different political traditions, the theorists of Blair's Labour Party are able to make an appeal across the political spectrum. They emphasize individual opportunity and community rather than equality. Social justice is expressed in terms of responsibilities and obligations as well as rights. There has been an explicit attempt to claim that Labour has become the party of 'one nation' in place of the the Conservatives. The liberal strand of the Labour Party's intellectual inheritance is emphasized for reasons that are both ideologically convenient and electorally strategic.

In government, Labour continues to strenuously oppose the high levels of taxation and public expenditure prevalent in continental Europe, claiming that it can deliver European levels of public service at American levels of taxation, an approach based on the 'third way', a modernised, neo-liberalized form of social democracy that hopes to embrace Anglo-American private economic initiative and continental European social compassion. As a result, having abandoned old-style Labour collectivism and 'tax and spend liberalism', the Blair government's watchword is prudence and responsibility, its policy to instinctively prioritize the needs of the private wealth-creating sector over the public wealth-consuming sector, when there is a conflict of interest between the two. Having adopted the privatization agenda of Conservative governments, Labour continues to pursue public–private partnerships (PPPs) in all forms of public service, most notably in transport, the London Underground, education and the NHS. So far, this has created a great deal of unease among many Labour backbench MPs and the trade unions, principally the GMB and UNISON, who have reacted strongly to the idea private firms should provide public services, while ministers continue to believe that the private sector can and will effectively provide public services.

Labour's current policy stance – and the policy record of the Blair government – reflects the fact that ideological differences between the parties (all too apparent in the 1980s) have narrowed significantly with the result that all parties are now avowedly pro-market. Although Labour still stands to the left of the Conservative Party, it is now a *centre party*, one able to draw support from the centre right as well as the centre left, able to mount a cross-class electoral appeal, and make significant inroads into Conservative support since 1992. This ability to win over and seemingly retain former core Conservative voters, particularly as class voting, the mainstay of the electoral process in the 1950s and 1960s, continues to decline, demonstrates why Labour is today an electorally successful catch-all party.

The plight of the Conservative Party has not been helped by its own failings, not least its unpopularity after eighteen years in government, poor leadership, party infighting, European obsessions, and an image of 'extremism'. Hamstrung by Labour's reinvention of itself as a centre party. the Conservatives spent the 1997 Parliament edging ever rightwards, obsessed with Europe, seemingly keen to turn back the political, social and economic clock back to the Victorian era, and unable to recapture political territory overrun by Labour. Of course, under Iain Duncan Smith, elected Conservative leader in September 2001, there is always the possibility that the party may stop 'edging rightwards' and prioritize vote gathering over policy purity, despite Duncan Smith's status as a right-wing leadership candidate elected in preference to the more left-wing Kenneth Clarke. Time alone will tell, but the desire to prosper electorally (some-thing the Conservatives have singularly failed to do since September 1992) often moderates a party's policy stance, something perhaps forshadowed by Duncan Smith's attempt to make the quality of public services the main plank of its attack upon the Blair government.

Of course, as Labour moved rightwards and the Conservatives foundered in the 1997 Parliament, the Liberal Democrats sought more political room to manoeuvre, keeping an eye out for the main chance. Labour's preparedness to cooperate with them while in government has waxed and waned since 1997, and although the parties agreed a raft of constitutional change just six weeks before the 1997 General Election, the Liberal Democrat subsequently found themselves on the sidelines. The innovative Joint Consultative Cabinet Committee set up in 1998 delivered little and was finally wound up in September 2001. While the Liberal Democrats welcomed many of Labour's constitutional initiatives, the one which is central to their own advance – reform of electoral arrangements for the House of Commons – has disappeared from the political agenda. Although the Jenkins Commission's proposals for reform of the electoral system attracted interest when they were released in October 1998, the government firmly kicked them into touch. Labour remained divided on electoral reform, Blair refused to champion it, Cabinet opinion was largely hostile and the issue was hastily shelved. The experience of new electoral systems for Scottish, Welsh and European elections in 1999 did little to win converts to the cause of change.

As a result, denied access to government, the Liberal Democrats remain uneasy bedfellows with Labour. As Labour straddles the centre ground of politics, inevitably flanked to its right by the Conservatives, the party increasingly finds itself to Labour's left, together with the Scottish Nationalists, Plaid Cymru, and the much smaller Greens and the Scottish Socialist Party and the Socialist Alliance. During the 1997 Parliament, policy differences between Labour and the Liberal Democrats, centred on tax and spend, increasingly became all too apparant. The Liberal Democrats excoriated Labour for its stewardship of the public services, savaging the government in language often reminiscent of Labour's charges against Thatcherite Conservatives in the 1980s. Claiming ministers had done too little, too late, and had squandered the opportunity to make lasting reforms, they proposed to increase income tax to pay for more spending in education and social services, and ran to Labour's left at the 2001 election. Of course, to prosper from a position on Labour's left means that the Liberal Democrats will need to make inroads into the Labour vote. The alternative, to attempt to replace the Conservatives, may be unlikely, given their current policies and political stance. Although having succcessfully built a firm base in the House of Commons with 52 MPs, it still remains to be seen if the Liberal Democrats' position to Labour's left will bring the party electoral benefits in the long term.

At the 2001 election, for the first time in British history, the majority of the electorate were probably no longer to the right of the Labour Party. That might change, but it is something that indicates the seismic changes witnessed in the policy stance of political parties since 1992, something that might in time herald a far-reaching, ongoing transformation in the politics of the British party system.

## Conclusion

In 2001, Labour won its impressive seats total by winning the support of just 25 per cent of the electorate. British politics is in a critical phase, and the coming parliament may well see the continued emergence of a more pluralist form of electoral and party politics, even if the plurality electoral system continues to benefit Labour at the expense of other parties. Declining levels of political participation seems a safe bet given recent trends. The structural changes surveyed in outline here pose individual and collective challenges to a polity that has long been one of the most stable in the world. The chapters that follow look in detail at distinct aspects of change in British politics, focusing strictly on what has happened since 1997 and what is in prospect in the early years of the new century.

In Chapter 2, Fielding considers the extent to which it makes sense to talk of a 'new politics' in the Blair years, and takes a resolutely sceptical line on the issue. Chapter 3 is a key contextual chapter. In it, Pierre and Stoker examine the complex nature of governance in the multi-level polity that emerged in the UK in the closing years of the twentieth century, and provide a framework within which many subsequent chapters operate. Hix in Chapter 4 focuses on one key element of multi-level governance, the supranational tier of the EU, and considers where Britain stands at the start of the new century. He pays particular attention to one of the issues of the moment, membership of the euro. In Chapter 5, Peele looks at the impact on law and the constitution of the reforms enacted since 1997, noting that it is in these domains that some of the most important effects are being registered. Holliday follows this in Chapter 6 by investigating the nature of the traditional powerhouse of British politics, the core executive, in the light of major structural reform, particularly after the 2001 election. He also considers the changing nature of executive and administrative politics in other parts of the British polity. In Chapter 7, Cowley examines legislatures and assemblies at all levels of UK governance, taking in the devolved assemblies, the Westminter Parliament and the European Parliament.

The focus changes a little in Chapter 8, where Dunleavy investigates the changing nature of British electoral and party systems in light of the 1997 and 2001 General Elections. Webb follows this up in Chapter 9 by considering how British parties are responding to the new demands of the electoral market. Scammell then looks in Chapter 10 at the structure of the media in the information age, and at its impact on politics. In Chapter 11, Margetts examines the shifting forms of political participation and protest that are being witnessed as conventional forms are displaced by new ones. Frazer reflects in Chapter 12 on contemporary meanings of citizenship, and on the ways in which British political culture is changing.

Economic policy is central to all governments' programmes, and the Blair government is no exception. Thain reviews new Labour's economic policy in Chapter 13, looking in particular at the important role of the Treasury under Brown in establishing the context for much policy-making and in shaping preparations for Britain's possible adoption of the euro. Welfare policy, deeply affected by core economic policy decisions, is analyzed by Alcock in Chapter 14. He considers the extent to which new Labour has a distinctive agenda in this broad sphere. In Chapter 15, Jordan addresses another important broad policy area, that of the environment, paying particular attention to transport and energy policy. The foreign and defence dimensions are investigated by Spear in Chapter 16, where the ability of new Labour to inject an ethical dimension into foreign policy is a major issue. In Chapter 17, Gamble provides a concluding summary analysis of the revolution in British government that is at present taking place.

# Chapter 2

# A New Politics?

STEVEN FIELDING

As the UK entered the new millennium, many commentators believed that British politics had been transformed. In their view, as Labour and the Conservatives appeared to have set aside their distinctive ideologies, the substance of party activity had been recast. In addition, declining participation in elections, devolution of power to Scotland and Wales, reform of the House of Lords, talk of regional assemblies in England and proportional representation, along with the increasing salience of the EU, seemed to indicate that the structure of political life was also in flux.

Labour under Tony Blair was seen as being at the forefront of this process. In 1994 Blair was elected leader of what he termed 'new Labour' and subsequently renounced many of his party's policies. After Labour's 1997 landslide general election victory, Blair outlined a 'Third Way'. In so doing, he was accused of aping the market-orientated approach of the Conservative governments led by Margaret Thatcher and John Major. After their defeat, the Conservatives also appeared to rethink established positions. Members of William Hague's shadow cabinet began to speak of the public sector in more positive terms: commentators thought the party's faith in market economics was weakening. Some claimed to see in this a 'post-ideological' or 'new politics', defined by the maverick Labour MP Austin Mitchell as consisting of: 'No passion. No poles. No fixed positions. No Blocks. No Right. No Left. Just multi-hued blancmange.'

Change, both superficial and profound is, of course, ever-present in social, economic and political life. However, the extent to which change has literally led to a 'new politics' is debatable.

## A 'new politics'

There have always been excitable commentators claiming to have detected the emergence of a 'new politics'; towards the end of the twentieth century the cry became ever more insistent. Pre-millennial tension encouraged a disparate gaggle of apparently authoritative intellectuals to argue that the West was experiencing massive economic and social transformations with profound political consequences. In Britain, many such observers were disillusioned Marxists who despaired of the left's inability to counter Thatcherite Conservatism. They considered the country was in the vanguard of what *Marxism Today* called the 'new times'. A major feature of the new politics is said to be a lack of significant disagreement between the parties, chiefly due to the impact of 'globalization' (Held, 1995). As will be outlined below, one of the agreed objects of policy after 1945 was to restrain the market through state intervention. By the mid-1970s, however, this was seen to be a more problematic proposition; by the late 1990s it was widely considered impossible. This change in perceptions of state capacity was due to three factors which, taken together, are generally held to constitute economic globalization. First, the power of financial speculators, considerable in any case, was said to have increased. The abolition of exchange controls, in conjunction with advances in computer technology, meant that governments either accepted the judgement of speculators or saw their currencies collapse. Whether they liked it or not, national leaders were steered in the direction of policies that favoured low inflation rather than low unemployment. Second, industrial employers were thought more willing and able to relocate their operations. Countries with high taxes and wages were considered in peril of seeing manufacturing take flight to low tax and wage societies. Finally, the level of international trade was said to have risen, putting a premium on competitiveness. As with the second factor, low labour costs and stable tax regimes were seen as imperative to success. Whatever their ideological complexion, governments across the world were told they had to please the financial markets so as to make their countries attractive to investors.

While few disputed that government capacity had declined since the 1970s, there was considerable doubt that globalization was quite the force it superficially appeared to be. Advocates of 'hyperglobalization' certainly believed that the nation state had become irrelevant (Ohmae, 1995). Yet, if financial markets were more powerful than hitherto, both the footloose nature of manufacturing and the increasing importance of international trade were questioned by some. Such sceptics believed 'globalization' was more smokescreen than reality, a concept designed to legitimize the restoration of capitalist interests after the 1970s world recession (Weiss, 1998). Others charted a more cautious path, thinking that governments retained an important economic role, albeit one significantly circumscribed by the developing world economy (Held *et al.*, 1999). Yet, even those who attacked it credited the term 'globalization' with great influence. If globalization was a 'necessary myth', it was one believed by most decision-makers across the world – in Britain especially (Hirst and Thompson, 1996; Marsh *et al.*, 1999). The potent nature of the 'myth' was enhanced by Communism's late 1980s collapse. If the Soviet bloc had been economically weak, its very existence constrained the progress of free-market capitalism (Hobsbawm, 1995). Communism's demise merely added to the triumphalism of market enthusiasts who now believed there was no alternative to societies based upon liberalized capitalism (Fukuyama, 1992).

If the dominant interpretation of international events seemed to compel parties towards the same macroeconomic policies, more domestic factors had a similar impact. Largely basing their views on American evidence, commentators pointed to the dominance of materially 'contented' voters among Western electorates as another check on party difference. Increasingly the only ones to participate in elections, members of the suburban middle class, were depicted as those who held the key to political power. All parties had to take account of their interests before those of any other group. Such people generally supported low taxes and government spending. This meant that no party could afford to advance policies specifically designed to help poorer members of society – who, anyway, tended not to vote (Galbraith, 1992). Apart from those processes that seemed to reduce the parties' room for manoeuvre, adherents of the new politics also alighted upon other developments which undermined the traditional class blocs that sustained partisanship in Britain and forced changes to the structure of political life.

The British economy underwent significant change during the 1980s and 1990s. Between 1979 and 1997 those employed in manufacturing fell from 32 per cent to 18 per cent, while the service sector rose from 58 per cent to 75 per cent of all workers. This transformation accelerated the decline of the 'traditional' manual working class and encouraged the further representation of women in the labour force. The rise of the 'knowledge economy' also meant that an increasing number of those in employment worked on the basis of their individual mental capacities (Leadbeater, 1999). In addition, post-war immigration meant that the population as a whole was more ethnically diverse. Consequently, Britain as elsewhere, was thought to be a less hierarchical and more permissive society than hitherto. People thought of themselves as individuals: class feeling, in particular, was in retreat (Giddens, 1994).

Established political parties were said to find adapting to this more complex social order difficult: representing the diverse interests it allegedly promoted cut against the grain of conventional political life. As a result, many lost faith in the parties and failed to participate in elections. The emergence of single-issue groups and direct forms of action further demonstrated the parties' irrelevance. Indeed, the universal battle between left and right, which had raged since the French and Industrial Revolutions of the later eighteenth century had, some claimed, ceased to mean much to the majority. The established working and middle classes which had sustained the conflict were breaking up while, owing to globalization state power, access to which had been its main prize, was no longer worth having (Mulgan, 1994, 1997). Cast adrift in a new world of flux, parties – which had once distinguished themselves through robust ideological argument – were now forced to adopt each other's characteristics just to stay afloat (Giddens, 1994). They also began to experiment with new forms of popular legitimation: hence proposals to devolve power, introduce referenda and reform the electoral system.

That change had occurred prior to the turn of the new century is, therefore, incontrovertible. The extent and meaning of this transformation is, however, debatable. Perception, it is argued here, is at some odds with reality. The desire to identify novel elements in contemporary politics led many observers to overlook underlying continuities with recent history. Others also over-simplified the character of that past and drew a spuriously clear line between 'old' and 'new'. To assess the novelty of the 'new politics', it is necessary to outline what it is thought to have replaced.

## The 'old politics'

The concept of the 'new politics' is juxtaposed with what political life is thought to have been like during the three decades following the Second World War. Yet, even a cursory investigation of this period reveals the extent to which it anticipated many of the themes familiar at the turn of the millennium. This is especially so with regard to the underlying substance of political activity; even in relation to the structure of politics, by no means everything is as new as it appears.

According to the classic view, the period 1945–75 saw both party leaderships in broad agreement over the essential basis of economic policy. Indeed, according to the leading authorities, Winston Churchill's wartime coalition government gave rise to a 'genuine fusion of purpose', inaugurating an 'era of consensus' defined as an 'historically unusual degree of agreement over a broad range of economic and social policies' (Addison, 1994; Jefferys, 1991). In contrast to the late 1990s, the contents of this 'agreement' included establishing a universal welfare state financed through progressive taxation and using government intervention to secure full employment. Such collective action embraced not only state ownership of some industries, but also the management of demand through manipulation of tax and interest rates as well as varying government spending, techniques associated with the ideas of John Maynard Keynes.

The nature of this alleged consensus is disputed: critics stress the continuing controversial nature of state intervention after 1945 (Pimlott,

1988). Moreover, some suggest it was only the election of Clement Attlee's Labour government in 1945 that led to the enhancement of state power. Labour's landslide forced Conservatives to accept much of Attlee's programme by the time Churchill was re-elected in 1951. Within the Labour party itself, many active members wanted the state to intervene far more than did their leaders (Fielding and Tonge, 1998). Others, in contrast, firmly believe the concept so flawed that it should be abandoned forthwith (Marsh *et al.*, 1999).

While 'consensus' is undoubtedly a problematic term it, nonetheless, indicates the extent to which, by the 1950s, both leaderships found themselves in broad, if imperfect, agreement over key economic policies. Echoing views expressed 40 years later, many intellectuals endorsed Daniel Bell's opinion that, across the West there was an 'end of ideology'. Yet, as will be argued in relation to contemporary politics, there was no 'genuine fusion of purpose'. As in the 1990s, the parties were confined by parameters based upon what was generally considered politically possible and economically necessary. Most voters were thought happy with what was described at the time as the 'mixed economy'; there seemed, moreover, no imperative economic case for change.

Moreover, if the leaderships adapted to what they took to be reality, this did not mean they had ceased to be ideological. That many commentators thought they had was due to the belief that ideologies comprised closed, fixed, wholly coherent systems of belief based on key precepts whose importance and meaning did not vary. Ideologies, especially those embraced by electorally orientated political parties are, however, more flexible than that: circumstances can alter the relationship between core concepts which may also be subject to reinterpretation (Freeden, 1996). Thus, despite appearances, Labour and the Conservatives continued to pursue, in a roundabout way, their long-established and distinct ends.

Labour's formal ideological purpose was contained in Clause Four of the party's constitution, first drafted in 1918 (Foote, 1997). This stated that the party sought to 'secure for the producers by hand or brain the full fruits of their industry by the Common Ownership of the Means of Production'. If nothing else, this denoted the party's general belief in the superiority of state over market with regard to promoting efficient production and greater equality. While some in the party read the clause literally, the leadership interpreted it in a flexible and cautious manner. Not wishing to alienate sceptical voters, even in 1945 the party promised to nationalise only natural monopolies and industries which had 'failed the nation'. By the 1950s, the leadership believed a more equal society could be built without a further significant extension of the public sector.

Modern Conservatism was, in contrast, concerned with reconciling an efficient market economy with the established social order (Norton, 1996).

How best to promote this equilibrium was constantly disputed. The election of 1945 bolstered the influence of reformers who argued that some state intervention was necessary. They asserted that limited nationalisation would strengthen the remaining – dominant – market economy and argued that the welfare state further legitimised the traditional order. They even pointed to the past to justify this accommodation, reviving Benjamin Disraeli's concept of 'One Nation' to demonstrate the party's long association with state paternalism. If the substance of post-war politics leads one to question the novelty of the 'new politics', this is less true of its structure. Even so, there remain many continuities.

First, the means by which politics was delivered was subject to limited criticism. In the aftermath of war, most believed in the utility of the British constitution: faith in the nation state – its ability to control its own destiny and maintain internal integrity – was supreme. Britain had, unlike other European nations, survived a world conflict intact; Labour politicians were also impressed by how easily the system allowed them to enact their manifesto. There was little belief, on either side of the political spectrum, that major constitutional reform was necessary. This lack of clamour for innovation was, however, historically unusual. The later nineteenth century had seen some radical Liberals call for a republic; even their more moderate colleagues sought Home Rule for Ireland, Scotland and Wales. The pre-1914 period had been one of constitutional turmoil as the Liberal government pursued Irish Home Rule and limited the power of the Lords. At the same time, members of the rising Labour party called for proportional representation and referenda. If the pace slackened after 1918, the minority 1929–31 Labour government, with Liberal support, would still have introduced electoral reform proposals had its life not been cut short by economic crisis. Post-war attitudes changed as Britain's economic performance became less satisfactory. Conservative and Labour governments of the 1960s sought entry into the EEC, a process completed by Conservative prime minister Edward Heath. The desire to 'modernize' the economy also involved casting a more critical eye on how the country was governed. In the late 1960s Labour attempted to reform the Lords but was defeated in the Commons. Heath also introduced wide-ranging changes to local government. This period saw the revival of demands for limited independence for the Celtic fringe; that led the 1974–9 Labour government to hold referenda on Welsh and Scottish devolution. Both failed to achieve necessary levels of popular support.

Second, it is indisputable that in the earlier period the two major political parties enjoyed higher levels of support than 50 years later. In the 1951 general election Labour and the Conservatives between them won 96.8 per cent of votes cast; 82.5 per cent of those entitled to vote did so. By 1997 these two parties accounted for the support of only 73.9 per cent of voters while turnout had fallen to 71.2 per cent. The basis for the parties' support is also thought to have been distinct. For most of the post-war period, Labour relied upon the support of two-thirds of manual workers while the Conservatives benefited from the votes of about three-quarters of the middle class. Nonetheless, this still meant they each required to win over significant minorities outside their main class bases to attain office. Consequently, both appealed to the whole nation rather than one particular class. Labour's big post-war victories prior to 1997 each followed this strategy. Labour won in 1945 describing itself – as would Blair – as the 'People's Party'; in the 1960s Harold Wilson sought to make Labour acceptable to the suburbs – just as Peter Mandelson did (Fielding, 1993). In practice, this meant the parties focused their attentions on the 'middle ground' of the electorate: skilled workers and the lower middle class. Such voters had weak political loyalties, determined by which party they believed was the most economically competent. Thus, as in 1997, both parties projected themselves as composed of talented economic managers best able to increase standards of living.

## A second 'consensus'

The 'post-war consensus' is generally agreed, even by those who believe in the term, to have ended during the 1970s. By then, the interventionism which had underpinned it was associated with failure. That state interference was to blame for Britain's economic problems is uncertain, but the ending of the post-war world boom which forced Britain and others into deep recession, did not exactly help. Thatcher's election as Conservative leader in 1975 coincided with a re-emphasis on the market within her party (Kavanagh, 1987). Many post-war Conservatives had seen state intervention as a necessary evil: by the 1970s it was bereft of necessity. Responding to Britain's faltering economic performance, Thatcher's predecessor Heath had won the 1970 election promising to reduce government interference. Events forced him to reverse course, although defeat in both 1974 general elections did not suggest he had won many friends for so doing. By the end of the decade, therefore, Thatcher had few economic or political reasons for adhering to even a watered-down version of Attlee's 1945 programme.

What became known as 'Thatcherism' was, therefore, less radical than is usually supposed. While opposed by One Nation Conservatives, the new leader still operated within the party's established ideological parameters. She aimed to liberate the market to preserve a social order circumstances now suggested was threatened by too much government. Moreover, the order Thatcher wanted to sustain was highly traditional, one in which trade union leaders knew their place, two-parent families were the norm and loyalty to the monarch was unquestioned. While anticipated by earlier attempts to make Conservatism popular with the masses, Thatcher's rhetoric made a strong appeal to well-off manual workers while reinforcing support within the expanding middle class. Her stress on individual freedom seemed in tune with cultural developments later noted by advocates of 'new times'. In the 1980s the Conservatives withdrew government from many areas occupied since the 1940s. The concept of progressive taxation was also undermined by the reduction of direct tax and its replacement by more regressive indirect taxes.

While the Conservatives easily distanced themselves from those policies taken to define the consensus, Labour's position was more difficult. Much of the post-war settlement had been dictated by the party's assumptions about state intervention. In this context, the 1974–9 Labour government proved painful as ministers attempted to pursue established policies. They found themselves forced by international currency speculators to curtail expenditure and allow unemployment to rise. Some tried to engage with this new context, which might be seen as early evidence of globalization. While endorsing equality as the ultimate object of policy, Labour's leaders questioned the form and scale of state action. Defeat by Thatcher prevented them developing these thoughts. Power within the party also fell into the hands of activists who accused their leaders of betraying 'socialism'. These activists formulated an alternative economic strategy which included more nationalization, enhanced regulation and higher taxes. Labour's appalling performance in 1983 demonstrated the unpopularity of these policies.

After defeat in 1987, Neil Kinnock determined to adapt to the new economic climate. Through a wide-ranging policy review, he argued that Labour had to embrace low inflation as government's immediate goal. He also recognized that taxing and spending had to remain at 'prudent' levels. After the review, Labour's economic policy proceeded from the assumption that, while the state had an important role, it was 'not to replace the market but to ensure that markets work properly'. By the time of the 1992 general election, Kinnock's left-wing critics wondered what difference there was between Labour and the Conservatives. However, while Labour policy was based on a highly creative interpretation of clause four, it still gave the state a more influential role than the Conservatives (Fielding, 1999). Moreover, Labour's object remained that of furthering equality – or 'social justice' as it was now called – so as not to frighten middle-class voters.

Enjoying only electoral triumph, Thatcher's stress on the market became unrelenting. The privileges of middle-class professionals, still the backbone of Conservative support, were scrutinized. Insecurity of employment, in the form of short-term contracts, was introduced to other salaried workers. By the early 1990s, there was a sense that the party had gone too far: its pursuit of economic efficiency through the market was endangering the social order (Gray, 1997). An early indication of Conservative troubles came in 1990 when the introduction of the controversial poll tax saw Thatcher replaced as leader by Major, who won the 1992 election. Major was, however, ideologically indistinct from Thatcher. His governments privatized what remained of the state sector and introduced market mechanisms into public services (Evans and Taylor, 1996). Major's ministers were unwilling or unable to address the concerns of many Conservative voters about the decline of public services, especially in health and education, and increasing evidence of fraying social cohesion. Following Thatcher, most thought these difficulties could be overcome by further curtailing state power. Ministers also initiated a 'back-to-basics' campaign which censured poorer members of society for contributing to their own poverty. To an increasing number of electors, such responses seemed more the problem than the solution (King, 1998).

It was at this propitious moment that Tony Blair became Labour leader. The party already rode high in opinion polls, but his objective was further to entrench Labour's support amongst former Conservative voters. This he calculated could be done only by assuring them that Labour adhered to most of Thatcher's policies. The new leader referred to his party as 'new Labour' and in 1995 revised clause four to dramatise how much Labour had changed. According to the new clause, instead of extending public ownership, the party was now committed to promoting a 'dynamic economy' in which the 'enterprise of the market and the rigour of competition' were central. Across the full range of social policy, Blair also encouraged the idea that individuals should become more responsible for their own lives and less dependent upon the state. In this, he echoed Conservative concerns that the welfare state had created a 'dependency culture'.

Blair's leadership signified, many suggested, Labour's abject surrender to Thatcherism (Hay, 1999). However, beyond the media spin, new Labour was 'older' than Blair wanted to admit (Fielding, 2000). Regarding clause four, as already indicated, Labour leaders had rarely looked on it as realistic. Moreover, Blair's clause stated that, while a 'dynamic economy' was desirable, it would have to be one 'serving the public interest, in which the enterprise of the market and the rigour of competition are joined with the forces of partnership and co-operation'. This still gave the state an economic role at variance with Thatcherite precepts.

In relation to social issues, Blair introduced a more populist gloss. As shadow home secretary he had promised to be 'tough on crime, tough on the causes of crime'. While being seen as a break with the past, Blair had merely asserted that crime should be punished and its underlying social causes overcome, which was a statement no previous Labour home secretary would have contested. Moreover, Blair – in contrast to Thatcher – adhered to a more liberal attitude to personal morality and advocated, for example, lowering the age of consent for homosexuals. If the new leader believed the unemployed should be less dependent upon the state, this was in the context of Labour's proposed 'welfare-to-work' programme. This initiative also qualified Blair's disavowal of raising taxes: it was, after all, to be financed by a windfall levy imposed on state industries privatized by the Conservatives.

Blair's leadership did, nonetheless, mark the culmination of the making of a second 'consensus', albeit one based upon an economic outlook at variance with its predecessor: if the first was Attlee's, the second was Thatcher's. Yet, the second 'consensus' was no less conditional and partial than the first: within the new parameters the parties still wished to pursue distinct goals. However, in the immediate aftermath of ascending to the leadership and winning national power, Blair, for obvious electoral reasons, wished to obscure that fact.

## The Third Way

If Labour easily won the 1997 general election, it did so less by applying new means and strategies than by applying tried and tested methods in an exceptionally focused and disciplined way. The party's message – that it was best able to run the economy – was promoted with a unique vigour; it was directed at the target group – disillusioned Conservatives – with an unprecedented ruthlessness. While much was made of the party's media tactics, these hardly constituted a revolutionary campaign. Moreover, without the widespread perception of Conservative incompetence and division, Labour's progress would have been much more difficult. The election was also fought on well-trodden ground: who were the best economic managers? Similarly, that so many in both the working and middle class believed Labour was best qualified was unusual but hardly unique: broad cross-class alliances had long been the prerequisite for winning power.

Nonetheless, the new Labour government was thought to have inaugurated a novel phase in British politics, a belief confirmed by Blair's assertion that his administration adhered to a Third Way, beyond the established positions of left and right (Blair, 1998b). This term generated much interest and was, unsurprisingly, developed by academics who already believed social and economic change required parties of the left to abandon old methods. Blair's Third Way rhetoric was very much their own (Giddens, 1998; Finlayson, 1999). According to Blair, the Third Way stood between Thatcherite Conservatism – leaving everything to the market – and Labour's post-1945 position – running everything through the state. On that basis, he claimed, 'New Labour is the new politics'. This assertion was, however, based on a crude caricature of the past: even Thatcher used the state when it suited her, whereas previous Labour governments gave the market a significant degree of autonomy. If inaccurate, these poles still defined Blair's position which, he stated, was based on a pragmatic use of market or state. What mattered was what worked, not what was dictated by ideology. Of course, Labour and Conservatives had always operated somewhere between the market and state while both had also claimed to embody the virtues of pragmatism.

Blair's rationale for the Third Way was that globalization was 'inevitable', even 'desirable'. He confirmed Labour's belief that government should now maintain 'strong, prudent discipline over financial and monetary policy'. If this had been established under Kinnock, Blair went further. Echoing the fashionable verities of the day, he claimed there was 'no right or left politics in economic management today' as 'the battle between the market and public sector is over'. Thus, the Third Way allowed for a further increase in the role of the market – if the case could be made. Minor state assets might be sold off if they served no useful purpose by remaining in public hands; private capital could be used to fund public projects if government finance was unavailable; and commercial service providers might be introduced should they be considered more efficient. Labour in power did all these things: it partially privatized the London tube and the air traffic control agency; extended the Private Finance Initiative; and allowed schools to be run by private companies. The state was now considered to be but one of the available means of facilitating collective ends.

Yet, if it was considered appropriate, Blair thought the state could still have an important role, albeit not one as direct as that assumed after 1945. Government, after all, needed to 'set a framework in which the potential and talent of our people is liberated, in which new businesses can be created and old ones adapt to survive'. It should also set minimum standards at the workplace and ensure a level playing field between employers and employed. This was why Labour in office introduced the EU's social chapter and a minimum wage, and gave trade unions a statutory right to be recognized.

## New political alliances

If the Third Way was more a development of existing themes than a clean break with them, it still marked Labour's further shift from the scale and form assumed by the post-war state. In that sense it might, as some have argued, be seen as evidence of the party's 'post-Thatcherism' (Driver and Martell, 1998). Yet such a description overlooks the extent to which the Third Way echoed similar innovations in other Western centre-left parties. Most prominently, the term was used by President Bill Clinton of the United States and the German Chancellor Gerhard Schröder. Despite their many national differences and historical peculiarities, such parties, like Labour, confronted globalization and electorates sceptical of government action.

Comparisons are often drawn between Blair and Clinton. Indeed, Blair has been accused of wanting to 'Clintonize' Labour. This said much about his desire to emulate Clinton's appeal to socially conservative middle-class voters who had last voted for a Democratic presidential candidate in 1976 (Rentoul, 1995). It led to the adoption of tactics employed by the successful Clinton presidential campaigns in 1992 and 1996 in which some leading Blair advisers had participated (Gould, 1998). This was, however, by no means unprecedented: in the early 1960s Harold Wilson enthusiastically purloined some of John F Kennedy's 1960 campaign themes (Rose, 1967). In contrast, as leader of a party which had never been socialist, located in a society which saw a national health service as tantamount to Communism, the American President had fewer concrete policy lessons to impart to Blair.

Labour had more in common with other European social democratic parties. These had also been historically based on the manual working class and looked upon state intervention as the means of transforming capitalism into socialism. Like Labour, they, too, had come to terms with globalization by distancing themselves from the working class, state action and the idea that capitalism was a temporary phase of economic development (Sassoon, 1997). Blair attempted to draw continental social democrats behind the Third Way banner, but with limited success. French prime minister Lionel Jospin was particularly scathing of something which claimed to be an alternative to socialism. In truth, the extent of new Labour's zeal for the market was unusual in European terms. Be it due to the impact of past authoritarian regimes, the influence of Catholicism or stronger indigenous Communist movements, continental Europeans took higher levels of state activity for granted. Even European Conservatives engaged in forms of intervention that horrified British Thatcherites. The Thatcher years themselves had made Britain's distinctive position even more apparent, encouraging voters to see the state in negative terms.

Labour's contemporary attitude to the market was, therefore, the result of Britain's different historical development. Yet, if a more market-based response to globalization than many continentals liked, Labour's Third Way was not wholly at variance with their concerns. Blair and Schröder especially shared similar views, expressed in a joint Third Way paper on the direction of economic and welfare policy (Blair and Schröder, 1999).

In outlining the Third Way, Blair emphasized the extent to which it drew on Labour's established outlook as much as that of Liberalism: the Third Way would reconcile the two (Blair, 1996a, 1998b). This said as much about Blair's tactical sense as it did about his ideological ambition. By the early 1990s, under Paddy Ashdown the Liberal Democrats embraced policies almost indistinguishable from those proposed by Labour. On becoming leader, Blair wanted to increase cooperation between the two parties. While Blair and Ashdown described this as creating a 'new, more constructive and more rational culture', which some suspected would lead to the parties merging, it derived from less novel and more base realities. Both leaders needed each other. The Liberal Democrats wanted a more proportional electoral system and many Labour members now supported change. An informal pre-election common front also promised to further marginalize the Conservative government and prepare the ground for a post-election coalition some thought likely. The 1997 result made coalition unnecessary but Blair still invited Liberal Democrats to sit on a cabinet subcommittee to discuss policy (see Chapter 6).

## The Conservatives in opposition

After the Conservatives' 1997 thrashing, the party's new leader, William Hague called for a 'fresh start' and advanced what he termed the 'British Way' – a deliberate counterpoint to Blair's Third Way. His room for manoeuvre was, however, limited. Hague confronted a situation in contrast to that faced by previous Conservative leaders after a Labour landslide. In the wake of 1945 the party could move much closer to Labour and still remain in touch with Conservative principles. After 1966 there was enough space to Labour's right to allow Heath to move towards the market without endangering electoral support. Hague's position was more comparable with that of Labour in 1951. Having lost to a party which had stolen many of their policies, Attlee and colleagues hoped Churchill's government would quickly revert back to pre-war Conservatism. Unfortunately, it did not and so Labour found it hard to criticise their opponents. Hague's situation was much the same. He could not distinguish his party from Labour by dramatically pushing economic policy in an even more free-market direction – this would have been electorally disastrous. Nor could he move too close to Labour – even his closest advisers believed the unsullied free market had to remain at the heart of Conservative doctrine (Willetts, 1997).

The Conservatives consequently adopted two responses to defeat. First, echoing the tactics of certain Republicans in the United States, Hague promoted a more 'inclusive' social agenda. In speeches he used words like 'caring' and 'compassion' because opinion surveys showed Conservatives were seen as antithetical to these terms. Hague also conceded that more public money could be spent on health and education – although this extra finance would not imply higher taxes. This attempt to win over doubtful voters, without compromising party ideology, needed an acute sense of balance not all possessed. When deputy leader Peter Lilley stated that he considered the free market had 'only a limited role in improving public services' he was thought to have gone too far one way and was sacked from the shadow cabinet.

This 'caring' Conservatism was, in any case, undermined by the party's opposition to most of the government's initiatives. Introduction of the minimum wage, social chapter and trade union recognition were seen as imposing excessive inflexibility upon employers. The indirect tax increases introduced by chancellor Brown were each met with woeful expressions. Labour's utilities tax was also resisted because Conservatives believed it would hurt shareholders' interests. When Brown's 1998 comprehensive spending review saw him pledge an extra £40 billion to health and education, his Conservative shadow described the chancellor as 'irresponsible'. This approach was consolidated at the party's 1999 conference which saw Conservatives reinforce their attachment to cutting taxes and reducing government spending (Conservative Party, 1999).

Hague opened up another front by identifying Conservatives with a defence of the 'British Way'. This was influenced by the 'civilized' or 'civic' Conservatism which leading thinkers and MPs David Willetts and Oliver Letwin had begun to develop. To their minds the 'little battalions' in society were vital to both order and liberty (Letwin and Marenbon, 1999). Hague claimed that even the limited advance of government under Labour after 1997 would destroy these little battalions and those uniquely British characteristics – such as 'our individualism and spirit of enterprise, our social mobility and our loyalty to local institutions' – which they fostered. This approach at least meant Hague did not have to rely upon purely economic arguments to distinguish his party from Labour. It also gave coherence to his otherwise eccentric opposition to Labour's banning of beef on the bone and hostility to fox hunting.

For all its apparent novelty, however, Hague had merely reinvented a well-established Conservative response to change, one as old as Conservatism itself. It was heavily indebted to the eighteenth-century thinker Edmund Burke. While they had never referred to a British Way, nineteenth-century Conservatives had adopted a comparable rhetoric to castigate reform-minded Liberals. Like the reviled Liberal leader William Gladstone, Blair was cast in the role of a meddlesome, cosmopolitan force wanting to impose foreign ways on a native people through an intrusive state. In this narrative, the Conservatives stood for sturdy indigenous values tested by time. If Hague did not wax lyrical about the 'roast beef of old England' he might as well have done.

## Political divisions

Despite some of the rhetoric of the Third Way, talk of a new consensus based on the irrelevance of left and right consequently needs qualification. One of the most important thinkers to believe this is the Italian Norberto Bobbio (1996), who argues that the question of equality is central to the left/right distinction. Bobbio's understanding of the term is relative rather than absolute. Thus, he does not mean the left seeks perfect equality but that, in contrast to the right, it wishes to reduce inequality and make natural inequalities less painful. In Britain, Conservatives long ago accepted the principle of legal and political equality; more recently, both parties formally adhered to gender and ethnic equality.

However, Labour and the Conservatives still assume discrete positions over income inequality. Conservatives rarely discuss equality except to attack schemes designed to increase it: Willetts argues that it is 'the key anti-Conservative concept' (Willetts, 1992; Gray and Willetts, 1997). By contrast, Labour has always sought to reduce inequality: according to some, this was the party's central historical objective (Ellison, 1994). Despite all their other policy changes, leading new Labour figures remained publicly committed to establishing what they generally referred to as a 'more equal society'. However, they asserted, the Blair government could not follow the methods employed by its Labour predecessors owing to changes in the social, economic and political context (Brown, 1999). During the immediate post-war period, poverty was less acute than it would become in the 1990s: full employment had largely eradicated it. Most people who wanted work could find it, while the real incomes of even unskilled employees rose. Labour leaders of this period believed they could further reduce inequality mainly by redistributing income – that is, taxing the better-off to finance improved welfare payments. In contrast, by the 1990s unemployment was endemic in many working-class communities. Yet, new Labour believed it could not be reduced by demand management due to globalization. It had also become politically perilous to increase tax rates to finance welfare payments sufficient to lift recipients out of poverty. In any case, as most of the unemployed were unskilled, they were unlikely to find work even in a buoyant job market as they lacked the necessary competence. For these reasons Labour ministers argued that it was better for government to invest in improving training opportunities rather than paying higher benefits.

That the unemployed could leave welfare dependency only if the state helped them develop skills was the basis of the 'welfare-to-work' programme launched in 1998. Financed by £3 billion from the utilities windfall tax, this promised to give the long-term unemployed appropriate work experience, training or education to make them more employable. Once in work, they could then benefit from other measures introduced by the government. These included a minimum wage, a lower starting rate of direct tax and the working families tax credit, all of which made the poorest members of the workforce better off.

Critics on the left of the party believed that if their leaders talked of reducing inequality they did not mean it. Brown, for example, defined his aim as increasing equality of *opportunity* rather than that of *outcome*. Yet, few post-war Labour leaders spoke of equality of outcome as desirable. While they wanted income inequality to decrease, like the Conservatives they saw merit in differentials, believing they promoted efficiency. The left also remained unhappy that new Labour had disavowed income redistribution through direct taxation and higher welfare payments. However, the rigour with which post-war Labour governments pursued these policies is doubtful, their performance in reducing inequality being much attacked at the time.

Labour doubters also overlooked the fact that chancellor Brown pursued redistribution by stealth, raising various indirect levies on the better-off to finance tax breaks for poorer workers. This led to a modest redistribution of income in the years following 1997. Indeed, the longer they remained in office, the more Labour ministers talked openly about tackling poverty. Blair's 1999 commitment to abolish child poverty marked a significant move from the restrictive promises made prior to 1997 and towards more familiar Labour ground. In opposition, Labour's leading figures had always stated that they did not want to abolish all forms of government intervention. Instead, they wanted to reinvent it in terms appropriate to the 1990s while, at the same time, remaining true to the party's established ends (Brown, 1995). The key example of poverty substantiates this rhetoric. In office, ostensibly working within free market parameters, Labour has moved cautiously in directions most Conservatives oppose. They thereby confirmed the continued existence of the party's distinctive purpose and the contemporary relevance of the left/right divide.

## The changing structure of politics

With regard to the structure of political life, many of the claims for a new politics cannot be sustained. While 1997 saw only 71 per cent of electors vote, active discontent with the party system remains muted. Moreover, those parties seeking to advance new issues, such as the environmentally inclined Greens, or pressure groups like Greenpeace, remain marginal. The two major parties, and Labour in particular, still dominate (Webb, 1995). The nature of the political process is, nonetheless, under greater scrutiny than for some time and the significance of constitutional issues unusually pronounced (Foley, 1998).

In 1997 Labour promised numerous constitutional changes. Yet, Blair had inherited much of this programme and was no enthusiast; devolution apart, in office he has been in no hurry to enact it. To Blair's mind, the purpose of reform was to conserve as much of the existing order as possible (Blackburn and Plant, 1998). Labour's promise to reform the Lords looked more like the last act of Edwardian Liberalism than a measure for the twenty-first century (see Chapter 5). The promise to introduce devolution represented more unfinished business – that of the Callaghan government of the 1970s. After their 1999 elections, the Scots found themselves governed by a Liberal–Labour coalition; the Welsh by a minority Labour administration. The very existence of these bodies will inevitably create some friction between centre and periphery. More than the threat of nationalism, Blair's difficulty is that both sets of electorates are more inclined to 'old' Labour policies than the English. However, the powers of the Scots parliament and Welsh assembly, are tightly circumscribed – even if the former enjoys modest tax-levying powers. The Labour leadership has, moreover, shown the alacrity with which it wants to maintain consistency between London, Cardiff and Edinburgh. Thus, the implications of devolution will be, if the government has anything to do with it, limited. Labour presented devolution as a means of saving, not destroying, the Union.

Perhaps the greatest threat to the Union resides in England. Having reluctantly accepted devolution, Hague questioned why Scottish MPs should influence English affairs. Condemned for raising the flag of English nationalism, his modest question had actually been asked many times before – usually by the rebellious Scots Labour MP Tam Dalyell. For the present, however, any 'English problem' is little in evidence. One possible way to circumvent its development is for Labour to give the English regions their own assemblies. Blair has, however, shown no enthusiasm for the federalization of Britain.

The question of electoral reform presently resides in limbo. Having appointed an independent Commission to recommend a more proportional system which, under the stewardship of Lord Jenkins it duly did, Blair has subsequently sat on the issue. The Jenkins formula – a compromise between the first-past-the-post system and a truly proportional set up – increases the chances of coalition government. Betraying his own caution, Blair is reluctant to put the matter to the people before safely securing re-election. The Conservatives oppose it, numerous Labour MPs are antagonistic – and, more importantly, the public seem less than enthusiastic. However, as Labour has already introduced proportional representation for Welsh, Scottish and European elections, it is clear how the matter is likely to be resolved. Should the Jenkins system be accepted, the probable implications for party politics appear clear. Many see it as guaranteeing Labour's grip on power for a generation, either on its own or in alliance with the Liberal Democrats.

The question of further integration within the EU is another matter Blair has avoided. This, again, is no new issue: it has split both parties since the 1960s. At first, it was Labour which suffered division; by the 1990s, Conservatives were most at loggerheads. The Conservatives had supported EEC entry, thinking it would help British industry by abolishing trade barriers. Since the 1980s, however, the European Commission has harmonized social and economic practices within the Union. This has had important constitutional implications: by 1992 European law took precedence over British statutes. Many Conservatives opposed this, arguing that it undermined national sovereignty while, in the form of the social chapter of workers' rights, it also imperilled the free market. In contrast, Labour leaders – in opposition at least – were more relaxed about the constitutional ramifications of harmonisation and broadly welcomed the chapter (Geddes, 1999).

At the time of the 1997 election, the next stage in the evolution of the EU, economic and monetary union (EMU), was in the offing. The most important element of EMU was the creation of a single currency, the euro, to which member currencies would be linked (see Chapters 4 and 13). Should Britain sign up to the euro, the substance of political life will be significantly altered: important economic matters, long the lifeblood of party debate, will be decided at the supranational level.

In contrast to Labour's cautious enthusiasm, Hague has committed the Conservatives to oppose EMU for at least a decade. Europe, like other issues with constitutional implications, was a matter on which he wanted to emphasize his party's differences with the government. This not only mobilized the Conservatives' core support but also made Hague's defence of the British Way appear more relevant. Labour's constitutional 'meddling', in particular the advance of what Conservatives like to describe as the European 'super-state', was another threat to Britain's native ways. However, while Blair's position on electoral reform and Europe remains opaque, and the implications of devolution and Lords reform continue to be modest, defending the 'British Way' will, in all likelihood, be little more than a minority pursuit.

## Conclusion

This chapter has been resolutely cautious. Terms such as 'consensus' and 'globalization' – along with the 'new politics' itself – are all too often taken to represent reality. They are, however, only partial or exaggerated representations whose connection to actual processes is, at best, problematic. This does not mean they are wholly false; it does mean they need to be applied with care. While the structure of political life is changing, it is doing so less dramatically and more slowly than some hope. Most strikingly, the major questions which articulate contemporary party debate and resonate with the public would have been familiar to Blair's post-war predecessors. First, how best can market or state deliver prosperity? Second, how much of the wealth generated by economic activity should be taken into public hands? And, finally, how best should government spend that money? Many of the assumptions which now provide answers to these 'getting and spending' questions have changed in the last 20 years. Nonetheless, as illustrated above, in responding to them, Labour gives evidence of remaining on the left; Conservatives indicate they continue to reside on the right.

# Chapter 3

# Towards Multi-Level Governance

JON PIERRE and GERRY STOKER

Governing Britain today is a more complex and challenging task than ever before. Collective interests are defined and pursued at four different institutional levels: the local authority, the region, the state, and the EU. To this list could be added experiments with metropolitan government (such as the new arrangements for Greater London) and also institutions operating below the local authority. We also note the growing regulatory and 'steering' role of transnational institutions such as the World Trade Organization and, to a lesser extent, organizations such as the International Monetary Fund (IMF) and the World Bank. Finally, we could add ad hoc international agreements which target subnational institutions as the main actors to attain them, such as the Rio, Tokyo and Osaka summits in the environmental protection sector. Even a quick glance at this multi-layered system suggests that the risk of incoherence, contradiction and confusion is overwhelming.

Furthermore, at each tier of government political leaders are confronted by contingencies and dependencies that significantly impair their ability to proactively 'steer' society in the traditional sense. Twenty years ago political institutions and political leaders were much more self-reliant and it was assumed – for good reasons – that the state governed Britain. Today, the role of the *government* in the process of *governance* is much more contingent. Local, regional, and national political elites alike seek to forge coalitions with private businesses, voluntary associations and other societal actors to mobilize resources across the public–private border in order to enhance their chances of guiding society towards politically defined goals.

Governing Britain – and indeed any other advanced western democratic state – has thus become a matter of multi-level governance. To understand the challenge of governing requires a focus on multiple locations of decision-making – in both spatial and sectoral terms – and the way in which exchanges between actors in those locations are conducted and managed. The first part of this chapter explores how best to conceptualise this emerging world of multi-level governance. The developing world of multi-level governance is, of course, populated by many new or reformed institutions. The Labour government elected in 1997 has produced an extensive programme of institutional reform ranging from the creation of the Scottish Parliament to reform proposals aimed at local government. These reformed institutions and the structure of governing institutions that they have joined are examined in the second part of the chapter. The third part of the chapter looks at some of the tensions and difficulties associated with the reform programme and emerging system of multi-level govern-ance. The concluding section contains alternate scenarios about the future of UK governance.

## The challenge of multi-level governance

The past few years have seen a growing interest among scholars in different models of multi-level governance (Marks, Hooghe and Blank, 1995; Kohler, Koch and Knodt, 1997; Smith, 1997). While much of this research has been focused on the EU, recent institutional reform at the regional tier of government has clearly encouraged the application of this conceptual framework on nation states as well. A baseline definition of multi-level governance is that it refers to negotiated exchanges between systems of governance at different institutional levels. Multi-level governance emerges as a coordinating instrument in institutional systems where hierarchical command and control mechanisms have been relaxed or abolished. It draws on bargaining rather than submission and public–private mobilization rather than public sector specificity. Most impor-tantly, multi-level governance makes no pre-judgements about the hierarchical order of institutions: global patterns of governance can hook up with local institutions just as local or regional coalitions of actors can by-pass the nation-state level and pursue their interests in international arenas.

Britain's delicate negotiations in the autumn of 1999 over the lifting of the ban on British beef imposed by the French government despite the view of the EU's scientific panel that there was no case for the ban illustrates a process where the hierarchical route was initially rejected in favour of a negotiation process. Given the interests of Britain's farmers in selling their meat and the potential of considerable delay if a more hierarchical legal route were pursued, the British government opted first for a governance solution.

A key message of the governance perspective is to challenge constitu-tional/formal understandings of systems of government. In the British case it provides a challenge to the 'Westminster model' (Gamble, 1990). From the perspective of this model the British political system was characterized by parliamentary sovereignty, strong cabinet government and account-ability through elections. The dominant image was of a unitary state directed and legitimated by the doctrine of ministerial responsibility. Governance suggests that institutional/constitutional perspectives, such as the 'Westminster model', are limited and misleading. The structure of government is fragmented into a maze of institutions and organizations. The 'Westminster model' in particular fails to capture the complex reality of the British system. It implies that in a unitary state there is only one centre of power. In practice there are many centres and diverse links between many agencies of government at local, regional, national and supranational levels. In turn each level has a diverse range of horizontal relationships with other government agencies, privatized utilities, private companies, voluntary organizations and community groups. There is a complex architecture to systems of government which governance seeks to emphasize and focus attention on.

Boldly put, at least in terms of its governance the UK is not united. Scotland, Wales and Northern Ireland in key domestic areas of decision-making can go their own way whether it is over university fees, beef on the bone or policies in relation to local government. Scotland, Wales and Northern Ireland have also developed to a degree their own relationship with the EU.

However multi-level governance remains a slippery concept. The conceptual discussion is frustrating on several accounts. First of all, it is interesting to note that much of the discussion on multi-level governance is still very much about government, as Smith (1997) points out. This is obviously unfortunate: the notion of multi-level governance should be reserved for something broader than inter-governmental relationships. The significance of multi-level governance is that it looks as such relationships more as nested than hierarchical. True, institutional levels are nearly always 'nested' but multi-level governance emphasizes negotiated arrange-ments between clusters of actors at different levels. Such negotiated arrangements are created not because the levels of governments are hierarchical or 'nested' – if they were then there would be little need for negotiations – but precisely because much of the contemporary governance defies hierarchical orders.

The academic literature on governance is eclectic (Jessop, 1995). Its theoretical roots are various: institutional economics, international rela-tions, organizational studies, development studies, political science, public administration and Foucauldian-inspired theorists. Its precursors would include work on corporatism, policy communities and a range of economic analysis concerned with the evolution of economic systems.

Theoretical work on governance reflects the interest of the social science community in a shifting pattern in styles of governing (Stoker, 1998). The traditional use of governance and its dictionary entry define it as a synonym for government. Yet in the growing work on governance there is a re-direction in its use and import. Rather, governance signifies 'a change in the meaning of government, referring to a new process of governing; or a changed condition of ordered rule; or the new method by which society is governed' (Rhodes, 1996, pp. 652–3).

Reviews of the literature generally conclude that the term 'governance' is used in a variety of ways and has a variety of meanings (Rhodes 1997a; Pierre and Peters, 2000). There is, however, agreement that 'governance' refers to the development of governing styles in which boundaries between and within public and private sectors have become blurred. The essence of governance is its focus on governing mechanisms which do not rest on recourse to the authority and sanctions of government: 'The governance concept points to the creation of a structure or an order which cannot be externally imposed but is the result of the interaction of a multiplicity of governing and each other influencing actors' (Kooiman and Van Vliet, 1993, p. 64).

To develop an effective crime prevention strategy requires more than giving the police more powers or resources or tougher sentences from the courts. To tackle car theft, for example, vehicle manufacturers may need to be encouraged to change the design of their cars. Insurance companies may need to provide incentives through reduced premiums to those that have their cars better protected. Individual car drivers might need to be encouraged to take more care over the security of their vehicle. Local authorities, schools, probation services and voluntary organizations may need to coordinate action aimed at discouraging 'joy-riders' and provide alternative outlets for their fascination with cars. Inspectors of garages may need to be vigilant in detecting the bases of organized car theft groups. The coordination of all these actors and their actions is a key element of the art of governance.

The processes of governance lead to outcomes that parallel those of the traditional institutions of government. As Rosenau (1992, p. 3) comments:

> To presume the presence of governance without government is to conceive of functions that have to be performed in any viable human system . . . Among the many necessary functions, for example, are the needs wherein any system has to cope with external challenges, to prevent conflicts among its members . . . to procure resources . . . and to frame goals and policies designed to achieve them.

Governance is ultimately concerned with creating the conditions for ordered rule and collective action. The outputs of governance are not therefore different to those of government. It is rather a matter of a difference in processes.

In political science (Peters, 2000; Pierre, 2000; Rhodes, 1997a), governance has emerged as a leitmotif in almost all subfields of the discipline. However, approaches to governance tend to develop from two different vantage points. One perspective is to look at governance as those formal or informal processes of coordination that lead to the resolution of common problems and challenges. Here, self-governing networks have been suggested to be the key instrument of governance and are said to be a predominant role in governance in Britain (Marsh and Rhodes, 1992; Rhodes, 1997a). The other perspective looks at governance in a more state-centric perspective and asks questions about how traditional institutions are transforming to meet the challenge of governance (Peters, 2000). In this latter perspective, the state is assumed to remain the key actor in governance by virtue of the vast resources, broadly defined, which it still controls and also by the legitimacy it enjoys as the sole actor in society which can properly define the collective interest.

Regardless what perspective we apply to governance, it must be remembered that governance is a highly charged political process; there is, on reflection, little to suggest that governance should be any less susceptible to conflict regarding goal definitions and defining priorities than the traditional view of government. Governance is not about the end of politics but it is rather about the playing out of conflict and cooperation in a broader arena than the formal institutions of government.

Ultimately the contribution of the governance perspective may not be at the level of causal analysis or a new normative theory. Its value is as an organizing framework. The value of the governance perspective rests in its capacity to provide a framework for understanding changing processes of governing. As Judge, Stoker and Wolman (1995, p. 3) comment, such conceptual frameworks

> provide a language and frame of reference through which reality can be examined and lead theorists to ask questions that might not otherwise occur. The result, if successful, is new and fresh insights that other frameworks or perspectives might not have yielded. Conceptual frameworks can constitute an attempt to establish a paradigm shift.

The value of such frameworks can be found in their identification of what is worthy of study.

The governance perspective works if it helps us identify important questions, although it does claim to identify a number of useful answers as well. It provides a reference point which challenges many of the assumptions of traditional studies of government. It asks us to look at the way we are governed through a different lens.

The rise in importance of the EU and the array of new devolved institutions make the case for shifting to a governance perspective even stronger. Twenty years ago the argument for a governance perspective could still be presented, even then Britain was not governed through one centre of power (Rhodes, 1988). The constitutional developments of recent years make the case for a multi-level governance focus even more compelling.

## Developing the differentiated polity: the Conservatives' legacy and Labour's programme

The Conservatives during their long period in office (1979–97) were often critical of the interest of others in what they liked to describe as 'constitutional tinkering'. However looking back at their years in power it is possible to identify a number of legislative and institutional reforms undertaken by the Conservatives that, it can be argued, have had profound constitutional implications.

First there are the developments in our relationship with the EU (see Chapter 4). The Conservatives passed the Single European Act of 1986 which amended the founding treaties of the EC. The Act increased the scope for majority voting in the EU and strengthened the powers of the European Parliament in the legislative process. Above all it created the single market – an area without frontiers in which the free movement of goods, persons, services and capital is ensured. The Act also included general commitments to better cooperation over economic and monetary policy with the EU. The Maastricht Treaty paved the way to the establishment of a single currency in Europe although the Major government negotiated an 'opt-out' for the UK. It also laid out provisions for greater cooperation in the areas of justice and home affairs and repeated earlier commitments to common foreign and security policies. Maastricht also established further restrictions on the use of the national veto in EU policy-making and established some modest citizen rights for all peoples resident in EU countries.

Second there is the reduction in the powers and responsibilities of elected local government and the expansion of a world of local quangos. The Conservatives presided over a reduction of the powers and capacity of local government. They established a range of tighter controls over local spending. They abolished the Greater London Council and six Metropolitan County Councils. They replaced local rates first with the disastrous poll tax and then with the council tax. They removed the business rate from local control. Yet at the same time they recognized the need to have a local capacity to deliver key objectives so set about establishing new appointed agencies – 'local quangos' as they are called – to undertake key tasks. Local authority responsibilities in further and higher education were taken away and free-standing colleges and universities established. Training and employment responsibilities were given to Training and Enterprise Councils (TECs) in England and Wales and Local Enterprise Companies (LECs) in Scotland and run by appointed business and other interests. Urban regeneration tasks were taken away from local authorities and given to Urban Development Corporations (UDCs) and a range of other partnership bodies.

Third there is the sale of public sector assets to the private sector including most of the major public utilities and nationalized industries, such as gas, electricity, water (in England and Wales), railways and telecommunications. Fourth there is the restructuring of central departments and the creation of over 150 agencies. Core civil service functions such as policy advice and the preparation of legislation were left in the departments but executive and administrative functions were devolved to arm's-length agencies in which nearly 80 per cent of civil servants now work.

Labour has left the structural reforms undertaken by the Conservatives largely untouched. A more positive rhetoric towards the EU can be observed but the rules of the game have not been fundamentally changed. One of the first actions of the Blair government was to sign up to the Amsterdam Treaty which strengthened citizenship rights within the EU still further. It made EU decision-making structures subject to the Convention of Human Rights (ECHR) and established an Ombudsman for Europe. Local government has received some greater encouragement (as will be discussed below) but there has been no bonfire of local quangos although a number are in the process of restructuring. Nor has there been any programme of renationalization. The reforms of civil service structure have also been left in place.

What Labour has done, however, is launch its own major programme of constitutional reform and restructuring. It has established three devolved assemblies in Scotland, Wales and Northern Ireland (see Chapter 7). A new Greater London Authority with an elected mayor and a separately elected assembly was elected in May 2000. Regional Development Agencies (RDAs) were established throughout the remainder of England in April 1999 and they are seen by some as a precursor for full-blown elected regional assemblies. A further wave of reform has been launched by new Labour with respect to local government.

It is possible to see some shared connections between Labour's programme of constitutional reform. There is an underlying commitment to embrace some devolution of power from Westminster to the 'nations', the regions and localities. There is a recognition that developing leadership capacity at sub-Westminster levels of decision-making is an appropriate response to the complexities of the emerging world of multi-level governance. Yet beyond these general factors it is important to recognize that there have been, and remain, particular driving factors behind each element of Labour's reform package.

The case of Northern Ireland makes the strongest argument for uniqueness. The move to a settlement was one of the great events of the Blair government's first year in office. The legislative Assembly is part of a broader agreement designed to bring peace and political progress to the province. The basic structure of the settlement is what political scientists call a 'consociational agreement'. It includes cross-community executive power sharing; proportionality rules applied throughout the relevant governmental and public sectors; community self-government (or autonomy) and equality in cultural life; and veto rights for minorities. These and other complex features of the Belfast Agreement are designed to regulate ethnic and national conflict.

The demands for a Scottish Parliament, too, reflect a complex set of demands and influences. The rise of Scottish nationalism and its political expression from the late 1960s in the ability of the Scottish National Party (SNP) to win a sizeable proportion of votes were key driving factors. The reaction of the mainstream UK political parties was mixed. An attempt at reform failed in the late 1970s. Crucially under John Smith's leadership in the early 1990s Labour committed itself to a parliament, a promise which the Blair government has been able to deliver.

A major role in Scotland was played by a body called the Scottish Constitutional Convention (SCC), which was set up in March 1989. The Labour Party and Liberal Democrats participated in the Convention along with representatives from local authorities, trade unions, churches and other organizations. The Convention delivered a blueprint for the future Scottish Parliament, demonstrated a capacity for cross-party and beyond-party joint working and led the growing elite and non-elite consensus that some form of political devolution for Scotland was essential.

The case of Wales is different again. There was and is undoubtedly greater ambiguity compared to Scotland about the nationalist dimension and the case for devolved government, a feature which explains the extremely close referendum vote in favour of reform in 1997 and the less developed nature of the proposed Welsh Assembly.

In London, the argument for a new strategic authority began almost as soon as the Greater London Council (GLC) was abolished in 1986. With the exception of the Conservatives there was cross-party support for such an initiative and a largely favourable reaction among the public. The particular form of the new GLA and the powers given to the new mayor,

Ken Livingstone, reflect the thinking of the Blair government rather than the product of a cross-party or political/civil elite consensus.

The regional dimension is not a strong focus for public opinion elsewhere in England, with the possible exception of the North East. RDAs and regional chambers are not the product of a ground-swell of regionalist sentiment but rather a pragmatic policy tool designed to deliver more effective economic regeneration. Strong advocates for English regionalism exist but they by and large recognize that their enthusiasm as yet is not shared by most people or all key members of the Labour government.

Equally in terms of local government it is difficult to point to a huge surge of popular opinion in favour of rejuvenating reform. However elite opinion (in reaction to the centralizing tendency so strongly expressed in the Thatcher years) has moved from the early 1990s onwards in favour of a radical overhaul which both gives local government a clearer role and enhances its democratic accountability. The proposals in the White Paper (DETR, 1998) reflect the particular preferences of the Blair government but also display a complex relationship with the Conservatives' previous reform agenda.

The Labour government has shown much more interest than the Conservatives in the democratic reform of local government. The democratic reforms focus on three issues: first, the encouragement of more systematic and effective forms of public consultation and participation; second, a range of electoral reforms aimed at one end of the spectrum simply to make voting easier and at the other end a debate about the introduction of proportional representation; and third a move to new political structures, including the option of directly elected executive mayors. The aim of these reforms is to restore accountability to the system and provide elected local authorities with the legitimacy they need to undertake the role of community leaders in a complex world of governance (Blair, 1998a).

Labour's agenda tackles head on two issues ducked by the Conservatives: the political management and organization of local government and its core role and purpose. As the Prime Minister's pamphlet indicates, the two issues are linked: 'At the heart of local government's new role is leadership – leadership that gives vision, partnership and quality of life to cities, towns and villages all over Britain' (Blair, 1998a, p. 13). It continues:

> Local government's credentials to be community leaders are weakened by its poor base of popular support . . . councils need to avoid getting trapped in the secret world of the caucus and the party group. They should let people have their say . . . But the heart of the problem is that local government needs recognized leaders if it is to fulfil the community leadership role. (Blair, 1998, pp. 14–16)

Thus at the centre of Labour's agenda is a concern to restore public trust and legitimacy to the political life of councils in order for them to take on a broad community leadership role. Labour has sustained a commitment to financial constraints although there are signs of relaxation. The announcements on public spending made in June and July 1998 indicate substantially more money for some local government services, especially education and social services, but limited growth in other areas. Capital spending is also likely to be increased above levels achieved under the Conservatives. Yet there is a strong element of caution in the management of local finances. Major levels of control remain in the hands of the centre, although there is considerable scope for local authorities to develop some modest additional revenue streams and some imaginative partnerships that are based on capital projects and release resources through effective asset management.

Labour clearly shares with the Conservatives and many in local government a belief in managerialism and consumerism in a general sense, although its emphasis is rather different. The best-value regime carries the potential of being a flexible and effective tool for improvements in local service delivery. There is also a strong theme in government circles on the virtue of developing 'joined-up' or 'holistic' approaches for tackling social and economic problems. Local government with its range of responsibilities and leadership roles has a particular contribution to make in this sphere.

The Conservatives' programme showed that change imposed in a heavy-handed, non-consultative manner is prone to considerable implementation failure and the production of a range of unintended effects (Stoker, 1999a). All this is not to deny that any reform process needs a clear vision and strong leadership. It is also appropriate for central government to insist that some reforms take place and for it to provide a package of sticks and carrots. To recognize that reforms can lead to unintended and perhaps perverse effects is not an argument against reform, but rather makes the case for more piloting, monitoring and effective implementation support. What is also needed – and was never delivered under the Conservatives – is a programme to build capacity and encourage ownership of the reform process within local government. Labour's approach to local public service reform is committed to providing a more flexible reform strategy.

First there are mechanisms to ensure the strident review of what is provided and to establish mechanisms for continuous improvement. At the national level the Comprehensive Spending Review constituted an initial mechanism for examining what was being achieved with public spending. At the local level the key mechanism is the Best-Value process introduced on a voluntary, experimental basis shortly after the election of Labour in May 1997 and a statutory provision for all local authorities in April 2000.

Best Value installs a comprehensive and intensive review of all services on the basis of locally driven priorities and procedures but policed through a national system of inspection and ultimately intervention in the case of failure.

Second there are mechanisms to encourage innovation and experiment. Pilots, zones and special projects of various sorts are used to promote new ways of working and break down institutional barriers and risk aversion within the public services. The aim is to encourage joined-up solutions and outcome-oriented thinking. In particular, there is an emphasis on using new information and communication technology to transform people's experience of public services. The possibilities in terms of providing more efficient and effective service delivery have only just begun to be realized. The potential offered by new information and communication technology requires a willingness to completely rethink the structure and operating norms of public services.

What is clear is that although central government has done a great deal to promote more flexible working it runs the risk of falling into two traps by concentrating efforts on special initiatives rather than mainstream programmes and budgets. Such an approach can lead to excessive demands being placed on the time of managers in the bidding game for initiatives. Second it downgrades the initiatives in the minds of managers and potentially creates confusion for the public (Oh no, not another joined-up pilot coming our way!).

The Conservatives did take steps to effectively institutionalize the multi-level governance characteristic of today's British polity, particularly through overseeing the expansion of the decision-making capacity of the EU and creation of privatized utilities responsible for the supply of basic services. Labour has taken the process of institutionalization still further with a programme of devolving responsibilities to the nations, regions and localities. Yet in neither case can the process of establishing an institutional framework for multi-level governance be seen as the product of some over-arching constitutional vision or blueprint. The British polity has changed not only in the way that it does its business but in its institutional structures. However what has been witnessed is not the playing out of one storyline but rather a complex variety of subplots and themes.

## Governance: unresolved tensions in the British polity

The specific new elected institutions installed by Labour – backed as most of them have been by endorsement through referenda – will be difficult if not impossible for any future government to reverse. However it would be a mistake to view the current system as stable: rather, all the evidence points to the British polity being in the centre of a period of continuing flux and change. There are a number of unresolved tensions and challenging questions that remain to be answered. Moreover multi-level governance itself is a daunting and complex task.

The first unresolved issue is the future relationship with the EU. Withdrawal from the EU seems to be an option for only those on the fringes of politics, although the UK Independence Party did win 7 per cent of the vote in the 1999 European Parliament elections (see Chapters 4 and 11). The mainstream issue is what should be the nature of a future relationship. Should the UK join the 'euro' single currency project? How quickly will the EU be expanded to incorporate other countries? Can the existing rather cumbersome decision-making structures of the EU be sustained in the light of any expansion? Is it possible to find a way of enhancing the democratic credibility and legitimacy of decision-making at that level? Given the low turnout in the 1999 European Parliament elections and general public opinion towards the EU this would appear to be a pressing but somewhat overlooked issue.

Whatever else it is, the EU is not a finished product. Equally there is no certainty about the future trends. There is no inevitability about the creation of a 'United States of Europe' – a new over-arching sovereign super-state. Equally it is not clear that, perceived as an alliance of nation-states for their mutual benefit, the appropriate institutional and decision-making structures have been found.

There are a number of tensions when it comes to the internal rearrangement of the British polity. Is an asymmetrical programme of different arrangements for different parts of the UK sustainable? The diverse nature of the devolution programme raises the issue of whether the different directions and pace of change will create tensions. In particular, some ask if Scotland goes storming ahead can Wales or the English regions be left behind? Will they be dragged along in the wake or alternatively provide a brake?

In Northern Ireland and Scotland big political questions about the fundamental break-up of the UK lie not very far below the surface. The prospects for a lasting settlement in Northern Ireland remain uncertain. In Scotland the SNP – a party committed to an independent Scotland – continues to provide a powerful political challenge to Labour. What would be the implications for the SNP winning a majority of Scottish seats in the UK parliament or winning coalition control of the Scottish Parliament? How will these tensions be managed? Will the (potential) future prospects of further more radical constitutional change make the pragmatic political running of new arrangements more difficult?

A tension – and a hotly debated issue at least among political elites – is whether the different electoral systems that drive the various parts of

Britain's multi-level governance system can coexist. National UK elections and local elections in England, Wales and Scotland use a majoritarian 'first-past-the-post' system. In Northern Ireland for some years a proportional single-transferable vote (STV) system has been used for European Parliamentary and local elections. A similar system was adopted for the Northern Ireland Assembly elected in 1998. Indeed all of the new elected institutions set up by Labour have gone for Proportional Representation (PR) systems that deliver a greater correspondence between votes cast and seats won. The Scottish, Welsh and London assemblies use an additional member system with some candidates elected on a 'first-past-the-post' system topped up by a list of candidates to achieve greater proportionality. The London Mayor was elected in May 2000 using the supplementary-vote system. The 1999 Euro elections were conducted with a proportional list-based system.

One concern might be whether these diverse systems are likely in themselves to confuse the voters. A more important issue, however, is whether it is possible to sustain the legitimacy of the different political institutions of the UK polity with such a variety of systems. Is one system better, and if so should not all institutions have it? Or is the public supposed to subscribe the view that each electoral system matches the needs of each institution? Having conceded ground to more proportional-based systems for the Scottish Parliament and other new institutions there does appear to be a substantial logic for Labour to extend the principle to local elections at least. In Scotland the Labour–Liberal Democrat Coalition have agreed in principle to move towards a PR system for local elections. The position over local elections is still the subject of debate in England and Wales. As for elections to the UK Parliament it would seem that notwithstanding the recommendations of the Jenkins Commission the Labour government is moving towards retaining the current first-past-the-post system. The key point is that with a variety of systems now in place it is clear that it is difficult to keep the PR debate off the agenda.

Can the public spending/taxation dimensions of the programme be managed? The debate about the fair distribution of resources between the different parts of the UK is likely to heighten and gain pace in the context of devolution. As one commentator has rather graphically put it 'if the Scots and the Welsh want more freedom it is inconceivable that the English will want to underwrite continuing public spending generosity towards them' (Travers, 1998, p. xiii). In 1996–7 Scotland enjoyed £4825 per head of public spending, compared with £4620 in Wales and £3885 in England. Northern Ireland exceeded them all with spending at £5484 per head. These differences reflect higher unemployment and greater needs in some areas, but the question remains: what is a reasonable level of difference?

In England there is an unresolved battle between the priority for local government capacity-building and the potential of regional-level institutions. It is possible that the two positions can be reconciled but the tension is real. It could become even more apparent if some of England's main cities go down the route of the strong executive mayor. Such figures may not take too kindly to strong regional agencies; on the other hand, they may work through and with them. A related issue is does devolution – especially in Scotland and Wales – squeeze the political space left for local government in those territories?

A more general and over-arching tension in the system of multi-level governance that is developing in the British polity is whether government – particularly central government where the greatest power has in the past resided – learn to accommodate itself to and work successfully in the world of governance. Can Britain both steer and cooperate in the EU? What are the appropriate limits on the political space afforded to the new devolved assemblies? Can local government be encouraged to modernize and at the same time have the degree of autonomy to make local rejuvenated institutions a prize worth competing for and holding?

The Anglo–American literature is striving hard to find adjectives to describe the 'light-touch' form of government appropriate to the circumstances of governance. 'Enabler', 'catalytic agent', 'commissioner', have all been offered to capture the new form of governing. Government in governance aims to give leadership, build partnerships, protect and regulate its environment and promote opportunity. In a more general way Kooiman and Van Vliet (1993, p. 66) classify 'the tasks of government in a governance' in the following way:

- (de)composition and coordination
- collibration and steering
- integration and regulation.

The first task involves defining a situation, identifying key stakeholders and then developing effective linkages between the relevant parties. The key issue is how to establish a *shared vision*. At the local level a community planning process is proposed but what of relations at higher levels and between tiers? The second is concerned with influencing and steering relationships in order to achieve *desired outcomes*. Labour says it wants to negotiate outcomes not the detail of processes but it is struggling to do so. The third is about what others call 'system management' (Stewart, 1996a). It involves thinking and acting beyond the individual subsystems, avoiding unwanted side effects and establishing mechanisms for *effective coordination*. The great challenge of 'joined-up' government has been taken up but far from met by new Labour.

It is not clear that most of those involved in government have the capacity – or, indeed, even the desire – to behave in tune with a governance 'mission statement' and governing style. Faced with the complexity and autonomy of a system of multi-level governance there is a strong tendency for political leaderships to seek to impose order and issue directives. This pressure to 'take charge' can be exaggerated by the way that the media covers news issues. Negotiating can be portrayed as a sign of weakness, as in the case of the argument with the French government over the lifting of the beef ban in Autumn 1999. If schools fail, or hospitals make mistakes the pressure on ministers to posture and claim that they are going to 'sort things out' can be considerable.

Government in these circumstances becomes a vast and unresolvable principal–agent problem. Governments may issue orders but lack the capacity to ensure compliance. The Labour government may face accusations of 'control freakery' but it should not be assumed that it can – even if wished – exercise effective control. Government in the context of governance has to learn an appropriate operating code which challenges past hierarchical modes of thinking. There is evidence of some success as well as failure in meeting the challenge.

The paradox of the governance perspective is that even where government develops an appropriate operating code governance failure may still occur. The idea of governance failure should not surprise us since both 'state' and 'market' are known to fail to some degree. Governance as an alternative coordinating mechanism is also likely to run into difficulties (Jessop, 1999) if the conflicts that governance is attempting to resolve have an 'either-or' character – matters of religion, race, language or ideology – then the compromise and messiness central to governance may be inadequate (Stoker, 2000). On a pessimistic interpretation this may be a difficulty that will continue to haunt Northern Ireland. Second multi-level governance often requires not only a capacity to coordinate action at different spatial levels but also an ability to manage different perceptions of time-scales. The long-term perspective of the EU and its slowness to take decisive action may be perceived as an affront by a campaigning voluntary organization looking for the resolution of a problem today and not tomorrow. Trust, patience and the sheer managerial capacity to join the various parts of the complex polity together may be lacking or unsustainable. Third the contingencies of politics may undermine governance. Electoral considerations may encourage politicians to break apart complex governance mechanisms for short-term advantage. London mayoral candidates, for example, have already heightened tensions by 'having a go' at Scotland's perceived public spending advantage.

That multi-level governance is not automatically successful should not cause undue alarm. Recognizing the potential incompetence of governance suggests the need for continued experimentation and learning. Jessop (1999) asks for participants to display a 'self-reflective irony' which recognizes the 'likelihood of failure' but requires them to 'proceed as if success were possible.' Rhodes (1997b) in a similar manner argues that government needs to pick up the skills of indirect management and learn how to operate a complex mix of tools.

The great challenge facing the British polity is that not only are the core institutions in a state of flux but that, at the same time, new skills, practices and ways of working are having to be forged in order to ensure the effective operation of multi-level governance. We need to check institutions against their capacity to deliver good governance that has governing capacity and democratic legitimacy. At the same time the polity is trying to redefine what are the principles of good governance and how they can be achieved in a complex multi-level system.

## Conclusion

An underlying theme of this chapter is that the UK's governing institutions and processes are in a state of flux. It may be helpful to conclude with a review of different scenarios of the future for multi-level governance from a British perspective.

The first vision of the future might be described as embracing *federalism* as the mechanism for driving multi-level governance. It is a scenario most strongly supported by the Liberal Democrats, by many in the Labour Party, but also in a broad sense underwritten by a number of campaign groups such as Charter 88. It celebrates the creation of multiple levels of decision-making at European, national, regional and local tiers. In institutional terms the challenge is to complete the move to a federalist structure which gives distinctive powers to different tiers and allows for cooperation between them. In England regional government should be created to match the new institutions in Scotland, Wales and Northern Ireland. Powers should be restored to local government. The UK Parliament should be reformed to make it more democratic and open; so too should European-level institutions. Measures are also necessary to extend the proportional principle in elections and to guarantee rights to information. Above all, this scenario embraces a pluralist vision of governance. Thus according to David Marquand (1998a, p. 10):

> Two implications stand out. The first is summed up in the old adage 'that power, like muck, is no use unless it be spread': to make a reality of self-government power must be diffused as widely as possible. The

second implication is that there must be checks and balances to ensure that power is not concentrated in an overmighty central state: that the ideal of self-government also entails a politics of pluralism, power-sharing and negotiation.

Embracing federalism means establishing a strong range of cross-checking institutions at different levels of governance and ensuring that those institutions are open and accountable and capable of working alongside private, voluntary and community interests.

The second scenario might be viewed as *holding back multi-level governance*. 'Enough and no further' appears to be a dominant view among the Conservative Party and some in the national media. Staying in the EU is acceptable but only if the powers of intervention of the EU can be reined back and there should be no more 'pooling of sovereignty' over monetary, economic or other matters. The internal constitutional tinkering undertaken by Labour is regrettable and should not be developed. The Conservatives have suggested that they will abolish RDAs and have ruled out a commitment to regional government. The concept of an English Parliament also appears to have been rejected. However the referendums that supported the establishment of the Scottish, Welsh and London bodies appear to have dissuaded the Conservatives from threatening to abolish them if they return to power in the UK Parliament. Above all the over-arching supremacy of the UK Parliament is not to be undermined any further.

The third scenario and one that has support among some in the Labour Government and many civil servants is that the future lies in *managing multi-level governance*. The view here is that although the task of governance has become more complex and the range of institutions involved more diverse there remains the need for a central core to provide direction and leadership. In this scenario the core is seen to reside around Westminster and Whitehall – among the political and managerial elites. Through regulation, manipulation and sheer organizational skill the aim is to ensure that the fragments both inside and outside government are brought together to achieve collective purposes.

For some, this managerial vision is what lies behind the rhetoric about 'joined-up' government. It is a matter of ensuring that all the institutions of multi-level governance are guided to perform in a manner commensurate with the ambitions and objectives of the central Westminster/Whitehall elite. Marquand (1998a, p. 9) refers to this approach as the 'dirigiste' option.

It is based on the premise that elected governments both can and should change social behaviour for the better by regulation and manipulation from the centre. Its exponents take it for granted that the democratic state has the legitimacy, the knowledge and the capacity to engage successfully in this sort of social engineering.

The assumption of the managerialist vision of the future is that government should and can learn the necessary skills and gain the necessary capacity to steer multi-level governance from a central core, which in turn finds its legitimacy through winning elections and reflecting the broad thrust of public opinion.

Given what has been argued in the earlier parts of this chapter about the complex forces and competing motivations that have so far contributed to the development of Britain's emerging system of multi-level governance it would seem reasonable to expect that the future is unlikely to fully follow the path laid down by any of these scenarios. Contingencies, the complexity of the forces at work and the unruly dynamic of politics will ensure that the future of multi-level governance remains to a substantial degree unpredictable. The challenge for political scientists is to understand the complex dynamics as best as we can and perhaps also contribute by way of evidence and reason to the debate about what are the best options for the future.

# Chapter 4

# Britain, the EU and the Euro

SIMON HIX

Europe has been a salient issue in British politics ever since Britain joined the EEC in 1973. For example, Labour's 1983 manifesto commitment to withdraw from the EC contributed to the party's isolation from the political mainstream until the late 1980s. In the early 1990s, the resignation of Foreign Secretary Geoffrey Howe over Margaret Thatcher's persistent isolation at the European level was a critical step in her eventual downfall. At Maastricht in 1991, when member states negotiated the treaty that established the EU, Conservative Prime Minister John Major proclaimed that he had protected British interests and stemmed the tide of further political integration. However, in the House of Commons ratification of the Treaty, a group of anti-EU rebels in the Conservative Party voted with the Opposition to inflict a crucial parliamentary defeat on his government.

Tony Blair then came to power in 1997 promising a more positive approach in Britain's policy towards Europe. However, when the European single currency (the euro) was launched in January 1999 by 11 of the 15 EU member states, Blair decided to exercise the 'Opt Out' negotiated by the Major government, and remain on the sidelines. The Labour government argued that it was in favour of British membership of the single currency if the 'economic conditions' – such as a convergence between the British and continental European economic cycles – were right. But, for most of the public, the mass media, the rank-and-file of the Labour Party and the other political parties, the issue remains essentially *political*: should Britain give up its macroeconomic sovereignty?

In the meantime, in the 1999 Amsterdam Treaty, the EU took another major step towards deeper 'political union'. This Treaty strengthened the powers of the Commission President and the European Parliament against member state governments, reinforced the provisions for common European foreign and defence policies, established a deadline for the abolition of border controls between the EU member states, and set up provisions for common EU immigration and policing policies. The next stage of institutional reforms, as the EU prepares for enlargement to central and eastern Europe, will probably take the EU a step closer to a genuinely 'federal union'.

Consequently, the specific question of Britain membership of the single currency, and the general question of Britain's place in the emerging EU political system, are the fundamental issues for the current generation of political leaders. How these questions are resolved will have a dramatic impact on Britain's position at the European level, on the British party system and on the careers of the current party elites.

## The EU and British politics

With the delegation of more and more competences to the European level in successive treaty reforms since the mid-1980s, EU policies now cover virtually all areas of public policy, including market regulation, social policy, environmental policy, agriculture, regional policy, research and development, interior affairs, citizenship, international trade, foreign policy, defence policy, consumer affairs, transport, public health, education and culture. The result is a new kind of multi-level political system in which political power is shared between the EU, national and subnational levels, and decisions taken at one level shape outcomes at others (see Chapter 3).

As a result, the impact of the EU on British politics is huge. On an administrative level, most senior British ministers and many senior civil servants spend many days each month commuting to Brussels for EU meetings. Much of the rest of their time back in Westminster and Whitehall is spent tackling questions relating to the EU agenda. More significantly, on a policy level, British government is severely constrained by policy outputs from the EU system. The British government is still sovereign in deciding most of the main areas of public expenditure – such as social security, health care, transport and public housing. However, this is only one aspect of policy-making. In the area of *regulation*, over 80 per cent of rules governing the production, distribution and exchange of goods, services and capital in the British market are decided by the EU. In the area of *macroeconomic policy*, despite the fact that Britain is not a member of the single currency, decisions by the European Central Bank (ECB) and the Council of Finance Ministers have a direct impact on British monetary, fiscal and employment policies. In the area of *foreign and defence policy*, Britain is bound by its commitments under the EU's Common Foreign and Security Policy (CFSP).

This places obvious strains on the British party system. Within the policy straitjacket of the EU, radical policy alternatives are infeasible. On the left, a neo-Keynesian demand-side macroeconomic policy is impossible in Economic and Monetary Union (EMU). On the right, a Thatcherite deregulatory supply-side policy is impossible in the 'social market' regulatory framework of the single market. This is less of a problem for the Liberal Democrats and the post-Keynesian leadership of the Labour Party, who are comfortable with the EU's macroeconomic and regulatory policy agendas. However, it is a big problem for many in the Conservative Party, whose deregulatory agenda is in direct confrontation with the policy regime that dominates the EU level. As Thatcher once put it, from this perspective the EU regulatory regime is 'socialism through the back door'.

European integration and this new policy regime have also reinforced certain policy ideas in British political debate. For example, with the acceptance of the delegation of power to the European level, and the consequent erosion of the classic notion of 'parliamentary sovereignty', European integration has been a catalyst for radical constitutional reform. With the reality of a division of powers between London and Brussels, other constitutional constraints on the Westminster majority – such as regional devolution, a bill of rights, an independent Bank of England and proportional representation – become plausible options. Similarly, the single market has increased the regionalization of economic production and hence increased demands for regional devolution to Scotland, Wales and the English regions. The possibility of leaving the UK but remaining part of NATO, the single market and even joining the single currency has reduced the cost and risk of independence for Scotland and Wales.

The British Foreign Office used to think of the Maastricht Treaty as 'the high water mark of integration'. But, with the pressures for common employment and budgetary polices in EMU, new policies to adapt to enlargement to Central and Eastern Europe, the removal of internal borders, and the development of genuine common foreign and defence policies, more and more powers are likely to be passed to the European level. Whether the Foreign Office likes it or not, the question of Europe will not simply go away.

## The 'British' position *in* Europe

On most *political* issues on the EU agenda – such as the speed of political integration, the allocation of new policy competences to the EU level and the allocation of powers between EU institutions – the position of the Blair government is almost indistinguishable from that of previous Conservative and Labour administrations. Britain has always been one of the member states most opposed to the creation of a federal 'United States of Europe'. As a result, in the Amsterdam Treaty negotiations, the election of a Labour government did not make as much difference to Britain's negotiating position as some other member states had hoped. The Blair government was strongly opposed to the extension of qualified majority voting (QMV) in the Council to a number of highly contentious policy areas (such as tax harmonization), decided to opt out of the provisions for the abolition of internal borders and common immigration policies and opposed any increase in the powers of the Commission and the European Court of Justice (ECJ). Like previous administrations, the Blair government is strongly in favour of enlargement to Central and Eastern Europe, but argues that Britain's voting weight in the Council should be increased to enable the larger member states to continue to dominate EU decision-making. The Labour government is strongly 'Atlanticist', arguing that the EU can develop a common defence framework only as part of the NATO Atlantic alliance.

Nevertheless, on some political and institutional design questions, the Blair government has pursued different policies to the Thatcher and Major administrations. Robin Cook, Blair's Foreign Secretary in the 1997 Parliament, was a key agenda-setter on the question of defence coopera-tion, with the proposal and negotiation of a joint Anglo–French declara-tion on a common EU defence policy.

In addition, on the issue of how to tackle the democratic deficit in the Intergovernmental Commission (IGC), Blair was instrumental in securing an agreement on increasing the powers of the European Parliament in the legislative process – *vis-à-vis* the member state governments in the Council – and in the investiture of the Commission. But unlike the other issues of institutional design, the question of European Parliament powers is more about long-term *economic* policy preferences than questions of national political sovereignty.

The EP's main legislative competences are in rules governing economic, social and environmental regulation in the EU single market. On these economic issues, the natural coalition in the EP, of Socialists and Christian Democrats, is closer to the Blair's 'social market' agenda than the more neo-liberal agenda of the Thatcher and Major governments. As a result, Blair was willing to see an increase in the EP's powers to counteract either a 'corporatist' or a 'neo-liberal' majority in the Council.

The story is somewhat similar on the *economic* issues on the EU agenda – such as common macroeconomic policies, reform of the EU's budgetary policies, industrial policy and regulation of the EU single market. Which-ever government is in power, the British economy has a particular position *vis-à-vis* the core economies of the EU. Britain has lower levels of welfare spending, lower levels of worker protection, generally lower wages, more liberal markets (in air transport and telecommunications, for example), is more open to the global economy and is stronger in certain economic sectors (such as financial services). As a result, on some economic issues the Blair government has pursued the same policies as the Thatcher and Major governments. In the single market, the Labour government is opposed to regulations that would threaten British industries – such as the Directive on harmonization of taxes on capital investments. Also, all British governments support the Commission's positions on free trade and liberalization of EU markets. In the Agenda 2000 negotiations on the reform of the EU budget, the Labour Chancellor Gordon Brown was adamant that he would not give up the special British 'rebate' that Thatcher negotiated in 1984. Finally, the Blair government decided not to join the single currency.

However, Labour also represents different economic interests to the Conservatives. To defend the interests of organized labour, in the IGC on the Amsterdam Treaty the Labour government signed the EU Social Chapter, which allowed policy-making on social and labour rights to be brought into the main EU Treaty. Also, because Labour does not have to rely on support from British farmers, the Blair government has been more active in pursing reform of the CAP than the previous Conservative governments. Thatcher and Major were in favour of CAP reform, but only if the interests of large British farmers were protected. Having received significant electoral contributions from the biotechnology industry, the Labour government was strongly in favour of an EU Directive allowing life forms to be patented. Tony Blair successfully put pressure on the British Labour Members of the European Parliament (MEPs) to mobilize and prevent the Socialist group in the EP from rejecting the Directive. During the British Presidency of the EU Council in the first half of 1998, the Labour government was instrumental in securing agreement on a number of new Directives on environmental protection.

Above all, Blair has been at the forefront of a campaign to persuade the other member state governments that the best way to address the problem of the high level of EU unemployment is to reform the single market to make European industry more competitive, to introduce labour market flexibility and to reduce the tax and regulatory burden on small- and medium-sized enterprises (SMEs). From the perspective of the other EU member states, this sounds very like the neo-liberal agenda of Thatcher and Major. However, in Blair's vision of the Third Way for Europe, these policies go hand in hand with continued high levels of welfare spending, environmental protection and health and safety at work, and some elements of neo-Keynesian macroeconomic policy. As a result, Blair's economic agenda is much closer to the mainstream of EU politics – such as the Social Democratic governments in Germany, Scandinavia and the Benelux countries, the Prodi government in Italy and the Aznar government in Spain – than the economic policies of the Thatcher and Major governments (Chapter 2).

Key differences between Blair and previous Conservative governments are illustrated in Figure 4.1. On the 'political dimension' of EU politics – on issues relating to the delegation of new policy competences to the EU level and the strengthening of supranational institutions *vis-à-vis* the EU governments (in the Council) – the Blair government is only moderately more 'integrationist' than the Major government. This explains why Blair will continue to oppose giving more powers to the EU institutions and extending QMV with EU enlargement, as these policies would lead to more movement from the status quo than Britain favours. On issues of national political sovereignty, then, British policy preferences have been relatively stable over time, as realist theory predicts.

However, on the 'economic dimension' in EU politics, with the establishment of EMU and the single market, the status quo is relatively regulatory (left of centre). Blair's position on labour market flexibility and further liberalization of the EU single market is on the same side of the status quo as the previous Conservative governments. However, Blair is closer to the EU mainstream on this dimension, and is hence able to build coalitions in the Council to back his economic agenda. For example, he was instrumental in securing the backing of Romano Prodi, a fellow 'Third Wayer', as the new Commission President. Moreover, this helps explain

**Figure 4.1**   *Strategic position of the Labour and Conservative governments in the EU*

(a)   The political dimension of EU politics

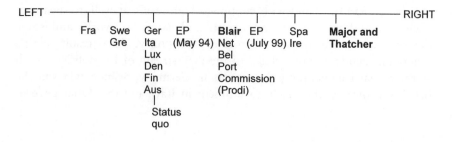

(b)   The economic dimension of EU politics

why Blair increasingly supported reinforcing the ability of the EP to amend legislation governing the single market. The majority in the EP, both before and after the 1999 European elections, is closer to Blair's position than to the status quo. This was not the case for Major, who hence tried to block an extension of EP powers. On issues that touch on competing domestic economic policy preferences, then, the British position in the EU has changed, as liberal theory predicts.

## The electoral environment: the public's position *on* Europe

There are two different types of support for a political system (Easton, 1965, 1975). On the one hand, 'affective support' is an ideological or non-material belief in the value of the political system. For example, in the case of the EU some citizens have an ideological belief in, or opposition to, the goal of European integration. On the other hand, 'utilitarian support' is the belief in a political system on the condition that the system increases the material (economic) well being of an individual. In the case of the EU, some citizens support the EU only if they think that it will make them better-off.

Research on public support for the EU, using the six-monthly 'Eurobarometer' European-wide polls (conducted by private polling agencies on behalf of the Commission), shows that both these types of support exist. On the one hand, citizens in the original member states of the EU, who have high levels of cultural identification with 'Europe', have high levels of affective support for the EU (Anderson and Kalthenthaler, 1996; Gabel, 1998b). Similarly, individuals who reveal 'post-material' values (such as environmentalism and peace) tend to have higher levels of support for European integration than 'materialists' (Inglehart, 1977). On the other hand, certain groups in society that clearly benefit from the process of market liberalization in the EU (such as private sector professionals) or receive funds from the EU budget (such as farmers) show high levels of utilitarian support for European integration (Gabel, 1998a; Gabel and Whitten, 1997). Public support for the EU in Britain can be explained using the same type of analysis.

A number of cultural, political and historical factors explain why the British public is less enthusiastic about European integration than most other EU citizens. Britain did not have the same experience of the Second World War as continental Europe, which experienced Nazi occupation and political and economic destruction. The British have a stronger cultural identification with the English-speaking world than with continental Europe (Inglehart, 1991). Also, because Britain did not join the EC until

1973, only a few generations have grown up with membership of a wider European polity a fact of political life. As Figure 4.2 shows, support for EU membership in Britain was about 10 per cent below the European average throughout the 1990s.

Nevertheless, changes in the levels of support for European integration in Britain have followed European trends rather than specifically British events. As Figure 4.2 shows, enthusiasm for the European project reached a peak across Europe, including in Britain, in 1990–1. At this time, most Europeans expected the EU single market, which was launched at the end of 1992, to bring economic rewards to all sectors of industry. Also, until this point, there was generally a 'permissive consensus' on the issue of European integration, whereby voters trusted their politicians to negotiate on their behalf in Brussels (Lindberg and Scheingold, 1970). But European states suffered an economic downturn in the early 1990s, and the permissive consensus collapsed in the process of ratifying the Maastricht Treaty in 1992 and 1993 (which was symbolized by the 'No' vote on the Treaty in the first of two referendums in Denmark). As Franklin, Marsh and McLaren (1994) put it: the anti-Europe 'bottle' had finally been 'uncorked'. This was as true in Britain as in the rest of Europe.

On the issue of the single currency, however, the pattern is somewhat different. In the run-up to the lauch of the euro, British opinion followed the general European trend. As Figure 4.3 shows, in this period British public

**Figure 4.2**   *Is your country's membership of the EU a 'good thing' or a 'bad thing'?*

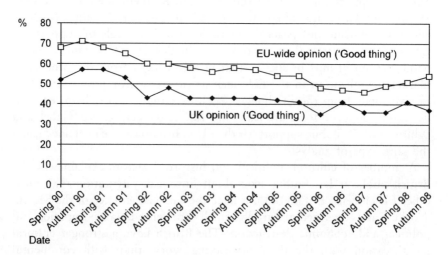

*Source: Eurobarometers* Surveys, 36–50.

opinion was approximately 20 per cent less enthusiastic about the single currency than the European average (of all EU member states, including the four non-members of EMU). This gap meant that whereas there was a clear majority in favour of the single currency in most European states, more people in Britain were opposed to the euro (48 per cent in Autumn 1998) than were in favour (36 per cent in Autumn 1998).

For a while, support for the single currency rose consistently in Britain and across Europe. In spring 1997, which was the peak of anti-single currency feeling in Europe, the British public was almost two-to-one opposed to the single currency. The British then became more pro-euro up to the launch of the single currency. However, throughout 1999 and into 2000, as the British economy continued to outperform the euro-zone and the euro weakened dramatically against the dollar, British support for membership of the single currency declined to record lows. If British opinion rejoins the European trend, and support for the single currency continues to rise across Europe – for example, as people get used to the existence of the currency – the gap between those opposed to British membership and those in favour will decline. But if support for the single currency across Europe flattens out – for example, if the euro continues to fall against the dollar or if the euro-zone continues to have high levels of unemployment and relatively low growth – then a majority of the British public will continue to oppose British membership.

Nevertheless, as the utilitarian approach to explaining public support suggests, there are also clear differences within the British public about European integration. As Figure 4.4 shows, different occupational groups

**Figure 4.3**  *Are you 'for' or 'against' your country joining the single currency?*

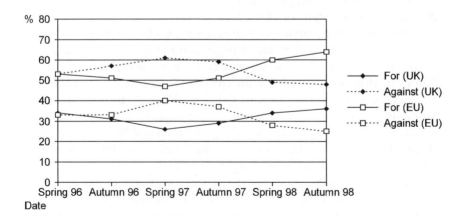

*Source: Eurobarometer* Surveys, 44–50.

have different attitudes towards the EU. Professional employees and owners of business (together with students, who are likely to join these groups) are the social groups which are most favourable towards the EU. These groups stand to gain the most from trade liberalization in the EU single market. For example, financial services firms in the City of London have comparative advantage in the EU single market, which has allowed them to attract capital investment from the rest of the EU and to be lead players in mergers and acquisitions in the financial services sector across Europe. At the other end of the social scale, the working class and small business owners are the most anti-European groups in Britain. Small businesses mainly compete for the domestic British market. Trade liberalization in the EU consequently means greater competition for small British firms. And for skilled and unskilled workers, trade liberalization leads to threats of capital flight and industrial relocation. In the middle, British white-collar employees (who can presumably attract capital investment) and British farmers (who receive significant funds from the EU under the CAP) are both moderately pro-European.

Utilitarian factors also explain the different levels of support between the British regions. As Figure 4.4 shows, Yorkshire and Scotland, which receive the most regional aid from the EU budget of the British regions (outside Northern Ireland), are both strongly pro-European. The other main beneficiary regions – Wales, the North East and the North West – are also moderately pro-European. In London and the South East, where the British financial services industry is located, people are relatively pro-European. In contrast, in the South West, where the fishing industry has suffered badly from EU fishing quotas (and which before the 2000–4 EU budget did not receive any regional aid from the EU), people are strongly anti-European. Similarly, in the West Midlands, which has seen its industries decline as competition in the EU single market has heated up, people are also strongly anti-European.

Turning to voting intentions, Figure 4.4 shows that none of the British parties has supporters that are strongly pro-European or strongly anti-European. However, Labour supporters are generally slightly more pro-European than Conservative supporters, and supporters of the Liberal Democrats, Greens and the Scottish and Welsh nationalists occupy positions between these two parties. Interestingly, SNP and PC voters are more anti-European than the average Scottish and Welsh voters. Also, those who declare no intention to vote in the next general election show very strong negative sentiment towards the EU.

This pattern of mass attitudes towards European integration in Britain presents a particular electoral environment for British party leaders. The median British voter is certainly more Eurosceptic than the EU average. The core class supporters of Labour – the skilled and unskilled worker

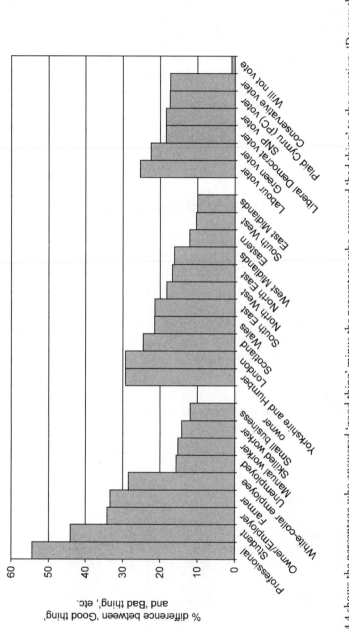

Figure 4.4 *British support for the EU, by class, region and party affiliation*

% difference between 'Good thing' and 'Bad thing', etc.

*Note:* Figure 4.4 shows the percentage who answered 'good thing' minus the percentage who answered 'bad thing' to the question: 'Do you think that the United Kingdom's membership of the EU is a "good thing", a "bad thing", neither good nor bad" or "don't know"?'.

*Source: Eurobarometer,* 44.2 Autumn 1996.

class – are strongly anti-European. However, this can be weighed against the moderately pro-EU views in Labour's core regions – the North of England and the peripheries. Conservative supporters are also divided. The small businessman is strongly anti-EU, but the professional and business elites are strongly pro-EU, and so are voters in the Conservative heartland of the South East. However, the Liberal Democrats probably find themselves in the most difficult position, seeking to appeal to class interests that are strongly pro-European, but with a core support base in one of the most anti-European regions (the South West). We now turn to how the party leaderships and the British elites have adapted to this electoral environment.

## The elite context: the emerging pro- and anti-Euro camps

Recent evidence shows that the British elite is more pro-European than the British mass public. In 1996, the *Eurobarometer* division of the European Commission conducted the first European-wide survey of elite attitudes towards the EU (EOS Gallup, 1998). In Britain, the pollsters interviewed 2500 elected politicians, senior civil servants, leaders of industry, leaders of the media and members of the cultural and intellectual elite. As Figure 4.5 shows, this social, economic and political elite is much more supportive of British membership of the EU and the euro than the mass public.

**Figure 4.5**    *British mass and elite attitudes towards the EU compared*

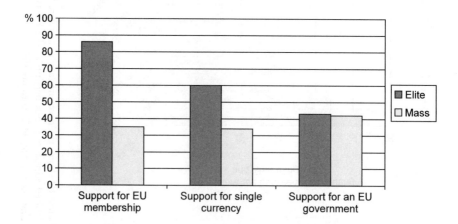

*Source:* Elite – Top Decision Makers' Survey, Autumn 1996. Mass – *Barometer*, 44, Autumn 1996.

However, on questions of 'political integration', such as whether there should be a 'European government accountable to the European parliament', the British elite shares the same sceptical attitudes as the mass public. This confirms the widely held view that European integration is largely an elite-driven project. However, this can also be explained by the fact that the British elite shows a mix of utilitarian and affective attitudes towards the EU. On the one hand, the British elite sees the economic benefits of European integration, which suggests a high level of utilitarian support for the EU. But the British elite is wary of giving up political sovereignty to Brussels, which suggests that like the mass British public the elite has a low level of affective support for the EU.

## Inter-party competition: a new cleavage in the British party system?

In most party systems in the EU, the issue of European integration cuts across the main left–right dimension of party competition (Hix and Lord, 1997). On both the right and left, pro- or anti-European positions are politically feasible. However, if parties try to take opposing stances on the question of Europe, they risk undermining internal party cohesion. To minimize internal divisions over Europe, the main political parties in most member states choose not to compete on the question of Europe, either by not discussing the issue in domestic electoral competition, or by saying exactly the same thing (Hix, 1999a). As a result, the European dimension tends to be articulated in domestic politics by extremist parties either on the right (such as nationalists and racist movements) or the left (such as Greens or ex-Communist parties), by anti-European movements (as in Denmark and France) or by rank-and-file members of the main centre-left or centre-right movements.

This was exactly the situation in Britain between the 1975 referendum on remaining in the EEC and the 1997 general election. Conscious of internal divisions in both parties, the Labour and Conservative leaderships colluded to keep the question of Europe out of domestic politics. Or, when the issue did arise, as in the mid-1980s with the question of Britain's rebate, or the early 1990s over the question of EMU, both main British parties adopted broadly the same moderately anti-European positions. Only the Liberal Democrats and the Scottish and Welsh nationals have consistently advocated a 'federalist' approach to the European project.

However, this cosy inter-party consensus broke apart with the fall of Thatcher, when divisions within the Conservative elite were a catalyst in her downfall. The Labour leadership began to see advantage in exposing the internal Conservative divisions, and so used ratification of the

Maastricht Treaty to inflict the first Westminster defeat on the Major government. As Labour became progressively more pro-European – openly supporting EMU in its 1994 European election manifesto – pressures grew in the Conservative party for a more explicitly anti-European stance. The final straw came for Conservative moderates with the 1997 election defeat. The result appeared to vindicate the claims of the anti-Europeanists that the party was defeated because it was too internally divided, and that it could only be united around an explicitly Eurosceptic stance.

This confluence of the European cleavage into the left-right divide in the British party system was also facilitated by the attitudes of the new intake of Westminster MPs in the 1997 election (Baker *et al.*, 1998). As Figure 4.6 shows, the new Labour parliamentarians were much more pro-European than the rump of Conservative MPs. For example, almost two-thirds of Labour MPs believed that British membership of the single currency is 'crucial for Britain's prosperity', as compared to about 10 per cent of Conservative MPs. Also, over one-quarter of Conservative MPs openly supported British withdrawal from the EU.

This new structure of party elite opinion enabled the new Conservative leader, William Hague, to adopt a more explicitly anti-European stance than any previous Conservative leadership. He ruled out British membership of the single currency at least until the end of the next parliamentary term (about 2006), and adopted the slogan of 'In Europe, Not Run By Europe' as the new guiding principle in this policy area. On the other side of the debate, with the support of most backbenchers, the Labour leadership promoted a 'constructive' European policy as part of its general policies of 'rebranding Britain' as a modern European nation, and advocating a 'Third Way' for Europe between American- and German-style capitalism. However, fearing a backlash at the electoral level and among sections of the Labour rank-and-file, Blair refused to declare whether he supported British membership of the single currency and consciously tried to keep the issue of British membership off the 1999 European election agenda.

As a result, at the end of the 1990s, the question of Europe is a major element of inter-party competition. This pattern of competition – with the main centre-left party on the pro-integration side and the main centre-right party on the anti-integration side – is almost unique in Europe. In the few party systems where Europe is part of left-right competition, as in Scandinavia, the centre-right tends to be more pro-European than the centre-left. Nevertheless, as 'Europe' represents a particular style of 'regulatory capitalism' compared to 'national' neo-liberalism or corporatism, Social Democrats across Europe have begun to see the European project as their salvation. Conversely, some centre-right parties are beginning to see Europe as a threat to their neo-liberal agendas – such

Figure 4.6   *Westminster MPs' attitudes towards the EU*

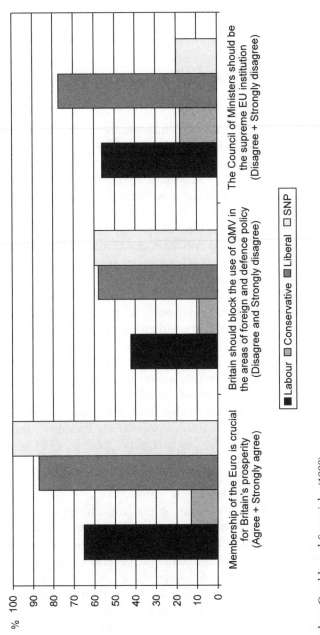

*Source:* Baker, Gamble and Seawright (1998).

as the free-market Liberal parties in the Benelux (Hooghe and Marks, 1998). In this interpretation, the structure of party competition in Britain on the question of Europe may actually be leading the European trend rather than being at odds with it.

## Interest groups, the media and the 'No' and 'Yes' campaigns

Interest groups representing British business, industrial sectors, trade unions, regional associations and political organizations (such as Greenpeace) were some of the first private organizations to establish offices in Brussels. British lobbying companies are also some of the leading players on the Brussels political scene – winning lucrative contracts from multinational British, European and American business to represent their views to the EU institutions. As a result, private British interests are extremely well represented in the EU policy process. From the perspective of some of the other member states, it often appears that 'the Brits run Brussels'.

As a result, British groups that have secured EU legislation promoting their interests have had an incentive to put pressure on the British government to continue to support the process of EU integration. For example, the City of London continues to urge the British government to support the further deregulation of financial services and the privatization of state monopolies throughout the EU. Similarly, the Confederation of British Industry (CBI), whose dominant members are export-oriented firms, is a strong advocate of British membership of the euro, on the grounds that it would lead to significant transactions costs reductions for its members. And, ever since Commission President Jacques Delors' famous 1988 speech to the Trades Union Congress (TUC), the leaders of the British trade union movement have been strongly pro-European – seeing Europe as the only hope for protection of their jobs and high levels of workers' rights and health and safety.

However, surveys by some of the anti-European newspapers have revealed that the rank-and-file membership of the CBI and the TUC are not as pro-European as their leaderships maintain. The leaderships of the two sides of industry see the economic benefits of the euro – a utilitarian attitude. But many of the members of the CBI and TUC prefer to oppose the definite loss of political sovereignty than consider the uncertain economic gains – attitudes that are more affective than utilitarian.

The Institute of Directors (IOD), which mainly represents the interests of small and medium-sized enterprises (SMEs), is also strongly anti-European. However, unlike the rank-and-file of the CBI, this position can be justified on utilitarian grounds. Whereas large multinationals compete in EU-wide and global markets, these SMEs mainly compete for the domestic British market, and hence see trade liberalization in the EU single market as a threat to domestic competition. Also, these interests prefer an independent British monetary policy, designed specifically for British economic interests, rather than a 'one size fits all' interest rate in a single European currency.

Turning to the media, very few of the British papers are overtly pro-euro. Speaking for financial and large business interests, the *Financial Times* is certainly the most pro-single currency paper. The *Guardian*, the *Observer* and the *Mirror* support Blair's argument that integration within Europe is inherently a 'progressive' policy – which will lead to international cooperation, economic growth, higher environmental and social standards and the chance of regaining influence on the global stage. *The Economist*, on the other hand, argues that European integration can increase economic and political freedoms, but it may be time to move to a federal design for the EU, with an explicit 'states' rights' clause and the establishment of powerful checks-and-balances on Brussels' regulatory powers.

On the other side, the *Daily Telegraph* and the *Sunday Telegraph* are openly anti-euro. Although the press relations' gurus in the Blair administration have consciously sought to fraternize with the editors and political correspondents in the *Mail* and the *Express*, this has done little to change their continued opposition to Labour's European policy. Also, despite being sympathetic to Blair in the 1997 general election, the Murdoch press – *The Times* group and the *Sun* – remains vehemently anti-European, and often verges on outright xenophobia, particularly against German Commissioners, government ministers or MEPs.

Finally, several pressure groups have been established on each side of the debate over British membership of EMU. Among a plethora of anti-European parties, movements and alliances, *Business for Sterling* and the *Save the Pound* campaign have emerged as the main contenders to lead the campaign for a 'No' vote in a future referendum on the single currency. These two groups already enjoy the support of the Conservative Party leadership, are backed by a several daily newspapers (including the Murdoch press), and have raised a considerable amount of funding from the business community.

Surprised by the volume of resources gathered by the 'No' camp, the *Britain in Europe* movement was set up in early 1999 as a main umbrella group for the various pro-European groups – such as the *European Movement* – and a focus for fundraising for a 'Yes' campaign in a single currency referendum. *Britain in Europe* is supported by Tony Blair and other leading Labour figures as well as prominent pro-European Conservatives like Ken Clarke. However, Blair refused to back the campaign until after the 1999 European elections. Following the poor performance of Labour in the elections, the formal launch of *Britain in Europe* was postponed, as Blair was reluctant to come on strongly in favour of the euro. A compromise was reached in summer 1999 whereby Blair agreed to take part in the launch of the campaign, alongside several leading pro-European Conservatives, on the condition that the campaign focused on the general issue of a positive attitude towards the EU and took a low profile on the euro.

## The 1999 European Parliament election

Research on European elections has generally affirmed Reif and Schmitt's (1980) thesis about the first European elections, that they are essentially 'second-order national contests' (Eijk and Franklin, 1996; Marsh and Norris, 1997). In all political systems, elections that decide who holds national executive office are the main – 'first-order' – political contest. As a result, political parties cannot resist the opportunity to use all other elections – European elections, regional and local elections, second chamber elections or elections to choose a ceremonial head of state – as 'beauty contests' on the performance of the party/ies that won the last 'first-order' election. These other contests are thus 'second-order'. In other words, European elections are not about European issues, but are about the fight for national government office between national party leaders.

The 'second-order' nature of European elections leads to two phenomena. First, there is less incentive for supporters of governing parties to vote, and turnout is generally lower than in national general elections, with governing parties suffering most. Second, because the elections are about national government office, people who do vote often vote differently than if a national election were held at the same time. Either they vote sincerely instead of strategically ('vote with the heart') or they vote for opposition or protest parties to punish governing parties ('put the boot in'). The combined effect is that governing parties tend to lose votes in European elections, and opposition parties, single-issue parties and protest parties win votes.

These 'second-order' phenomena have always been a feature of European election in Britain, and this was again the case in June 1999. Table 4.1 shows that, as in 1994, the elections were won by the opposition parties – Labour in 1994 and the Conservatives in 1999. Whereas Labour was consistently standing at 50 per cent in opinion polls in the build up to the 1999 election, with a lead of between 15 and 20 per cent over the Conservatives, it achieved a dismal 28 per cent of the vote, almost

Table 4.1   *The 1994 and 1999 European election results*

|  | 1994 % of Vote | Seats | 1999 % of Votes | Seats |
|---|---|---|---|---|
| **Mainland Britain** | | | | |
| Conservative Party | 27.9 | 18 | 35.8 | 36 |
| Labour Party | 44.2 | 62 | 28.0 | 29 |
| Liberal Democrats | 16.7 | 2 | 12.7 | 10 |
| UK Independence Party | 0.8 | | 7.0 | 3 |
| Green Party | 3.2 | | 6.3 | 2 |
| Scottish National Party | 3.2 | 2 | 2.7 | 2 |
| Plaid Cymru | 1.1 | | 1.9 | 2 |
| Pro European Conservatives | – | | 1.4 | |
| Other parties | 2.9 | | 4.4 | |
| **Northern Ireland** | | | | |
| Democratic Unionist Party | 29.2 | 1 | 28.0 | 1 |
| Social Democratic and Labour Party | 28.9 | 1 | 27.7 | 1 |
| Ulster Unionist Party | 23.8 | 1 | 17.4 | 1 |
| Sinn Fein | 9.9 | | 17.1 | |
| Alliance Party | 4.1 | | 2.1 | |
| Other parties | 4.4 | | 7.7 | |
|  | 1994 | | 1999 | |
| Voter turnout in Mainland Britain | 36.1 | | 23.1 | |
| Voter turnout in Northern Ireland | 48.7 | | 57.7 | |
| Average voter turnout across Europe | 56.8 | | 49.4 | |

8 percentage points behind the Conservatives. Part of this can be explained by the turnout of only 23.1 per cent, which was the lowest ever in any nation-wide British election, and considerably lower than the average across Europe in the 1999 contest. As in all 'second-order' contests, and so soon after the local elections in May, many supporters of the governing party stayed home in the 1999 European election. The other main reason was that some of the Labour voters who did turn out decided to vote for other parties – such as the Greens. The Greens had done very well in the 1989 European election, with 15 per cent of the vote, but did not expect to reach the 6 per cent they achieved in 1999. Some anti-European Labour voters may also have supported the UK Independence Party (see Chapter 11).

These smaller parties were also helped by the introduction of Proportional Representation (PR) for this election. This was the first time that PR was used in a British-wide election, with a system of multi-member regional constituencies. Under this system, the smaller parties could argue that a vote for them would not be wasted, as they had a much better chance of winning a seat than under the old first-past-the-post system. As the allocation of seats shows, the introduction of PR ensured that three smaller parties won seats for the first time, and the Liberal Democrats gained 8 new seats, despite seeing their vote fall by 4 per cent since 1994. However, the increased opportunity for smaller parties under PR did not encourage more people to vote. In fact, some commentators claimed that the system of PR used in the elections may have encouraged people to stay at home. There was not much publicity about how the new system worked, voters were not able to vote for individual candidates under the closed-list system, and the length of the ballot papers (with over 10 parties and 100 candidates in most regions) was widely ridiculed by the press. The result in Northern Ireland, which has always used a single-transferable vote (STV) system for European elections, was the same as in 1994, with two seats going to Unionist parties and one to the Republican SDLP. The only surprise was that Sinn Fein, building on its success in the elections for the Northern Irish Assembly, almost beat the Ulster Unionist Party (UUP) for the third seat.

A third reason behind the switch in fortunes of Labour and the Conservatives was that some voters did express their attitudes towards the EU in their electoral preferences. Contrary to the standard 'second-order' theory of European elections, a proportion of voters in all member states – who are either strongly pro- or anti-Europe – does use these elections to express a preference about Europe (Blondel, Sinnott and Svensson, 1998). This proportion has a greater impact on the outcome when the turnout is especially low, as was the case in Britain in 1999. Whereas Blair consciously tried to play down the significance of the elections, in the knowledge that the introduction of PR would mean that Labour would lose at least 20 seats, Hague used the elections as a chance to illustrate the difference between the two parties on the question of Europe. Also, whereas Labour did not even issue its own manifesto (simply using the manifesto of the transnational Party of European Socialists), the Conservatives issued and widely publicized an openly Eurosceptic docu-ment. The Conservative leadership and rank-and-file also used the list-PR system to weed out, or place low down on the party lists, some of the 'federalist' sitting Conservative MEPs. Two such MEPs – John Stevens and Brendan Donnelly – withdrew their positions on the Conservative party lists and founded the 'Pro European Conservative Party', which presented a list in every region in mainland Britain. But, with such a low turnout, the strongly anti-European elements of the British electorate were able to mobilize. This enabled the UK Independence Party to win 7 per cent and the ('Anti-European') Conservative Party to win almost 36 per cent (see Chapter 11). In contrast, only 19 per cent of those who bothered to vote supported overtly pro-European parties: the Liberal Democrats, the Pro European Conservatives, and the two nationalist parties. In other words, the Conservative Party did gain some support from their anti-European stance in the 1999 European election. However, they were also helped by the continued existence of the 'second-order' effect (which meant that some anti-European Labour supporters probably voted for anti-European parties) and the low turnout (which meant that many Labour supporters stayed home, and vehemently anti-European voters mobilized for the contest).

## Conclusion

Because of his strategic position closer to the mainstream of EU politics, new Labour has a greater chance than perhaps any previous British government of being 'at the heart of Europe'. This partly explains why Blair has been reluctant to cater to the views of the median British voter – who is moderately Eurosceptic – or to bend to the whim of the British press – sections of which are vehemently Europhobic. Blair has not openly come out in support of British membership of the single currency, but continues to argue that European integration is in Britain's interests and that, given the right economic circumstances, it might be appropriate for Britain to join the euro. However, another reason for Blair's continued support for Europe is the position of his electorate, the economic interests he would like to attract and the attitudes of his parliamentary elite. The British professional middle class, and the British economic, political and cultural elite, are as pro-European as almost any in Europe. So, too, are the financial services sector, export-oriented manufacturing firms and the trade union movement.

The Conservative rank-and-file, Conservative MPs and the Conservative press are adamantly opposed to British membership of the single currency, and the race to succeed Hague in 2001 was heavily influenced by Europe, with the Eurosceptic Iain Duncan Smith beating the pro-European Ken Clarke to become Tory leader. Moreover, such attitudes are hard to change as they appear to be based on 'affective' (non-material) attitudes about British sovereignty, rather than 'utilitarian' (economic) attitudes about whether the single currency will increase individual economic well being.

Consequently, in a referendum on British membership of the euro the two sides of the contemporary campaign would be almost the reverse of the 1975 battle over British membership of the EEC. The moderate wings of Labour and the Conservatives are pro-European, but most Labour parliamentarians and supporters are now in favour of Europe, and most Conservative parliamentarians and supporters are now opposed. This might suggest that, as in 1975, the 'sensible' side of the campaign, based on the views of the moderates and presenting the economic case for membership, would win a referendum quite easily. However, there are two key differences this time. First, the tabloid media is almost universally hostile to Europe. Second, whereas public opinion on Europe in the early 1970s was relatively 'soft', and could hence be turned around in a relatively short time, the British public's attitudes towards Europe have 'hardened' since the early 1980s. In other words, if Blair decides to get off the fence and advocate British membership of the single currency, it will be an uphill battle.

# Chapter 5

# The Law and the Constitution

GILLIAN PEELE

'A central theme of this book is the extent to which constitutional reforms engineered by the 1997 Labour government have complemented other political developments to create new patterns of authority in the British state. Gradually, the UK is becoming a multi-layered and pluralistic democracy quite different in structure and culture from the older, heavily centralized system of government of the pre-1997 period. This chapter will focus on the constitutional characteristics of this emerging new polity, emphasizing especially the implications for the UK's legal institutions. One of the most significant, if unintended, effects of Blair's constitutional initiatives is to expand the role of law and the judiciary in the political system.

The role of the UK judiciary was, of course, already changing before 1997. The current programme of constitutional change makes a qualitative difference however as measures such as the incorporation of the European Convention on Human Rights (ECHR) and devolution bring judges to the centre of the political system and legitimizes a range of new tasks for them. Increasingly, the judges will have to resolve morally, politically and socially contentious issues as they weigh claims under the ECHR in British courts. Judges will become more visible simply because of an increase in the number of conflicts they will have to resolve, including challenges to the validity or *vires* of legislation passed by devolved bodies. Although these changes to the legal system have been brought about by parliamentary action, they will highlight institutions, processes and personnel that have generally escaped intense examination by students of politics. We can thus expect, in addition to a greater role for the British legal system, extensive debate about the competence and legitimacy of its officials.

## The changing structure of the British state

Dramatic though the series of constitutional reforms initiated by the Blair government have been, they must be placed in the context of a long-term process of adaption and reform dating from at least 1979. Over that longer period the EU had steadily become a significant factor in all aspects of British politics and policy-making. The scope of EU policy initiatives had increased and, although Britain initially remained outside the single currency, few doubted that the process of integration of the British economy into the wider European one would continue. The UK had come to terms with the constitutional superiority of EU law over Westminster legislation.

The evolution of the EU and Britain's role in it interacts with the Blair government's constitutional agenda. Few policy-making sectors can now be seen simply as national preserves so that the transfer of power to devolved assemblies inevitably raises complicated questions of multi-level decision-making. Even law and order, an area originally seen as primarily of national concern, is increasingly affected by European policy. The EU itself has become more sensitive to regional issues and more skilled at dealing with federal and quasi-federal states (St John Bates, 1997); it is thus likely that straightforward relationships between the UK national government and the devolved authority will be transformed as the EU or Edinburgh, Cardiff or Belfast seek to establish direct contacts by-passing London. The EU's dispute resolution process itself involves a much greater use of legal instruments than the UK's domestic government had traditionally done and the European Court of Justice (ECJ) is an important instrument of European integration. After the Amsterdam treaty, the EU became more concerned with issues of social and civil rights (Vibert, 1999). This development implies a direct relationship between the EU and its citizens in areas previously viewed as of exclusive national concern. The expanding scope of the EU's agenda means that UK political elites – including the judiciary – have to be more aware of, and open to, different styles of policy-making as well as increasingly sceptical about claims of national sovereignty. Formal powers and informal intellectual influences thus reinforce each other, eroding the autonomy of the English legal system.

In addition to the continuing changes brought about by Britain's membership of Europe, the British state has been changed as a result of indigenous developments. There has been an 'increasing preoccupation' with the potential uses of administrative law as judicial review became more widely available (St John Bates, 1997). Judicial review has become more salient politically mainly as a result of the British judges' own determination to construct a system of administrative law appropriate to the modern state. From the 1960s onwards legal challenges to administrative decisions became more common, although the increase in judicial review of ministerial decisions was disliked by both Labour and Conservative governments: few politicians in power welcomed a strong judiciary checking the executive.

Blair's reforms were grafted on to a state structure losing some of its traditional characteristics. One important legacy of the 1980s and 1990s which the Blair government accepted was the new style of public administration marked by deregulation, privatization and agencies (Hood, 1998; Hood and Scott 1996). This new public management created novel problems of accountability within the state. Finally, although this change was perhaps as much one of culture as of structure, the British state had become less marked by reliance on informal understandings than by regulation. Thus debate about the proper standards of conduct in public life and the desire to eliminate 'sleaze' led to the establishment of a standards commissioner to supplement the informal system of self-regulation by MPs, while legislation in 2000 created a new regime to regulate party funding (Committee on Standards in Public Life 1995; Neill 1998).

## A changing political culture?

The demands for greater formal regulation and for more effective instruments of accountability reflected wider cultural changes as well as greater exposure to the practices of other political systems. Wider international influences were also important in shaping a greater concern with human rights and civil liberties as well as with social rights. 'Rights-consciousness' was not limited to the high ground of moral principle, however. Within the UK, government-led initiatives under Margaret Thatcher and John Major had led to a growth in support for consumer rights both in the private sector and, more radically, within the welfare state. League tables and performance indicators became an important part of the health and educational sectors, producing at the very least greater openness and debate about service delivery standards.

## Labour and the law

One crucial shift in the political culture related to the Labour Party's attitude to the role of law in the modern state. The British left had a long-standing suspicion of the judiciary, which was seen as reactionary, drawn from a narrow social class, politically biased towards the Conservative Party and isolated from the mainstream of British life. For the trade union movement the struggle with the judiciary in the late nineteenth and early twentieth centuries was part of its collective memory. The battle over the 1971 Industrial Relations Act reawakened the historical antagonism between organized labour and the law. Although analysts are divided about how much discretion the judges in fact have, many on the left took the view that judicial neutrality was a pretence, cloaking the exercise of value preferences. And the values of the British judiciary often seemed inherently conservative – favouring, for example, property rights against welfare rights and government against civil liberties (Griffiths, 1977).

For Labour in the 1990s, however, the potential role of the law was very different. Britain's membership of the EU was one factor creating a new legal framework and transforming the relationship between policy-makers, politicians and lawyers. EU law is directly applicable in British courts and takes precedence over national law (Slynn, 1992). While the integrationist approach of the ECJ had in the 1980s and 1990s incurred hostility on the right (see, for example, Neill, 1994–5), the left had been generally more favourable to its rulings in such areas as pension entitlements, workers' rights and environmental action.

Similarly in opposition between 1979 and 1997 (in marked contrast to its attitude between 1964 and 1979) Labour had recognized that the growth of judicial review was unlikely to be reversed and there had been a marked growth of sympathy for the judges in their efforts to check the executive. Crucially, also, one impediment to a larger judicial role had been taken off the political agenda. The Thatcher governments' revision of industrial relations law had (unlike Heath's attempt to reform Britain's trade union laws) successfully subordinated trade union activity to comprehensive legal regulation.

These extensions of the judicial role were part of the new British state and for the most part new Labour had no quarrel with them in principle. More positively, law began to be seen as a tool for improving British democracy as a growing concern with rights and for strengthening accountability focused attention on public law. In this context, questions such as the availability of judicial review, access to justice and the need for a justiciable bill of rights within the UK formed a new agenda for Labour, enabling it to make common cause with like-minded groups such as Charter 88, Justice and the Constitutional Reform Unit (CRU).

The years 1979–97 also changed the judiciary. First, the judges became less complacent about the ability of traditional common law methods to protect civil liberties, and some senior judges publicly advocated a bill of rights (Scarman, 1992). Calls for constitutional reform reflected the widespread awareness of the extent of the power of the British executive and the limits of traditional restraints on its powers (Ewing and Gearty, 1990). Secondly, legal and penal policy saw dramatic and public conflicts between Conservative ministers and judges in the 1990s. The political salience of law and order issues made Home Secretaries anxious to appear tough on crime by stiffening sentences. Important elements within the legal profession – notably the Bar Council – also became alienated from the Conservative government's attempt to bring market-oriented reforms to the restrictive practices of the legal profession itself – the so-called 'bar wars' (Rozenberg, 1995). In fact, the 1997 Labour government was as keen as its predecessor to modernize the delivery of legal services, a cause which also found crucial support within the solicitors' branch of the legal profession. Labour was thus confronted with a world in which law inevitably played a larger part, in which many of the old prejudices had become irrelevant and in which there was both more antagonism between the judiciary, the bar and the Conservatives and much greater sympathy between Labour and the legal elite. By successively electing two lawyers, John Smith and Tony Blair, as leaders, Labour seemed symbolically to embrace the profession.

Blair's Lord Chancellor, Lord Irvine of Lairg (who had been his pupil master when Blair was a young lawyer) was determined to exercise a broader political role than his predecessor, Lord Mackay of Clashfern, had done. Labour's programme of constitutional reform gave him a key role as chair of a number of Cabinet committees. In addition to the Lord Chancellor, there are two other important legal figures within the government (but not in the Cabinet). The Attorney General, Lord Williams of Mostyn, and his deputy, the Solicitor General, Ross Cranston, are the government's law officers formally responsible for giving it legal advice. (The Lord Chancellor in theory does not do so because it might interfere with his position as head of the judiciary. In practice, however, it is likely that Lord Chancellors do from time to time give informal advice to their Cabinet colleagues, pointing up the conflict inherent in the office itself.) Although Irvine was the lawyer who attracted most attention in the 1997 Blair administration, Lord Falconer, Blair's first Solicitor General, who was promoted to the Cabinet Office, became a key government coordinator.

In addition to a series of constitutional reforms, Labour's 1997 manifesto also promised a modernization of the legal system. In many respects, the legal system seemed a prime target for a problem-centred approach to government, emphasizing 'joined-up government'. Although the idea of bringing all legal responsibilities within a single ministry of justice had been debated at least since the 1918 Haldane Committee, the administration of the legal system in the UK remained split between two government departments, the Lord Chancellor's Department (LCD) and the Home Office. The Lord Chancellor exercises responsibility for the court system, judicial appointments, law reform and legal aid and presides over a department which though small has been growing in importance. (Until 1971 there was no departmental structure at all – simply a Lord Chancellor's office – but following the Courts Act 1971 it gained departmental status.) Two executive agencies work within LCD: the Court Service and the Public Trust Office. The Home Office exercises responsibility for the criminal law and penal policy as well as the police, prisons and the probation service. By contrast with this divided structure, Scotland after 1999 chose to unite all responsibilities for legal administration within a single Ministry of Justice.

Traditionally, the LCD has been set somewhat apart from the mainstream of domestic policy. In recent years, however, its special status has been eroded as a result of tighter cost controls (in turn a result of spiralling legal aid costs), greater parliamentary scrutiny (a product of greater political interest) and a relative strengthening of policy direction by civil servants. The multiple functions of the Lord Chancellor and the physical separation of the LCD staff from their political head have tended to make its officials isolated (Egan, 1999).

The difficulties occasioned by the division of responsibilities for legal matters between departments has long been compounded by the complexities of different legal jurisdictions. The English and Welsh jurisdictions are identical except that Welsh may be used in court proceedings in Wales. Scotland's legal system is, however, very different from that of England and Wales. It has its own legal system administering a distinct body of law which owes more to Roman law than to English common law. In contrast with the 1978 devolution legislation, the Scottish court system is now wholly devolved. Criminal cases are heard in sheriffs' courts and the High Court of Justice (HCJ) while civil cases are heard in sheriffs' courts and the Court of Session. Although the House of Lords is the highest court of the system for Scottish *civil* cases, it does not hear *criminal* appeals from Scotland. Northern Ireland's legal structure is slightly different again and terrorism has caused modification of the criminal law.

## Tensions in Labour's approach

Beneath the general commitment to a range of constitutional reforms and to legal modernization there were, however, some unresolved tensions and ambiguities within the government about both constitutional reform and legal policy. First, it was unclear how far constitutional reform reflected a deep-rooted commitment within the Cabinet to the creation of a new legal and constitutional order with genuinely different values from the old political system. Did the government really accept the creation of a new balance between the state and the individual and between the centre, devolved governments and the regions even at the expense of a strong state? Or were the Scottish Parliament and Welsh Assembly (and, indeed, many of the other changes advanced) primarily minimal responses to difficult political situations and awkward commitments?

The handling of Freedom of Information legislation was indicative of these value conflicts. Although a freedom of information bill had been promised since 1997, the legislation was delayed to the dismay of civil liberties' groups and Labour backbenchers. Legislation is likely to be passed providing a general right to information, but the exceptions to the right include important areas such as material related to policy-making and information about incidents where legal proceedings are likely. Moreover the Information Commissioner, who would enforce the legislation, has powers only to *recommend*, not to compel, the release of information.

Similarly it was unclear how far British politicians would be able to adjust their constitutional thinking to take account of structural change. One of the oddities of the UK's membership of the EU was the capacity of senior politicians at the time of British entry to deny the constitutional implications of British membership and the determination of politicians of all parties since 1973 to cling to the myth of parliamentary sovereignty. Blair's government was similarly cautious in relation to its constitutional reforms.

Thirdly, it was unclear how far the individual measures of constitutional change were to be regarded as a coherent package. The series of measures introduced in rapid succession after 1997 were handled as individual self-contained pieces of legislation, initiated by different lead departments and drafted by different draftsmen. There were crucial differences of outlook between Irvine and Home Secretary Jack Straw over both the Human Rights Bill and freedom of information legislation. Nor was it clear how much thought was given to monitoring the interaction and operation of the constitutional reforms post-enactment.

Tensions also emerged in relation to criminal justice and the penal system. Crime was a high electoral priority and the 1997 Labour government was determined not to be seen as soft on law and order. Its approach to social policy emphasized the individual's obligations as well as rights in society. There were new initiatives to cope with anti-social behaviour (such as social exclusion orders) and to impose curfew orders on young people. As with civil justice there was a drive to speed up the process of justice and the Crime and Disorder Act of 1998 attempted to reduce delays. These measures brought Straw into conflict with civil liberties bodies such as *Liberty* and did not find an entirely sympathetic audience among Labour MPs.

Finally the handling of legal issues could not be divorced from the central question of public spending. In the debate on the Human Rights Act it was pointed out that access to justice was one of the most fundamental of rights and that it would be negated if individuals were deterred from using the legal system on cost grounds. Yet no Lord Chancellor could ignore the soaring costs of legal aid (which had been in crisis in the 1990s) and the Treasury search for economies in legal administration. For many lawyers, greater control of the legal system in the name of administrative efficiency threatened judicial independence and the integrity of the law, especially if it was suggested that there might be alternative forms of dispute resolution that were cheaper than the courts. The dilemma was one which the Labour government, despite its intention to build new bridges to the legal profession and the judiciary, could not avoid.

## The constitutional agenda

The speed of Labour's constitutional reform programme concerned some observers (Hazell, 1999). Devolution, House of Lords reform and the incorporation of the ECHR dominated Labour's first two years in power, but there was in addition legislation on the electoral system, regional government and a directly elected mayor for London as well as a series of enabling referenda and other measures. The delicate task of trying to re-establish devolved government for Northern Ireland required a good deal of ministerial and legislative time. But enacting constitutional reform was in some ways only the beginning: how it was implemented would be crucial, and one important factor in determining how these reforms would be implemented was the court system and the judges (Craig and Walters, 1999).

### Devolution

Although the reorganization of territorial jurisdiction within in the UK stopped short of creating a federal system, clearly the reforms would produce jurisdictional conflicts similar to those found in a federal system such as the United States or Germany. Different degrees of devolution were deemed appropriate for Scotland and Wales (see Chapter 7), and hence it may be assumed that Scotland rather than Wales will throw up the larger number of conflicts. The spirit of the devolution legislation for Scotland was more innovative and radical than that of 1978. Edinburgh's Parliament was not expected to replicate Westminster's procedures and it rapidly established its own legislative methods and a new approach to working methods and public relations. Matters such as the formation of the executive (which in 1978 had been left to convention) were given statutory basis and the role of the Secretary of State for Scotland was reduced so that he no longer acted as the channel of communication with the sovereign.

Whereas the Welsh Assembly was given a series of enumerated powers and the power to scrutinize secondary legislation, the Scottish Parliament was given a general legislative competence. The Scottish Parliament can pass primary as well as secondary legislation. Its legislative power is limited, however, by the retention by Westminster of specified subjects (such as defence and foreign policy) and by other provisions in the Scotland Act, notably clause 28. Clause 28 makes a provision *ultra vires* if it affects a territory outside Scotland, modifies the parent legislation, relates to reserved matters, is incompatible with Community law or European Convention rights or affects the role of the Lord Advocate.

Special procedures formal and informal are provided to deal with resolving questions of *vires* or legislative competence. Informally, it is expected that there will be extensive consultation at the drafting stage of bills. Formally, the Speaker or Presiding Officer of the Scottish Parliament, who is given a major constitutional role, must satisfy himself that a proposed measure is *intra vires* before giving approval for its introduction. There is a provision that bills may be reconsidered between passage and the Royal Assent if there are concerns about *vires*. If there is a dispute between Scottish executive and the UK government, the dispute will be resolved by the Judicial Committee of the Privy Council (JCPC), which will also consider disputes about 'devolution issues' (conflicts over the validity of measures) arising after the Royal Assent or referred to it in the course of ordinary court proceedings.

The use of the JCPC (rather than the House of Lords) recognizes the need to give special status to 'devolution issues'. The UK has no specialized constitutional court and constitutionally significant cases are handled in the ordinary court system which has as its highest court the House of Lords. The JCPC seemed a better forum for the resolution of 'devolution disputes' for positive and negative reasons. On the positive side its constitutional jurisdiction in relation to the Commonwealth had given it some expertise in conflict of powers' cases. More negatively, there was a feeling that although the judicial functions of the House of Lords are carried on quite separately from its legislative work, there might be a suspicion of bias if the House of Lords had to resolve a disputed use of legislative power between Westminster and a devolved body. The composition of the House of Lords judicial committee and the JCPC is very similar, but the JCPC has the advantage that it can include Scottish and Northern Irish judges as appropriate (Boyd, 1997); and it can sit outside London.

How much work the JCPC will have to do is unclear and the incidence of disputes over *vires* will reflect the broader political relationships between Westminster and the devolved bodies. In Scotland's case it seems likely that there will be an effort to grant the Scottish executive as much autonomy as possible. Thus although the UK government has the power to challenge legislation passed by the Scottish Parliament, it has pledged not to use those powers to challenge legislation on policy grounds but to limit itself to cases where there is doubt about the *vires* of legislation in the technical sense.

Inevitably devolution issues will arise in the course of ordinary court proceedings, not just in Scotland or Wales but throughout the UK. Special procedures are needed to ensure definitive resolution of these issues as with points of EU law. The Attorney General may require a case raising a devolution issue to be transferred from any court to the JCPC. If a devolution issue arises in court proceedings, the court may refer it to the JCPC, although such a referral is not mandatory if the court feels competent to decide it.

It remains to be seen how judges will operate the devolution legislation. They will have to be aware that they moving into a new constitutional era and interpret the legislation with political sensitivity as well as flexibility. Certainly we may expect here to see a movement by the judges towards a more purposive or teleological approach to statutory interpretation and away from the 'plain-words' method of resolving meaning. It is also highly likely that the increased caseload arising from devolution disputes will place additional strain on the courts, and especially on the JCPC and on the Attorney General's office.

## The Human Rights Act 1998

If the devolution legislation raised the possibility of the judiciary having to deal with federal-style conflicts of jurisdiction, the legislation incorporating the ECHR into British law increased the likelihood that British judges would have to address problems which turned much more explicitly on political and moral values and general principles than on rules of law and precedent. And even with the adoption of the so-called 'British model' of incorporation so carefully devised to avoid a head-on conflict between the judges and parliamentary sovereignty, it seems likely, as Lord Kingsland suggested in the House of Lords, that incorporation will be a 'defining influence' on the balance of power between the legislature and the judiciary.

The legislation has an impact across the legal system creating new rights and remedies against public authorities (Outhwaite and Wheeler, 1999). Labour's 1997 white paper (*Rights Brought Home*) (Home Office, 1997a) and the Human Rights Act 1998 created a model of rights enforcement which is a compromise between strong models of rights protection (which allow the judiciary to enforce civil rights against primary legislation) and weaker declaratory models.

The incorporation of the ECHR changes UK law in a number of ways. First, section 3 of the Human Rights Act requires the judges to interpret all legislation in a way that is compatible with Convention rights if it is at all possible. This change in statutory interpretation is important, pushing the judges to the use of a purposive rather than a literal standard of statutory construction. In the past, some judges had tried to take account of the ECHR's provisions (for example, protecting freedom of speech); but they were on weak ground without formal incorporation. Now they *must* take account of the ECHR. Secondly, the Human Rights Act makes it unlawful for any public authority to 'act in a way which is incompatible with a Convention right' and provides judicial remedies where rights have been violated. The Act also makes it possible to rely on Convention rights as a defence in judicial proceedings. Incorporation of the ECHR thus creates many new causes of action in public law and makes it inevitable that judges will have to resolve difficult value conflicts. Thirdly, the Act provides a novel mechanism for dealing with cases where the Convention and legislation conflict. Where a judge finds legislation incompatible with the ECHR (and cannot remove the incompatibility by interpretation) she must make a declaration of incompatibility. The legislation provides that a minister may, by order, amend the legislation to make it compatible with the Convention. This so-called 'fast-track' for dealing with legislation which violates the ECHR assumes that in many cases the government will wish to remedy the conflict. It leaves the government and Parliament free to resist a judicial declaration of incompatibility if it wishes to do so. Much thus depends on the willingness of a government to comply with judicial decisions. And much is also likely to depend on the attention and time ministers can themselves devote to these issues. Unfortunately, the new legislation does not yet provide for a monitoring organization (similar perhaps to Northern Ireland's advisory committee) to review compliance with the legislation and draw attention to problems with it.

The areas likely to be affected by the new legislation are extensive, affecting a wide range of public bodies as well as hybrid bodies with mixed public and private functions such as regulatory authorities. Freedom of speech protections may make many forms of censorship suspect. The impact on the law of medical negligence could be dramatic not least because Articles 2 and 3 of the Convention which protect the right to life and forbid torture or inhuman and degrading treatment are *absolute* rights. Failure by a public body such as the NHS to provide life-saving treatment cannot therefore be defended on resource grounds (Outhwaite and Wheeler, 1999). Family law is also likely to be affected, as are provisions governing discrimination where there has also been a tightening of protections offered by EC laws. Privacy and confidentiality acquire new protections as a result of incorporation; and the Convention provides important new rights in connection with the operation of the legal system itself and access to justice.

In some ways the impact of change may be less severe because in some areas the UK has already responded to ECHR rulings or anticipated legal challenges to its practices. Thus a recent privacy case saw the ECHR condemn the UK government's ban on homosexuals in the military. Much recent family law has been drafted with the Convention provisions in mind (Outhwaite and Wheeler, 1999). But there will probably be extensive use of the Convention to promote substantive claims in civil law and as a defence in criminal law. The effect of this increased use of the Convention could be to change the culture and to make public bodies more sensitive to individual rights. It could also provoke a backlash if policy is changed by court action in directions out of harmony with public opinion or if reliance on Convention rights appears to result in technical acquittals. The challenge for the judiciary will be to develop a jurisprudence of human rights which does not bring it or the Convention into acute public controversy.

## House of Lords reform

Reform of the second chamber was in many ways the most puzzling of the Labour constitutional reforms. Theoretically the case for the abolition of the right of hereditary peers to sit in Parliament was very strong; Labour's problem was how to reform the composition of the Lords without at the same time increasing its legitimacy and thereby threatening the supremacy of the Commons.

The process of Lords reform was staged rather than achieved in a 'big bang' single step. In 1999 the right of the hereditary peers to sit and vote in the upper chamber was removed by law. The original intention had been to exclude *all* hereditary peers but an amendment had the effect of preserving 92 hereditary peers as working members of the House of Lords until such time as a new formula could be agreed. A Commission under Lord Wakeham was given the task of finding a new formula for the House of Lords. It was told to take account of other constitutional developments such as devolution and that the supremacy of the Commons had to be maintained.

One solution to the problem of composition (which might have worked earlier) was a wholly appointed chamber. This had many advantages, not least of posing little threat to the House of Commons and of avoiding the need for a different electoral system. A wholly nominated House could also be constructed to maximize expertise and would allow the nomination of minority parties and cross-benchers. On the other hand, nomination appeared both undemocratic and created a massive opportunity for patronage. It seemed likely that the government would decide to slow further reform of the Lords following Wakeham's cautious recommendations released in January 2000, but following the General Election, a White Paper was published in November 2001. It proposes that only 20 per cent of members be elected, 20 per cent appointed independents and 60 per cent nominated by the political parties in line with their share of the vote at the previous General Election, with the last 92 hereditary peers losing their role.

Reform of the second chamber focuses attention on the peculiar position of the Law Lords, the lords of appeal in ordinary who are given life peerages on appointment. Historically the House of Lords has always had an important role as a judicial body and until the nineteenth century all peers were able to play a part in judicial proceedings. Today, the exercise of the House of Lords' judicial functions is a specialist task undertaken only by 12 law lords and peers who have held high judicial office. The presence of the Law Lords in a legislative body, however, may be thought to offend the separation of powers and *Justice*, an all-party group, recommended in May 1999 that the Law Lords should no longer sit in the House of Lords. It was suggested instead that there should be a new supreme court with a fixed number of judges who would sit in their own purpose-built building rather than as at present in the House of Lords itself. This supreme court could take over both the Law Lords' role as the final court of appeal and the functions exercised by the JCPC resolving devolution issues.

The position of the Lord Chancellor has come in for special criticism in relation to the separation of powers because he is not merely the head of the judiciary (though he does not often sit on cases) and a member of the House of Lords. He is also the presiding officer of the House of Lords and a member of the Cabinet. In the view of *Justice*, the Lord Chancellor's position as head of the judiciary should be taken by the Lord Chief Justice as the senior justice. Although there is theoretical merit in this argument, it is unlikely to be implemented swiftly. Certainly Irvine wished to retain all the functions of the Lord Chancellor's office, arguing in this respect as in many others that the British constitution was full of anomalies and that the incumbents of the office knew how to separate their various functions. It is possible that the Court of Human Rights itself may force the issue by ruling a similar overlap of functions in Guernsey contrary to the ECHR.

## The efficiency of the legal system

Few denied that these constitutional changes, especially incorporation of the ECHR, had serious implications for the UK legal system. Even if the changes turned out to be smaller than anticipated there remains the question of how suited the British judicial system is to *any* such expanded role.

## The composition of the judiciary

Any changes to the power of an institution will shift the focus of attention to its composition and the related question of who appoints the judiciary. There are different ways of defining the judiciary. Table 5.1 gives the official number of judges at different levels of the system as at 1 May 1999, and shows the number of women at each level (Lord Chancellor's Department, 1999). Politically the most sensitive appointments are those to the senior judiciary – judges of the High Court, the Court of Appeal and the House of Lords. One 1999 survey pointed to the continuing predominance of public school and Oxbridge in the educational background of the judiciary (*Labour Research*, 1999). There is also a near absence of female judges at the senior level, although as the official statistics show the position with regards to women judges is slightly better at the lower levels of the judiciary. This imbalance is significant because women are numerically expanding in the law, representing 43 per cent of its recruits but severely under-represented in the higher reaches of the profession. (Table 5.1 gives number of women judges at various levels of the judiciary.) There is also concern about the low level of ethnic minority recruits.

*Labour Research*'s criticism of the composition of the judiciary was in part sharpened by the awareness of the new role which judges will play in the British system, in part a reflection of disappointment that Labour had made so little difference. Indeed its calculations showed eight out 10 of those appointed since Labour came to power had been to public school (and hence presumably from an upper-middle-class background), compared with a figure of 69 per cent for judges overall (*Labour Research*, 1999). In fact, only on the age criterion had Labour's advent to power made a positive difference, with Labour's appointees being on average 55 years of age compared with the average age of 60 for the judiciary as a whole.

Two broad factors are important in skewing the composition of the judiciary towards white males from public school backgrounds. The first is its career structure, the second the appointments process itself. The career structure is important because the overwhelming majority of judges are recruited from the private bar, a small subset of the legal profession with its own close networks and culture and one which has traditionally demanded some degree of personal financial means to enter. Although it is theoretically now possible for solicitors to reach the judiciary, the Law Society, which represents the majority of the 80,000 lawyers practising in Britain, feels that its members are discriminated against in the judicial selection process.

## The appointments process

The Lord Chancellor is solely responsible for all judicial appointments below the level of the Court of Appeal. Appointments to the two highest courts, the Court of Appeal and the House of Lords, are made by the prime minister who takes advice from the Lord Chancellor but is not bound by it.

Table 5.1 *The number of women and former solicitors at different levels of the judiciary, 1 May 1999*

| | | Former Barristers | Former Solicitors | Total |
|---|---|---|---|---|
| Lords of Appeal in Ordinary | Women | – | – | – |
| | Men | 12 | – | 12 |
| | Total | 12 | – | 12 |
| Heads of Divisions | Women | – | – | – |
| | Men | 5 | – | 5 |
| | Total | 5 | – | 5 |
| Lords Justices of Appeal | Women | 1 | – | 1 |
| | Men | 34 | – | 34 |
| | Total | 35 | – | 35 |
| High Court Judges | Women | 8 | – | 8 |
| | Men | 88 | 1 | 89 |
| | Total | 96 | 1 | 97 |
| Circuit Judges | Women | 31 | 5 | 36 |
| | Men | 453 | 69 | 522 |
| | Total | 484 | 74 | 558 |
| Recorders | Women | 69 | 9 | 78 |
| | Men | 717 | 80 | 797 |
| | Total | 786 | 89 | 875 |
| Assistant Recorders | Women | 51 | 16 | 67 |
| | Men | 289 | 46 | 335 |
| | Total | 340 | 62 | 402 |
| Assistant Recorders in Training | Women | 18 | 2 | 20 |
| | Men | 88 | 4 | 92 |
| | Total | 106 | 6 | 112 |
| District Judges | Women | 5 | 47 | 52 |
| | Men | 13 | 313 | 326 |
| | Total | 18 | 360 | 378 |
| Deputy District Judges | Women | 9 | 89 | 98 |
| | Men | 23 | 646 | 669 |
| | Total | 32 | 735 | 767 |
| Metropolitian and Provincial Stipendiary Magistrates | Women | 11 | 2 | 13 |
| | Men | 25 | 55 | 80 |
| | Total | 36 | 57 | 93 |
| Acting Stipendiary | Women | 5 | 13 | 18 |
| | Men | 20 | 57 | 77 |
| | Total | 25 | 70 | 95 |

*Source:* Lord Chancellor's Department (1999).

Just how much political influence is involved in the process is unclear. It is difficult to believe that a prime minister with Blair's legal connections would not take a strong interest in legal appointments.

Some reforms to the appointments process were introduced by Mackay in an effort to make the process more transparent. There has been open competition since 1994 for the position of circuit judge. Mackay also introduced interview panels to undertake an initial sifting and interview of applicants. Irvine has ended the practice of appointing High Court judges by invitation and has introduced competition for these posts in addition to reviewing the procedures of appointment and reporting on the process to Parliament (Peach, 1999). Nevertheless there remains pressure (from groups such as *Justice* and the Howard League for Penal Reform) for a Judicial Appointments Commission to replace government nomination. It is not clear whether a more political role for the judiciary should entail more political input rather than less. Some observers have suggested a confirmation process akin to that of the US Senate, an idea which has gained support in the Conservative Party (Malleson, 1999). This has been introduced in Scotland for key judicial appointments. Although Labour was initially in favour of a Judicial Appointments Panel, Irvine has backed away from the idea, possibly for fear of alienating the judiciary (Malleson, 1999). Members of the senior judiciary have expressed their strong opposition to any process which would entail the public questioning of judges to ascertain their political views (Gibb, 1999b). Given the fact that recruitment to the judiciary is difficult in a climate where top barristers earn far more than judges, this opposition has to be taken very seriously.

## Judicial values

Any discussion of judicial attitudes must draw a distinction between the values displayed inside the courtroom in the process of reaching decisions – judicial methodology – and the attitudes of judges outside the courtroom. The traditional view of judicial methodology was that British judged interpreted but rarely made the law. Judicial discretion and judicial law-making powers were denied as politicians and senior lawyers colluded in what most now regard as a myth of neutral decision-making. It is indeed more appropriate for the political scientist to note that although lawyers and judges speak of the process of decision-making as though it were objective, it is in fact highly pragmatic both in relation to the interpretation of common law and of statute. Identifying precisely how the judges exercise their discretion is a difficult process. One problem is that the highest court – the House of Lords (which has an average caseload of perhaps 40 cases per year) – sits not as a whole court but in panels. Which judges hear a case can make a difference (Robertson, 1998). However, distinctions between judges are not to be measured in terms of self-consciously held beliefs or ideologies but rather differences of emphasis. Judges have the power to change their own working rules. Thus the House of Lords in a 1966 practice statement declared its willingness to depart from precedent from time to time; and in 1992 they changed the rule which had prevented them from referring to the parliamentary record to resolve an ambiguity in a statute (*Pepper* v. *Hart 1992*). At first sight this last development looked like a liberalizing move away from canons of interpretation which emphasize the literal meaning of the words towards a more purposive approach. The ability to refer to *Hansard* to clarify a statutory ambiguity may have the effect, however, of limiting judicial ability to adapt to new circumstances by freezing an interpretation 'within the contemporary understanding of the government of the day' (Robertson, 1998). In fact, it is likely that the freedom given by *Pepper*, like the other instruments of judicial construction, will be used selectively and in a *post hoc* fashion.

Outside the court the opinions of judges can affect the legitimacy of the wider legal system. Once judges would be appointed from barristers who had also had political careers; but it is now rare to see a combination of the professions, although of course the Lord Chancellor will normally have a strong partisan association. In the recent past judicial participation in public debate had been limited by the operation of the so-called 'Kilmuir rules', which prevented judges from appearing on television. These rules were repealed by Mackay in 1987 and the early 1990s saw an increase in judicial participation in public debate. Judges who are members of the House of Lords may also contribute to debate on legislation. This freedom may be seen either as an abuse of the separation of powers or as a useful way of adding to the expertise of the House. Moreover judges are frequently asked to chair sensitive commissions of inquiry.

It is unlikely that the judges could be shielded from political debates or administrative tasks, even if there was a strong argument for doing so. Clearly there is a need to avoid them becoming involved in partisan debate but that is relatively unlikely. The controversy over Lord Hoffmann's participation in General Pinochet's extradition hearing, despite the judge's links to Amnesty International, underlined the extent to which the British judicial system is in transition. Clearly Hoffman thought that he could trust himself to act fairly in the case; but the lawyers for Pinochet – and, as it turned out, Hoffmann's fellow Law Lords – thought the judge should have disqualified himself. Hoffmann's 'error' had the merit of opening wider debate about the extent to which an individual judge's attitudes were public knowledge. As became apparent later, many London law firms were creating files on judges in the hope of finding evidence which might disqualify a judge who might be unsympathetic to their client (Gibb, 1999a). This trend alarmed the Lord Chancellor and in September 1999 the senior judges, Lord Bingham, Lord Woolf and Sir Richard Scott called in five cases where challenges to judges had been made. But it is a sign of a changing legal culture which can no longer be operated on informal understandings. Greater prominence for the judiciary and a more political role will undoubtedly affect the behaviour of all the players in the legal system, requiring a robustness on the part of the judges themselves and a willingness to be subject to greater public scrutiny.

## Access to justice

How adequate is the legal system itself in coping with its existing role, let alone any additional strain placed on it by extra cases generated by new civil rights litigation or devolution? One measure of the increased demand for the resolution of disputes by the courts is the increase in the number of judges from 288 in 1970 to 3000 in 1998.

Two major problems dogged the courts in the 1990s: the overload on the civil justice system and the mounting cost of legal aid. The 1997 Labour government quickly established a review committee under Sir Peter Middleton to look in tandem at two reforming initiatives of its predecessor – the Woolf Report, on the structure of the civil courts (published as *Access to Justice*, Lord Chancellor's Department (1996a), in 1996) and the 1996 report on legal aid (*Striking the Balance*, Lord Chancellor's Department (1996b)). Middleton endorsed Woolf's findings that much of the cost and delay inherent in the civil system could be tackled by better case management and the use of different tracks for different kinds of cases, though he urged greater attention to the systematic implementation of the reforms. The first phase of those reforms was put in place in April 1999, with the rest scheduled over the next two years. As a result there are now effective timetables for civil cases, a three-track system for allocating cases according to monetary value and complexity and a system of judges in place by judicial area to help oversee the effective management of the caseload.

In the highly controversial field of legal aid, Middleton's concern that the cost of legal aid could not be controlled and that its resources were difficult to target led to the framing of a new approach. On the civil side it was suggested that much money could be saved if alternative dispute mechanisms to the courts were used, if contingent fee arrangements were made and if cases had to be subject to a merit test before granting public funding. On the criminal side, budgetary control could be imposed if a Criminal Defence Service (composed of salaried lawyers) and a small group of law firms handled criminal legal aid work rather than allowing the defendant complete freedom of choice among lawyers. There was fierce opposition to these changes, especially from the legal profession but also from those who saw the direction of change pointing towards a more limited and state-controlled legal aid system than the one introduced in 1949. The 1999 Access to Justice Act came into operation in April 2000. Although less sweeping than critics originally feared, it makes provision for a new Legal Services Commission (LSC) to replace the Legal Aid Board. The LSC will manage the Community Legal Service (which will deal with civil legal aid on the basis of a Funding Code which contains criteria for the application of public money to civil disputes) and the Criminal Defence Service which will provide some but not all of legally-aided criminal defence work, leaving the rest to firms who have been given government contracts.

## Conclusion

A series of high-profile constitutional reforms is restructuring the UK state and changing its institutional arrangements. In the new multi-layered polity there is greater scope for judicial activism and dispute resolution by the courts. This enhanced role will put new pressure both on the judges themselves and on the wider legal system. There will be demand for greater public accountability of the judicial system, both in terms of its ability to provide the necessary services and in terms of the opportunities for those who exercise power within the system. Although the Labour government has set in motion some modernizing policies and developed initiatives from its predecessors, these have proved highly controversial and may have undesirable side-effects in terms of access to the legal system. Legal reform is unlikely to go off the political agenda, but neither the British legal profession nor perhaps the government will be able to control the direction of change completely. In part this is because the UK's legal system is now subject to a variety of political and intellectual influences. Two external influences – the ECJ and the reorganized European Court of Human Rights – are bound to have an increasing influence on English jurisprudence as well as a direct impact on the substance of law. Equally the increasingly global nature of legal business – where mergers have created multi-national giants – have produced new players with interests beyond the nation state. All these circumstances suggest that not merely is the pace of change in the legal system likely to quicken but the lawyers are likely to play an ever-greater role in the governmental process.

# Chapter 6

# Executives and Administrations

IAN HOLLIDAY

Until about 30 years ago, analyzing the UK executive and administration was a fairly straightforward matter. The executive was based in London, and transacted the vast bulk of its business in Westminster and Whitehall. The administration was much more dispersed, with both the central state and local government employing substantial numbers of people outside London. But the home civil service was at least unified in the sense that it operated as a single organization with common rules, codes and structures, and even in local government the extent of administrative variance was frequently limited. Today things are more complex because of EC/EU membership since 1973, an administrative revolution spearheaded by Next Steps reforms since 1988, and devolution to the UK subnations since 1998–9. This chapter looks chiefly at the nature of the UK core executive following these changes, and also at the EU executive and the emergent devolved executives. It examines change in the administrative dimension of UK politics, focusing on central and local government. There are three main tasks: to explain the increasingly variegated nature of the executive and administrative dimensions of the UK state; to assess how power is being redistributed within UK executives and administrations; and to consider whether the changes that are currently taking place are helping Labour to deliver on its much-trumpeted promise of 'joined-up government'. The implications for UK democracy are also briefly considered.

## The UK core executive

The heart of the UK state, and the key driving force in UK politics, is the core executive. It is not altogether easy to identify. The 'core executive' is not a government department, like the Foreign and Commonwealth Office or the Department of Health, and it is not even a government office, like the Prime Minister's Office or the Cabinet Office. Instead, it is a concept developed by political scientists to mark out those parts of central government that are engaged not in one particular policy domain, or in supporting one specific part of government, but instead in coordinating

88

and possibly directing government policy across the whole range of business. The concept is, then, functional, in that it focuses on the tasks the core executive seeks to perform (Dunleavy and Rhodes, 1990, p. 4). As it happens, the concept, though not the actual term, is increasingly becoming part of the way in which individuals who work in the central state see things. To insiders, the set of individuals and offices that operates as the core executive now tends to be known as 'the centre' (Burch and Holliday, 1996, p. 1). The slightly ominous ring to the term is by no means accidental.

Adopting a functional perspective, the UK core executive may be defined as Cabinet (including, of course, the Prime Minister), Cabinet committees, the Cabinet Office, the Prime Minister's Office, parts of the Treasury, the major government law offices and those central elements engaged in managing the governing party's parliamentary support base (Figure 6.1). Since Labour took office in May 1997, several important changes have been made to its structure and operations.

## Cabinet and Cabinet committees

Looked at on paper, there is little to mark out the Blair Cabinets from any of their post-war predecessors. In June 2001, Tony Blair appointed 22 members of Cabinet, among them a new Minister Without Portfolio and Labour Party Chairman, Charles Clarke. A further three individuals – the Minister for Transport, the Minister of State for Work and the Government Chief Whip in the House of Lords – also attend Cabinet meetings without being members. There is nothing unusual in any of this. What is unusual is the use now made of Cabinet. In the early 1950s, Cabinet might meet more than 100 times a year, with the post-war record of 108 meetings being set in 1952 (Hennessy, 1986, p. 100). By the early 1970s, the number of annual meetings was down to a little over 60, which meant that Cabinet often met twice a week when Parliament was in session. In the 1980s and 1990s, that number fell still further to around 40 because both Margaret Thatcher and John Major held just one Thursday morning Cabinet per week when Parliament was sitting, and none when it was not (Burch and Holliday, 1996, pp. 44–5). Tony Blair makes yet more limited use of Cabinet. Weekly Cabinet meetings now rarely last more than an hour, and have been known to finish in 30 minutes. In place of a formal agenda, business is grouped under a series of headings, though Blair does not always take items in the order in which they appear. 'Cabinets,' Hennessy (1998, p. 11) has written, 'are now extraordinary affairs and not just because of their brevity'. Cabinet is unlikely to disappear from British political life altogether, but only deeply divisive matters requiring real consensus across government now get properly debated and decided there.

**Figure 6.1**   *The UK core executive*

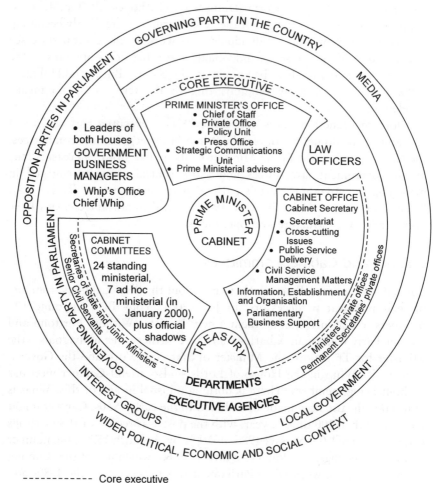

GOVERNING PARTY IN THE COUNTRY

OPPOSITION PARTIES IN PARLIAMENT

GOVERNMENT BUSINESS MANAGERS

MEDIA

CORE EXECUTIVE

PRIME MINISTER'S OFFICE
- Chief of Staff
- Private Office
- Policy Unit
- Press Office
- Strategic Communications Unit
- Prime Ministerial advisers

- Leaders of both Houses

- Whip's Office Chief Whip

LAW OFFICERS

PRIME MINISTER

CABINET

CABINET OFFICE
Cabinet Secretary
- Secretariat
- Cross-cutting Issues
- Public Service Delivery
- Civil Service Management Matters
- Information, Establishment and Organisation
- Parliamentary Business Support

CABINET COMMITTEES
24 standing ministerial, 7 ad hoc ministerial (in January 2000), plus official shadows

Secretaries of State and Junior Ministers Senior Civil Servants

GOVERNING PARTY IN PARLIAMENT

Ministers' private offices Permanent Secretaries' private offices

TREASURY

DEPARTMENTS

EXECUTIVE AGENCIES

INTEREST GROUPS

LOCAL GOVERNMENT

WIDER POLITICAL, ECONOMIC AND SOCIAL CONTEXT

- - - - - - - - - - -   Core executive

*Source:* Adapted from Burch and Holliday (1996), Figure 0.1.

It is actually many years since Cabinet was a real decision-taking forum: the work of central government has long been done elsewhere. In the course of the twentieth century, Cabinet committees increasingly became the places in which that business which flowed up from government departments into the core executive was really decided. This remains the case to a considerable extent, though an assertive Prime Minister with an enhanced support base (analyzed below) mean that business does not flow up from government departments quite so much. Instead, some business now flows down from the

Prime Minister and his immediate circle of advisers into subordinate parts of the government machine, notably ministers in their departments.

All that said, Cabinet committees retain a clear importance under Blair, and those individuals who sit on, or better still chair, key Cabinet committees remain critical members of the government. In June 2001, 34 standing ministerial committees and sub-committees of the Cabinet were created. Both types of committee are shown in Box 6.1, with the chair and number of members given. All ministerial committees have a shadowing official counterpart on which civil servants sit and shape (sometimes in important ways) the business that is to appear before ministers.

Looking at who chairs standing ministerial committees and sub-committees, we find that the key individuals are Prime Minister Tony Blair (who chairs four), Deputy Prime Minister John Prescott (five), Chancellor of the Exchequer Gordon Brown (three), Home Secretary David Blunkett (four), and Lord Chancellor Lord Irvine (four). Apart from Chief Secretary to the Treasury Andrew Smith (who chairs two committees), no other minister chairs more than one standing committee. By recent standards Blair has a full complement of Cabinet committees, but he makes less use of them than did any of his immediate predecessors. Again, this is in line with the trend of recent change. At the start of the Thatcher years the total number of Cabinet committee meetings (ministerial and official) fell by one-third from its late 1970s levels. By the start of the 1990s the number was down to one-half of late 1970s' levels. Under Major the number continued to fall, though less steeply, and the creation of ad hoc committees was also restricted as Cabinet committee business became more streamlined and routine (Burch and Holliday, 1996, p. 45). The number is down still further under Blair. Cabinet committees have in no sense been written out of the policy process, but there has been something of a shift away from them.

The obvious question is where that portion of business that would once have been transacted in Cabinet committee or, just occasionally, Cabinet, is now being handled. The answer is complex. Some strategic thinking takes place in ad hoc meetings of senior ministers convened by Tony Blair outside of Cabinet Committees, but further policy planning takes place in meetings involving the Prime Minister, his closest officials and advisers, and a senior minister and their advisers or, in some cases, between the PM and a senior minister alone. By far the most important of these bilaterals are Blair–Brown, which take place several times a week. Blair–Prescott meetings also constitute an important axis on the domestic front. Blair's personal rapport with Irvine, who (for this reason) chairs or sits on key Cabinet committees, makes meetings with him important. In the latter stages of the 1997 Parliament Blair was close to Lord Falconer (then Minister of State in the Cabinet Office), though his strategic place in the government was less substantial. Former Northern Ireland Secretary Peter Mandelson also remains a significant figure in the Prime Ministerial entourage. On a quarterly basis Blair meets key ministers and officials to check progress on the government's programme (*Economist*, 1999b). More detailed cross-departmental policy development takes place in the welter of units, task forces, reviews and groups created by this government (of which more later).

## The UK executive office

Supporting the work of key politicians in the core executive are leading civil servants. Formally, they are located in two distinct parts of the central state, the Prime Minister's Office and the Cabinet Office. However, a further trend visible in recent years has been effective fusion of the work of these two offices to the point at which they have become a single executive office in all but name (Burch and Holliday, 1999).

---

### Box 6.1  Standing ministerial committees and sub-committees of the Cabinet, September 2001

*Chaired by the Prime Minister, Tony Blair*
DOP         Defence and Overseas Policy (6)
IN           Northern Ireland (6)
CSI          Intelligence Services (5)
WR          Welfare Reform (6)

*Chaired by the Deputy Prime Minister, John Prescott*
DA           Domestic Affairs (20)
ENV          Environment (19)
CNR          Nations and Regions (20)
DA(SER)      Social Exclusion (13)
DA(N)        Energy Policy (8)

*Chaired by the Chancellor of the Exchequer, Gordon Brown*
EAPC         Economic Affairs, Productivity and Competitiveness (18)
PSX          Public Services and Public Expenditure (8)
EAPC(E)      Employment (12)

*Chaired by the Home Secretary, David Blunkett*
CJS          Criminal Justice System (8)
DA(ACF)      Active Communities and Family Issues (13)
DA(D)        Drugs Policy (5)
CJS(CR)      Crime Reduction (13)

$\longrightarrow$

---

→

*Chaired by the Lord Chancellor, Lord Irvine*
CRP        Constitutional Reform Policy (11)
CRP(EC)   Incorporation of the European Convention on Human Rights (21)
CRP(FOI)  Freedom of Information (21)
CRP(HL)   Reform of the House of Lords (10)

*Chaired by other ministers (as shown)*
EP         European Issues (22) *Foreign Secretary, Jack Straw*
GL         Local Government (16) *Secretary of State for Transport, Local Government and the Regions, Stephen Byers*
LP         Legislative Programme (14) *Leader of the House of Commons, Robin Cook*
SCI       Science Policy (9) *Secretary of State for Trade and Industry, Patricia Hewitt*
PSX(E)    Electronic Service Delivery (7) *Chief Secretary to the Treasury, Andrew Smith*
PSX(L)    Local Public Service Agreements (9) *Minister of State, Department for Transport, Local Government and the Regions, Nick Raynsford*
DA(ABS)  Adult Basic Skills (10) *Secretary for Education and Skills, Estelle Morris*
DA(EQ)   Equality (11) *Minister of State, Cabinet Office, Sally Morgan*
(DA(F)    Fraud (9) *Chief Secretary to the Treasury, Andrew Smith*
DA(OP)   Older People (17) *Secretary of State for Work and Pensions, Alastair Darling*
DA(RR)   Rural Renewal (10) *Secretary of State for Environment, Food and Rural Affairs, Margaret Beckett*
ENV(G)   Green Issues (18) *Environment Minister, Michael Meacher*
SCI(BIO)  Biotechnology (11) *Leader of the House of Commons, Robin Cook*

*Notes*:
1. For each committee, Cabinet Office designation and title are given.
2. Number of members is shown in brackets. Membership figures include government ministers (both in and outside the Cabinet) but do not include individuals like the Chief Medical Officer and the Chief Scientific Adviser,
3. In some cases ministers who are not members of a committee may be sent all the papers and invited to attend as necessary. In many cases ministers may be invited to attend committee meetings for matters in which they have a departmental interest.

*Source*: Cabinet Office website, available at < http://www.open.gov.uk/ >.

The Prime Minister's Office, located in 10 Downing Street, is headed by the Prime Minister on the political side and by his Chief of Staff, Jonathan Powell, on the official side. Powell held the same position in the Leader's Office in opposition, and was made a temporary civil servant when Blair became Prime Minister. The position of Chief of Staff is new, and is an attempt to generate greater coherence both within the Prime Minister's Office and between it and the Cabinet Office. Before the 2001 election the five main elements of the Prime Minister's Office, with approximate staff numbers in brackets, were as follows:

- Private Office (6): works directly to the Prime Minister
- Political Office (6): handles the Prime Minister's direct political business (including constituency matters)
- Press Office (12): oversees government relations with the media
- Policy Unit (13): engages in policy initiative
- Strategic Communications Unit (6): seeks to ensure all ministers are 'on message' and to coordinate their press relations; reports to the Press Secretary.

After the 2001 election, significant changes were effected in the structure of Downing Street. While Jonathan Powell, the Prime Minister's Chief of Staff, retained overall management of Downing Street, the Private Office and Policy Unit have been merged into a Policy Directorate under the leadership of a career civil servant, Jeremy Heywood, the Prime Minister's Principal Private Secretary. Two other directorates have been established, Communications and Strategy and Government Relations. Communications and Strategy, headed by Blair's close adviser, Alastair Campbell, deals with press relations, political communications, policy presentation and strategic planning. Campbell, the Prime Minister's Official Spokesperson, 1997–2001, no longer takes the lead in briefing the news media, and this task has been given to two career civil servants. Government Relations, headed by Anji Hunter, and then by Lady Morgan, deals with relations with ministers, governmental departments, devolved administrations, the Labour Party and other outside bodies. The unity, effectiveness and profile of the office as a whole have increased under Powell, with the result that ever more business flows into and out of it.

The Cabinet Office, located chiefly at 70 Whitehall (with a connecting door to the Prime Minister's Office), is led on the political side by Blair but since the 2001 election is administratively headed by the Deputy Prime Minister, John Prescott On the official side the head is Sir Richard Wilson (Cabinet Secretary and Head of the Home Civil Service). Following a review undertaken by Wilson at the start of 1998, the Cabinet Office was substantially reorganized. The most significant changes were, however, made to those parts dealing with civil service management and public service delivery, and are therefore examined later in the chapter. The element of the Cabinet Office that is most relevant here is the Cabinet Secretariat, which oversees business passing through Cabinet and its main committees. It is divided into five parts:

- Central
- Constitution
- Defence and Overseas
- Economic and Domestic
- European.

In addition to reforms within Downing Street, the Cabinet Office, only nominally under the control of the Deputy Prime Minister, John Prescott, continues to be brought ever further within the ambit of Downing Street. The number of Cabinet Office ministers was increased in June 2001, among them several loyal Blairites, including Charles Clarke and Sally Morgan. An Office of Public Service Reform, a Delivery Unit and a Forward Strategy Unit, all based in the Cabinet Office and reporting to the Prime Minister, have been set up, designed to advance reforms in public services, particularly in four key areas, health, education, crime and transport. The Downing Street Policy Directorate's influence over the Cabinet Office has been significantly strengthened – and the Prime Minister's influence over European, foreign and defence policy enhanced – by the appointments of Sir Stephen Wall as the Prime Minister's European Union Adviser (while remaining the head of the European Secretariat in the Cabinet Office) and Sir David Manning, Britain's Ambassador to NATO, as the Prime Minister's Foreign Policy Adviser on all other foreign issues.

Since 1997 the Cabinet Office also acts as the institutional home for special units created to deal with important policy issues that cross departmental boundaries. Following the Wilson review, four such units were located there:

- Social Exclusion Unit, formed in December 1997
- Performance and Innovation Unit, formed in July 1998
- Women's Unit, transferred from the Department of Social Security in July 1998
- UK Anti-Drugs Co-ordination Unit, brought fully into the Cabinet Office in July 1998.

Having any one of these units in the Cabinet Office would not be particularly unusual. Having four units dealing with cross-cutting issues is unprecedented. Moreover, each is more interventionist than any of its predecessors, and brings in expert outsiders to work alongside civil servants.

The discrete changes made within the Prime Minister's and Cabinet Offices since May 1997 are important in themselves and have enhanced central capacity within the UK state. However, of greater significance is the increased coordination and integration of these two offices which makes them, in effect, a single executive office. The main aspects of this integration are: a roving brief for Powell in bringing together the work of the two offices; a weekly planning meeting in 10 Downing Street chaired by Blair and attended by Mowlam, Powell, Miliband, Wilson and the heads of the four main parts of the Cabinet Secretariat; and increasingly close policy-making links between the Policy Unit and the Cabinet Secretariat.

## The rest of the core executive

The elements of the core executive that have not yet been analyzed are parts of the Treasury, the major government law offices and those central offices engaged in managing the governing party's parliamentary support base. Here the main changes have focused on the Treasury, which has enhanced its profile at the centre of the state (see Chapter 13). It helps that the current Chancellor is powerful even by the standards set by some of his predecessors. Brown was a leading contender for the Labour Party leadership that Blair in fact won, and remains a formidable figure in the party and government. His personal authority, not to mention his forceful personality, have made him a critical figure in driving Labour's agenda forward. But the character of the present Chancellor does not explain all of the change witnessed since 1997. Structural reforms have also been made, by far the most important of which was the early introduction of a Comprehensive Spending Review (CSR). This is a three-year forward-planning mechanism by means of which the Treasury has increased its control of departmental spending plans. In the past departmental budgets were agreed on an annual basis, and the Treasury could find itself forced into a corner at the end of a particularly difficult spending round (which, in recent decades, most have turned out to be). Now the Chancellor chairs a Cabinet committee (PSX) before which ministers must explain and defend their spending claims over a three-year period. The Treasury is therefore in a position to ask tough and pointed questions about budgets that stretch well beyond the current political fixations and cannot be sneaked through on a wave of media frenzy. Indeed, the Treasury is now able itself to play a role in shaping departmental spending plans and priorities. There is also a second dimension to the CSR, which is that in being allocated cash by the Treasury departments have to sign a Public Service Agreement imposing clear delivery targets on their future performance. The Treasury has always been critical where money – taxing and spending – is concerned. The CSR is an important new weapon in its perennial battle with government departments.

The other changes worth noting here concern the government's business managers, the most important of whom are the Leaders of the two Houses and the government Chief Whips in both Houses. Under Blair the Chief Whip in the Commons, Hilary Armstrong is a member of Cabinet. Perhaps more significantly, the staff and offices of the government's business managers are now more closely integrated into the Cabinet Office than ever before. These innovations reflect the government's strong concern to leave as little as possible to chance in managing its parliamentary support base, a concern that parallels the control imposed by the leadership on the wider party both before and after the 1997 general election.

## Blair's core executive

What is being witnessed under Blair are yet further reinforcement of the Prime Minister's position at the heart of the executive domain, yet greater attempts by the executive to coordinate its internal operations and yet more refined efforts by the executive to manage its relationships with the wider world (including the media). In some ways what Blair has done is retreat still further than did any of his predecessors into the executive domain in order to project from a position of strength on to the wider Labour Party and country as a whole. Data gathered in the late 1980s showed that Thatcher was the least parliamentary Prime Minister of modern times (post-1867) (Dunleavy, Jones and O'Leary, 1990, pp. 136–7). Blair has surpassed even her record of parliamentary non-attendance. It would be wrong to exaggerate, but there is a sense in which government is increasingly by referendum, focus group and opinion poll, which are now important means by which the executive seeks to relate to the public. Similarly, Thatcher was a notoriously directive Prime Minister, yet the core executive over which she presided was nothing like as unitary and focused as the one that exists now. Finally, Thatcher's press secretary, Bernard Ingham, held by many to be the most controlling of Press Secretaries, was surpassed by Campbell, whose management of the Whitehall (not just Downing Street) press function in the 1997 Parliament was more sophisticated and directing than anything seen before.

None of this is to suggest that the Blair core executive has solved all the problems that beset each and every one of its predecessors in coordinating and directing the vast range of business in which contemporary UK governments are engaged. Much still slips through the net for one reason or another. Indeed, the present government has generated a degree of executive fragmentation – in the units, task forces, reviews and groups that it so favours – that could actually make imposing any sense of central direction on government policy harder rather than easier. Beyond that, there is plenty of resistance in the wider executive to control mechanisms launched from the centre, and as in all governments a certain amount of policy entrepreneurship and empire-building is certainly taking place. Ministers like Jack Straw (now Foreign Secretary) and David Blunkett (now Home Secretary) were not to start with members of the Labour government's central core, but they, particularly Blunkett, have increasingly been regarded as 'heavy hitters'. They form part of a second tier of key ministers. A third tier comprises the territorial ministers and others. Finally, there are of course tensions within the central core itself. On a personal level, rivalries abound, not simply between the Prime Minister and his Chancellor as frequently (and exaggeratedly) reported in the press, but also between other members of the Big Four. Just as important are institutional tensions at the centre. Two very established government departments, the Treasury and Foreign Office (since 1968 the Foreign and Commonwealth Office), spent much of the twentieth century observing the emergence of an increasingly powerful core executive focused on the Cabinet and Prime Minister's Offices. This emergence has not been entirely to the liking of civil servants and ministers in these departments, and at least partly underpins the institutional conflict that has surfaced on a series of occasions since 1985 (when UK participation in a single European currency first became a dominant issue in domestic politics). Under Brown, the Treasury has made a clear bid to gain, or regain, power through the CSR and the linked Public Service Agreements (see Chapter 13).

Blair's core executive is therefore more substantial and more integrated than any of its predecessors, reflecting the trend change since the start of the twentieth century. This change has been driven by the pressures of administration and the possibilities opened up by technology as much as by the 'power lust' of central actors. The core still remains reactive to policy initiatives taken elsewhere, from the rest of the central state to the EU and yet more distant places. Moreover, it continues to provoke a reaction on the part of those elements of the state with most to lose from a centralization of power in and around Number 10.

## The EU executive

The EU is a strange set of institutions with no single organization that can be identified as an executive. The Council of Ministers comes closest, for it is here that representatives of the executives of member states come together to agree policy. However, this is equally true of the European Council. Beyond that, the European Commission also possesses some executive functions, including the exclusive right formally to initiate policy by issuing white papers and the like.

Since the mid-1980s the major change to have affected the *Council of Ministers* is the introduction of qualified majority voting (QMV) and its use in an increasing number of policy areas. The result is that there is usually no such thing as a national veto, which means that the UK, and all other member states, can be outvoted even on important issues. The rather less fractious relations the UK has had with the EU since 1997 mean that fewer squabbles get reported in the press, but it remains the case that the UK government position sometimes either has to be modified or is actually rejected outright. The latest revisions to EU governance, contained in the Amsterdam Treaty (which came into effect on 1 May 1999), did not greatly extend the use of QMV: out of more than 60 policy areas requiring unanimity pre-Amsterdam, only five were switched to QMV (Geddes, 1999, p. 49).

The *European Council* tends to operate rather informally and can be strongly affected by shifts of personnel. In the late 1990s the two biggest changes of this kind were the replacement of Major by Blair as UK Prime Minister in May 1997, and the replacement of Helmut Kohl by Gerhard Schröder as German Chancellor in September 1998. More generally, the EU experienced a shift to the centre-left. This had no institutional implications for the European Council itself, but it did generate a shift in the political context within which major EU initiatives were shaped. Initially it was thought to have prompted something of a move away from neo-liberal economics towards a focus on the social dimension associated with German Finance Minister Oskar Lafontaine. However, Lafontaine's resignation in March 1999, five months into the life of the new government, turned attention to the more important Blair–Schröder axis, which in June 1999 resulted in publication of the modernizing Anglo–German paper, 'Europe, the Third Way, *die neue Mitte*'. This document and Blair's 'good war' in Kosovo were held to indicate that he had succeeded in realizing the Majorite dream of positioning the UK 'at the heart of Europe'. However, French resistance to the charms of the Third Way and increasing German scepticism suggested that the dream had still not been turned into reality by the start of the new century. The UK's non-participation in the euro was also critical here.

Under the self-confident leadership of Jacques Delors, the *European Commission* was a major factor in the EU's integrative surge of the late 1980s and early 1990s, which produced first the single European market and secondly the euro. By the late 1990s the 20-person Commission was on much more uncertain ground as it struggled with the linked challenges of Eastern enlargement and institutional re-engineering. It also found itself enveloped in a series of corruption scandals that an increasingly assertive European Parliament was not slow to exploit. On 15 March 1999 the Commission headed by Jacques Santer resigned *en masse*, and a replacement under new President Romano Prodi eventually took its place. Only four members of the outgoing Commission were given portfolios in the new one. More important was a small amount of institutional restructuring undertaken in the process. In taking no portfolio himself, Prodi enhanced his room for manoeuvre in directing overall Commission business – much as, say, Blair directs UK government business. He also appointed two Commission Vice Presidents (Neil Kinnock and Loyola de Palacio) in an attempt to give the Commission a clearer sense of hierarchy. Finally, he is said to have secured from each Commissioner a promise to resign if asked to do so. There is, however, no provision in the EU's core treaties for this.

In some ways the EU executive is gradually becoming more streamlined and focused. However, the European Central Bank (ECB), created in 1998, is a key functional agency not answerable to an executive. It is possible that this is how EU politics will develop in the future, with a proliferation of agencies not linked to an over-arching supranational executive.

## The devolved executives

At the same time as central capacity within the UK state has been enhanced, so reforms have been put in place to devolve power away from London to three of the UK's constituent subnations, Scotland, Wales and Northern Ireland, as well as to a reconstituted strategic authority for London (see Chapters 3 and 7). This is one of the apparent paradoxes of the Blair government. In the three subnations, elections held in July 1998 (Northern Ireland) and May 1999 (Scotland and Wales) produced assemblies from which executives have been drawn.

The UK's is an instance of asymmetric devolution in the sense that distinct regions are being given different sets of powers at variable times and speeds, although there are as yet no firm plans to move beyond regional development agencies and appointed regional chambers in England (the case of London excepted). Among the three UK devolved executives, the greatest powers have been given to the Scottish and the smallest to the Welsh (Chapter 7). In Scotland the executive comprises a ministerial team of 22 (including two law officers), of whom 11 sit in a Cabinet headed by the First Minister (initially Donald Dewar and since his death by Henry McLeish and then Jack O'Connell). Statutory powers in relation to devolved matters were transferred to Scottish ministers on 1 July 1999. In Wales on the same date statutory powers were devolved to the Welsh Assembly, which delegated executive powers to then First Secretary Alun Michael. He in turn delegated some powers to the eight Assembly Secretaries who make up the Assembly Cabinet. This arrangement was retained when Rhodri Morgan replaced Michael as First Secretary in February 2000. Problems with the peace process meant that the 12-member Northern Ireland executive was not formed until December 1999, when powers were also briefly devolved. These various differences reflect the distinct historical circumstances of entry into the union, and the equally distinct contemporary context of nationalist political pressures (Holliday, 1999).

Relationships between the devolved executives and the rest of the UK state were managed in the period immediately before and immediately after the first assembly elections through a series of settlements – known as 'administrative concordats' – negotiated first by officials and subsequently by politicians in Whitehall and the devolved capitals. The existence of a functioning Northern Ireland assembly in Stormont for the half-century to its abrogation in 1972, and the wholesale transfer of almost all its powers to the Northern Ireland Office, means that disengaging the new Northern Ireland polity from the rest of the UK state has been less difficult than disentangling its Scottish and Welsh counterparts. Even though a Scottish Office was created in 1885 and a Welsh Office in 1964, both were substantially integrated into the mainstream of UK government business. From 1999 the Scottish Office became known as the Scottish Executive, and had six main departments: Justice, Health, Rural Affairs, Development, Education and Enterprise and Lifelong Learning. It also had three central offices: Secretariat, Corporate Services and Finance. From 1999 the functions of the Welsh Office were transferred to the Welsh Assembly. However, in both cases the list of devolved powers goes beyond those formerly controlled by the territorial offices. More importantly, the existence of the devolved assemblies means that new lines of accountability are now in place and need to be catered for. Whereas prior to devolution all national business could ultimately be resolved in Whitehall, since devolution this has not been the case. One institutional response is creation of a Joint Ministerial Committee between the UK government and the devolved administrations, backed up by official committees and a joint secretariat. A wider response was formation of British–Irish institutions, as part of the 1998 Good Friday Agreement, on some of which the devolved executives have representation alongside their national counterparts from the UK and Ireland.

Relations with the EU are critical to all three subnations. Their economies are more open than the UK economy as a whole, they are important recipients of inward investment and partly for this reason are heavily reliant on EU markets for export business. In addition, substantial parts of all three subnations are eligible for support under the territorial aspects of EU structural programmes. Beyond this, important policy sectors, such as agriculture, fisheries and forestry, have a vital EU policy component. Indeed, all three territorial offices have long been in the anomalous position of being substantially implicated in EU business whilst having the policy lead in no single area. All subnational input has been fed through the UK central state in Whitehall, and in more ad hoc ways through secondment of officials to relevant EU organs such as the

Commission, the Council of Ministers and the UK's permanent representation in Brussels (UKREP). Developing a new relationship with Brussels and a proper role in the EU policy process are therefore highly important for all three devolved executives, and equally quite problematic for the central state. In all three cases the relevant Acts make formal relations with the EU a reserve matter for the UK government. However, in each case responsibility for observing and implementing aspects of EU policy is devolved.

The fact that the devolved executives in Scotland and Wales are dominated by Labour means that some of the tensions that could one day characterize relations with London may not be seen in the early years of their existence. Labour's lack of a secure majority in both the Scottish Parliament and the Welsh Assembly means that a tension-free existence cannot, however, be taken for granted. Indeed, the resignation of Alun Michael as Welsh First Secretary in February 2000 may be only one of many central devolved tensions. More generally, there is certain to be some institutional friction as the new executives seek to flex their muscles and the established executive in London seeks to protect its turf.

## The administrative dimension

The administrative changes now affecting the UK state are many and varied. The big reform of the late Thatcher and Major years, the piecemeal creation of Next Steps executive agencies, had largely worked its way through the system by the time the Labour government entered office and was not contested (Theakston, 1997). In the process, Next Steps took around three-quarters of UK civil servants into executive agencies. The largest is the Benefits Agency (of the Department of Social Security), which employs more than 70 000 staff, administers more than 20 kinds of social security benefit, and disburses more than £80 billion of public money. Although the Blair government has not launched a reform initiative of this magnitude, it has nevertheless sponsored important administrative changes in both central and local government.

At the very heart of the UK state, some administrative changes formed part of the general restructuring of the Cabinet Office undertaken in July 1998 following the Wilson review. The Office of Public Service, formed in the early 1990s, was closed down; the most significant successor sections are Civil Service Management Matters and Public Service Delivery. The latter contains the Regulatory Impact Unit, the Central IT Unit, the Modernizing Public Services Group (incorporating the Service First Unit and the Effective Performance Division) and the Modernizing Government Team. These units oversee many of the Labour government's administrative reform initiatives, working alongside Cabinet committees (Central IT Unit and MISC 4; Modernizing Government Team and MISC 7), task forces (Regulatory Impact Unit and the Better Regulation Task Force) and ministers (Central IT Unit in advising on IT strategy). This is a further instance of policy being driven from the core executive.

The most distinctive administrative innovation of the Blair years is a task-force approach to government. 'May the taskforce be with you', stated the *New Statesman* in August 1997 as such bodies began to litter government departments (Daniel, 1997). Task forces are typically given a specific brief, a clear deadline and a set of outsiders to work alongside civil servants. No one can say precisely how many task forces, units, reviews, advisory groups and so on have been created since May 1997, but a count at the end of Labour's first year or so in office came up with the figure of 227 (Barker, 1998). The number is certainly now over 300. The key aspects of this approach are the use of outsiders and a willingness to ignore traditional departmental boundaries in the search for policy solutions. The most important task forces – in fact called units – are the four now located in the Cabinet Office to deal with cross-cutting issues (see above).

The reliance on task forces reflects the government's preference for a partnership approach to problem-solving and administration. Individuals with hands-on experience from both the public and private sectors are the key to good policy-making. Formal institutional boundaries, both within the state and between it and civil society, must not be allowed to stand in the way of the central task of finding 'joined-up' solutions. 'What counts,' insists Blair, 'is what works.' It is, of course, hard to find anything intrinsically wrong with this, though in practice it tends towards what *The Economist* has dubbed 'a new corporatism' (*Economist*, 1999a). Most remarkable in many ways is the fact that there are now very strong links between the Labour government and big business: 28 of the FTSE-100 companies have donated either their chairman or their chief executive as a part-time adviser to the government. 'This is a departure,' notes *The Economist*, 'not just for the Labour Party, but for British government as a whole' (*Economist*, 1999a, p. 48). Whether a new cronyism – the point of the frequently-heard 'Tony's cronies' jibe – will in fact emerge and prove embarrassing to the government in the long term remains to be seen.

Beyond the central state, local government has also had some experience of the Blairite drive for administrative efficiency and effectiveness. Taking 'better value' as the central theme of its modernization programme, the Labour government has sought to move away from what was widely perceived as a Conservative assault on local councils by being nice as well as nasty. The continuing nastiness comprises a series of controls on local government spending and operations. On the spending side, central government retains important reserve powers to control local government finance. On the operations side, the four main strands of 'best value', which has replaced compulsory competitive tendering (CCT), are service targets (based largely on the Thatcherite 3Es of Economy, Efficiency and

Effectiveness), annual local performance plans, new external audit and inspection requirements and consultation with the public. The balancing niceness comprises the abolition of CCT just mentioned, a Central–Local Partnership forum created in June 1997 and chaired by the Deputy Prime Minister (who is also Secretary of State for the Environment, Transport and the Regions, DETR), arguably more money for local authorities and the possibility that well-performing ('beacon') councils will one day be given significant discretionary powers.

It would be a mistake to mention only the rather controlling side of Labour's administrative philosophy. Another part of that philosophy is a strong commitment to electronic service delivery, evident in the *Modernizing Government* initiatives already listed. Moreover, anyone who has conducted research into the operations of the British state will have found this government to be far more open than any of its predecessors, in large part because it has built on the Major government's decision to place a wealth of information on the Web. In this respect the change that has taken place in the few years since the mid-1990s is huge. The Blair government has also created a People's Panel run by the Modernizing Public Services Group in the Cabinet Office (see Chapter 11). This comprises 5000 representative individuals, randomly selected, who are consulted three times a year on how public services are delivered and how that delivery can be improved. Any public sector organization can make use of the panel, which is claimed as a world first at national level. Early studies focused on transport, local democracy and complaints handling. More generally, the Modernizing Public Services Group oversees a large array of initiatives designed to improve public service delivery (Box 6.2). It should also be noted that the government now issues an Annual Report at the end of each parliamentary session, though the early ones were highly self-serving. Nevertheless, each of these elements represents a genuine attempt to make the state more responsive to the real wants and needs of British people, and more transparent in the ways in which it goes about meeting those wants and needs.

It is worth mentioning some elements that are missing. There has been no major restructuring of government departments (Prescott's rather mammoth department excepted), and no attempt to run a big reform programme through the civil service. Genuine freedom of information legislation is being resisted in the time-honoured fashion, at least in England. (It is being addressed separately by the Scottish Parliament.) Incorporation of the European Convention on Human Rights (ECHR) into British law will nevertheless take place in October 2000. This is a little later than intended to allow more time for officials to prepare themselves for a new era in which human rights provisions (a novel concept for the UK) become actionable in domestic courts.

---

## Box 6.2 Key elements of *Modernizing Government*

**Opening up government**

- Public services to be made available 24 hours a day, 7 days a week where there is a demand (e.g. NHS Direct by the end of 2000)
- Change of basic details (e.g. address) to be notifiable to all parts of government electronically and in a single transaction
- All dealings with government to be deliverable electronically by 2008

**Changing the way civil servants work**

- Enhanced focus on delivery, with permanent secretaries being made personally responsible for ensuring key departmental performance targets are met
- Possibility of financial reward for civil servants who identify financial savings or service improvements
- 'Learning Labs' to encourage new ways of frontline working by suspending rules that stifle innovation
- Drive to remove unnecessary regulation, with departments required to submit Regulatory Impact Assessments for policies that impose new regulatory burdens

*Source:* Cabinet Office website, available at < http://www.open.gov.uk/ >.

---

The chief characteristic of the Blair government in the administrative domain is its pragmatism and willingness to learn from anyone with good ideas. The private sector is often held to be an important repository of such ideas, but the true core of this government's administrative approach is its refusal to take a clear line on the virtues of public versus private sector management. Best outcomes are the focus of attention, and the processes by which they are attained are comparatively unimportant.

## Conclusion

The UK state is becoming ever more complex as a result of domestic changes and EU membership. The two key questions concern the ways in which power is being shifted, and the extent to which government is becoming 'joined up'.

The issue of power is always tricky, not least because it is hard to distinguish clearly the power of a specific individual and that of the office he or she occupies. The considerable power possessed by Blair and Brown, the two most important figures in the government, derives at least in part from the personal authority they have built up over the years. A new Prime Minister or Chancellor would not have their power. In the long run, what we are most interested in is the way in which distinct offices within the UK state are empowered or disempowered. Taking this as the main issue, it is clear that a real measure of power has been shifted from London to the newly devolved executives. This is a genuine break with the past and an important institutional change that could have unpredictable knock-on effects in years to come. It could also be argued that the Labour government's willingness to bring outsiders into parts of the policy process that have until now been dominated by civil servants will have the lasting effect of dispersing some power away from Whitehall and into the hands of key outsiders. This seems quite likely.

Perhaps the most intriguing question focuses on the core executive, and the extent to which it is being empowered by the Labour government. It is here that ultimate control over many strands of policy-making is exercised, and to an increasing extent. It is clear that the capacity of the core executive to direct policy has been enhanced. But we should not get carried away with either the extent of change, or the degree of power now concentrated at the core of the UK state. *The Economist* argues that Blair has replaced the 'percolator' conception of government with a 'cafetière' concept. Policy no longer bubbles up from government departments into the core executive, to be thrashed out in Cabinet committees. Instead, it is 'settled from Mr Blair's sofa and often communicated to other ministers by mobile phone' (*Economist*, 1999b). The image is certainly neat, and it does bear some relation to what is going on. But it also has to be said that this is a considerable exaggeration of the extent both of recent change and of contemporary core executive capacity. Creeping centralization of power in the core executive is a phenomenon of virtually the entire twentieth century (Burch and Holliday, 1996, ch. 1), as any review of the Thatcher years will confirm. Perhaps more important is the fact that the core executive remains a comparatively small set of institutions that simply lacks the capacity to impose policy on the whole of Whitehall. For this very reason, a large amount of power is still located elsewhere, notably in traditional government departments.

As for 'joined-up government', it is evident that this comprises a determinedly fluid approach to problem-solving, and an attempt to reduce the number of seams in the web of public services. In those places where power is properly located, it should be exercised efficiently, effectively and without concern for traditional boundaries between distinct parts of government (such as departments) or between the public and private sectors. In fact, structural boundaries are best ignored in the search for policy advance. This is certainly characteristic of the present government.

The question is whether an aspiration to fluidity can be turned into a functioning policy process that is more effective than its more structured predecessor. There are good reasons to think it cannot. On the one hand outsiders may well find the attractions of 'public service' begin to pall when results are something less than spectacular, or government popularity begins to wane. On the other, established structures are still in place, and for all sorts of reasons – institutional, cultural, personal – are likely to reassert themselves.

Finally, it can be argued that these changes make two distinct deals with UK democracy. The devolution reforms genuinely do enhance democracy, for they open up the political process to a greater number of inputs. However, the administrative philosophy of the present government also places some restrictions on democracy. The Blair government is actually not particularly interested either in democratic inputs or in truly open government. The key is to get the right solution to perceived political problems. Public perceptions are best measured through opinion surveys of one kind or another. Right solutions are best delivered pragmatically by experts drawn from both the public and private sectors. Things like a genuine Freedom of Information Act are likely only to get in the way of effective government. In 'Blair's Britain' the task of executives and administrations is to take regular soundings of the public mood and to respond in the most effective way possible.

# Chapter 7

# Legislatures and Assemblies

## PHILIP COWLEY

The study of the British Parliament used to be the academic equivalent of stamp collecting. While a small band of academic anoraks found it fascinating, everyone else – including the vast majority of political scientists and political observers – saw it as a dull and essentially irrelevant topic. British politics was said to be 'post-parliamentary' (Richardson and Jordan, 1979, p. 191). Parliament had ceased to be an important part of the policy process. It served merely to rubber stamp policies presented to it by the executive. Given this, there was little point in studying it. The same dismissive comments are frequently made of the European Parliament. Even as late as 1998, and despite progressive increases in its powers, one British newspaper described it as a 'multi-lingual talking shop' (*Independent,* 14 June 1998). If turnout is any guide, the British public share that view: only 23 per cent could be bothered to vote in the European Parliament elections in June 1999.

Despite the low esteem in which the existing legislatures are held, a central part of Labour's package of constitutional reform was the creation of yet more legislatures and assemblies. In the early years of the twenty-first century there will be four new such bodies in the UK operating alongside, and sometimes in competition with, the Westminster and European parliaments:

- the Scottish Parliament
- the Northern Ireland Assembly
- the National Assembly for Wales
- the Greater London Assembly.

This division in the nomenclature – one 'parliament' and three 'assemblies' – has historical roots but is not helpful. It is better to see three of the new institutions – those in Scotland, Northern Ireland and Wales – as legislatures: that is bodies that have the ability to give assent to measures of public policy (Norton, 1990, p. 1). The fourth – the Greater London Assembly (GLA) – is an assembly in the strict sense of the word: it lacks the ability to legislate.

108

What unites them is that, in contrast to the existing institutions, the new bodies tend not to be seen as dull or irrelevant. Particularly in Scotland and Wales much has been made of how the new institutions will be different from Westminster. They will be part of a new form of politics, more open and inclusive than Westminster. In part this is simply because they are new, invested, as new bodies usually are, with high (unrealistic?) hopes and aspirations. But it is also because the variants of proportional representation adopted for their election makes majority rule unlikely. At Westminster, by contrast, it is the norm for one party to control the majority of the seats in the House of Commons. Since 1945, minority governments have been rare and coalition governments non-existent. No UK executive since the war has contained members of more than one party, and most have been confident of commanding a majority in the Commons, if not in the Lords. The contrast between the new legislatures and Westminster is therefore striking.

## The new institutions

The four new institutions are all very different to one another, in terms of both composition and powers, as Table 7.1 shows.

Table 7.1   *The new institutions*

| Name | No of members | Method of election | Powers |
|---|---|---|---|
| Scottish Parliament | 129 | 73 by SMP<br>56 from regional lists | Primary/Secondary legislative power<br>Tax-varying powers |
| Northern Ireland Assembly | 108 | STV (6 per Westminster seat) | Primary/Secondary legislative power |
| National Assembly for Wales | 60 | 40 by SMP<br>20 from regional lists | Secondary legislative power |
| Greater London Assembly | 25 | 14 by SMP<br>11 from London-wide list | Largely consultative, but with power to alter budget by two-thirds majority |

## Scottish Parliament

The Scottish Parliament is both the largest and the most powerful of all the new legislatures. It has full legislative powers – such laws being known as Acts of the Scottish Parliament – over a wide range of policy areas. One writer on the subject argued that the areas not reserved by Westminster cover 'almost every area of domestic legislation affecting the ordinary Scottish voter' (Burns, 1999a, p. 44). This is going too far: the reserved powers are considerable in their scope; even in the domestic sphere they include many areas of direct concern to the 'ordinary', as well as the extraordinary, Scottish voter. However, even with these exceptions, the Scottish Parliament enjoys a substantial legislative vista covering health, education and training, local government, economic development and transport, law and home affairs, the environment, agriculture, fisheries and forestry and sports and the arts.

The Parliament also has limited tax-varying powers, being able to vary (which, in practice, means being able to raise) the rate of income tax in Scotland by up to three pence in the pound. Before the 1997 general election Labour promised not to use this power in the first Scottish Parliament. However, even if they had not committed themselves in this way, the power of the Parliament to raise its own revenue is minimal, since it gives it control over just £450 million out of a total Scottish Office Budget of £14.6 billion (Bogdanor, 1999, p. 239). Thus even when legislating on those areas over which it has competence, the Parliament has to do so within the confines of a budget almost exclusively determined by the UK government through the Barnett formula. It may re-prioritize spending – by taking money from one pot and putting it in another – but unless it is willing to cut severely some existing spending programmes it can do so only at the margins.

## Northern Ireland Assembly

Proposals for the other new legislatures were contained in Labour's 1997 election manifesto. By contrast, proposals for the Northern Ireland Assembly emerged from the on-going 'peace process' as part of the Good Friday Agreement. Its somewhat bloated size – roughly one Member of the Northern Ireland Assembly (MNIA) for every 11 000 people in Northern Ireland – was an attempt to ensure that all the parties involved in the peace process received some representation in the Assembly (although even with this inclusive approach the Ulster Democratic Party failed to get elected). The Assembly has the power to pass primary legislation – Acts of the Northern Ireland Assembly – over a range of policy areas. Although the legislative vista of the Assembly is smaller than that of the Scottish

Parliament, it is still considerable. In addition, although the Assembly does not enjoy tax-varying powers, these have not been ruled out in the future.

The Assembly first met in a 'shadow' capacity, without legislative or executive powers, gaining its full powers only when the various other bodies created by the Good Friday Agreement are established. That was originally supposed to have happened by February 1999. On 15 July 1999 the Assembly met to appoint members of the Northern Ireland executive, but as a result of disputes over the decommissioning of weapons, the meeting collapsed when the unionist parties refused to nominate any members. A deal was finally reached allowing the Assembly to gain its full powers in December 1999. Continuing problems with arms decommissioning led to temporary suspensions of the Assembly and Executive subsequently.

## National Assembly for Wales

The National Assembly for Wales, more commonly known as the Welsh Assembly, has no tax-raising powers. Nor does it have the power to pass primary legislation. Rather than being part of a process of legislative devolution – as in Scotland and Northern Ireland – it is part of a process of executive devolution: the powers formerly held by the Secretary of State for Wales, over a range of domestic policy areas, have been transferred to the Welsh Assembly. One of the most common statements made about the National Assembly is that its inability to raise revenue or to pass primary legislation means it will be toothless. It is true that it has fewer powers than the legislatures established in either Scotland or Northern Ireland. Yet this is not the same as being toothless; the Assembly has the power to allocate the budget: around £7 billion in 1999. As importantly, it has the power to make subordinate – more commonly known as 'secondary' – legislation. Subordinate legislation exists where primary legislation has delegated decisions to another body. This body used to be the Secretary of State; it is now the Assembly.

Much subordinate legislation is minor, 'a mass of abstruse technicalities' (de Smith and Brazier, 1994, p. 362). Yet it can also cover important areas of public policy (Page, 2000). Decisions about whether, when, or how, primary legislation is brought into effect are often made by subordinate legislation. This is true, for example, of regulations concerning beef on the bone, tobacco advertising and most EU legislation. However, the Assembly's power to make policy via subordinate legislation will be patchy. It will represent 'a haphazard collection of miscellaneous powers reflecting the almost arbitrary decisions taken by administrations over the last 50 years about what to include in primary legislation and what to leave for secondary legislation' (Silk, 1998, p. 74). In some areas, these powers will be minor or trivial. In others, they will be more significant.

Not only will the Assembly's powers be patchy, they will also be dependent on the goodwill of Westminster. If primary legislation is loosely drafted, it gives greater power to the Assembly than if it is tightly drafted. 'If, for example, an Act were to provide that "Provision be made for Wales by Order as the Assembly sees fit", that would yield considerable autonomy to the Assembly. If, however, it were to provide that "Provision for Wales shall be by Order by the Assembly in like manner as for England in this Act", the Assembly would have very little autonomy' (Bogdanor, 1999, p. 256). It is quite possible that there may develop new practices in the style of primary and secondary legislation that make it very difficult to extrapolate from existing patterns exactly what the delegated legislative powers will mean and how they will be exercised.

If there is a tendency to over-state the degree of power enjoyed by the Scottish Parliament, then there is an equal tendency to under-state the degree of power enjoyed by the National Assembly. It is more than a talking shop. It has teeth: small teeth, perhaps, but teeth nonetheless.

## Greater London Assembly

The Greater London Assembly (GLA) is the smallest and weakest of the new bodies. Most of the power in the Greater London Authority rests with the directly elected Mayor rather than the Assembly (Loveland, 1999). The Assembly must be consulted on most issues. It can make proposals to the Mayor, and can issue reports on his or her activities and on other matters relating to London. But the Mayor is under no obligation to do anything in response other than to respond. Members of the Assembly sit on a variety of London-wide bodies – such as the London Development Agency (LDA) – but they are chosen by the Mayor, as is the Deputy Mayor. Organizations such as Transport for London (TfL) – the body replacing London Transport – are responsible to the Mayor rather than to the Assembly. The only significant power held by the Assembly is the ability to amend the Authority's budget. That requires a two-thirds majority in the Assembly, rather than a simple majority.

## Composition of the new institutions

There are, then, many differences between the new institutions. There are, however, also some important similarities. First, the three new legislatures and the London Assembly are all unicameral: they have no second chamber – such as the House of Lords, or the US Senate – to act as a check on the activities of the first. Second, and more importantly, the variants of proportional representation used in the election of their members make majority rule in that one chamber unlikely, if not impossible. As Table 7.2 shows, in the first elections to the legislatures, no one party won a majority of the seats in any of the bodies. Single-party government in London is also unlikely (Rallings and Thrasher, 1999, p. 189).

Indeed, in Northern Ireland – again, in order to ensure an inclusive approach to politics and to address nationalist fears that the Assembly would entrench a unionist majority – coalition behaviour is institutionalized. Rather than belonging to the largest party or parties, membership of the executive is divided up between the political parties, in proportion to their strength in the assembly. In addition, voting in the Assembly is not conducted on the basis of a simple majority. Rather, all Assembly members have to register themselves as nationalists, unionists or 'other'. Most votes require either parallel consent (a majority of those voting, including a majority of both unionists and nationalists) or a weighted majority (60 per cent of those voting, including at least 40 per cent of both unionists and nationalists). In Scotland and Wales there is no institutional requirement for coalition building – one party *can* take all the seats and form the executive alone – but given the electoral system, majority rule is unlikely.

Coalition or minority governments are not unknown in Britain. Of the 60 years between 1885 and 1945 only 10 saw one party command a majority in the Commons (Searle, 1995). Similarly, British local government has extensive experience of coalition (see, for example, Laver, Rallings and Thrasher, 1987; Mellors, 1989). However, in the second half of the twentieth century there has been no coalition government at Westminster – except in the sense that all British political parties, being broad churches, are themselves coalitions of various groupings – and only rarely has there been a minority government.

In multi-party systems, like many of those in mainland Europe, coalition-building between parties is a fact of national political life and

Table 7.2  *State of the parties in the new legislatures, 1999*

| Scotland | | % | Wales | | % | Northern Ireland | | % |
|---|---|---|---|---|---|---|---|---|
| Lab | 56 | (43) | Lab | 28 | (47) | UUP | 28 | (26) |
| SNP | 35 | (27) | PC | 17 | (28) | SDLP | 24 | (22) |
| Con | 18 | (14) | Con | 9 | (15) | DUP | 20 | (19) |
| LD | 17 | (13) | LD | 6 | (10) | SF | 18 | (17) |
| Others | 3 | (2) | Others | 0 | (0) | Others | 18 | (17) |
| Total | 129 | | | 60 | | | 108 | |

a voluminous (and often complicated) academic literature has grown up to explain, and occasionally predict, the way these coalitions form (McLean, 1987). This literature is grouped around three basic theories:

- minimal winning coalition
- minimum size coalition
- minimal connected winning coalition.

The idea of the minimal winning coalition comes from the work of von Neumann and Morgenstern (1947). They argued that the winning coalition would consist of the smallest number of parties needed to deliver a majority of the votes in the legislature. In both Scotland and Wales, there are three minimal winning coalitions that consist of two parties: Labour plus the Conservatives, Labour plus the Liberal Democrats and Labour plus the nationalists (PC in Wales, SNP in Scotland). No other coalition of just two parties can yield the 65 or more needed for a majority in Scotland, or the 31 votes or more needed in Wales. A larger coalition is unnecessary and, since it would involve sharing the spoils of office between more parties, undesirable from the parties' point of view.

The concept of the minimum-size coalition is associated with William Riker (1962). Riker pointed out that von Neumann and Morgenstern took no account of the size of the parties involved. Riker argued that it was better to share the spoils of government out among as few MPs as possible, and that therefore the winning coalition would be the minimal winning coalition of the smallest size. In both Scotland and Wales, this is the coalition of Labour with the Liberal Democrats. In Scotland, this involves 73 votes, fewer than Labour plus SNP (91) or Labour plus Conservatives (74). In Wales, this involves 34 votes, fewer than Labour and PC (45) or Labour and the Conservatives (37).

The problem with both of the above theories is that they ignore a party's ideology. Every party is assumed to be able to form a coalition with every other party, no matter what their beliefs or policies. Axelrod (1970) argued that this was unrealistic: parties will be able to form coalitions only with parties that are adjacent to them on the ideological spectrum. This – the idea of the minimal connected winning coalition – is intuitively attractive. Parties are not completely promiscuous: they will not jump into bed with just anybody. As a result, most comparative studies find that models attempting to explain coalition-formation without including some measure of ideology perform badly (Laver and Schofield, 1990). The problem with including ideology in the models is measuring it – not least because parties may be adjacent on one ideological dimension but apart on another (Taylor and Laver, 1973) – but in both Scotland and Wales the minimal connected winning coalition is almost certainly that of Labour plus the

Liberal Democrats. Both are (probably) adjacent to each other on the ideological spectrum, and in both Scotland and Wales this combination produces a minimal winning coalition of two parties.

In Scotland the outcome of the post-election negotiations was a coalition between Labour and the Liberal Democrats. Since this was predicted by all three theories, this might be seen as predictable and/or as a triumph for coalition theorists. However, none of the theories predicted the initial outcome in Wales, where Labour governed as the largest party, but in minority status. Yet despite taking all the seats in the executive, Labour still had to negotiate with the other parties in the Assembly, and coalition theory suggested that Labour was more likely to be willing and able to achieve informal compromises with the Liberal Democrats than with any other party or parties. Indeed, by October 2000 political reality (and coalition theory) emerged victorious, with Labour entering a formal coalition with the Liberal Democrats.

## Procedures and structures

Largely overlooked in the run-up to devolution was the question of how the new bodies would function. Even the Acts that established the legislatures were (deliberately) vague about this. They provided a skeleton around which the legislatures were expected to arrange their own flesh. In Scotland, this was done through an all-party Consultative Steering Group (CSG), which drew up draft standing orders that were then presented to the Parliament (CSG, 1999). The equivalent body in Wales was the National Assembly Advisory Group (James, 1998).

A common theme in the work of these groups was that they did not see the Westminster Parliament as a model to emulate. Rather, they saw it as one to reject (see, for example, Crick and Millar, 1995). The UK Parliament was perceived to suffer from four main flaws:

- archaic working practices
- not open and inclusive
- unnecessarily confrontational
- failing to operate as an effective check upon the executive.

By contrast, the new legislatures were to be modern and family-friendly, they would facilitate the development of consensus and they would keep the executive in check.

These were ambitious aims. From the start there was a conscious effort to facilitate openness – through information technology and the like – which has even extended to the architecture: the new Welsh Assembly building is made predominantly of glass to emphasise the transparency of government in Wales. There was also a deliberate attempt to break away from some of the Westminster-based practices not seen as desirable: the new legislatures, for example, utilize electronic voting and sit for 'business hours', rather than having late-night sittings. Much more difficult to achieve, however, are the last two aims: to develop consensus and to operate as an effective check on the executive.

MSPs, according to one commentator, 'should put aside their sectional and adversarial interests and work together for the common good of Scotland' (Burns, 1999b, pp. 52–3). Perhaps they should, but will they? Westminster politics may be somewhat confrontational, but Scottish politics hasn't always been a love-in either. The same goes for Wales and (especially) Northern Ireland. As Box 7.1 shows, debate in the Welsh Assembly can be more than a little reminiscent of the Westminster Parliament at its worst.

Of course, the lack of a majority in all the new bodies makes things different from Westminster. But this will not necessarily engender consensus. In Scotland, for example, the coalition of Labour and the Liberal Democrats simply creates one governing bloc; the other parties form a *de facto* opposition bloc. Relations between the two blocs could be much the same as between the two sides of the House of Commons. The important thing for Labour is to keep the Liberal Democrats on board. There is no incentive to develop genuine consensus with the other parties. Confrontation is just as likely as at Westminster. In Wales – where there is no majority coalition – and in Northern Ireland – where, as outlined above, there is the requirement for cross-community support – things may be more fluid. But even here, there are likely to be groups – such as the

---

### Box 7.1 New politics?

The Presiding Officer: I call the National Assembly to order.

Rod Richards: Point of order. What is the situation when the Secretary for Agriculture and Rural Development has failed to turn up to answer questions on agriculture when the industry is in turmoil?

The Presiding Officer: That is not a point of order.

The First Secretary: Point of order. Can we check the time on the clocks in the Chamber? According to my watch it is just approaching 2pm now.

Rod Richards: It has gone 2pm.

The First Secretary: You do not know what time of day it is anyway.

Dafydd Wigley: Just get on with it.

*Source:* National Assembly for Wales, *Official Record*, 21 July 1999.

Conservatives in Wales, or the anti-agreement parties in Northern Ireland – which are almost permanently excluded from the governing process.

Placing checks on the executive is likely to be even harder. In the three new legislatures the main vehicle by which this is hoped to be achieved is the committee (see, for example, Jones, 1998; Burns, 1999b). Each new legislature has an extensive committee structure. In Scotland there are eight so-called 'mandatory' committees, such as those investigating procedures and subordinate legislation, along with eight subject committees. The latter combine legislative and scrutiny work. They will benefit from a permanent membership – rather than being established ad hoc as are the legislative committees at Westminster – which should help build up a body of expertise (see, for example, Shaw, 1998). They will be expected to examine a bill before it goes to the plenum of the Parliament for a vote on its principle – thus being able to inform the plenary debate – and they will then examine it in detail, line-by-line, after it has been approved in principle. Subject committees will also be able to initiate legislation.

In Wales, there are three types of committee. Five 'subcommittees', similar to the Scottish mandatory committees, examine, *inter alia*, equal opportunities, standards of conduct and the drafting of legislation. Four regional committees – covering Mid, North, South-East and South-West Wales and each consisting of members from that part of Wales – advise the Assembly on matters affecting the regions. Six subject committees each shadow the responsibilities of an Assembly Secretary, the members of the Welsh executive. The subject committees work closely with the relevant Assembly Secretary, who is also a member of the committee, and monitor the implementation of existing legislation in their subject area, as well as advising on proposed legislation affecting their area (Hornung, 1999). As in Scotland, the chairs of the committees are distributed according to the composition of the Assembly. In four of the six committees, therefore, a Labour Assembly Secretary has to work with committee chairs from a different party (and with committees on which Labour members are in the minority).

These procedures, and the others like them, are designed to facilitate scrutiny. That, however, is all that standing orders can do: they can facilitate scrutiny. They cannot ensure it. The principal determinant of the extent to which the legislatures will act as a check on their executives is the political will of the elected legislators. If that is lacking even the best designed legislature will soon resemble a rubber-stamp. The first question time in the Scottish Parliament was seen as being more courteous than at Westminster, but also as including planted questions from Labour's backbenchers 'every bit as nauseating as the worst of Westminster' (*Times*, 18 June 1999). Covering the Scottish Parliament, the parliamentary sketch-writer of *The Times* 'found the old politics alive and reassuringly well'

(*Times*, 3 November 1999). The standing orders adopted by the Welsh Labour Party to govern its Assembly group have been described as giving 'maximum power to party apparatchiks' (Betts, 1999, p. 22). If this is the shape of things to come, then even if the new legislatures prove to be somewhat better behaved than Westminster, they are unlikely to become much more effective in checking the activities of the executive.

The full extent to which the new legislatures will realize their potential will become clear only in the years to come. Legislatures are 'vibrant entities' (Longley, 1996, p. 39), which change over time, as customs and conventions grow up affecting the way they perform. Predictions made now about their behaviour and influence are likely to be proved embarrassingly wrong. But it might be better to be slightly sceptical about the way the legislatures will perform than to be starry-eyed and hopeful, as some – although not all – of the current literature on the new bodies has a habit of being.

## Modernizing Westminster

In addition to creating the new legislatures, Labour's programme of constitutional reform includes changing those that already exist. Reforms to the Westminster Parliament were trailed in Labour's election manifesto. They were:

- modernization of the House of Commons
- reform of the scrutiny of European business
- making Prime Minister's Questions (PMQs) 'more effective'
- reform of the House of Lords.

## Modernization of the House of Commons

The main vehicle for the modernization of the Commons – and the means by which procedures for dealing with European business were reformed – was the Select Committee on the Modernization of the House, established in June 1997. For the most part, the Committee's recommendations have been neither radical nor particularly novel. Most of the recommendations on reforms to the legislative process contained in the first report (HC 190, 1997) had long been advocated (see, for example, Hansard Society, 1993). The recommendations on ways to improve the scrutiny of European business in the seventh report (HC 791, 1998) were almost identical to those suggested by the Select Committee on European Legislation in 1996. The one more imaginative idea is the parallel debating chamber, to be known as 'Westminster Hall' (HC 194, 1999). Yet this is the exception rather than the rule. Those who expected 'modernization' to bring about radical change will be disappointed.

It is also possible to criticize the committee's lack of focus and of clearly defined aims. Of its first 10 reports, only two – the first and the seventh in the first session – had the potential to enhance the scrutinizing role of the Commons. The others were designed for cosmetic or tidying-up purposes, or for the convenience of MPs. 'Though these aims may be desirable, they are not central to the strengthening the House in its relationship to government' (Norton, 1999). Indeed, it is possible to argue that some of the proposals – such as the changing of the parliamentary timetable, recommended in the first report of the second session, in order to make the House more 'family-friendly' (HC 60, 1998) – will detract from the ability of the Commons to hold the government to account.

Changes to PMQs were announced on 9 May, before the Modernization committee was even established. Making PMQs 'more effective' involved moving it from two 15-minute slots on a Tuesday and Thursday to one half-hour slot on a Wednesday. In opposition, Tony Blair had thought the amount of preparation required twice a week was a 'ridiculous use of a prime minister's time' (Draper, 1997, p. 36). However, the shorter 15-minute sessions had advantages for prime ministers. The new half-hour session allows for greater persistence in questioning, something William Hague has frequently used to his advantage. As a result, Blair has had some sticky moments in the 'more effective' PMQs.

## Reform of the House of Lords

Of all the direct reforms to the UK Parliament, reform of the House of Lords is the most dramatic; it is dealt with in some detail in Chapter 5. Given its importance to the UK Parliament, however, a brief discussion is also necessary here. The first stage of reform – the removal of the hereditary peers – was enacted by the House of Lords Act, with the exception of 92 hereditary peers who are to remain until the second stage of reform is implemented. The details of this second stage were farmed out to a Royal Commission, chaired by the Conservative peer Lord Wakeham.

Even where we know the shape and form of the revised Lords there is no certainty about how it will function. A concern repeatedly raised during the debates on the House of Lords Bill was that a Lords predominantly made up of appointed peers would be an emasculated body, unable to act as a check on the Commons. Yet more doubt surrounds the role of the Lords (if it is called that) after stage two has been implemented. The terms of reference given to the Royal Commission make it explicit that the Commons is to remain the dominant chamber of Parliament (Cm 4183,

1999, p. 35). Yet even if stage two results in a second chamber with no extra formal powers, the added legitimacy given to the chamber as a result of the absence of the hereditary peers may make it *more* effective in challenging the Commons. This is particularly the case if any or all of those in the second chamber are there as a result of election. The pre-reform House of Lords – knowing its legitimacy was limited – frequently exercised a self-denying ordinance. This may well cease once it has been fully reformed. The Lords may end up putting up a greater fight against the Commons than it ever used to.

## By-products of other reforms

The greatest of the reforms to the UK Parliament will not be those trailed in Labour's manifesto. Rather, they will be the indirect reforms, those that occur as a result of Labour's other constitutional policies (Hazell, 1999). The enactment of the Human Rights Act, for example, acts as a *de facto* constraint on the activities of Parliament (see, for example, Judge, 1999). The clearest example of such an indirect effect is that of devolution.

The establishment of the new legislatures has had (and will continue to have) a profound effect on Westminster, one that was little considered before devolution. Some of the changes are already apparent, in the abolition or downgrading of procedures that are no longer necessary once so many responsibilities have been devolved to the new legislatures (HC 185, 1999). But there may also be behavioural or attitudinal changes that will take longer to become clear. MPs currently spend a considerable amount of time dealing with constituency matters (Norton and Wood, 1993). Outside of England, such matters may now start to be the concern of the members of the new legislatures. Westminster MPs sitting for seats in Scotland, Wales and Northern Ireland may find they have little or nothing to do. The Conservatives have called for them to be paid less than English MPs on precisely this ground.

More problematic will be any attempts to deal with the so-called 'West Lothian' question, named after the constituency of the MP for West Lothian, Tam Dalyell, who asked it repeatedly during debates on devolution in the 1970s (Dalyell, 1977). (He was not, though, the first to raise it, as is sometimes claimed. Gladstone had identified similar problems with his proposals for home rule to Ireland, see Bogdanor, 1999.) This 'question' – why should Scottish MPs have the right to vote on legislation affecting people in England, when those in England have no right to vote on legislation affecting people in Scotland – always used to be an argument against devolution. *Mutatis mutandis*, a rarely discussed 'North Down' question relates to any functioning Northern Ireland Assembly (although the absence of any devolution of primary legislative powers means that a

West Cardiff question does not arise). Now devolution is a reality, however, these have become practical problems rather than theoretical debates.

It is possible to dismiss the West Lothian question in principle, by arguing that since the UK Parliament retains absolute sovereignty – a point made explicit in the devolution legislation – it can choose to legislate on whatever it likes, whenever it likes. It can, should it so wish, abolish the devolved bodies – without consultation with them or with the voters in the country concerned – and can continue to legislate on areas over which a devolved body had competence (Burrows, 1999). 'Nothing, therefore, could prevent English MPs from voting on Scottish affairs except the House of Commons itself – dominated, as it always is, by English MPs' (Miller, 1998, p. 169). Seen from this perspective, then, the answer to the West Lothian question 'is to stop asking it', a phrase used by the Lord Chancellor, Lord Irvine. In principle, this is a neat argument – one worth having up your sleeve in a tutorial – but in practice it is clearly futile. Whatever the legal theory, in practice devolution establishes bodies with their own legitimacy and power. Only *in extremis* will the UK Parliament be able to assert its formal power over them.

The West Lothian question is not amenable to any easy answer. In partial response, the Boundary Commission has been told to end the over-representation of Scotland in the House of Commons. (No similar instruction has yet been issued for Wales or Northern Ireland.) Reducing the number of MPs in this way lessens the issue, but it does not remove the basic problem. One solution, increasingly advocated by some, is for devolution in England, either to an English Parliament (a solution usually advocated by those on the right), or to a series of regional bodies (more often advocated by those on the left). There is as yet no great demand for this in England, nor any realistic possibility of it happening. In the short- to medium-term, the response to the West Lothian question will be internal reform to Parliament. The Procedure Committee (HC 185) suggested a new procedure for any bills that relate exclusively to one part of the UK, comprising a Second Reading Committee consisting solely of MPs elected from that part of the UK.

In a similar vein, the Conservatives advocated what they termed 'English votes on English laws' (Hague, 1999), proposing restricting the voting rights of MPs from areas with devolved legislatures. This would mean, for example, that only English MPs could vote on domestic legislation affecting England, and on which the Scottish Parliament would legislate in Scotland. This is not a new plan. It was considered, and rejected, by Gladstone when he was drawing up his plans for Irish Home Rule in the 1880s and 1890s (Bogdanor, 1999, pp. 30–1). Its fundamental problem is what happens when a government elected with a majority of UK seats is dependent for that majority on MPs sitting for non-English seats. The government is then not able to enact much, if any, of its domestic legislation in England. It would either have to abandon the legislation – and face almost certain electoral defeat at the next election – or change the rules and over-ride the views of the English MPs using Scottish and Welsh votes. This could lead, as one senior Conservative MP pointed out in response to Hague's plan, to a 'constitutional crisis' (Davis, 1999).

## Ignoring Westminster

At the same time as the UK Parliament is being modernized and reformed, so it has been described as being marginalized (for an enjoyable if ever so slightly barmy example see Redwood, 1999, esp. chs 5 and 6). This complaint consists of four main strands: majority, discipline, arrogance, and the reform of the House of Lords.

- *Majority*. The government enjoys the largest parliamentary majority seen since 1935. It is Labour's largest ever. The government is therefore likely to survive the entire parliament without suffering a single defeat in the Commons, something that has not happened since the 1966–70 parliament.
- *Discipline*. Government MPs have two conflicting roles. First, to support the government under whose colours they were elected. And, second, to scrutinize that government. The balance between these two roles is difficult to achieve. Since May 1997 the complaint has been that many Labour MPs have ignored the second role, and instead given unquestioning support to the government. New methods of whipping – including tighter standing orders and electronic message pagers – have led to criticisms that Labour MPs are too slavishly following the party line. Whereas the complaint used to be that Labour leaders were not in control of their party, it is now that they are too much in control.
- *Arrogance*. Partly because of the first two factors, and partly as a result of the personality of the individuals concerned, a third criticism has emerged: that Labour ministers are arrogant and dismissive of parliament. Important policy announcements are often made outside of Westminster and then reported to Parliament later, a tendency publicly deprecated by the Speaker. The Prime Minister is an infrequent attender in the House of Commons. The change in PMQs attracted negative comment not because of what was done, but because of how it was done – by fiat, without consultation with the other parties.
- *House of Lords*. The only defeats the government suffered in the first two sessions of the parliament came from the House of Lords. Many

resulted from the presence of the hereditary peers. Removing these peers led to charges that Blair wishes to emasculate the second chamber, and remove the one last significant check on his behaviour within parliament.

Under Labour, then, Parliament has a marginalized role in the policy process. Yet it was ever thus. The first problem with most of the criticisms made of Parliament under Labour is not that they are wrong – because they are not – but that they pretend to be describing something that is new (Cowley, 2000). Lamenting the decline of parliament was a popular sport throughout the twentieth century.

Defeats may be non-existent in this parliament, but – with one exception, the period from 1974 to 1979 – they have been rare or non-existent in every parliament since the war (Norton, 1980; Cowley and Norton, 1996). Blair may attend parliament infrequently, but the decline in prime ministerial participation in the business of the Commons is nothing new (Dunleavy and Jones, 1993). Nor is the Blair government the first to prefer to announce policy outside of the House of Commons. An earlier Speaker, Bernard (now Lord) Weatherill frequently had to persuade a reluctant Margaret Thatcher to come to the Commons to report on a policy decision. It was, she said, 'a nuisance'. Blaming the Blair government for the decline of parliament is therefore about as sensible as blaming it for the loss of America.

The second problem with most of the criticisms made of Labour's relationship with Parliament is they misunderstand or misrepresent what is currently taking place.

- Rather than being the result of harsh whipping or spineless back-benchers, some of the discipline that exists on the Labour benches results from agreement. Many Labour MPs – particularly the newer ones – are cohesive not because they are sheep-like but because they are happy with what the government is doing: it is the cohesion of those who are perfectly happy to be cohesive.
- But when they are not happy, Labour MPs are prepared to vote against their party. The first session saw more rebellions than in the first sessions of eight of the post-war parliaments; the largest saw 47 MPs vote against their party over the issue of lone-parent benefits (Cowley, 1999). The second session saw an even larger rebellion, when 67 voted against planned cuts in disability benefit. By the end of the second session, almost one in three Labour backbenchers had voted against the government at least once in the parliament (Cowley and Stuart, 2000).
- While the Blair government does contain some autocratic ministers – as do all governments – it also contains a considerable number who are

prepared to discuss and debate privately with their backbenchers. Where genuine consultation has not taken place, or where the government has adopted a macho stance – as with lone parent benefit or disability benefit – rebellions have been noticeable. Where the government has adopted a more consultative approach, being prepared to sugar the legislative pill – as with the treatment of asylum seekers in June 1999 – rebellions have been muted, if not non-existent.

- The large majority has seen some parts of the Commons becoming more assertive. This is particularly true of the Select Committee system, both the Departmental Select Committees, and other bodies, such as the Public Accounts Committee (Wolstenholme, 1999) These have provided an alternative route for the effective scrutiny of ministers.

- While it is possible that reform of the House of Lords will lead to a weakened upper chamber, it is (as argued above) just as likely that it will lead to one which is more assertive, and better able to act as a check on the executive.

So Parliament *is* marginalized. But it always has been; and things are not significantly worse now than they were 10, 20 or 50 years ago.

## The European Parliament

The European Parliament is even more misunderstood than the UK Parliament. Far from being a 'multi-lingual talking shop', it is now a significant player in the formulation of European legislation. It began as the Common Assembly of the European Coal and Steel Community (ECSC) in 1951. The Common Assembly was small (78 members), had no electoral mandate (its members were appointed from within national parliaments), and had no legislative powers. The European Parliament of today is large (626 strong; the UK delegation consists of 87), since 1979 has been directly elected (although the low turnout in EP elections somewhat limits its mandate), and has accumulated substantial legislative powers. These powers grew in a piecemeal fashion:

- Initially, the Assembly had the power to be consulted. By 1964 it was consulted on all legislative proposals and by 1968 most non-legislative texts (Shephard, 1998, p. 169).

- In 1979, in the *Isolucose* case, the European Court of Justice (ECJ) ruled that although the Assembly – which from 1962 had re-styled itself as a Parliament – had only the power of consultation, it had to have given its opinion on a piece of legislation before the Council could adopt it. *De facto*, this gave the Assembly an indefinite power of delay, 'a first, though essentially negative, role in the Union's legislative process' (Westlake, 1998, p. 774).

- The first positive role – known as the cooperation procedure – resulted from the Single European Act which came into force in 1987. In certain policy areas, mainly but not exclusively those relating to the establishment of the Single Market, the Parliament – as it was now officially called – had the power to amend or reject draft legislation. The Council could overturn decisions of the Parliament, but only by an unanimous vote. If such unanimity could not be secured, the Parliament could and did exercise real power.

- The codecision procedure – introduced as a result of the Treaty on European Union (more commonly known as the Maastricht Treaty) in November 1993 – yet further strengthened the position of the European Parliament (although see Tsebelis and Garrett, 1997). For the first time the Parliament gained the right of ultimate veto in a range of areas. The areas covered by the codecision procedure were extended by the Amsterdam Treaty in 1997.

In a remarkably short space of time, then, the Parliament has gone from an insignificant talking shop to a situation where 'it is possible to argue that the European Parliament now actually exercises greater sway over laws than do at least some of the national legislatures of the EU's member countries' (Scully, 1997, p. 69). Its most impressive show of force came in 1999 when it precipitated the resignation *en masse* of the Commission.

It still lacks many powers. It has, for example, no power to initiate legislation of its own, being forced to react to measures placed before it. And the power that it does have is patchy, being dependent on the policy area under examination. In some areas, consultation still applies. Yet there is now elite-level recognition of the powers of the European Parliament. National governments recognize its powers, as do interest groups (Mazey and Richardson, 1993; Shephard, 1999). The current problem for the European Parliament is not a lack of power. Rather, it is the lack of recognition or understanding at mass-level, where the public neither knows nor cares much about it (Wallace and Smith, 1995).

## Conclusion

The creation of three new legislatures and one new assembly provided an abundance of riches for psephologists. A range of new elections – all with different electoral systems – to examine was almost too good to be true. A similar feast awaits the student of legislatures. Now that the new legislators are safely installed in their new legislatures, attention can turn to what they will do. Although often overlooked, attention should also turn to the impact that their establishment will have on the Westminster Parliament.

The new legislatures have high hopes invested in them. Not only are they to be open, inclusive and consensual but they are also to act as a check on the executive. As should be obvious from much of this chapter, this writer is sceptical about the likelihood of all of this happening. That said, most writing on the way the new legislatures will work is at best little more than educated guesswork, at worst it is wishful thinking. It will take a considerable period of time – 8–12 years (that is, two–three terms) at a minimum – before we have enough systematic and continuous data on the way the new legislatures are performing to allow us to move much beyond guesswork.

However, the more established legislatures can give two important insights into what might happen. First, Westminster shows how difficult it is for a legislature to act as a check on the executive. Even when an institution has considerable formal powers – and the Westminster Parliament's formal powers are pretty much second to none – if it fails to utilize them, it will have only limited effect on policy. So, insight one is: powers do not mean power. The extent to which their powers are utilized is the first great imponderable about the new legislatures.

Second, the European Parliament shows that influencing legislation is not the sole or even the main function of a legislature. The European Parliament does not lack powers, or even genuine power (although it could probably do with a little more of both). But the European Parliament lacks much sense of legitimacy or engagement with its citizenry. The UK Parliament, by contrast, has such an engagement, and bestows such legitimacy upon the government. So, insight two is: power is not enough. The second imponderable, therefore, is the extent to which the new bodies manage to connect with their electors.

The third imponderable is the effect that the new institutions have on Westminster. The process of 'modernization' has been slow. It has not resulted in dramatic change at Westminster. Far more dramatic changes are likely to flow from the establishment of the new legislatures as the Westminster Parliament adapts to new political realities. The effect of this, too, will become clear only in the years to come.

# Chapter 8

# Elections and Party Politics

## PATRICK DUNLEAVY

Suppose you gave an election, but nobody changed their mind and very few people came. This quick characterisation of the 2001 General Election has a lot going for it. The parties' vote shares from the 1997 election were reproduced again, almost unchanged. The transfer of House of Commons seats between the parties was inconsequential. And turnout at the polls plunged to its lowest total ever in Britain's history as a liberal democracy. Buttressed by an even more than usually unfair electoral system, the Labour government was returned to power for another four to five years. In democratic terms this seemed a mixed kind of phenomenon, perhaps signalling that British citizens had reached a settled state of mind which they were happy to maintain, or perhaps signalling only a conditional endorsement of the government, given the way that the electoral system would work. Either interpretation is consistent with a polity that is potentially storing up fundamental legitimacy problems for the future.

In party political terms the outcomes are much easier to characterize. For the first time in its 101-year-old history, Labour won re-election for a second full term of government with a secure working majority and in a convincing fashion. The unsuccessful Tory leader, William Hague, fell on his sword at breakfast time the morning after polling day, inaugurating a prolonged leadership contest. By winter 2001 the Conservatives, now headed by Iain Duncan Smith, seemed mired in desperate terrain. In opinion polls (measuring how people say they will vote if a general election were held 'tomorrow') their support fell as low as 25 per cent, compared to Labour's hegemonic 57 per cent. Three and a half years to the next election is a long time in politics. But already a Labour third term in 2005 seemed feasible, even a fairly safe bet, given the mountain which the Tories have to climb, and the extent to which the Westminster electoral system now protects Labour seats from adverse swings.

In party system terms, 2001's complete stasis cemented in place an already prolonged period of apparent Labour dominance, itself following on from a long period of Conservative hegemony throughout the 1980s and most of the 1990s. Like Labour now, the Tories were largely immune to opposition challenges for a long period, at least from the 1982 Falklands War until the UK's exit from the European Exchange Rate Mechanism (ERM) in September 1992, if not for all their eighteen years in office.

Periods of close competition between the major parties have become a rarity in Britain for at least three decades now, even though a major alternation of alignments and of government has occurred. Is the UK, then, locked into a long cycle of 'punctuated equilibrium' conditions, where long periods of hegemony for one governing party are interspersed by tectonic shifts of the political landscape, causing an alternation in power and the near-ruin of the previous hegemon?

To address this and the other issues above we need to examine how the 2001 election continued and changed previous trends; the roles of Britain's multiple election systems, turnout and issue mix in conditioning voters' alignments now; and the impacts of 2001 on the parties' electoral strategies and on the party system.

## Recent political trends and the 2001 election

The Conservatives went into the 2001 general election needing a miracle to win, and in the end did not come anywhere close. There was a minuscule swing towards them, with their vote increasing by 1 per cent and Labour's declining by just over 2.5 per cent. The Liberal Democrats picked up an extra 1.5 per cent support, the Scottish and Welsh nationalists held their own, and the 'others' declined slightly from the 1997 peak achieved with the intervention of the now defunct Referendum Party. The first two rows of Table 8.1 show the almost identical votes result, and the even clearer stasis within the House of Commons. Labour lost six seats in England and one in Scotland, but picked up a seat in the south west. The Conservatives lost three seats in southern England and the Midlands but made up for it elsewhere, to gain one seat net. The Liberal Democrats added 6 more seats to their *annus mirabilis* total from 1997, giving them 52 MPs, more than at any time since the war. The result was the least change after a full term election ever in Britain's history as a democracy.

Yet the hegemonic Labour position in the general election scores was not reflected in other main contests during Blair's first term. Table 8.1 shows that Labour support was fully 9 percentage points higher in the 2001 and 1997 nationwide contests than in any of the intervening elections. (In making this point I have compared the party's general election showings in Scotland and Wales, not shown in Table 8.1, with the devolved Scottish Parliament and Welsh Assembly elections). Even in Westminster by-elections using the same electoral system as general elections, Labour's vote share was 10 per cent less than its nationwide vote. Variations in the other parties' votes were very much less, with the Conservatives centring on 31 per cent in all contests except the European election, when their populist position gained them 5 per cent more vote share. The Liberal Democrats consistently achieved 15–19 per cent, but gained a modest boost in the by-elections. The Scottish National Party and Plaid Cymru did very

Table 8.1  Votes: shares and seat shares for the major parties in elections, 1997–2001

| | % share of votes | | | | | | % share of seats | | | | | |
| --- | --- | --- | --- | --- | --- | --- | --- | --- | --- | --- | --- | --- |
| | Lab | Con | Lib Dem | SNP/ PC | Green | Other | Lab | Con | Lib Dem | SNP/ PC | Green | Other |
| General election 1997 FPTP | 44 | 32 | 17 | 2 | 0.3 | 5 | 65 | 23 | 8 | 1 | 0 | 0.3 |
| Scottish Parliament election 1999 AMS | 34 | 15 | 13 | 27 | 4 | 8 | 43 | 14 | 13 | 27 | 1 | 2 |
| Welsh National Assembly election 1999 AMS | 36 | 17 | 13 | 31 | 3 | 2 | 47 | 15 | 10 | 28 | 0 | 0 |
| European Parliament election 1999 List PR | 28 | 36 | 13 | 5 | 6 | 12 | 33 | 41 | 12 | 5 | 2 | 7 |
| London Assembly election 2000 AMS | 30 | 29 | 15 | na | 11 | 15 | 36 | 36 | 16 | na | 12 | 0 |
| Sixteen Westminster by-elections (1997–2000) FPTP | 32 | 29 | 24 | 9 | na | 6 | na | na | na | na | na | na |
| General election 2001 FPTP | 42 | 33 | 19 | 3 | 1 | 3 | 64 | 26 | 8 | 1 | 0 | 0.3 |

*Notes:* The European Parliament results are for the UK as a whole, including Northern Ireland parties in the 'Other' columns.

well in the devolved elections, but slipped back to their customary lower levels of support in the Westminster contests. Support for 'other' parties boomed in mid-term, with the Greens winning representation in the Scottish Parliament, London Assembly and European Parliament, but then collapsing again in 2001 to less than 1 per cent of the total vote. The UK Independence Party won three MEPs in 1999 but only 1.5 per cent of the vote in 2001.

Thus Labour alone among the major parties seemed to operate at two quite different levels of support, a general election level and an other elections level, while the two main opposition parties were much more stable. If we look at opinion poll data for the 1997–2001 period, however, right through the mid-term elections and in by-elections, the public's general election voting intentions remained eerily consistent. Labour support was almost certainly overrepresented somewhat in many mid-term polls that put it in the high 40s (or even over 50 per cent). But the governing party held a commanding poll lead over the Conservatives throughout Blair's first term, quite different from its lacklustre mid term ability to turn out the votes.

The stability of the 2001 result extended also into the social structuring of the vote. There was no gender gap at this election, with Labour and Conservative vote shares exactly the same across men and women, but men very slightly less likely to vote Liberal Democrat. In social class terms Table 8.2 shows how far class politics had changed from the early 1990s, with Labour commanding the largest share of support in all social groups except the AB professional and upper non-manual category, and commanding a third of support even there. The Con/Lab odds ratio for each occupational class is the proportion voting Conservative divided by the proportion voting Labour. In the heyday of class voting we could compare these odds ratios and typically find that the number for the AB group was six times or even seven times larger than that for the DE group. In 2001, however, the AB group was only 2.2 times more likely to vote Conservative

Table 8.2   *Percentage in each occupational class voting for the main parties at the 2001 General Election*

| Party supported | AB category | C1 category | C2 category | DE category |
|---|---|---|---|---|
| Labour | 33 | 39 | 47 | 50 |
| Conservative | 40 | 35 | 29 | 27 |
| Liberal Democrat | 21 | 20 | 18 | 18 |
| Others | 6 | 6 | 6 | 5 |
| Total (%) | 100 | 100 | 100 | 100 |
| Con/Lab odds ratio | 1.21 | 0.90 | 0.61 | 0.54 |

*Source:* Rowe (2001).

rather than Labour than were the DE group, a very modest difference indeed. By repeating the 1997 outcomes closely this result also creates a problem for those political scientists who still argue that class remains the most important feature of British politics and claim that no consistent process of 'class dealignment' has occurred in modern times.

In one aspect though, the 2001 election was highly unusual. The turnout in any UK election has never been lower. Figure 8.1 shows the raw turnout data for general elections since 1945, and the 12 per cent decline since 1997 immediately stands out. As recently as 1992 turnout reached 78 per cent, so the 2001 result represents an unprecedented drop of 19 percentage points across two successive elections. Virtually all media and political science commentaries have blurred the significance of this calamitous fall by characterizing it as 'the lowest since 1918' when turnout was 58.9 per cent, or 0.3 per cent less. The implied suggestion here is that 2001 is within the range of previous results, hence quite likely to be reversible and to prove a one-off anomaly. Perhaps people were just turned off by William Hague's failure to provide a viable opposition, and will return to the twentieth-century norm of 70+ per cent participation next time round.

But in fact there is no valid comparison with 1918, for several reasons. In both the 1918 and the 1945 elections the turnout was artificially lowered by the overseas location of a significant number of male electors in the armed forces. In addition, 1918 was the first ever genuinely liberal democratic

**Figure 8.1   *Turnout in Britain since 1945***

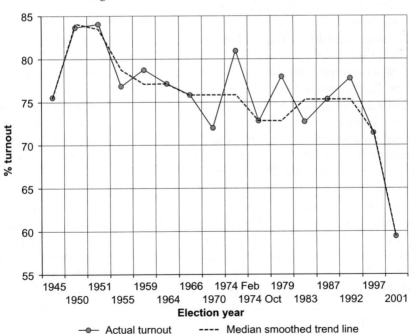

election held in the UK. No less than 40 per cent of male voters (those without property) gained the franchise for the first time, plus all female voters aged 28 or more. The first election held under any new franchise rules or any election system is likely to produce lower turnout, for the simple reason that many new electors are unaware that they can now vote or of how to do so. Similarly with all the disruptions of wartime movements and so many new voters eligible, it is likely that the 1918 register was not a very accurate one. So there are multiple good reasons to believe that in 1918 turnout was artificially much lower than it would have been under normal conditions: the next election, in 1923, attracted over 71 per cent turnout. Thus 2001 stands alone.

The fall in the general election turnout at and after 1997 is distinctive because it occurred at the same times that participation in all other established forms of voting has also declined sharply by at least 10 percentage points, more or less across the board. Across all the Westminster by-elections in Labour's first term turnout averaged just 40 per cent, in seats whose general election average was 68 per cent. This staggering decline even lead to one Labour MP winning a safe seat (Leeds Central) with less than a fifth of electors voting. The regular turnout in European Parliament elections was already low at a consistent rate just over 34 per cent, across all four European contests from 1979 to 1994. But in 1999 it fell dramatically to 24 per cent, less than one in four voters. In the 1992 local council elections as many as 45 per cent of London voters went to the polls. By 1999 just 36 per cent did so, even with the added attraction of a referendum on creating a London Mayor and Assembly. Turnout in all English local elections fells to 29 per cent in 1999 and stayed there in 2000. In some council by-elections turnout almost disappeared, reaching 6 per cent in some Liverpool wards.

When the first devolution elections took place in 1999 under proportional representation systems, the 'low' turnouts of 58 per cent of Scots and under half of all Welsh voters attracted a lot of (English) media criticism, with arguments that devolution had failed to engage voters' attention. Even for Scotland some political scientists proclaimed confidently that the contest for the Edinburgh Parliament was still a 'secondary election' in voters' eyes. But in the 2001 general election the Scottish turnout was only 58 per cent (down 13 points on 1997), compared with 59 per cent in England and 62 per cent in Wales (both down 12 percentage points). The interesting question of whether devolved bodies could compete successfully with Westminster to be the prime focus of politics in their country was thus a close draw between Westminster and the Edinburgh Parliament for Scots. But for Wales the National Assembly in Cardiff still remained less interesting to voters than UK politics. The special dynamics of Northern Irish politics were evident again, for here turnout went up 1 point in 2001 to 68 per cent.

Explaining the sharp collapse in British citizens' willingness to vote, and thinking through what may happen next, are important issues. Some commentators argued early on that a major turnout decline was imminent, seeing it as the entirely foreseeable consequences of sticking with the conventional British voting system. Often termed 'first-past-the-post', this system is much more accurately described as 'plurality rule', since the winning candidate need only get more votes than anyone else (a plurality) in a local contest, and there is no fixed winning post (like 51 per cent support) which they must achieve. (In 1992 a close four-party Westminster race in Inverness was won by a candidate with just 26 per cent of the votes.) Plurality rule privileges the Labour and Conservative parties over all competitors, so it was controversial for successive Tory and Labour governments to stick with it long after it became clear in the early 1970s that Britain was definitively established as a multi-party system. Plurality rule elections in the UK cannot represent modern diverse voting patterns accurately. So to retain them risks de-legitimizing the polity by ensuring the repeated 'wasting' of millions of votes for third and fourth parties at each election.

A second view ascribes falling participation to the end of the sharp left–right politics of the Cold War era, an influence reinforced by the strong consensualism of Blairite politics. Whatever its other defects the Thatcherite period in British politics was a strongly mobilizational one. Turnout levels were probably artificially maintained at high levels in the 1980s and the early 1990s by the stark partisan conflicts of that era, and the apparent promise or threat of major changes over economic policies, taxation levels, privatization and the welfare state. On this interpretation they then collapsed sharply from the mid-1990s onwards because the prospect of radical changes in the welfare state receded in favour of a consensus on stabilizing economic management and improving the major public services again, leaving little at issue between the Conservatives and new Labour.

A third interpretation of the turnout collapse points to the unique difficulties confronted by European social democratic parties in assembling a sufficiently large coalition to win majority control of government (Przeworski and Sprague, 1986). Under plurality rule the British threshold for gaining governmental power is very low, requiring an election winner to assemble at most around 41 or 42 per cent support in order to win a completely artificial absolute majority of Commons seats (Colomer, 2001). The period of Conservative hegemony reflected the relatively even split in the opposition to first Thatcher and then Major between the Labour and the Liberal Democrat voters. After John Major's humiliating 1992 exit from the ERM, Labour was able to reverse this situation, and won a first term in 1997 with a unique coalition of working-class and disgruntled non-manual voters. But in order to retain 'middle-class' support the government was forced to steer a small 'c' conservative course, suppressing public expenditure below the Tories' planned levels in 1997–9, cutting back welfare eligibility and starting only a late and carefully controlled boost to public spending in the 2001 election run-up. On this interpretation, the low turnout in 2001 reflected working-class Labour voters reacting to the dashing of many ambitious hopes by sitting on their hands. Turnout fell only slightly more in Labour's safe areas (over 13 per cent) compared with Conservative and Liberal Democrat seats (11 per cent, or less), but from an already lower base.

A fourth 'sociological' explanation points to the differential collapse of turnout among younger and middle-aged voters, compared with the stronger 'civic-duty' behaviours of the elderly. Age-cohort effects, of course, are long-standing, with young people voting least and pensioners most. But as the younger cohorts' participation rates decline to minorities, and party activists are more and more exclusively middle-aged or more, the traditional mechanisms pulling people into participation may be ebbing away. The bleakest critics point out that factors differentially associated with higher turnout levels in the past (such as being in non-manual occupations, years in education and the proportion of graduates in the workforce) have all been growing strongly in the contemporary UK. So the actual declines in aggregate voting levels charted above are all the more serious, because overall turnout trend should have been gently upwards for most of the last three decades. This observation suggests that the underlying propensities for people to vote (given their social characteristics) have fallen even further and faster than the aggregate national data suggest. One possible contributory factor here has been the UK's shift away from a very centralized mass media system. In the early 1990s there were effectively still only four national TV channels, governmentally constrained to show a quota of political news every day, especially in campaign periods for fear of losing their licences or funding cuts. But in the current more differentiated media system there is no necessary 'mass' experience of political news. With dozens of TV channels and thousands of Web sites open to them, most people can now pursue an evening's viewing without necessarily encountering any political news at all – removing at one stroke a key support for majority interest in politics.

These views suggest differing perspectives on future possibilities. If low turnout is particularly a Blair/new Labour problem then the prospects for the next election in 2004–5 could be for a further sharp decline. If the UK's problem is part of a wider post-Cold War phenomenon then the experience of other liberal democracies in industrialized countries and using similar electoral systems could be relevant. Falls in turnout of a similar scale have occurred recently in Canada, Japan and South Korea. Perhaps all liberal democracies like these, in advanced economies and without proportional systems, are headed for US turnout levels, permanently hovering around 50–55 per cent? Critics argue that this trend reflects a 'culture of contentment' in which only the middle-class vote, relatively immune to the growing problems of a politically inactive underclass, who are increasingly excluded from the focus of public policy as a result (Galbraith, 1992). In rational choice terms, if the working-class or left-inclined part of the electorate begins to abstain differentially, then the median position among those still voting simply shifts further over to the right. 'Rational' politicians of both left and right will simply have to adjust their polices to reflect the new mid-point of the electorate. For Britain, this account implies that if the party leadership can keep on setting policy flexibly, new Labour need not worry about greater non-voting among its traditional support bases. So long as there is no ideological backlash within the party's ranks, and no image problem with voters, the Blair (or possibly future Brown) leadership can continue to set party policy almost unilaterally. New Labour may be able to move progressively rightwards with impunity and still win against a disorganized Tory opposition.

## Britain's multiple electoral systems

Looking back at Table 8.1 there seems to be a straightforward difference between Labour's strong support in the nationwide plurality rule (or 'first-past-the-post') general elections and the party's apparent weakness in the other main mid-term elections, held under proportional representation systems. However, Labour's mid-term weakness applied also to local council elections and to Westminster by-elections, both held using plurality rule. Undeterred by such complicating evidence, numerous Labour critics of electoral reform have insistently made the argument that proportional representation is bad for the party's chances of forming a government. They lament Labour's failure to win majorities in either Wales or London (actually owing to Blair's disastrously mishandled interventions to rig party elections), and they deplore the necessity of being in coalition governments in all three mainland devolved bodies. A more sophisticated version of this Labour 'tribalist' reaction underpins a great deal of the prime minister's cooling towards electoral reform, especially the decision not to act on the 1998 Jenkins Report, which called for a minimally proportional system to be introduced for the House of Commons. Labour critics of reform have been quick to notice that voting for fourth or fifth parties (such as the Greens, UK Independence, left-of-Labour parties and far-right parties) is stronger under PR systems and weakest for Westminster contests.

Yet, despite these misgivings, Labour in its first term enacted radical innovations for all Britain's new voting systems, and has continued to discuss creating new PR systems. It is just possible that the Jenkins system has not yet been utterly buried, since Labour promised a review of Britain's proportional systems for 2003 in order to maintain Lab–Lib tactical voting in 2001. The Labour–Liberal Democrat coalition running the Scottish Executive is considering proposals to introduce the single transferable vote system for local council elections there, a step strongly favoured by the Liberal Democrats and the Scottish National Party. In England five cities voted in referenda during 2001 to introduce directly elected Mayors, who will be chosen using the Supplementary Vote system first designed for electing the London Mayor (on which see below). And in autumn 2001 the second Blair government itself unveiled plans for a completely new PR election. Their much-criticized plans for a mainly appointed 'reformed' House of Lords none the less included 100–120 MLs (Members of the Lords) who would be elected at the same time as the general election, using the List PR system already employed for the European Parliament elections (see below). Thus already enacted and proposed changes have created a permanently mixed polity in the UK. Over time voters will gain more and more experience of using new proportional representation (PR) systems, in tandem with the established plurality rule approach.

The most important British PR system, used in Scotland, Wales and London, is a version of the 'additional member system' (AMS) popularized by Germany's experience in the post-war period. Here some local MPs are elected by plurality rule in conventional single-member constituencies, while the rest are allocated in a compensating manner within larger regions to 'top up' parties underrepresented from the local results. The 'classic' AMS system used in Germany (and in New Zealand since 1996) elects half the MPs locally and half in top-up areas. But Labour successfully insisted on having a majority of MSPs locally elected in the consensual plans for the Scottish Parliament drawn up by a Lab–Lib coalition in the Scottish Constitutional Convention in the early 1990s. The Convention also devised a system of small top-up areas which maintained constituency contact, even for top-up MSPs. Labour later copied the Convention approach in a more rigged variant for choosing the members of the Welsh National Assembly. By contrast, when Labour ministers came to design the Greater London Assembly (GLA) arrangements they were determined to have a very small body, that would not rival the London boroughs. The GLA was eventually restricted to just 25 members. An AMS system was again adopted, with 14 local members representing large two- or three-borough constituencies, and 11 top-up members elected from London as a whole, both measures supposed to ensure that GLA members took a 'strategic' view of London's problems.

Table 8.3 shows that the three 'British AMS' systems share numerous features. All elect a majority of representatives in local constituencies. They elect top-up or additional members for areas that are either small and accessible to citizens or well recognized by them. And they allocate top-up seats using a method called the d'Hondt rule which slightly favours large over small parties (also used in the UK's European elections under list PR in June 1999). Neither the Scottish nor the Welsh schemes specified a legal minimum threshold of votes needed to win seats. Instead they kept down the total number of local and top-up seats elected within each top-up area (a measure called the 'effective district magnitude'). This kept *de facto* votes threshold needed to win a seat fairly high, an approach which the Jenkins proposals followed closely. However, in London for the first time in any British election ministers built in a 5 per cent legal threshold (instead of leaving the 3.5 per cent level which would otherwise have applied). This safety feature aimed to prevent racist parties winning one of the 25 seats, theoretically possible if a great many parties entered competition. In 2000 with massive numbers of parties, the British National Party won 2.7 per cent support across London.

The unimplemented Jenkins Commission's proposal for the Commons shares most of the key features of British AMS but it is distinctive in two respects. First, Jenkins argued for the absolute minimum number of top-up MPs, less than a fifth of the total, a step which meant that the system might be 'broadly proportional' but could not guarantee proportionality as the other systems do (Dunleavy and Margetts, 1999a; Dunleavy, Margetts and Weir, 1998b). Second, the Jenkins Commission was heavily influenced by the Liberal Democrats' pressure for more voter choice (the reason why the Liberal Democrats have traditionally backed the single transferable vote, a system still anathema to Labour people). Instead of using plurality rule in electing the four-fifths of constituency members in their scheme, the Commission called for the 'alternative vote' (used in Australia) to be employed instead, thereby guaranteeing that all MPs would have (bare) majority support in their local areas. The Commission also wanted 'open' lists to be used at the top-up stage, so that voters could if they wish vote for specific candidates instead of having to accept a fixed ordering set by each party (see below). Both these complicating features contributed strongly to making the Jenkins Commission scheme seem much more complex than British AMS, and in no small part explain its subsequent failure to attract much public support.

A second set of systems in Table 8.3 use the 'closed-List' PR method with candidates elected to represent regions. In 1999 voters chose members of the European Parliament by casting a single vote between slates of party candidates in regional multi-member constituencies, with between 4 and 11 seats in each. Parties then won seats in proportion to their votes, with candidates being allocated seats in the order that they were placed on their party's list, again using a d'Hondt rule. Critics argued that Labour's scheme was an unwise fix, designed solely to smooth the transition from its huge majority of MEPs elected under plurality rule in 1994 to a necessarily reduced seats' share under PR. Closed-list voting was also argued to be off-putting for voters, especially after Labour adopted a thoroughly

Table 8.3 Key features of existing British proportional representation systems and currently proposed systems

| 'British AMS' systems | Assembly size | Mix of local: top-up seats (%) | Constituency members elected by | Top-up areas (if used) used | Top-up seats per area | Effective district magnitudes | Exclusion threshold % |
|---|---|---|---|---|---|---|---|
| Scottish Parliament | 129 | 57:43 | Plurality rule in 73 Westminster constituencies | 8 former Euro constituencies | 7 | 15–17 | 5.6 |
| Welsh Assembly | 60 | 67:33 | Plurality rule in 40 Westminster constituencies | 5 former Euro constituencies | 4 | 11–13 | 7.1 |
| Greater London Assembly | 25 | 57:43 | Plurality rule in 14 double or triple London borough areas | Greater London | 11 | 25 | 3.8 |
| Proposed Jenkins Commission's 'AV+' system for Westminster | 659 | 83:17 | Supplementary vote in 543 redrawn Westminster constituencies | 80 counties and parts of metro counties in England; top-up areas in Scotland and Wales as above; 2 new areas in Northern Ireland | 1 or 2 | 5–11 | 8.3 |

| List PR systems | Assembly size | Other elements in Assembly | UK Elected members | Areas used | District magnitudes | Exclusion threshold % |
|---|---|---|---|---|---|---|
| European Parliament | | 539 MEPs from other EU countries | 87 | Government standard regions in England, plus Scotland, Wales and Northern Ireland | 4–11 | 7–20 |
| Government proposal for reformed House of Lords (autumn 2001) | c. 600 | c. 500 appointed MLs (Members of the Lords) | c. 100–120 | Government standard regions in England, plus Scotland, Wales and Northern Ireland | Probably 6–14 | Around 6–14 |

| Mayoral systems | Election system | Second counting round threshold | % of 'eligible votes' needed to win | % of total votes needed to win |
|---|---|---|---|---|
| London Mayor | Supplementary Vote (SV) | Top two candidates from first round | 58% in London 2000 Depends on number of candidates and the fragmentation of the vote | 49% in London 2000 Depends on number of candidates and the fragmentation of the vote |

*Notes:* The effective district magnitude is the number of seats considered by the electoral system in allocating seats. The exclusion threshold is the percentage votes level a party needs to win in order to be guaranteed that it will win a seat (Rae et al, 1971).

undemocratic method for selecting its candidates which favoured existing MEPs. Historically Euro election turnouts in Britain since 1979 were very low anyway but under the new system, and with a deliberately low-key Labour campaign designed as a damage-limitation exercise, turnout plunged to just 24 per cent. Labour's vote share was heavily eroded by defections to fourth and fifth parties and by abstentions among its core voters. In July 1999 the Labour National Executive Committee voted to scrap closed-list PR, and to explore instead a version of AMS for the next Euro elections due in 2004. However, once the 2001 general election turnout fell by 12 per cent under plurality rule, it became less plausible to believe that the List PR system had contributed particularly to the turnout decline in 1999, which now seemed to be part of an across-the-board shift in British politics.

A small-scale rehabilitation of list PR seemed to be signalled by the government's autumn 2001 plans for choosing 100–120 elected members of the reformed House of Lords. The Lords election would take place on the general election polling day, but with a separate closed-list ballot paper showing each party's candidates for between 5 and 14 regional seats in the Lords. With their single vote people would again only be able to pick between one of the 'closed' lists of candidates in the order set out by each party. The relative vote shares of the parties would determine how many seats each got, again using a d'Hondt formula. This approach will guarantee the major parties' predominance, but in the biggest regions like London and the South East the Greens and UK Independence Party might be able to elect some MLs. Given the 'deliberative' and revising chamber roles envisaged for the Lords, early critics saw the use of closed lists as especially problematic – even more so given the government's proposal that half the MLs would anyway be appointed by the parties to reflect their votes shares in the general election. Alternative arrangements would include a 'flexible list' approach, where voters could endorse a particular candidate within a party's list, moving her up the ranking if a lot of voters did the same; or a fully 'open list' where voters cannot just tick a party box, but must put a cross against a particular candidate. Usually in open or flexible lists the party's hierarchy of candidates still dominates who is elected, because rational parties anyway put their most popular candidates at the top of their lists in order to attract more votes. But flexible or open lists give voters more influence over a party machine that tries to exclude particular candidates or push them down the lists, and thus they may help to weaken unthinking party discipline – surely a useful feature in a revising chamber?

The final system just beginning to be used is the Supplementary Vote (SV) for local mayors. Each voter can vote twice, for a first and second preference candidate. First preferences are counted and if no one wins over 50 per cent, then the top two runners only stay in the race and all other candidates are eliminated. The second preferences of eliminated candidates are then examined, and any 'eligible votes' relating to the top two candidates are added to their respective piles of votes, while those for other eliminated candidates are discarded as ineligible. The winning candidate will have a majority of the eligible votes (58 per cent in the case of Ken Livingstone's decisive win in London in 2000), but maybe not a majority of all votes (48 per cent for Livingstone). This system is a great advance over plurality rule for choosing a single office-holder, however. In the 1999 race for Tokyo's governor the winning candidate under plurality rule gained fewer than one-third of all votes in a 19-candidate race. By contrast Livingstone's mandate was impressive and clearly helped him build a stable Labour/Liberal Democrat/Green coalition in the Greater London Assembly. The few towns and cities adopting elected mayors will use SV too, and since fewer candidates should contest other mayoralties than in London, the system should give clear majority support to winners.

Westminster elections developed over centuries and provided the source code for the plurality-rule elections used in all the English-speaking and Commonwealth countries around the world. So we perhaps should not be surprised that the Jenkins Commission proposals for even modest change still lie unimplemented. But all the new electoral systems set up since 1997 have been proportional ones, reflecting essentially the strained legitimacy of plurality rule, which continued in 2001. Labour won 64 per cent of Commons seats with just 42 per cent of the vote, a huge 'leader's bonus' effect secured at the expense of all other parties. For the second time in their post-war history the Conservatives were severely underrepresented, as were the Liberal Democrats even though they boosted their share of seats to nearly one in 13 of the Commons seats. If we subtract each of the parties' votes shares from their seat shares in Table 8.1 we obtain a set of positive and negative deviations; we can then discard the + or − signs, add up the total deviations, and divide by 2 (to eliminate double counting) to get a measure called the 'deviation from proportionality' or DV score. The DV score shows what proportion of the MPs elected are occupying seats that they are not entitled to hold in terms of their party's share of the national vote. In 1997 this measure was 21 per cent, and in 2001 it was 22. But the maximum DV score for a liberal democracy is not (as you might expect) 100 per cent. Instead it is set by $(100 - V1)$, where $V1$ is the share of the largest party. We can regrade the DV score to get a new measure called the adjusted DV or ADV score, where 0 indicates pure proportionality and 100 indicates a result at the limit of being a liberal democracy at all. For example, some local council elections (such as those in Newham borough in London) regularly assign all council seats to the largest party, which gives an ADV score of 100 per cent. On this measure the 1997 election rated 32 and the 2001 rated 33 per cent, very high levels of disproportionality. In fact we could say that Westminster elections are fully a third of the way along from pure proportionality and towards complete disproportionality for a liberal democratic system.

But even this national-level figure is a radical underestimate of how unfairly the electoral system operates on the ground, because pro-Labour biases in all the major metropolitan areas, northern England, Scotland and Wales are offset by a strong pro-Conservative bias still operating in southeast England and the eastern region. Looking at the picture for individual regions controls for this effect, and shows that across much of the country plurality rule works in a much less proportional way than the national data suggests. In Yorkshire and Humberside, for instance, Labour won 84 per cent of the seats in 2001 with just 49 per cent of the votes. The normal DV score here was 45 per cent, and the ADV score was an astounding 88 per cent – so that Yorkshire at this election was nine-tenths of the distance away from pure proportionality towards not being a liberal democracy at all.

With only one round of PR elections undertaken so far, we still have few clues about how (if at all) voters' alignments will change when plurality-rule elections for Westminster and local councils coexist for a long period with PR elections everywhere else. One interpretation of the votes outcomes in Table 8.1 is that in the 1999 mid-term PR elections voters correctly anticipated that a more pluralist politics would be viable, and were prepared to take chances in voting nationalist in Wales or for other parties like the Greens or left-of-Labour parties. On this view the two general election results and the stable opinion poll dominance for Labour reflect the fact that voters would not do the same in a general election – perhaps because the big national issues are more vital to them, or perhaps because they recognize that Westminster elections under plurality-rule voting still favour so much the two largest parties.

Another argument is that electors' ideological ties to the major parties have been loosening for a long period (Sarlvik and Crewe, 1983; Rose and McAllister, 1986) and may loosen further under the influence of PR. For example, in both 1997 and 2001 there was a lot of 'split-ticket' voting by people casting votes for different parties in the general election and local elections held on the same day (see Rallings and Thrasher, 1998). The same phenomenon played a major role in the devolved AMS elections in Scotland and Wales in 1999 where people had two votes (for local and top-up members), and even more in the London elections in 2000 where people could express four preferences in all (two for Mayor, and local and top-up votes for the Assembly). Almost a quarter of Scottish and Welsh voters split their votes in 1999, and over a third of London voters in 2000. It will be interesting to see if these patterns solidify in the 2003 and 2004 elections for the devolved bodies, but there were few signs in 2001 of these more conditional party loyalties producing distinctive changes in voting behaviour at Westminster elections.

## Party competition in a multi-party system

To understand the roots of both the 1997 and 2001 results it is important to take account of two factors:

- where parties are located in ideological and policy terms on the left–right spectrum
- how credible and effective a party seems to voters as a potential government, especially in terms of its political leadership.

A long line of public choice analysis stretching back to Downs (1957) and Hotelling (1929) has argued that parties can best maximize their vote by adopting the position of the median voter, the person in the electorate who has equally as many people on their right as on their left. For simplicity's sake let us take it that the distribution of voters across the left–right space is even. (It does not change the analysis if in real life there are more voters in the centre ground.) Then we can show the median vote as a centrist person, MV in Figure 8.2. Let us assume that voters always vote for their nearest party. So voters who are more left-wing than Labour or more right-wing than the Conservatives would always keep on voting for their party, even if it moves towards the median position. For these more 'extreme' voters there is nowhere else (effective) to go. For instance, left Labour people will find it hard to find a viable left alternative to vote for so long as Labour (however de-radicalized it becomes) at least stays left of the Liberal Democrats, and of the Scottish National Party or Plaid Cymru outside England. But by shifting position towards the median voter either Labour or the Conservatives in the British system could acquire more support from centrist voters, without losing their 'core' voters' support.

We have a difficulty in comparing the 2001 election with 1997, because all the parties stayed in pretty much the same policy positions, understandably enough for Labour and the Liberal Democrats who did so well out of these stances in 1997. It is very hard indeed to explain why the Conservatives after losing so badly in 1997 changed their position so little under William Hague. Essentially his approach firmed up a right-wing policy critical of the European Union and monetary union. He also attempted to tap some populist issues like fears about immigration and asylum seekers. But at the same time Hague tried to move centrewards in broadening the Conservative's social representativeness. Again the Tory leadership pledged to create £8 billion of tax cuts but at the same time as protecting key public services like the NHS and state education by maintaining Labour's spending plans for them. These offsetting policy changes tended to cancel each other out in most citizens' minds, with the result that the Tory policy position remained little changed over Blair's first term. Had Hague been a strongly effective leader in public opinion terms this approach might yet have been sustainable, but in fact he was held in relatively low esteem by a majority of voters. Apart from considerable skill in handling PM's question time, Hague had no great qualities to offset against Blair's commanding leadership position and strong poll ratings on most aspects.

So to see how the model works we really need to apply it to the major transition from Labour's marked defeat in 1992 to its strong showing in 1997, shown schematically in Figure 8.2a and 8.2b. One of Tony Blair's most decisive impacts on the Labour party, strongly promoted by his electoral strategists Peter Mandelson and Gordon Brown, was to move the party firmly rightwards, away from the distinctively left-wing position it still held even at the 1992 general election, towards a systematically centrist stance by 1997. For instance, Labour's 1992 election pledge to raise the top rate of income tax for high earners was completely scrapped, and instead the party pledged that there would be no income tax rise if it won office. 'Policy-making by focus group' was also introduced, allowing the Labour leadership to fine-tune their commitments so as to remove or marginalize unpopular commitments. And the party's long-standing Clause Four in its constitution (pledging Labour to achieve public ownership of the means of production) was replaced with a piece of innocuous waffle.

Comparing the positions of the three main British-wide parties on the horizontal axes in Figures 8.2a and 8.2b, it should be apparent that Labour's centrewards shift was the only significant movement in ideological terms between 1992 and 1997. The Conservatives under John Major did not become more right-wing in this period, but on the other hand they made no move to try and match Labour's shift to the centre. Indeed, apparently overconfident that voters would not back Blair, or perhaps hypnotized by the extent of changes which he introduced in Labour's policy positions, the Conservatives failed to make even the most basic adjustments of their own stance to try to match Labour's popular appeal. The Liberal Democrats also made no move, despite dallying with pledges for marginal increases of income tax. Their leadership recognized that their party was in danger of being squeezed between Labour and the Tories. But they had few options about continuing to present themselves in centrist ideological terms, since Liberal Democrats compete against the Tories in southern and rural England, but against Labour in northern and urban England.

However, where the parties stand on the left–right ideological scale is not the only determinant of how much support they receive. How voters see the *effectiveness* of voting for a party is also important. If a party looks well run, and in particular well lead, then voters will see its pledges as more credible, more likely to be implemented and hence of greater value. Tony Blair's almost immediate achievement on winning Labour's top post in 1994 was to seem a much more plausible and reassuring party leader than either of his predecessors, John Smith (who died after only a short period at the top) and Neil Kinnock (whose popular credibility was always

**Figure 8.2** *The left–right positions of the parties, and the effectiveness of the party leaderships, 1992 and 1997*

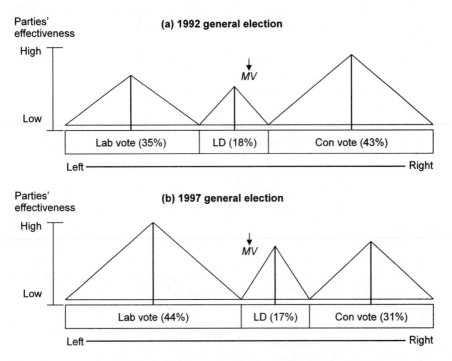

*Note:* The centre of each party-umbrella shows where the party's manifesto-policy stood on the left–right dimension, and how effective voters judged the party leadership to be. *MV* = median voter's position.

rather strained). Again, Blair took no chances with his reputation, managing to build on it by a series of carefully timed internal party reforms which put to rest most previous public anxieties about the power of the trade unions or of activists with unrepresentative views within Labour's ranks. Comparing Figures 8.2a and 8.2b it can be seen that in 1997 Labour was a far more credible potential government, so that in addition to *changing* and enlarging its appeal by moving centrewards it also *widened* its appeal by appearing for the first time as a more viable government than the Tories, and a more effective party for centrist voters to back than the Liberal Democrats.

The Conservatives lost votes so badly in 1997 not only because they made little or no move to match Labour's repositioning towards the centre ground but chiefly because their own effectiveness in the public's eyes declined very markedly after sterling was ignominiously ejected from the ERM in September 1992, almost as soon as John Major was re-elected. The tumult in financial markets then triggered a large rise in interest rates with devastating effects on mortgages and jobs for several years. The legacies of this crisis dogged Major's whole administration, and along with signs of internal Tory faction fighting over Europe and apparently weak leadership from Major it proved a major liability. From around 1995 onwards the Conservatives were also damaged by the growth of numerous 'sleaze' stories (Dunleavy and Weir, 1995).

The Liberal Democrats were also beneficiaries with Labour of the Conservatives' tribulations. Their leader in 1997, Paddy Ashdown, was the most long-established of all the party leaders then, and had acquired a reassuring *gravitas* over the years and very good public visibility for a Liberal Democrat politician. His deal with Labour for joint action on constitutional reform boosted Ashdown's credibility as a serious player further, and along with a tacit division of constituencies for 'high-effort' campaigning between the two parties it made the Liberal Democrats seem a much more important political force than for generations. Thus although the Liberal Democrats *were* squeezed in 1997 by Labour's shift to the centre, and their national vote fell from its 1992 level, their increased effectiveness produced a sufficient countervailing widening of their appeal. Attracting support from disillusioned Conservatives and tactical voting by Labour supporters in normally Tory constituencies meant that the number of Liberal Democrat MPs more than doubled in 1997. These gains were maintained at the 2001 election under Ashdown's successor, Charles Kennedy. Despite Labour's inaction on the Jenkins Commission's electoral reform plan, a project dear to the Liberal Democrats' hearts, Kennedy managed to stitch together a very limited understanding with Labour on avoiding divisive campaigning competition in many key constituencies, which might have let the Conservatives win them back.

Does Labour's almost exact replay of the 1997 result in 2001, and the current dim-looking Conservative prospects of staging a major recovery, imply that the British party system is moving decisively towards a pattern of Swedish-style social democratic dominance? Is the UK now back in a dominant party system, only switching the identity of the dominant party from the Tories in the 1980s to Labour now? Triumphalist new Labour strategists and much of the media, looking far ahead to a third Labour successive term of office, might subscribe to this analysis. But there are important caveats and qualifications worth noting. To begin with Figure 8.3 shows that both 1997 and 2001 were highly unusual elections in terms of the seats/votes ratios of all three major parties. These two results sit far away from the basic seats/votes relationship for the 1945–97 period shown as the earlier regression line in each of the party's graphs. In the post-war period both Labour and the Liberal Democrats have never won so many seats on such a small share of the votes. Nor have the Conservatives ever fared so badly in the post-war period or been so severely underrepresented twice consecutively in terms of seats than in the last two elections.

We know from Table 8.1 that despite the artificial seats landslides

**Figure 8.3** *The relationship between votes won and seats won (percentages of the total), 1950–2001*

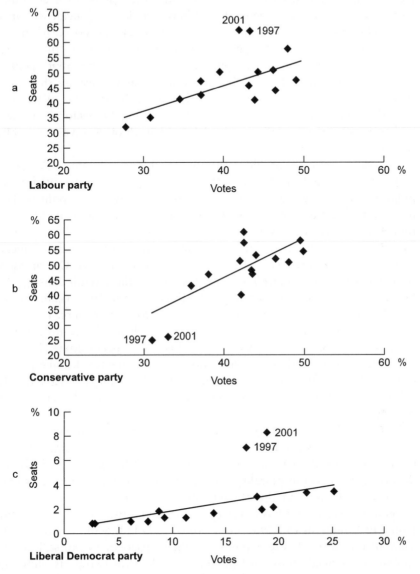

Labour party — Votes / Seats

Conservative party — Votes / Seats

Liberal Democrat party — Votes / Seats

produced by plurality rule, neither 1997 nor 2001 were 'critical' or 'realigning' elections. In both contests no new party or radically different electoral coalition came into being, unless you can count under this heading the effective but submerged cooperation of Labour and Liberal Democrat leaders, activists and voters to get the Tories out in 1997. (But this factor was not present in 2001, although a tactical voting effect was maintained.) Even in 1997 the parties' support bases only changed incrementally from what existed before. And the results for every other contest except the two general elections provides no evidence of a thorough-going Labour hegemony, reaching through to every corner of the political system. Instead it suggests in many ways a return to the normal politics of mid-term slumps, despite the Conservatives' apparent inability to either change their basic policy positions so as to increase their vote share or to secure credible leadership. Labour also came out of its mid-term slumps in a very traditional manner, by playing the electoral–business cycle successfully, especially via the delayed launch of massive new public services spending.

Just as Westminster provided the source code for plurality-rule voting world-wide, so the British party system has always been represented in the political science literature as a *locus classicus* of two-party politics. For many establishment observers this picture remains undisturbed, even though the Conservatives and Labour have jointly commanded less than 75 per cent of the total vote in an extensive sequence of general, European and local elections held since 1974, and did so again in 2001. On this view the current long-lived pattern of voting is merely 'the seventh phase in the history of Britain's two-party system', which remains 'remarkably resilient', because it is 'so compatible with the practice, procedure, traditions and culture of the House of Commons, with all its ramifications' (Harrison, 1996, p. 206). Adopting a historical perspective Harrison concludes that the traditional British dominance of the two leading parties is well able to withstand this latest temporary 'disruption' in an apparently substantial series of such episodes stretching back to the eighteenth century.

The main difficulty here is to know what the phrase 'two-party system' means any more, beyond the uncontested fact that the two biggest parties in Britain are likely to go on commanding artificially high levels of MPs at Westminster thanks to plurality-rule voting. Two-party dominance seems to mean no more than the obvious institutional corollaries of a voting method that since 1974 has always given around a fifth of the seats in the House of Commons to parties not justified to hold them in terms of their share of the national vote. Labour and the Conservatives can still jointly run an unreformed House of Commons as a kind of two-party club and marginalize the influence of other underrepresented parties on the conduct of business. And one or other of the big two can still normally count on forming a majority government on their own. But is this all that a 'two-party system' means – a kind of sustained joint exploitation of the third- and fourth-party voters in the electorate by the party leaders of the majority?

The alternative view is that a 'two-party system' genuinely rooted in voters' alignments and affections exists only where the two leading parties attract the continuous support of the vast majority (say, 90 per cent) of voters. In the US the Democrats and Republicans easily meet this criterion in every legislative election (although not in the presidential contests of 1992 or 1996). And of course in the US the plurality-rule system converts citizens' votes into seats as accurately as the PR systems in western Europe. But the United States is now the only large and mature liberal democracy where a living, breathing two-party system endures, well supported by voters. Elsewhere, even in current or former plurality-rule countries like Canada, India or New Zealand (now using AMS) nothing like this configuration exists, and even Australia has substantial third-party representation in its Senate. British politics too has moved a world away from having anything in common with the American template: Table 8.1 shows that the effective number of parties in Britain was already over three in the 1997 and 2001 general elections, and rose to around four in the mid-term elections of 1999 and 2000. In Scotland and Wales a permanent four-party system now exists both in voters' alignments (mirrored in the Scottish Parliament and Welsh Assembly) which is radically different from the three-party politics of England. In Northern Ireland the main British parties no longer even contest elections, and there is a completely different party system with around 10 to 12 separate parties.

Across all three of mainland Britain's party systems voters have also moved a long way from the 'classic' picture drawn by political scientists in the 1960s and 1970s of people with customary, 'natural' or unquestioning party loyalties (Butler and Stokes, 1970). Throughout the period since then numerous election surveys operating in this tradition (see Heath and MacDonald, 1988) and countless opinion polls, both concerned chiefly with predicting who will win governmental power, have consequently asked respondents only about their first preferences across the main parties. But this approach has disguised from political scientists the extent to which voters actually have well articulated preference structures, in which their behaviour is shaped by first-, second- and third-party preferences as much as by their top choice (Catt, 1996; Dunleavy, 1996).

These patterns are not accidental, but deep-rooted now and long-lived. In no currently foreseeable future will we see a return to Labour–Conservative conflicts defining the main dimension of party competition in Scotland or Wales. Even in London, the heart of England, the weakening grip of two-party conflicts was evident at an institutional level in the run-up to the Greater London Authority (GLA) elections in 2000, when Ken Livingstone ran for mayor and won as an independent candidate. And in the 1999 European elections, the success of fourth and fifth parties (the Greens and the UK Independence Party) in winning multiple seats in English regions notched up another small milestone in the arrival of multi-party politics, even if it was in a 'second-order' and PR election (see Chapter 4). Across most established liberal democracies (except the US), the dominant trend of party system change in the last 30 years has been towards a greater fragmentation of political alignments. The evidence still suggests that party system change in Britain will continue to move in the same direction, especially when (if) Labour's current support levels begin to weaken.

## Conclusions

At the 1997 and 2001 elections a new mould of Labour dominance in British politics seemed to many observers to becoming semi-permanently set in place, dramatically reversed the Tory hegemony of the 1980s and early 1990s. But despite Labour's commanding Commons majorities (179 in 1997 and 166 in 2001), the shape of future British politics still seems contestable. In the four mid-term elections the combined Conservative–Labour share of the vote was just 60 per cent in the European elections, 53 per cent in Wales, 49 per cent in Scotland and 59 per cent for the GLA poll. Even when plurality rule applied in the 2001 general election, Labour and the Conservatives still won only 75 per cent of the votes cast. Their combined grip on voters' positive allegiances nonetheless collapsed. In 1992 nearly 26 million voters endorsed one or other of them, but in 2001 only 19 million people did so – a decline of more than a quarter. Labour won decisively in 2001 with the support of nearly a million *fewer* voters than it had gained in its humiliating defeat in 1992.

Of course, the Tories' problems explain most of the two-party decline, with their support base slipping from an admittedly exceptional 14.1 million votes in 1992 to just 8.4 million in 2001, a staggering drop of 40 per cent in eight years. With a new policy review set in place by Ian Duncan Smith there are still few signs in Tory ranks of any new policy change ideas which are remotely commensurate with the scale of the party's difficulties. Their best hopes remained pinned on the possibility of a referendum on joining the Euro in autumn 2002 or 2003, which would still be very hard for Blair to win, and a hope that policy dissatisfactions under Labour will continue to grow, eventually causing a public opinion revulsion from Labour. More radical policy changes, like reconsidering the party's attachment to plurality rule and opposition to electoral reform, remain firmly off the Conservative agenda.

After allowing for the turnout rate, Labour in 2001 won its impressive seats total by winning the support of just 25 per cent of the electorate against the Conservatives' 19 per cent. This is a strangely weak basis on which to announce a new Labour hegemony. At a general election, those actually voting respond more conservatively to national issues and recognize that voting for small parties under plurality rule might 'waste' their votes. But as a protracted coexistence between plurality-rule and PR voting systems unfolds further, the emergence of a more pluralist form of electoral and party politics in Britain still seems a safe bet, amid declining levels of political participation. By the next general election in 2005, will the UK rival the United States' low turnout rates?

## Chapter 9

# Political Parties: Adapting to the Electoral Market

PAUL WEBB

In recent years British political parties have attempted to transform themselves into increasingly sophisticated electoral organizations in order to adapt to an increasingly fluid political environment. This has been most apparent in the case of new Labour, whose name has become a byword for coordinated party discipline and slickly professional election campaigning. Even so, there remain factors which constrain the development of such 'electoral-professionalism' (Panebianco, 1988; Webb, 1992b). For Labour these are currently most likely to arise, paradoxically, from the Blair government's agenda of decentralization of state power. For the Conservatives, despite William Hague's attempt to modernize his party organizationally, the main limiting factor continues to be internal party dissension over questions of policy and leadership.

Why is there greater scope for electoral competition in Britain than hitherto? In part, it flows from well known processes of electoral change such as dealignment and realignment (Crewe, Sarlvik and Alt, 1977; Crewe and Thomson, 1999; Evans and Norris, 1999), and in part from the growing variety of elective offices which parties prize and compete for. While the first of these developments is relatively long-term, dating back to the early 1970s, the latter is far more recent, owing much – once again – to the Blair government's agenda of constitutional reform. Partisan dealignment has generally rendered the electoral market more open. The main indication of such dealignment has generally been regarded as the erosion of partisan identification. In Britain, the proportion of voters claiming some sort of partisan identity (roughly 90% in 2001) had barely dropped since the 1960s, but the percentage claiming to be very strong partisans fell appreciably (from 44 per cent to 16 per cent). These figures provide a clear sense of the opening of the electoral market, in so far as weak partisans and non-partisans are known to be more likely to switch allegiance than strong partisans. In 1997, for example, some 74 per cent of very/fairly strong partisans voted for the same party as in 1992, whereas

151

only 48 per cent of very/fairly strong partisans did (see Webb, 2000, ch. 2). Moreover, dealignment has been complemented by processes of electoral realignment which have boosted the electoral standing of minor parties, and thereby changed the nature of party competition at regional and constituency levels. The pattern of constituency contests in Westminster elections is thus no longer dominated by the major parties to the same extent as hitherto. Whereas in 1970 some 92 per cent of such contests in Britain were direct confrontations between Labour and Conservatives, in 1992 just 65 per cent were. This shift in the pattern of competition at constituency level dates very clearly from February 1974 (Johnston, Pattie and Fieldhouse, 1994, pp. 260–1).

Furthermore, the competitive significance of minor parties has been enhanced by constitutional reforms introduced by the Labour government since 1997. Devolution creates a new tier of elective office for the parties to contest: control of the Scottish Parliament and executive at Holyrood, and the Welsh Assembly in Cardiff, are new and valued prizes which each of the main parties and the nationalists must organize themselves to compete for. Much the same can be said about the new Greater London Assembly (GLA) and mayoralty. What is more, prevailing patterns of party support in Scotland and Wales and the use of various PR electoral systems in elections for the Scottish Parliament and assemblies in Wales and London significantly improves the representative position of minor parties in all these contests: they will not simply be dominated by the major parties (see Chapter 8).

Thus, since 1974 proportionally fewer voters have strong partisan loyalties, elections to the Westminster parliament are no longer the only important ones, and the major parties no longer dominate the competition for votes right across Britain. These changes imply that there are now fewer electoral certainties. Though initially disconcerting for the major parties, they have shown themselves able to respond and adapt, especially at the level of internal organization. In various ways they have sought to transform themselves into sophisticated professional organizations which are better suited to the requirements of an increasingly competitive electoral marketplace.

## Changing models of party organization

Political scientists generally recognize that party organizations have changed historically as their primary purposes have altered. The most widely acknowledged initial account of these changes was provided by the French political scientist Maurice Duverger. In his classic work *Political Parties*, first published in English in 1954, Duverger argued that in the pre-democratic era parties were purely parliamentary alliances of elites who banded together for the purpose of coordinating legislative action; such parties lacked extra-parliamentary national organizations and grassroots memberships. This elitist organizational ideal type was referred to by Duverger as the *cadre party*, and its rather restricted form of local organization as the *caucus*. By contrast, the democratic era saw the invention of the *mass-branch party*, a form of political organization which depended on large numbers of grassroots members, and a more centralized national structure. Fundamental to the purpose of the mass party was the political education and integration of the newly enfranchized masses: 'Without members, the party would be like a teacher without pupils' (Duverger, 1954, p. 63).

Thus, as the central functions of parties shifted from coordinating legislative action to politically integrating the masses, their typical organizational structure changes. Though no British party conformed precisely to either of Duverger's ideal types, clearly the older Conservative and Liberal parties had pre-democratic origins and structures resembling those of the cadre party, while Labour had more in common with the mass-party model. By the 1960s, however, political scientists were pointing to a further evolution in the purpose and style of major parties. Most notably, the German writer Otto Kirchheimer (1966) argued that such parties were substituting electoral ambition for their role as social integrators. Kirchheimer wrote in the context of the controversial debate about the warning of the ideological conflict that engaged social and political theorists during the 1960s. Like a number of other observers, he perceived an attenuation of ideological conflict in Western societies. He credited this to the development of more fluid social class situations and the secularization of societies once firmly influenced by organized religion. His conclusion was that:

> the mass integration part, product of an age with harder class lines and more sharply protruding denominational structures, is transforming itself into a catch-all 'peoples' party. Abandoning attempts at the intellectual and moral *encadrement* of the masses, it is turning more fully to the electoral scene, trying to exchange effectiveness in depth for a wider audience and more immediate electoral success. (Kirchheimer, 1966, p. 185)

This entailed parties such as Labour in 'trying to hold their special working class clientele and at the same time embracing a variety of other clienteles' (Kirchheimer, 1966, p. 186). Such a process involved an amelioration of the 'expressive' function of these parties: that is, the tendency to articulate grievances, ideas and demands on behalf of a specific social constituency. Instead, the *catch-all* party, bent on attracting a wider electoral audience, had to 'modulate and restrain' such expression – hence, the erosion of ideological rhetoric and conflict. This transformation of West European parties involved not only ideological change, but also organizational changes affecting the respective positions of party leaders and members; specifically, Kirchheimer expected a 'downgrading' of the members' role within the organization, and a concomitant growth in leadership power. This argument was subsequently embraced and embellished by other writers, notably Angelo Panebianco (1988, pp. 262–7), who regarded the internal rebalancing of power as vital to the strategic autonomy required by leaders in order to implement their preferred electoral strategies.

Taking our cue from these authors, we might say that the major British parties, driven by the imperatives of electoral competition, have sought to:

- Adopt a political marketing approach which places strategic influence in the hands of opinion-research 'professional'.
- Alter their internal balance of power so as to enhance the strategic autonomy of leaders, although it is far from accurate to suggest that this coincides with a straightforward 'downgrading' of the role of grassroots members.
- Enhance their financial situation, though this only partly coincides with Panebianco's expectation that parties would exploit the resources of the state to achieve this.

The remainder of this chapter is dedicated to a closer examination of these three developments in respect of the major parties.

## Party competition and political marketing

Much academic attention has been devoted to the development of election campaigning in Britain since the 1980s (see especially Franklin, 1994; Kavanagh, 1995; Scammell, 1995; Rosenbaum, 1997; Scammell, 1999), reflecting widespread interest in the evolution of campaign methods and styles. Prior to the era of mass access to television (around 1960), election campaigns were characterized by limited (and relatively late) preparation, the use of traditional party bureaucrats and volunteer activists, direct communication with electors through public meetings, rallies and canvassing (plus indirect communication via partisan newspapers) and relatively little central coordination of campaigning across the country. Televisualization of campaigning gradually altered this traditional model, mainly by producing a far greater emphasis on indirect communication with voters via TV, but it was really only after 1979 that the modernization and professionalization of campaigning took a 'quantum leap' forward in

Britain (Scammell, 1995, ch. 2). By 1987, both major parties had adopted a model of campaigning which differed from the traditional approach in a number of important respects, including: careful campaign preparation centred around the role of specialist campaign committees established well in advance of the election; greater exploitation of media and marketing professionals; a 'nationalization' of campaigning with resources and coordinating power concentrated at the centre; greater emphasis on the party leader; and television as the dominant channel of communication. During the 1990s, campaigning techniques continued to develop with the arrival of new telecommunications technology (especially cable and satellite technology, and the Internet) helping to generate innovations such as the 'narrowcasting' of specific campaign messages on targeted groups of voters.

More generally, the advent of the 'permanent campaign' has rendered the influence of marketing professionals so pervasive that the adaptation of party messages to suit target constituencies has reached new heights. Specifically, it can be said that campaigning, at least for the major parties, has evolved into fully-fledged *political marketing*. Though often used as a form of short-hand for modern advertising and promotion techniques, writers like O'Shaughnessy (1990), Scammell (1995) and Wring (1996a, 1996b) have argued that there is more to it than this; rather, it entails a qualitative shift in the strategic influence of marketing professionals such as opinion researchers. While there is nothing particularly new in British parties using professional pollsters to gauge public preferences (Kavanagh, 1995, ch. 6), hitherto the product remained sacrosanct in so far as the underlying strategic aim was to 'sell' the existing package of policies and leaders. The adoption of a political marketing approach implies that consumer demand is now privileged; it is the *product* rather than the market which is regarded as malleable, as the emphasis shifts to the satisfaction of consumer wants (Scammell, 1995, pp. 8–9).

This clearly implies that political marketing experts have taken on a strategic significance for the major British parties. Indeed, it is abundantly clear that the major British parties have evolved into highly professional, market-oriented organization which are geared to the needs of virtually permanent campaigning.

## Labour

The party which now best exemplifies a highly professional and media-orientated approach to political marketing is undoubtedly Labour, though it was not always thus. For many years, the best that professional expertise had to offer was eschewed by the party. In part this flowed from sheer financial necessity, since Labour has rarely been in a position to match the

Tories for resources, but in part too it reflected ideological disinclination. This sentiment was never so prevalent within the Conservative Party, and Labour has therefore faced the greater challenge in adapting to the electoral–professional requirements of an era of intensified party competition. Between 1983 and 1987, Labour took the first steps towards electoral–professional adaptation under the leadership of Neil Kinnock, but it was only during the party's policy review of 1987–9 that the strategic influence of marketing professionals (in the shape of the now disbanded Shadow Communications Agency) started to be felt (Hughes and Wintour, 1990, pp. 137–9). Throughout the 1990s the pace of reform picked up, coming to the triumphant fruition in May 1997. It is widely thus acknowledged during the 1990s. In particular, this is credited with helping forge Labour's strategic goal of targeting potential swing voters in 'middle income, middle Britain' for the 1997 election (Seyd, 1998, p. 60).

In the 1997 election campaign the professionalization of Labour's political marketing reached new heights. This reflected not only the harsh lessons taught by repeated electoral failure, but a willingness to learn directly from the campaigning approach of sister parties overseas, especially the Democrats in the USA (Braggins, McDonagh and Barnard, 1993). The party shifted its media and campaign operations away from the national headquarters in Walworth Road (south-east London) to a large open-plan office development at Millbank on the Thames embankment, and within a short distance of Westminster and various news media offices. The Millbank operation incorporated purpose-built media facilities, and there were significantly more central staff than at previous elections. Moreover, orchestration of the national campaign was probably greater than hitherto, with regional and local figures kept meticulously 'on message' through a variety of personal, computer and telephone links. The centrality of election campaigning to new Labour's entire style of organization and operation was underlined when the party chose to shift its national headquarters from Walworth Road to Millbank on a permanent basis in the autumn of 1997.

## Conservatives

The Conservatives have generally effected a far smoother transition to the age of political marketing, even though in recent years they have clearly been surpassed by Labour (Cockett, 1994, p. 577). The arrival at the helm of Margaret Thatcher in the 1970s generated a qualitative shift in the party's exploitation of modern campaigning techniques. In particular, the role of experts such as the Saatchi & Saatchi advertising agency attracted an enormous amount of attention after 1979. Although the Conservatives had used advertising professionals before, Saatchis were unique in being the first to assume full-time control of all aspects of publicity and opinion research, and in being heavily involved between elections. This enabled them to work with the leadership on long-term campaign strategy. As Scammell puts it, 'they effectively transformed the role of marketing specialists in British politics from technicians to strategies' (Scammell, 1999, p. 733; see also Scammell, 1995, pp. 119–22). Saatchis' sustained relationship with the party was later supplemented by the introduction of new public relations and marketing approaches to the staging of annual conferences, direct mailing of targeted supporters, telephone canvassing and computer-aided communications (Scammell, 1999, p. 576). Under John Major in 1992 and 1997, the influence of the marketing experts was maintained over issue terrain and campaigning style (Scammell, 1999, p. 242). There is no doubting the party's continuing commitment to the techniques of modern political marketing.

## Liberal Democrats

No other parties in Britain have taken the art of professional political marketing as far as the major two parties, not least because of the cost implications. Labour and the Conservatives are considerably wealthier than any other party and can spend far more on their election campaigns; in 1997, the Conservatives spent £28.3 million nationally and Labour £14.9 million, while the Liberal Democrats' campaign cost just £2.3 million (Neill, 1998, 3.21–3.24). This imposes obvious constraints on investment in advertising, opinion research and professionalization. In total, the party spent just £300,000 on advertising during the campaign, compared to the £14.4 million which the Tories devoted to all forms of advertising and the £5.7 million spent by Labour. Nevertheless, even the Liberal Democrats are showing signs of a growing sophistication and professionalization in their marketing operations. Three features of recent campaigns demonstrate this. First, the party has become notably more inclined to invest resources in opinion research. For the 1997 election, this was started years in advance of the expected polling day and focused particularly on target seats where the party felt its best chances of electoral success lay. Second, the party ran a more coordinated national campaign. This was judged vital both to the strategy of targeting resources and efforts at selected seats and to the goal of keeping all contributions to the party's campaign 'on message'. A new national 'Communications Centre' was established at the national party headquarters in Cowley Street (Westminster) and this was the engine that drove the coordinated campaign. Its work, moreover, was supported by a network of regional media coordinators (Bonham-Carter, 1997). The third feature of contemporary Liberal Democrat campaigns which shows how they have moved some way towards professional political marketing is the party's growing willingness to focus on the leadership. In Paddy Ashdown in 1992 and 1997, its strategists were convinced that they had a highly marketable electoral commodity, and the leader's personal campaign was judged crucial to the overall party campaign (Holme and Holmes, 1998, p. 10). In short, while it would be an exaggeration to suggest that the Liberal Democrats conform closely to the electoral–professional model, there is no doubt that they are professionalizing their approach to political marketing.

## The changing balance of power within parties

It has long been orthodox to regard the major British political parties as dominated by their parliamentary leaderships, regardless of any formal pretensions to democracy which they might maintain (McKenzie, 1955). Until relatively recently, the Conservative Party made few claims to be a democratic organization, which is hardly surprising in view of the party's cadre–caucus origins. Nevertheless, the party's grassroots have been able to exercise a certain informal influence over elites (Kelly, 1989). Labour, on the other hand, has since 1918 maintained an idiosyncratically federalist model of democracy in which the delegates of affiliating organizations (such as trade unions, socialist societies and local constituency parties) exercised votes at the Party's formally sovereign annual conference. Recent reforms, however, imply that orthodox accounts of intra-party power require significant revision in respect of both parties.

### Labour

Since 1980 Labour has made a number of constitutional changes that have potentially and actually affected its internal distribution of power, and many of these reforms have been promoted under the label of 'decentralization'. Overall, such reforms have almost certainly not been designed to enhance the power of individual members in making policy, though they may well have done so in choosing candidates and leaders. In fact, many of Labour's reforms since 1987 have probably been motivated by the desire to enhance the autonomy of the leadership (at the expense of backbenchers and grassroots activists). In this way the leader is afforded the capacity for maximum strategic flexibility in shaping policies that s/he believes will appeal to the electorate.

The policy-making process has been radically recast since 1997 by the introduction of the *Partnership in Power* reforms. Planning for this preceded the general election, and drew in part on other recent innovations, such as the *National Policy Forum* (NPF) which Conference approved in 1990. In essence, Labour's modernizers wished to avoid what they regarded as some of the critical failings of the past – in particular highly visible conflicts between Labour governments and key components of the extra-parliamentary party such as Conference and the NEC. Endorsed by Conference in the autumn of 1997, *Partnership in Power* established a new two-year 'rolling programme' of policy formulation. While it is certainly the case that this allows for input by individual members, local branches and their representatives, the rolling programme approach nevertheless enshrines a powerful role for the leadership. While the first year of the programme is intended to be about consultation and the development of a range of policy options, the second year is designed to narrow these down to final proposals on which Conference then votes. In this way, the new system's apologists hope that detailed policy confrontations between front-bench politicians and extra-parliamentary actors will take place in 'policy commissions rather than being stored up for set-piece battles at party conference' (Taylor and Cruddas, 1999). The *Joint Policy Committee* (JPC), comprising members drawn from the front bench and the NEC and chaired by the leader, shapes the initial agenda for detailed consideration by the NPF (comprising 175 members representing all parts of the party) and the various *Policy Commissions* (comprising small numbers of politicians, NEC members and other cooptees, Labour Party, 1997, p. 16). While individual members can make submissions to the Policy Commissions and the NPF, policy documents are bounced back and forth between these bodies and the JPC so many times that the party leadership gets ample opportunity to respond to or dilute input it does not favour (see Figure 9.1). Furthermore, having been through this process once, proposals are then subjected to a second year-long round of consultation and modification before Conference gets to vote on the final policy recommendations. Clearly, the intention is to create a system of policy-making which is iterative and consensual, so that Conference might no longer be the venue for highly publicized (or 'gladiatorial') conflicts. Although conference remains nominally sovereign, its agenda is fundamentally determined by a process of which the parliamentary elites are likely to remain in control.

To be sure, the membership had little real influence under the old system of party policy-making. Nevertheless, early though it is to offer definitive assessments of the new system, certain developments already seem to point to enhanced leadership control. Thus, the agenda of NPF debate is heavily influenced by front bench politicians, given that initial policy drafts are submitted by ministers. Moreover, senior party officials act as 'facilitators' of NPF discussions and have considerable interpretive power when drafting NPF reports and statements. Finally, the NPF meets in private, which clearly undermines the capacity of party dissidents to mobilize

**Figure 9.1**  *Labour's two-year 'rolling programme' of policy-making*

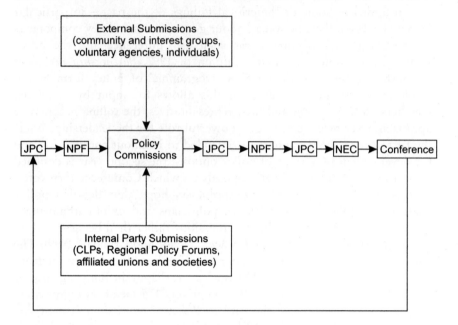

*Source:* Labour Party, 1997: 17.

opposition to the leadership (Seyd, 1999). Therefore, it seems likely that the leadership has engineered a process by which it guides debate from the outset, and maximizes its opportunities for hindering the articulation of public opposition.

Labour's policy-making process has been further modified in recent years by elements of plebiscitary democracy. This was first evident in 1995, when Tony Blair used a ballot of individual members to approve a major and highly symbolic change to Clause Four of the party's constitution. Though ostensibly democratic, this model of constitutional change clearly served to bypass the constituency labour party (CLP) conference delegates that Labour's modernizers believed were likely to resist such change. Furthermore, in 1996 Blair introduced another such referendum on what he promised would become the main features of the forthcoming election manifesto. This offered members the chance to give a simple 'yes' or 'no' answer to the question of whether they would support the overall package of policies likely to be included in the formal manifesto. As in the case of the Clause four ballot, the position was emphatically endorsed by the membership, but the process itself was not without its critics. Indeed, to many observers the plebiscitary model of democracy has always suggested the manipulation of gullible masses by cynical elites (Lipow and Seyd,

1996). In this case it might be said that the 'charismatic leader' bypassed the party's formal 'legislature' in order to address directly the mass membership, offering it a crude choice between support and opposition for something that was relatively bland and uncontentious to the progressive mind. Radicals could argue that while what was on offer was not necessarily insupportable, there was a real problem over what was *excluded* from the package.

It should be said that during the 1990s processes of candidate and leadership selection have witnessed a more definite picture of growing membership influence (Webb, 2000, ch. 6). However, even these changes do not necessarily serve to curtail the power of the leadership. The membership ballots which now are central components of both processes mean that the influence of local party activists who have often been regarded as ideological radicals (May, 1973; Kogan and Kogan, 1982; Norris, 1995) has almost certainly been the diluted by the voting power of non-activists presumed to be more moderate. As Peter Mair says, 'it is not the party congress or the middle-level elite, or the activists, who are being empowered, but rather the "ordinary" members, who are at once more docile and more likely to endorse the policies (and candidates) proposed by the party leadership' (Mair, 1994, p. 16).

However, the logic of new Labour's internal organizational transformation has been disrupted, paradoxically, by the impact of the Blair government's own agenda of constitutional reform. Specifically, the decentralization of power to the Scottish Parliament, the Welsh Assembly and even the London Mayoralty tends to weaken the grip which Millbank and the Leader's Office have sought to maintain. In respect of Scotland, for instance, there were a number of instances in the first few months of the new Parliament's operation which revealed the capacity for tension between London and Edinburgh, even within the Labour Party. The potential for such conflict was all the greater for the fact that the government in Edinburgh was a coalition, and the Labour First Minister, Donald Dewar, was obliged to be as sensitive to the demands of his Liberal Democrat partners there as he was to the dictates of Downing Street. This was best illustrated by the row over university tuition fees. Introduced across the UK by Westminster after the 1997 election, the Scottish Liberal Democrats pledged to rescind them north of the border in the Holyrood elections of May 1998. This placed Dewar in obvious difficulty, in that he could not simultaneously please both his coalition partners and the Cabinet in London. Furthermore, Dewar's willingness to demonstrate his independence from London was underlined when he sacked his own Chief of Staff, John Rafferty, for daring to go over his head and seek Downing Street's intervention in a row over Scottish affairs.

The nomination of a party candidate for the London Mayoralty proved no less vexing for Labour. While promoting the introduction of a Mayor for the capital as a way of enhancing democratic accountability, the leadership was desperately keen to prevent Ken Livingstone, left-wing MP and former Leader of the GLC (abolished by Thatcher in the mid-1980s) from winning the party nomination (Cohen, 1999). However, the selection process was not easy to control given Livingstone's widespread popularity with London voters and grassroots party members. When a party short-listing committee flirted with barring Livingstone over a matter of policy detail concerning the London Underground, it appeared that New Labour's strategists were struggling to accept that decentralization of the sort they had championed implied a degree of latitude for Mayoral candidates to establish their own platforms (see Chapter 11). Overall, then, the party has generally sought to distribute power in such a way as to maximize the strategic autonomy of the leadership, while still providing participatory incentives to its members. But the desire to 'modernize' the state and politics in Britain has sometimes threatened to undermine new Labour's fabled cohesion and discipline.

## Conservatives

If anything, the Conservative Party underwent even more far-reaching organizational reform in the wake of the 1997 election than Labour. Central to this was *Fresh Future*, a document setting out 'the most radical changes to our party's institutions since Benjamin Disraeli'. according to party leader William Hague. Interestingly, the document was suffused with the rhetoric of participation and democratization, as Hague declared his bold intention to 'build the single greatest mass volunteer party in the Western world' (Conservative Party, 1998, p. 1). Once endorsed by the party membership (in March 1998), the *Fresh Future* reforms initiated a constitutional revolution for the Conservative Party. For the first time, a 'single and unified' party was created in the sense that local membership bodies (the constituency associations), the national headquarters (Conservative Central Office in Smith Square, Westminster) and the parliamentary party were drawn together into a single structure.

Among other things, the new constitution handed Central Office the formal right to intervene in the running of local constituency associations. Indeed, local Conservative constituency association members have always exercised considerable autonomy in matters of candidate selection, and it remains their task to make the decisive choice at a final selection meetings for Westminster candidates. However, *Fresh Future* has accorded party members similar rights over the selection of European parliamentary and London mayorality candidates. Moreover, given the multi-member nature of the European constituencies under the list-PR system introduced in 1999, the members have been given the task of generating a rank-order of candidates. This constitutes an undeniable extension of democratic rights to party members, who can genuinely claim to be better endowed than Labour Party members in this respect.

However, the clearest extension of democracy within the party is apparent in the method of selecting the party leader. Since 1965, leaders have been elected by a system of exhaustive ballots among Conservative MPs. Though the precise rules for election have varied over time, when William Hague was elected in July 1997, they stated that a successful candidate needed to win the support of an overall majority and to achieve a clear margin of at least 15 per cent over any other rival. The new constitution replaces this with a system in which the parliamentary party has the right to act only as the preliminary selectorate whose function (via a system of ballots) is to reduce the number of candidates to just two; the final choice then rests with the party's mass membership, who will cast their votes (on a one-member, one-vote system) in a national postal ballot. Though it cannot be denied that this provides for leadership election by a greatly increased suffrage, two features of the new system are worth bearing in mind. First, the rules probably make it harder to depose incumbent leaders than hitherto. Second, it must also be recognized that the leader is now leader of the *entire* party, whereas before he was leader of only the parliamentary party. This is significant in so far as it implies that the leader now gains authority over all other sections of the party (including, for instance, Conservatives MEPs, Members of the Scottish Parliament and the Welsh Assembly – and of course, the hitherto autonomous membership). Thus, the prices exacted on the members for their involvement in the election of the leader is a new kind of *formal* homage which they are obliged to accord him or her.

However, new constitutional provisions alone cannot guarantee a cohesive and disciplined party. Groups within the Conservative Party called for genuine democratic participation by party members, and demanded greater openness and accountability in the party's management as well as the right to elect the Party Chairman and Treasurer. Both offices have traditionally been within the sole gift of the leader. Following William Hague's resignation Iain Duncan Smith was elected leader, beating Ken Clarke in the membership ballot, Michael Portillo (who had between 1999 and 2001 been widely regarded as heir apparent) having been eliminated by one vote in the parliamentary ballot. The greatest problem for the contemporary Conservative Party remains that of internal tension over questions of policy and leadership. To this extent the Tories resemble Labour in the early 1980s: recently turned out of office by the electorate, then trounced a second time at the polls and appearing ill at ease with itself over vital issues. The trickle of defectors from Conservative ranks since 1997, such as MPs Peter Temple-Morris and Shaun Woodward and

MEPs James Moorhouse, John Stevens and Brendan Donnelly, its testament especially to the continuing power of the European issue to divide the party. Overall, then, the Conservatives resemble Labour in seeking to establish a blend of leadership autonomy and participatory incentives for members, but the political contingencies of the period mean that they remain far more poorly equipped to compete for national elective office.

## Liberal Democrats

Overall, the Liberal Democrats can be regarded as a comparatively democratic party which offers individual members clear incentives to participate. To a significant extent, the cadre party origins of the old Liberal Party – never quite so obvious anyway as in the case of the Conservatives – have been further diluted by the influence of the SDP after the foundation of the new party in 1988. The Liberal Democrats have a federal structure, though not one which in any sense resembles Labour's. Rather, the Liberal Democrats exemplify a more orthodox form of territorial federalism, with distinct 'state parties' in England, Scotland and Wales, and a federal party for Britain as a whole. (Unless otherwise specified, the following discussion focuses on the federal party organization.)

Liberal Democrat members have significant participatory rights in matters of policy-making, leadership election and candidate selection. Thus, a national postal ballot of members is used to elect not only the leader of the parliamentary party, but also the party President (effectively the head of the extra-parliamentary organization). Such elections are an innovation derived from SDP practice; previously, Liberal leaders were elected by a special convention of constituency party representatives (Finer, 1980, p. 83). Moreover, party members can now send representatives to a conference that is sovereign in defining party policy; the old Liberal Assembly had no such formal power. Policy development may be initiated by either the Federal Conference or the *Federal Policy Committee* (FPC) (a majority of whose members are directly elected by conference representatives). Policy working groups are then appointed by the FPC to take submissions and produce a consultation paper for dissemination to local parties, regional and state party conferences, before a final draft is put to the Federal Conference by the FPC. In practice, the FPC drafts general and European election manifestos. Finally, postal ballots of party members are used to select candidates for parliamentary, European and regional elections. Stephen Ingle does not exaggerate greatly when he states that the Liberal Democrats have constructed 'a system of politics which seeks to empower ordinary people in a thoroughgoing manner which, in their periods of dominance, the major parties have not equalled in fifty years' (Ingle, 1996, p. 130). This is hardly surprising for a party which had few MPs at the time of its birth and relatively little corporate or state financial backing: its members are its lifeblood and need to be offered participatory incentives to maintain their enthusiasm. Nevertheless, despite the participatory ethos and constitution of the party, Charles Kennedy, like his predecessor as Liberal Democrat leader, Paddy Ashdown, still retains considerable autonomy in practice: it is normal, for instance, for the party leader to chair and direct the work of the pivotal FPC (Ingle, 1996, p. 116).

## Conclusion

Overall, the separate organizational evolutions of the main parties have produced a situation in which rank and file members have considerable rights over matters of leadership and candidate selection, but lack direct influence over policy-making. This is almost certainly calculated by the party leaderships to provide a blend of incentives for citizens to join, run local campaigns and legitimize major strategic decisions by the leadership, while permitting the latter the necessary degree of autonomy required to make such decisions. This is a difficult blend to achieve, but one required of all leading electoral organizations today.

## Developments in party funding

According to Angelo Panebianco, the electoral–professional party will be funded largely by either the state or a number of contingently linked interest groups (Panebianco, 1988, p. 265). This is because, in seeking to attract votes from a broad range of social groups, it will want to avoid becoming too heavily dependent on particular interests; from this perspective, it is far better to derive resources from a variety of groups or a 'neutral' source such as the state itself. In fact, developments in British party funding in recent years do not fully bear out such a pattern, although there have been some significant changes which are relevant to the needs of modern electoralist organizations, and which approximate the spirit if not the letter of Panebianco's ideal-type.

First, Labour has wrought a remarkable reduction in its financial dependence on the trade unions over the course of a little more than a decade. In 1983, some 96 per cent of all central party income (including General and General Election Funds) could be traced to the unions (Webb,

1992b, pp. 20–2). Within a decade no more than two-thirds could, and by 1997 the figure stood at just 40 per cent (Neill, 1998, p. 31). How has this been achieved? Largely through a determined and conscious effort to professionalize the task of fund-raising, an activity for which the party now employs external specialists on fixed-term contracts. This has proved especially successful in generating small personal donations. Labour claimed to raise some 40 per cent of its funding from such sources by the late 1990s. Some 70,000 members pay a regular monthly subscription, while a further 500,000 make ad hoc donations each year (Neill, 1998, p. 32). A particular success has been the party's *Business Plan*, established in the late 1980s in order to attract individual donations through activities such as fund-raising dinners. Within five years of its foundation, this accounted for nearly one-fifth of the Labour Party's central income (Fisher, 1996, p. 80). After the 1997 election, a new High Value Donors Unit and the *1000 Club* were established, both with the aim of increasing income from relatively large contributors (Neill, 1998, pp. 32–3). These changing financial connections demonstrate graphically the transformation of new Labour at the levels of both political linkage and organizational style.

Even Labour has not always found it easy to raise the money required to meet the spiralling costs of modern election campaigning, however. Thus, it is perhaps not surprising to discover that parties and external observers have often lamented the state of chronic under-funding which appears to have afflicted the main British parties, notwithstanding the undeniable real income growth they have enjoyed (Webb, 2000, ch. 8). Though less troubled than hitherto during the 1990s, it is interesting to note that the former General Secretary of the Labour Party, Tom Sawyer, estimated in 1998 that his party required an average of £20–25 million per year across the course of an electoral cycle in order to function properly, whereas its average annual income during the 1992–7 parliament was just £12.6 million (Neill, 1998, p. 36). For their part, the Conservatives considered their own income of more than £20 million in 1996 inadequate for their needs (Garner and Kelly, 1998, p. 204). Indeed, throughout the 1990s the Conservatives have consistently run an accumulated debt (often approaching £20 million). Despite shedding staff and benefiting from a remarkable burst of generosity from donors in time for the 1997 election, the party went into opposition facing another large deficit and further staff cutbacks. The Liberal Democrats plainly have relatively meagre resources, spending only a fraction of either majority party during election years.

In view of this, it is hardly surprising that a second recent development in party funding has been an increase in state subventions. In 1975, subsidies were introduced in Britain for opposition parliamentary parties (the so-called 'Short money'), and in 1996 a similar, though more modest, scheme ('Cranborne money') was established in respect of the two leading parties in the House of Lords. Indeed, in 1998, all parties argued that the

Short money scheme required augmenting considerably if opposition parties were to perform their parliamentary duties effectively, and the Neill Committee on Standards in Public Life (asked to investigate issues of party funding by the Blair government soon after coming to office) concurred by recommending that it be increased by as much as three times (Neill, 1998, pp. 102–3): this proposal was accepted by the government (Cm. 4413, 1999, para.6.8).

However, the Short and Cranborne schemes remain the only direct financial subventions to political parties provided by the state in Britain, and it is interesting that the major parties have not sought to exploit the possibilities of state funding to a greater extent, as the electoral–professional model implies they might. The Conservatives have long maintained their opposition to state funding for extra-parliamentary parties. After the 1997 election, however, their ability to raise money was severely reduced and they became acutely aware of the financial pressures on an opposition party. For its part Labour, which had seemed ready to break the bipartisan consensus on the issue earlier in the 1990s, changed its position once it resumed office in 1997. Though still conceding that 'there is a case in principle for various forms of state aid', Labour now suggested that the demands of 'fiscal prudence' meant that the time was not right to prioritize the needs of parties.

The Neill Committee therefore concluded that a better way of limiting party debt would be to impose legal limits on election campaign expenditure. Since the Corrupt and Illegal Practices Act of 1883, individual candidates in local constituency contests have been subject to very tight campaign expenditure limits, but the legal case of *Rex* v. *Tronoh Mines* in 1952 established that such limits did not apply to the general campaign expenditure of national parties. This, allied to the advent of televisual communication techniques, explains why the parties have focused ever more effort on their national campaigns. However, such campaigns are costly and have fostered a so-called 'arms race' mentality in parties desperate to outspend their rivals. Between 1983 and 1997 the Conservative Party's national election campaign expenditure increased by more than three times in real terms, and Labour's by more than five times (Neill, 1998, p. 43). The Neill Committee therefore recommended that no party contesting more than 600 seats in Westminster elections should be permitted to spend more than £20 million (at 1998 prices) on its national campaign (over and above specific constituency campaign expenditure). The government proposed to enact the recommendations, and to extend them to European and devolved elections as well (Cm. 4413, 1999, paras.7.14–7.17). Given that the Conservatives spent £28.3 million and Labour £26 million in 1997, it seems reasonable to conclude that, should this recommendation be effectively policed, it could indeed be expected to curb the profligacy of the major parties in election years.

Labour, long criticized by its opponents for being financially beholden to the unions, has thus significantly reduced this state of dependence. The value of state subsidies has been modestly increased. And the scope for financial profligacy in the face of ever-increasing campaigning demands has been legally restricted. Overall, these changes in funding should serve the organizational needs of modern electoralist parties, even though they do not accord precisely with the specifications of the electoral–professional party thesis.

## Conclusion

The main political parties in modern Britain are best understood as electorally motivated organizations compelled to act within an increasingly competitive and uncertain electoral market. In general, parties will seek to compete by convincing electors that they are reputable, competent, cohesive and credible, and have more attractive policies and politicians than their rivals (Webb, 2000, ch. 5). It is not enough, however, for parties merely to state their respective cases in terms of these characteristics. First, they need to be attuned to the nature of public opinion and adept in the arts of campaigning and political communication, which is why the two main parties have embraced political marketing and the Liberal Democrats have followed as best they can in this direction. Second, they need to protect or enhance the autonomy that leaders require in order to make crucial strategic decisions about party policy. However, in practice this has often proved a politically delicate undertaking, given that it has had to be balanced against the need to 'democratize' aspects of internal party decision-making which flows from a recognition of the continuing importance of members to modern parties (Seyd and Whiteley, 1992; Whiteley, Seyd and Richardson, 1994; Scarrow, 1996). This requires participatory incentives for the grassroots. Moreover, the decentralization of the British state and the contingencies of intra-party conflict over policies and personnel have demonstrated how they can constrain the power of party leaders. Finally, parties need to be adequately resourced in order to meet the exponentially growing costs of modern campaigning and marketing, which explains (in part) the recent changes in party funding. In general, the pace of internal party organizational change has grown notably during the 1990s, and is now being matched by new external regulatory frameworks for party politics. It can, moreover, be safely predicted that these features of modern British political life will endure.

# Chapter 10

# New Media, New Politics

MARGARET SCAMMELL

The twentieth-century story of communications ended as it began: in a state of revolution. At the start of a new century though, the tale is not merely or mainly of technology but of social transformation. Apocalyptic visions of the information society assail us at every turn. Media are sometimes presented as the route to new glories, enablers via the Internet of a truly participatory public sphere. Equally they are said to be the means to new dystopias: creating new inequalities, widening existing ones, fostering economic imperialism and American cultural dominance.

These are exciting times for the media. Formerly discrete domains, publishing, television, film, music, computers and telecommunications, are converging into one massive 'infotainment' industry that is predicted to be the most dynamic economic sector in the world as we enter the new millennium. Already, in 1998 Microsoft was listed by the *Financial Times* as the world's biggest company. The world number two, General Electric, owns the US network NBC. AOL–Time Warner forged the largest merger in history. Meanwhile, other media moguls, such as Disney and Rupert Murdoch's News Corporation are spreading into more countries and leisure sectors. In Britain, an avalanche of new media output, especially in TV, radio and Internet, hit the market over the 10 years from 1988 to 1997 (Table 10.1).

Table 10.1  *Expansion of Media Output in the UK: 1988–99*

|  | *1988/9* | *1997* | *% change* |
|---|---|---|---|
| Magazine titles | 2042 | 2438 | 19 |
| TV channels | 4 | 60 | 1400 |
| Commercial radio | 60 | 188 | 213 |
| Cinema multiplex | 14 | 118 | 743 |
| CD-ROM titles | 390 | 16762 | 4198 |
| Web pages | 0 | 132 million | Infinity |

*Source:* Henley Centre (December 1998).

How will these changes affect political communication in Britain? We should beware the rhetoric of revolution. Predictions of total upheaval in media markets have been with us at least since the early 1980s. Yet, the BBC and ITV remain intact as the centrepieces of British television, while the same newspapers command the national scene. It is a safe bet that their dominance, albeit in weaker form, will continue until well after the next general election. Reports of the death of mass media are greatly exaggerated. However, it is clear that British media are indeed restructuring in response to the risks and opportunities of new technology and under pressure of intense competition with an increasingly significant global dimension.

As yet, the picture is complex and uneven. Optimism and anxiety collide at every turn. The prospect of increasing media abundance and greater consumer choice is coupled with fears of fragmentation of audiences, a new divide between rich and poor, and the loss a unified national arena of high-quality news formerly created by our arrangements of public service broadcasting. We see global opportunities for British media business, linked to acute concerns at the overwhelming predominance of the US in the cultural industries. We are sure of immensely increased resources of information, but we are unsure of public reaction. Media resources have expanded much more quickly than consumer willingness to spend time and money on them. Public attention is now the scarce resource.

However, we can be sure that in the foreseeable future at least, media changes will make life more difficult for the major parties. This chapter will make the following broad arguments:

- Taken as a whole, the media are becoming more powerful economic and political actors
- Competition for audiences will become fierce as choice increases across more TV channels, the Internet and other leisure alternatives
- The role of the BBC, as the cornerstone of public service, will become simultaneously more crucial and more threatened
- Taken in combination, these changes will increase media autonomy from the parties; the gulf between media and party agendas will increase
- Parties, already pressured by weakening voter allegiances, will respond with an intensification of the techniques of political marketing.

Overall, then, the media are becoming more, rather than less important in politics. The elusive quest for media effects will increasingly seek evidence of influence on the political system as a whole, broadening considerably from the current emphasis on individual effects upon voters. First, though, let us look more closely at how change is impacting on the various sectors of the UK media market.

## The media market in the UK

### Television

The terrestrial TV market share in Britain is high by comparison with the US and some European countries. In June 1999, the Independent Television Commission (ITC), commercial TV's regulator, reported that 24.5 per cent of UK homes were subscribing to cable. This compares to more than 40 per cent in Germany and 90 per cent in the Netherlands. Table 10.2 demonstrates the steady evolution of the UK television market. Cable/satellite make their first breakthrough in 1991 and progress slowly but surely, to about 13 per cent of total audience share in 1998. BSkyB is easily the most important player in the cable/satellite market, its success driven in large measure by its exclusive rights to broadcast live sport, especially Premiership football.

The battle for audiences is increasingly being played out on the football pitches, with BSkyB and OnDigital joint-owner Granada strengthening their bargaining hands for broadcast rights by buying shares in top clubs, including Manchester United, Leeds United and Liverpool. BBC1 and Channel 3 (ITV) are the main losers in the new market, with BBC1's audience share dropping below 30 per cent in 1998. This was thought to be the threshold below which the BBC might struggle to retain government support for its licence fee funding. Nonetheless, BBC 1 and 2 together hold some 40 per cent of the audience, while the four main terrestrial channels between them retain about 83 per cent.

It is too early to gauge the impact of the new digital channels. However, on the basis of audience research figures into viewing in cable/satellite homes, one might project the BBC share slipping further to about 27 per cent and ITV's to about 34 over the next five years or so. Overall, then, the TV picture is one of increasing abundance of channels, gradual fragmentation of the audience, terrestrial BBC and ITV losing their former stranglehold on the market while at the same time remaining the largest forces.

The change is evolutionary but nonetheless profound compared to the period from 1955 to 1990 when the BBC/ITV duopoly had a guaranteed 90-plus per cent of the national audience and ITV a near-monopoly of advertising revenue. The market response has been a series of alliances and takeovers, with commercial terrestrial TV clustering into super-groups. Granada commands the north and owns London Weekend Television; Granada and United News and Media between them in 1999 controlled 10 of the 15 regional Channel 3 licences and are joint owners of ONDigital.

Table 10.2    *Annual audience shares for television, 1981–98*

| Year | Channel | | | | | |
|------|------|------|------------------------|------|------|---------------------------|
|      | BBC1 | BBC2 | ITV (inc. GMTV) | CH4 | CH5 | Others (Cable/ Sat) |
| 1981 | 39   | 12   | 49   | –    | –    | –    |
| 1991 | 34   | 10   | 42   | 10   | –    | 4    |
| 1992 | 34   | 10   | 41   | 10   | –    | 5    |
| 1993 | 33   | 10   | 40   | 11   | –    | 6    |
| 1994 | 32   | 11   | 39   | 11   | –    | 7    |
| 1995 | 32   | 11   | 37   | 11   | –    | 9    |
| 1996 | 33.5 | 11.5 | 35.1 | 10.7 | –    | 10.1 |
| 1997 | 30.8 | 11.6 | 32.9 | 10.6 | 2.3  | 11.8 |
| 1998 | 29.5 | 11.3 | 31.7 | 10.3 | 4.3  | 12.9 |

*Notes:* Shares before 1996 have been rounded to nearest whole number.
*Source:* BARB.

The major ITV companies are pressing government to relax further regulations, which restrict Channel 3 holdings to 15 per cent of total UK audience, citing the importance of domestic strength to maintain standards and ward off foreign predators. Further concentration is likely. Scotland is pursuing its own path, with Scottish Television increasingly opting out of national ITV networked programmes. The once-secure ITV arrangement of regional TV companies united round a UK networked core is looking increasingly fragile. Moreover, the regulatory framework is being stretched across the conflicting pressures of protecting British companies from foreign competition, and thus allowing some concentration of ownership, and keeping the domestic market healthily pluralistic. The strains are more pronounced, if less remarked, in Scotland. Scottish Television, following its takeover of Grampian, reaches 90 per cent of the Scottish audience and it owns the influential newspapers, the *Herald* and the *Evening Times*. The 15 per cent *UK* audience ceiling looks increasingly inappropriate for the post-devolutionary politics of Scotland, and has prompted calls for the devolution of broadcasting legislation powers from Westminster to Holyrood (Schlesinger, 1998).

How might these developments affect the reporting of politics? It is well known that the structure of the media market is directly correlated to the amount and type of electoral news in TV bulletins (Norris *et al.*, 1999). The more competitive and deregulated the market, the less space for substantive issues, and the more news is focused on softer personality, campaign hoopla and horse-race topics. The pattern holds true both across countries and within countries.

In Britain successive elections have borne this out, with the BBC news devoting significantly more time, proportionately and absolutely, to policy and issues, than ITV – or, at the 1997 election, Sky News (Goddard, Scammell and Semetko, 1998). However, by comparison with other countries, British TV overall is remarkable for the amount of time and resources it expends on elections. Since the Broadcasting Act of 1990, which reduced the statutory obligations on ITV, media watchers have been looking for signs of slippage in public service commitments. In fact, television passed the tests of the 1992 and 1997 elections well. There was no significant slackening by either BBC or ITV in the time given over to electoral news.

However, the predicted effects of increased competition and lighter regulation are at last becoming evident on ITV. A 1999 study of British TV trends concluded: 'Commercial television has effectively vacated political and economic current affairs, which is now covered almost exclusively by the BBC' (Barnett and Seymour, 1999). ITV's rescheduling of News at Ten became the touchstone of the 'dumbing down' debate about British television. For some it was the clearest sign yet of a break with the tradition established when ITV was first introduced to complement the BBC in 1955, and when the BBC moved its news bulletin from 9.00 to 10.00, ITV was forced to abandon the idea and reschedule its news back to 10.00. That tradition demanded obligations of public service from *both* the commercial and the public sectors, a highly unusual system by world standards where it is normally only the public broadcaster that is so committed. Increasingly, however, the BBC will have to stand alone as the public service carrier, aided only by Channel 4 with its relatively small audience.

The consequences of this are, first, that there will be less prime time political news on the mainstream commercial channels. Politics is not an audience winner, and as the competitive pressures mount and 24-hour news channels become more widely available, the ITC is likely to be even less minded to insist on unpopular programming in the name of public service. Ironically, then, while overall the availability of news expands considerably through the 24-hour channels (Sky News, BBC's UK 24,

Radio 5 Live), the audience reach of high-quality news may well decline as mass television retreats into an entertainment-driven ratings war. An indicator of this is the decline in the ITV news audience. In August, 1998, for example, News at Ten took four of the top 30 places in ITV's ratings, gaining a maximum of 6.5 million viewers. In August 1999, ITV news managed just one hit in the top 30 with a top audience of 5.1 million.

Second, we might expect the force of competition to affect reporting styles on the mass channels: not only less political news, but proportionately more emphasis on softer, human interest issues, personality and performance. Third, that, therefore, that the news market is becoming both more demanding and complicated for the parties. They are under intensified pressure for interviews and stories from an expanded news media while, at the same time, being offered dwindling space in prime time on the mass networks. Parties, therefore, will have to work harder to reach the same number of people and will face a tougher struggle to influence news agendas. As a result, it is both a predictable and rational response for parties to seek to professionalize their communications, as Labour is already doing: following the mass audience in tabloid press and broadcast news, exploiting opportunities on suitable chat shows and rationing appearances on the smaller-audience hard news programmes (see below).

The future shape of British political broadcasting depends in large measure on the BBC. The BBC has been accepted by all post-war governments as the cornerstone of quality for the broadcast system as a whole; it is effectively the custodian of national standards. The BBC's self-proclaimed burden is to enhance 'citizenship and democracy, guaranteeing access to the full range of information necessary for individuals to make informed choices' (BBC, 1999). This responsibility will be both more acute and more difficult to fulfil over the coming years. The BBC's first problem is the much-noted dilemma of matching its high aspirations to its desire to retain a mass national audience. The BBC has resolutely refused to follow the normal route for public broadcasters in competitive markets, confining itself to those bits of worthy programming, serious politics, high art, minority interest, which are insufficiently profitable for the commercial sector (Barnett and Curry, 1994). Its defence of its licence fee has for the last 20 years been predicated precisely on its ability to combine mass popularity with quality programming. Clearly, its diminishing share of the audience threatens this defence.

At the same time, the BBC is cross-pressured by a desire to compete in the global economy. Both the Major and Blair governments have encouraged it to develop commercial interests and pursue a world role. Of all British television companies, the BBC is the best placed to compete internationally. There is no British commercial company that comes remotely near the international profile of News Corporation, never mind the US giants (Table 10.3 and 10.4). The BBC has an annual income of some £2.1 billion (*Economist*, 7 August, 1999), greater than the total of advertizing revenue for all the terrestrial commercial TV companies combined. It boasts the world's largest news-gathering operation and a globally renowned brand image of quality. Under director-general Sir John Birt, the BBC launched a number of commercial services for cable and satellite, starting with UK Gold (jointly with Thames TV). Internationally, it broadcasts the news service BBC World and, in partnership with Discovery Communications Inc., is launching BBC America and documentary channels. In the words of its mission statement, BBC 2000: 'The BBC aims to be the world's leading international broadcaster; the world's first choice for international news on radio, television and online and the leading showcase for British creativity and talent, through programme sales and channels overseas.'

This vaulting and relatively new ambition chimes with the objectives of the Labour government. The government sees significant export opportunities in the media industry, and through the Graham report, *Building a Global Audience* (DCMS, 1999), has encouraged British TV to rethink programming better to fit overseas schedules and tastes. The US dominates the world trade of TV programmes, despite the efforts of the EU to encourage exchange between member states. The EU's *Television without Frontiers* directive that members' broadcasting services should transmit at least 50 per cent European material 'where practicable' is virtually meaningless for cable and satellite services. McChesney (1998) cites this example as a case study in the evolution of media policy 'to a largely market *über alles* position' in which commercial imperatives over-ride former policy commitments to national public service and domestic cultural production. Britain lags a distant second to the US in TV trade and such success as it has is largely due to the BBC. The BBC's role, therefore, is changing substantially in response to the global market. It is both the main guardian of domestic production and the spearhead of the export drive. It is a moot point whether it will be able to reach all its goals simultaneously: a leading commercial player on the world stage, a mass audience broadcaster domestically *and* the bastion of British public service. The fear is that the BBC is over-stretching. Something may have to give and the worry is that it may simultaneously lose its mass audience *and* its reputation for authoritative factual broadcasting as it is increasingly forced to scrap for ratings among the quiz shows. Thus, at one and the same time, the BBC has lost much live sport, notably test cricket and virtually all football, *and* it stands accused of 'dumbing down' in its attempts to keep its audience. The *Independent on Sunday*, under the headline 'BBC: Barren, Banal and Confused', launched a 'dumbwatch crusade' against what it deemed to be falling broadcast standards (Robins, 1999). BBC radio and TV political

Table 10.3    *Media ownership: the global players and British interests*

| Media Companies: top tier global players | Whole or main ownership interests |
|---|---|
| AOL–Time Warner Inc. Dulles, VA and New York Revenue: $30.421 billion (Dec 1999) | TV; Cable (CNN, Cartoon Network, HBO); Film (Warner Bros); Internet (AOL, Compuserve, Netscape); Magazines; Music; Telephony; Retail; Sport/Theme Parks |
| The Walt Disney Co. Burbank, Calif Revenue: $23.420 billion (Dec 1999) | TV (ABC network, Disney TV); Cable (sport, Disney, History); Film; Internet; Publishing; Music; Retail; Sports/Theme parks |
| Sony Corp. Tokyo (media/ entertainment only) Revenue: $19.364 billion (March 1999) | Film (Columbia); Music; Computer games; Cinema; JSkyB (cable/satellite) |
| Viacom New York Revenue: $12.858 billion | TV (Paramount); Cable (MTV, Movie Channel); Film (Paramount); Publishing (Macmillan); Theme Parks |
| News Corp Ltd. Australia Revenue: $13.064 billion (June 1999) | TV (Fox); Cable/satellite (BSkyB, Fox, Star); Film (20th Century Fox); Newspapers (NYPost, Times/Sun); Magazines; Publishing (HarperCollins); Internet; Sport (LA Dodgers, 10% shares in Manchester Utd and Leeds Utd, Chelsea) |
| *British International players* | |
| BBC Revenue: £3.2 billion (licence fee income 1998) | BBC World Service (radio); BBC World (TV); UK Gold; BBC America |
| Pearson Revenue: £3.4 billion (Dec 1998) | FT; Penguin; Simon & Schuster |

*Source: Financial Times*, company financials.

Table 10.4  *Market share of major TV exporters, September 1996–August 1997*

| Source of imported programmes[1] | | | | | |
| Market | UK (%) | US (%) | Australia (%) | France (%) | Germany (%) |
| --- | --- | --- | --- | --- | --- |
| Australia | 16 | 71 | | 1 | 0 |
| Canada | 5 | 87 | 0 | 1 | 0 |
| France | 8 | 72 | 2 | | 9 |
| Germany | 3 | 87 | | 4 | 1 |
| Italy | 1 | 66 | 0 | 3 | 3 |
| Japan | 10 | 83 | 0 | 0 | 0 |
| Netherlands | 9 | 74 | 4 | 2 | 2 |
| Spain | 3 | 69 | 0 | 3 | 0 |
| Sweden | 12 | 64 | 10 | 1 | 0 |
| US | 35 | | 0 | 1 | 1 |

*Note:*
[1] Excludes feature films.
*Source:* 'Building a Global Audience: British Television in Overseas Markets', Department for Culture, Media and Sport (January 1999).

presenter John Humphrys berates what he sees a trend to soft and 'populist' news (Humphrys, 1999): 'out goes the difficult stuff and in comes the story to which we can "relate". Or the private lives of the famous. Or crime. Or consumer affairs.'

The BBC's board of governors' appointment of Greg Dyke to succeed Birt is the clearest signal that the corporation will carry the fight to retain its mass audience. Dyke was a controversial choice, since he is openly a Labour supporter and donated £50000 to Blair's leadership and general election campaigns. Opposition leader William Hague warned the board that Dyke's appointment would be 'totally unacceptable'. *The Times* owned by Murdoch, waged a sustained campaign against him and reacted furiously to his selection. 'The governors have scripted a tragedy for the BBC', said an editorial, on the morning following the announcement (25 June, 1999). The BBC, it declared, will lose all credibility as an impartial broadcaster. However, the far more general media response was welcoming, and the Murdoch objections were regarded as a self-interested desire to avoid a highly competitive rival at the BBC. Dyke is clearly widely respected by his peers, and the most common concern had much less to do with suspicions of political bias than with his well-known populism (Horsman, 1999). His declaration to put 'education into the BBC's frontline' seems to signal an expansion of digital and on-line services, and not a move into high-brow territory on BBC1 (Dyke, 1999).

The BBC has proved remarkably resilient. It has defied various government threats since the 1960s to break it up, privatize it and scrap the licence fee. All the while, it has grown bigger adding new radio stations, TV satellite and digital channels and its massive Web-site, BBC ONLINE. It won at least a minor victory in February 2000 when the government agreed to increase the licence fee by 1.5 per cent above inflation each year until 2007. More than any other player in the British market, the BBC's survival as an institution looks assured. The question now though is: what *type* of BBC? What priorities should it pursue? A British Airways of the airwaves, or the keeper of the conscience for national broadcast quality? The first acid test of whether it can successfully combine mass appeal with high quality public service will come with its coverage of the next general election.

## Newspapers

Survey after survey confirms that television is the most important source of national news for the overwhelming majority of the population (Svennevig, 1999). At the same time, media effects studies repeatedly show that the press, rather than TV, has the greater influence on voting behaviour (Miller, 1991; Curtice and Semetko, 1994; Norris *et al.*, 1999). This is not so surprising. The press, unlike TV, has no obligations of fairness or balance and the tabloids in particular tend to be vigorously partisan. Changes in press ownership and partisanship therefore may have significant political impact. There is no doubt that the Labour leadership believed that tabloid hostility in 1992 had damaged their election prospects. A post-defeat strategy document by Philip Gould cautioned that the press had contributed significantly to Labour's negative image and helped set an anti-Labour agenda (Butler and Kavanagh, 1997, p. 47). Equally, they believed that press support, especially from the former enemy the *Sun*, contributed substantially to the 1997 landslide (Scammell and Harrop, 1997). Courting the tabloid press then has become a systematic part of Labour strategy. Politicians may over-estimate the power of the press to swing votes: research has generally found significant but *modest* effects. Nonetheless, Labour's determination to win over the tabloids is both understandable and sensible (Table 10.5).

Labour had a fantastic press in 1997, for the first time gaining more support than the Conservatives. This was a remarkable turnaround from the Thatcher years when, excepting the *Mirror* and the *Guardian*, Fleet Street was at war with Labour. The new government's press support strengthened after the election when the *Express*, then owned by Labour

Table 10.5   *Newspapers: circulation, ownership and party preference, 2000*

| Paper | Owner | Circ. April 1997 | Circ. April 1999 | Circ. change (%) | Party pref. (GE 1997) |
|-------|-------|------------------|------------------|------------------|------------------------|
| DM | Ass. Newspapers | 2151 | 2336 | 8.6 | Con |
| M | Mirror Group | 3084 | 2985 | −3.2 | Lab |
| E | MAI/United (Lord Hollick) | 1220 | 1099 | −9.9 | Con (now Lab) |
| DS | MAI/United (Lord Hollick) | 648 | 605 | −6.6 | Lab |
| S | News Int. (R. Murdoch) | 3842 | 3746 | −2.5 | Lab |
| TG | Hollinger/C. Black | 1134 | 1046 | −7.8 | Con |
| G | Scott Trust | 401 | 402 | 0.2 | Lab |
| TM | News Int. (R. Murdoch) | 719 | 744 | 3.5 | No party |
| I | Mirror Group | 251 | 224 | −10.8 | Lab |
| FT | Pearson | 307 | 368 | 19.9 | Lab |

DM = *Daily Mail*      TG = *Telegraph*
M = *Mirror*           G = *Guardian*
E = *Express*          TM = *The Times*
DS = *Daily Star*      I = *Independent*
S = *Sun*              FT = *Financial Times*

peer Lord Hollick, switched into the Labour camp. However, there are several reasons why this transformation is more *dealignment* than realignment. The new press allegiances are weaker and more issue-contingent than in the Thatcher years, when there was a clear left–right ideological party divide. The enthusiasm for Blair in 1997 was at least partly driven by the opinion polls and by exasperation with Major. Great issues, rather than party loyalties, now arouse the editorial passions. The euro, for example, was ultimately decisive in 1997 for *The Times* (anti), the *Independent* and the *Financial Times* (pro). The *Sun*, meanwhile, has tempered its infatuation with Blair with unremitting hostility to Labour's pro-euro stance. 'Is THIS the most dangerous man in Britain' its front page said of Blair and his willingness to 'scrap the pound' (24 June, 1998). Even Labour's most reliable friend, the *Mirror*, has demonstrated some independence, appointing as its chief political reporter the staunchly 'old

Labour' Paul Routledge, author of *Mandy*, a scathing biography of Peter Mandelson.

The fashion for columnists, with often contrasting views, has blurred the once single clear voice of the opinion pages. This is especially, but not exclusively, true of the broadsheets. As Seymour-Ure says (1998): 'Papers now have editorial voices, not a single editorial voice.' It is a more distanced and pluralist approach befitting the mood of an electorate increasingly detached from strong party loyalties. At the same time the style of news is changing, from relatively straight reporting of events to a more interpretative and critical journalism, less closely attached to the agendas of parliament. Journalists and politicians now mingle as equals, according to *The Times* columnist Peter Riddell (1998) and this produces the risk 'of journalists thinking they are more important than politicians, and hence presuming to determine what is rightfully the province of elected politicians'.

Will the press continue to be the most powerful political force in the new media market? After all, analysts predict that newspapers will be one media sector to decline as a result of general abundance of new choices (Henley Centre, 1999). In the short term, and certainly up to the next general election, the answer is 'yes'. National newspaper readership is still relatively high in Britain although total circulation has declined slightly since 1997 (Table 10.5). The *Sun* remains easily the dominant paper by circulation. Under its current editor, former *New York Post* man David Yelland, it managed to stem the slide in sales by 1999. It has pursued an aggressive pricing policy in its traditionally weaker market of Scotland, at the expense of the Mirror's stablemate, the *Daily Record*. As the next election approaches, the *Sun* will again be the paper to watch most closely, followed by the no longer slavishly partisan *Mirror* and *Mail*, the only tabloid to have significantly boosted its circulation in the past few years.

## Party communications in the new media environment

The trends of change generally indicate a less comfortable media environment for the parties. Equally, they predict the response of intensified party attention to the techniques of news management and political marketing (see Chapter 9). Labour has reacted in precisely this way, most obviously through the courting of the tabloids. Famously, Blair before the 1997 general election, and Gordon Brown in 1998, flew to address Murdoch executives on the Barrier Reef and in Idaho. Where Neil Kinnock, as Labour leader, once banned News International journalists from his Westminster briefings, new Labour has deliberately fostered warmer relations cemented through personal links. Peter Mandelson, in particular, through his early 1980s' experience at London Weekend Television, was well-placed to establish a network of influential media contacts. Mandelson's friendships with key media figures, notably Rupert Murdoch's daughter, Elizabeth, head of BSkyB and Sir John Birt (BBC) are much-reported (Routledge, 1999, pp. 201–8; see also Oborne, 1999). Through determined courtship and good fortune, there is now a Labour-friendly climate in the major media boardrooms of the land. Not just Murdoch, but Dyke at the BBC, Gerry Robinson at Granada and Lord Hollick at United are all pro-Labour. This is a highly desirable outcome for Labour but does not translate into a propaganda comfort zone. TV news is legally bound to be impartial; the Opposition and its remaining press support are sure to monitor the BBC for any hint of bias. Murdoch's support is issue-contingent – and, besides, worn more lightly than his desire for commercial success.

Labour has taken the practice of political marketing in Britain to new levels. Not everything it has done in government is new. Thatcher also was served by an exceptionally powerful press secretary (Sir Bernard Ingham), who sought to extend Number 10 control over the Whitehall publicity machine, in a manner that prefigured Alastair Campbell's efforts in the 1997 Parliament (Scammell, 1995). Moreover, marketing in politics is not a simple effect of media. It is a more complex political market now, with weaker voter allegiances and a proliferation of interest groups, single-issue and regionally-based parties all competing for voter interest. Devolution in Scotland and Wales, coupled with proportional representation which benefits minor parties, will exacerbate these developments. All this encourages parties to pay more attention to campaigning and to developing policy strategically, in line with their interpretations of the attitudes of floating and weakly aligned voters (Scammell, 1999).

Nonetheless, Labour's approach does stand out. Labour is unashamedly wedded to communications. As Campbell told the House of Commons Select Committee on Public Administration (1998): 'In opposition we made clear that communications was not something that you tagged on at the end, it is part of what you do. That is something we have tried to bring into government.' Marketing was intrinsic to the transformation of Labour. Communications, especially through Mandelson, but also Philip Gould and Campbell, became a power base for the modernization project led by Blair and Brown. When Blair marched into Downing Street on 1 May 1997, the fabled Millbank spin doctors came in with him among his closest entourage. This is the key difference compared to the Thatcher communications regime. Party campaigning has been transplanted into Whitehall, with many of the same personnel and the same methods. They have brought with them, according to one critic (Riddell, 1998), a greater interest in the broadcast studio than the Commons, which seems to be regarded as 'merely one part of a communications strategy, rather than a central aspect of democratic accountability'. They have transformed governing, more clearly than any predecessor, into permanent campaigning.

Those methods include an abiding faith in the importance of driving the news agenda (Gould, 1998). To this end, Number 10 tightened its control over the whole government publicity process. Labour-friendly journalists, former colleagues of Campbell at the *Mirror* and from Millbank have been recruited into Ministry press offices. Number 10 has established a Strategic Communications Unit, whose members include Labour-supporting journalists Philip Bassett (ex-*The Times*) and David Bradshaw (ex-*Mirror*), and who write the seemingly endless flow of signed Blair columns for the tabloid press. Blair is more likely now to be read in the *Sun* than heard in the Commons. In August 1999 Downing Street set up a new version of its Millbank 'prebuttal' unit, initially headed by former BBC head of political research, Bill Bush, to anticipate reaction from press and opposition and prepare government responses.

Most controversially, though, government's communicators have been regularly accused of bullying critical journalists and refusing to cooperate with 'hostile' news programmes (Jones, 1999). Paul Routledge claims his impending appointment as political editor on the *Sunday Express* was blocked by pressure from Campbell and Lord Hollick, although this was denied by its editor Rosie Boycott. Since then, the *Sunday Express* has sacked Amanda Platell, now working at Conservative Central Office, after she sanctioned a controversial story concerning Mandelson allegedly visiting gay nightclubs on an official visit to Brazil. In late 1999 Shadow Home Secretary Ann Widdicombe was threatening to sue the *Sunday Express* for dropping her weekly column, claiming political motivation. Alastair Campbell has been involved in a public dispute with the BBC over claims that government ministers were favouring soft talk shows, such as Des O'Connor and Richard and Judy, and deliberately avoiding confrontational interviewers, such as Jeremy Paxman. In a letter to *The Times* (30 June, 1998), Campbell agreed that Ministers were reluctant to appear on *Newsnight*, with its 'dwindling audience'. He wrote: 'As one minister said to me recently when I was trying to persuade him to appear on the programme: "What is the point of me traipsing out to W12 late at night so that Jeremy can try to persuade the public that I'm actually some kind of criminal?"'

All eyes at present are on Labour's communications, and the Conservatives, outgunned and struggling in the polls, seem scarcely to be playing in the same league, despite a number of reported 'image' changes. Their cause is seriously hampered by the loss of the *Express* and the *Sun*.

The latter's editor put the size of their task in perspective when he cited as one of his favourite *Sun* front pages the picture of William Hague as a dead parrot: 'this is an EX-party' (MacArthur, 1999).

## Conclusion

There is a vast mismatch between the popular, and politicians', perceptions of media as enormously powerful, and the consensus of social science research, which finds only modest effects. A deluge of recent work, mostly from the US, blames media for a catalogue of ills, such that 'video-malaise' is the new orthodoxy. Arguments are advanced that television is 'privatising our lives' (Putnam, 1995, p. 681), destroying the community networks which constitute social capital; fostering couch-potato passivity (Hart, 1994); inducing voter cynicism (Patterson, 1993; Cappella and Jamieson, 1997). This would amount to a cogent case for a powerful and harmful media, were it not for one thing: the conclusion of media effects research, which persistently says the opposite. Research into media effects at British elections, for example, not only finds minor effects on voting and public agendas, but also suggests that the media's strongest influence is beneficial. News watching is positively associated with political knowledge and interest (Newton, 1999; Norris *et al.*, 1999) Who is right and who is wrong? Perhaps it is possible that, in a sense, both are right, that media are both powerful *and* limited. Increasingly research is dissatisfied with the over-simple 'powerful media/minimal effects' dichotomy and is seeking more subtle answers, looking at indirect, long-term and system effects (MacLeod, Kosicki and MacLeod 1994).

Take the case of agenda-setting. It is not surprising that media have little effect in election campaigns, where most issues are already well known and voters are driven by bread-and-butter domestic concerns. Equally, we would be astonished if media coverage were not influential in new and relatively unknown matters – GM foods, for example, or foreign affairs. US special envoy to Yugoslavia, Richard Holbrooke (1999) claimed that Western intervention in Kosovo and non-intervention in Rwanda was intimately related to coverage, and lack of it, on television. The impact of media on foreign policy (the so-called 'CNN effect') is a new cottage industry of media research. Again, one would be surprised if media coverage dictated foreign policy, but equally staggered if it had no influence. It is abundantly obvious that politicians believe that media influence public opinion and political reputations, on crucial matters of competence and credibility. This perception affects party behaviour, not just in communication styles, but in internal power structures and almost certainly in the formation of policy (Shaw, 1994; Scammell, 1995;

Herbst, 1998). The question is less *whether* media impacts on policy, but how and when.

The impact of the Internet is the hottest new topic in town. The Internet hugely increases information available to the public, enables interactive communications, opens space to marginalized groups and enhances dissident power against governments. It may prove a boon to citizenship. It may simply increase the knowledge-rich/poor divide or undermine professional journalistic standards with an anarchic rumour mill. The Web probably *will* transform political communication. It may become *the* public face of government departments and organizations. Not yet, though. For the moment its use for the parties is limited to mainly an archive resource (Ward and Gibson, 1998). Its value is restricted by take-up – in 1998 just 16 per cent of UK homes, predicted to increase to 40 per cent by 2003 – and by the self-selecting nature of Web audiences. It is not an obvious tool for reaching the non-aligned and politically uninterested. We are left then with the irony that, for all the high-blown rhetoric of the new media of Internet and multi-channel TV, the old media will continue to be the more important political influence going into the next election and probably well beyond that.

# Chapter 11

# Political Participation and Protest

## HELEN MARGETTS

In Britain today conventional forms of political participation are down, particularly voting. Voting for certain types of political party has risen, however, and the increasing plurality of political parties in Britain is likely to be fuelled by current and future constitutional change. Devolution and the introduction of elected mayors might also do something to raise the astonishingly low profile of British local government among the British public, as it has in London. Political protest, demonstration and violence are all on an upward trend. These activities are carried out by a diverse range of interests – the environment, anti-capitalism and fox-hunting were all the subject of demonstration in the 1995–9 years. There has been far less political action from women and ethnic groups. Democratic innovations at central and local levels proliferated during the 1990s – but largely in a top-down fashion, provided or even mandated by central government. In contrast, the Internet and electronic forms of communication look like offering the most opportunities for all kinds of political behaviour in the future.

## Voting and the increasing plurality of political parties in Britain

The 1997 general election saw turnout decline significantly, from 77.7 per cent in 1992 to 71.5 per cent, the lowest level since 1935. The 2001 General Election produced a considerable further decline to 59.4, a drop of some 12 per cent, the lowest turnout since modern politics began. Turnout has subsequently continued to decrease at European and local elections. Locally it dropped to an overall average of 30 per cent across English councils with elections in 1998; the average for metropolitan councils was 25 per cent, down from 31 per cent in 1996; London remained higher than average at 35 per cent. Turnouts in both the 1998 and 1999 local elections were the lowest since local government reorganization in the 1970s (Rallings and Thrasher, 1999). At the by-election Michael Portillo won in Kensington and

Chelsea in November 1999, the turnout was only 29 per cent, barely half the figure registered at the 1997 general election. The new List Proportional Representation (PR) electoral system did not revive turnout for the June 1999 European elections, which dropped to 24 per cent overall (varying from 10 to 40 per cent across constituencies). This figure, down from 36 per cent in both 1994 and 1989, was the lowest ever in a national election in Britain, and the lowest across the EU (although in Northern Ireland, turnout was much higher than in the rest of the UK, as it was in 1994).

Voters showed more enthusiasm for Scottish devolution, with turnout in the referendum for the new Scottish Parliament at 60 per cent, and no region lower than 50 per cent. In Wales, turnout was significantly less, at 42 per cent. These national differences were retained in the elections to the new legislatures on 6 May 1999: 58 per cent in Scotland, 46 per cent in Wales. In London, although 72 per cent voted in favour of the new London Mayor and Assembly, only 33 per cent actually participated in the referendum. However, the almost complete lack of opposition to the proposals, the absence of a 'no' campaign and an extremely weak 'yes' campaign may in part explain these figures.

Although the act of voting remains in decline, voting for certain types of parties has risen. The cumulative vote obtained by the traditionally termed 'other' parties doubled from 3.5 per cent in the 1992 general election to 6.8 per cent in 1997: 1678 candidates stood for fringe parties or under an independent label, almost twice as many as 1992 (Norris, 1997, p. 18). The single-issue Referendum party, opposed to Britain's EU membership, was the most successful, polling 3 per cent of votes. Voting for parties outside Britain's three main parties continued in elections to other tiers of government after 1997, fuelled by constitutional change. The use of List PR for the European elections, and the additional member system for the Scottish Parliament, the Welsh Assembly and the London Assembly, all give smaller parties a chance. In the 1998 local elections the Green Party's share of the vote in the 10 per cent of available seats it contested rose significantly to over 10 per cent in London and 7 per cent across the rest of the country. The party won 27 seats in 16 authorities above the level of town and parish councils. In the 1999 European elections, the Green party gained 6.2 per cent of the vote, less than half of its historic 15 per cent in the 1989 European elections, but enough to gain two seats for the first time under the new List PR system (under which it would have gained 10 seats in 1989). The United Kingdom Independence Party, launched in 1993, fielded a full list of candidates in all regions of the UK and gained 7 per cent of the vote. The party won seats in three regions (South West, South East and Eastern) and narrowly missed being elected in two further regions. The new Scottish Parliament and Welsh Assembly gave a boost to voting for the Nationalist parties; the SNP gained 35 seats out of 129. But in the European elections, too, the SNP retained two seats with over 27 per cent of the vote while in Wales, Plaid Cymru took two seats for the first time with 30 per cent of the Welsh vote.

Planned changes to the election and leadership of local government (DETR, 1999) may further contribute to the increasing plurality of parties in British politics. Directly elected mayors, if introduced, may also do something to overturn the staggering anonymity of local government in Britain. In other European countries, local government is seen more 'as a political institution through which communities govern themselves', its existence denoting the right to local self-government, rather than a set of organizations created solely to secure the provision of a series of services as in Britain (Stewart, 1996b, p. 41).

In a MORI survey in Britain in 1998, 72 per cent of respondents (and 90 per cent of young people) claimed to know little or hardly anything about their local government (MORI, 1998). A table of media mentions across all UK press for London local authorities in the early 1990s showed the incredibly low public profile of even the capital's government, with Westminster at the top with 338 in a year (owing largely to several allegations of corruption during the period), followed by Lambeth with 180 (also owing in part to allegations of corruption) and Barking at the bottom with two; just under two-thirds of local authorities received less than 50 press mentions in a year. The London Mayor and Assembly have attracted considerable publicity since their election, particularly in the London press. During 2001, the modernisation and possible privatisation of London's Underground (a key issue in ensuring that Ken Livingstone was denied the Labour nomination for Mayor) was for the first time a high-profile discussion point in both the national and local media. In opposing privatisation, Mayor Livingstone and his transport chief, Bob Kiley, found themselves pitted against ministers, both sides engaged in a war of words that eventually ended up in the High Court ruling in the government's favour.

As well as voting for the main political parties, other mainstream measures of political participation remained low in comparison with the past. In 1992 Labour party membership was 280 000, lower than at any time since 1930. The Conservative party is organized locally and has rarely published its total membership figures, but appears to have lost more than half its members since the 1950s. An initiative called the 'Conservative Network' is advertized as a 'new style of political participation' (Conservative Party Web site, 1999). Members of the network do not have to belong to the party, but are encouraged to stand for public office, given 'social and political networking opportunities' and campaign training. The intention is presumably to attract younger members: by 1995 the average

age of party members was 62 (Heywood, 1997). Between the years of 1990 and 1995 the membership of the Green Party dropped from almost 20 000 to under 4000 and experienced only a modest recovery to around 5000 in 1999. Membership of TUC-affiliated unions remains steady at the 7 million (about one in three of the workforce) recorded by Evans (1997). In the late 1990s, there were other indicators of low levels of involvement in political institutions: in a survey of the 'People's Panel', 51 per cent of respondents said that they did not feel very much involved in the local community and only 5 per cent said 'a great deal'. Only 2 per cent said they were involved with a political party, and none that they were involved with a Housing Association (HA) or an NHS trust. The principal kind of institutional involvement was through arts or sports activities (which presumably could involve belonging to a gym, a rather weak form of political participation), at 18 per cent, and charity work, at 15 per cent. Of those surveyed, 52 per cent were involved in none of the activities about which they were questioned.

## Protest and demonstration

In contrast to voting, involvement with political institutions and party membership, political protest, demonstration and even violence have continued to increase since the 'dramatic upsurge in single-issue protest activity and unconventional forms of political participation' observed by Evans (1997). The anti-capitalist movement proved itself alive and kicking with a rally in London in June 1999 organized by the anarchist organization 'Reclaim the Streets'. The rally caught the police unawares, leading to 84 arrests and £2 million pounds worth of damage to the City of London. Another march took place on 29 November 1999, timed to coincide with a meeting of trade liberalisation talks hosted by the World Trade Organization in Seattle. Two thousand protesters attended a primarily peaceful rally which ended in violence outside Euston station. In Seattle itself around 100 000 protestors took part in what was probably the biggest protest in the US since the Vietnam war. City authorities imposed a 7p.m. to dawn curfew, armed state troopers and the FBI reinforced city police, a state of emergency was declared in parts of the city and the opening ceremonies of the talks were cancelled. Both protestors and representatives of developing countries excluded from the talks proclaimed victory when the talks themselves proved unproductive.

As with the first half of the 1990s, political protest and sustained political activity were dominated by environmental activism, particularly focused on roads and the countryside. The anti-roads' movement, building on sustained activity during the earlier 1990s, was by 1999 claimed as evidence of a new social movement emerging in Britain. 'Consideration of the lack of organization, the limited material resources, and the novelty of the tactics created in the movement, shows that these protests are qualitatively new, differing in kind from the earlier environmental interest groups' (Doherty, 1999, p. 291). The increased membership and hence income of groups such as Greenpeace and Friends of the Earth (411 000 and 230 000 in 1993) meant that by the end of the 1990s they had come to be regarded as almost 'establishment', relying too heavily on their income from membership to risk radical activity. Doherty suggests that although they represented the radical end of the spectrum of British environmental groups at the beginning of the 1990s, they were neither very democratic nor participatory in practice, and so offered no opportunity for radicals to express alternative ideologies through protest (Doherty, 1999, p. 278). Road protests began outside these groups because much of the impetus of ecological protest came from those who were dissatisfied with their passive character.

Environmental activity reached unprecedented heights during the 1990s with another locus: the protection of the countryside against food production, in particular the introduction of trials of genetically modified (GM) crops into the British countryside by the company Monsanto, a long-time producer of such crops in the US, where reactions against this method of food production had been minimal. The British environmental lobby feared that heavy doses of insecticide and herbicide used on the GM crops would kill all other plants and insects and that GM crops would cross-pollinate with native plants. Large interest groups returned to radical action alongside the new breed of environmental activists. A spate of direct-action protests took place in the summer of 1999. Trashing of crops, local referenda and protests located around specific trials on specific farms all served to keep the issue alive in the press and national debate while creating distinctive local patterns of activity. The Soil Association, the UK's leading certification and campaigning organization for organic food and farming, placed itself firmly against genetically engineered crops, as it became increasingly difficult for even the best-intentioned of producers with 'organic' status to be sure that products were free of any GM food. In 1999, *Newsnight* suggested that even 'Linda McCartney Vegetarian Sausages' contained traces of genetically modified soya.

Meanwhile, the British public as consumers seemed to be having an effect through consistent lack of appetite for GM food. MORI polls commissioned by Greenpeace in 1999 suggested that 73 per cent of the UK public did not want GM crops grown and 74 per cent of the public 'expressed concern' with the idea that ministers might redefine organic standards to incorporate organic crops that might have cross-pollinated with GM crops (MORI Polls and Surveys, 17 and 30 June 1999).

Questioned on five food safety-related issues for the 1999 People's Panel, three in five people were concerned about new food technology, such as GM food – even more than BSE/CJD (54 per cent), the key food scare of the first half of the 1990s. The big supermarkets responded more quickly than government, with Sainsbury's being congratulated by Friends of the Earth when it became the first to proclaim all its own-label food GM-free. This noble move had a sound commercial foundation, as worries about issues such as GM foods and pesticides had persuaded 39 per cent of shoppers to change their buying habits (*Guardian*, 22 November 1999). Although nearly half of those questioned also said they trusted super-markets less than a few years ago, the survey highlighted an even greater mistrust of the government over food issues – only one in five shoppers surveyed trusted it to tell the truth about food safety.

By April 1998, Monsanto realized that it had seriously misjudged levels of consumer concern over GM foods in Europe, and launched a $1 million advertising campaign to transform public opinion in the UK. The campaign was spectacularly unsuccessful. By November 1998, leaked internal documents showed that Monsanto was considering 'crisis manage-ment tactics' amid a society-wide collapse of support in Britain and Germany, and in April 1999 it failed in a high court bid to silence campaigners from the pressure group Genetix Snowball, who had trashed the firm's crops. The company had long campaigned on the basis that GM crops would tackle problems of world hunger – but by May 1999 even this argument was failing, when Christian Aid called for a five-year freeze on crop technology development, saying that GM giants would 'force the world into famine'. By November 1999, international concern about GM food had fed back to the US, where Democrats and Republicans joined in launching a bill requiring all GM food sold in the US to be labelled, and a coalition of 60 US consumer organizations called for a moratorium on GM foods. By October 1999, Monsanto announced it had suspended research into the 'Terminator' gene, which would allow the creation of crops bearing sterile seeds. The company chairman told a November 1999 Greenpeace conference in London: 'We have probably irritated and antagonized more people than we have persuaded.' In the same month the government announced that no GM crops would be grown commer-cially in Britain until at least the spring of 2003, to allow time for a panel of independent scientists to assess trial plantings and see whether they damaged the biodiversity of the wider countryside. However, anti-GM campaigners remained unsatisfied with the three-year trial period, seeing it as leading the way to full-scale farming: 'What happens when the three years is up?', asked the Soil Association.

Environmental activism of a kind was also evident among a section of the population traditionally less given to political protest in Britain – those living in the countryside, particularly farmers ruined by the BSE crisis and other food scares, and countryside populations concerned about the urban bias of policy-making in the Labour government. The issue around which these disparate interests consolidated was fox-hunting, after a Private Member's Bill sponsored by Labour MP Mike Foster looked likely to achieve success in banning it. In July 1997, an estimated 100 000 people on the 'Countryside March' gathered in London's Hyde Park to protest against the destruction of the British countryside. In spite of the organizers' claim to represent the concerns of the countryside community as a whole, 40 per cent of the marchers gave fox-hunting or hunting with dogs as the single main reason for being there and only 28 per cent claimed to be marching primarily for the rights of rural people. Supporters of fox-hunting tried to link this issue to matters of wider popular appeal, such as conservation, by claiming that the end of fox-hunting would mean that hounds and horses would have to be destroyed, and employment, pointing to the number of jobs that would be lost in the countryside through the disappearance of hunting. The 'Countryside March', organized by the Countryside Alliance (previously the British Field Sports Society), became an annual event. The second march in 1998 was attended by over 250 000, including the Conservative leader William Hague, the Liberal Democrat leader Paddy Ashdown and Labour's Environment Minister Michael Meacher. It was preceded by the lighting of a chain of 7000 beacons across the English countryside with several hundred in Foster's Worcester constituency. In spite of the failure of Foster's bill owing to lack of parliamentary time (or the Labour government's fear of the opposition it had provoked), there were rallies in six cities in 1999, with a claimed 20 000 attendance at each, specifically aimed at preserving fox-hunting against the threat of a revival of the legislation. The landowning community were turning to forms of political behaviour formerly the preserve of the left. In 1998, MORI found that four out of five of the 200 000 participants at the Countryside March on 1 March 1998 were Conservative voters; 47 per cent of marchers were in the AB class group and only 5 per cent from the DE group.

## Participation of women and ethnic minorities

There is a long-held debate in feminist literature as to whether a women's movement exists in Britain. If there is, it was not evident during the latter half of the 1990s. The gains for social representation made in the 1997 election, when 120 women entered the House of Commons, 102 representing the Labour Party, were followed by general disappointment with the new intake of women, disparagingly termed 'Blair's babes' by the media for their lack of willingness to step out of line. Harriet Harman, then Secretary of State for Social Security, aroused particular public outcry in 1997 when introducing controversial legislation which cut benefits to lone parents. There was little evidence of feminist-based political activity during the period. Perhaps surprisingly, several feminists turned their interest to a major event of the decade in terms of mobilisation ('a kind of emotional revolution of the streets', as the *Independent* put it on 3 September 1997) – the mass mourning of the death of Princess Diana and her lover in a road crash in Paris in 1997, which could only with heavy socio-cultural reworking be described as political (see Watts, 1999). Some feminists took the event to constitute a major feminist crossroads (Birchill, 1998; Campbell, 1998; Wheeler, 1998). Some claimed that the life and death of Diana had forged new links between the public and private (Attwood, 1999, p. 159). Critics dismissed such claims as evidence of a feminism which appeared to have abandoned collective action for 'a fascination with signs and symbols . . . and mistakes the only lesson to be learnt from the death of Diana – Don't get in the car if the driver's pissed'.

Outside England, however, women's representation received a boost in the elections to the new Scottish Parliament where women account for 40 per cent of Labour MSPs. In Wales, even more remarkably, given the traditional male predominance of the Welsh Labour party, half of all Labour Assembly members are women. As Coote (1999) put it: 'Westminster now looks out of step, with women occupying only one in six seats.' She also observed that 'the absence of any fanfare is curious . . . one might have expected a celebratory word or two from Millbank or Downing Street, acknowledging that Labour's positive action strategy had won through for women and democracy'. By twinning constituencies in Scotland and Wales and obliging each pair to select one male and one female candidate, Labour increased the numbers of Labour women elected and set an example for other parties. The campaigning of Scottish women meant that the same strategy was introduced in Wales through a more resistant Welsh Labour party. The very success of such a strategy may be the explanation for the Labour party's lack of attention – uneasy after the abandonment of a plan to introduce all-women shortlists in some constituencies in Britain which was declared illegal (some commentators suggest that the reason the Labour party never contested the ruling was that they were happy with the decision). Coote claimed that while feminist women had been influential in the party and on its policies during its dark years of the 1980s and the early 1990s, the new Labour leadership in power had surrounded itself with a coterie of young white graduate males who had had 'little exposure to the dialogue with feminism that was so influential in the early 1990s. For many of them, the women's agenda is "yesterday's problem"' (Coote, 1999). In consequence, Coote remarked: 'The Third Way is gender-blind.'

Black political mobilization has also had a low profile during the period and the parliamentary representation of ethnic minorities has lagged behind that of women. There was only a net gain of three black MPs in the 1997 general election (eight compared to five in 1992). At local government level it is estimated that there are 400 black and Asian councillors out of a total of 23 000 (Huq, 1998). Race differences in participation remain under-studied. Opinion polls in general fail to distinguish ethnic groupings in their demographic characteristics, owing to the difficulties in locating sufficient black respondents. Most opinion polls reported in the media provide a picture of white Britain. Verba, Lehman Schlozman and Brady (1995) overcame this problem with respect to race and participation by using over-sampling for Blacks, Latinos and inactive Anglo–whites. Using a weighting design they were able both to analyze in sufficient detail the participatory behaviour of specific ethnic groups and to rescale upwards from the groups to a national random sample. Such methods have not yet been replicated in British conditions, and we are more reliant on the observations of social and cultural commentators. In 1998, the sociologist Stuart Hall suggested that one reason why we might not expect to see black political movements in Britain at the end of the twentieth century was that 'we now have a situation where black British culture could be described as confident beyond measure in its own identity . . . blackness is no longer necessarily a counter or resistance identity, as it was in the 1970s' (Hall, 1998b, p. 39). Hall claimed that black British identity had emerged from the 1980s (a period when the majority of black people saw the decline of the welfare-state culture, the principal material support of the urban under-privileged to whom they largely belonged) with a distinctively individualist cast: 'the period when black politics was the politics of community struggle seems to me profoundly in recession. Political consciousness around race has increasingly taken the form of people seeing that they've got to carve out something for themselves' (Hall, 1998b, p. 42). Thus black women especially are taking the route of night-time learning and multiple part-time jobs rather than the role of community activism. Like Coote's view of new Labour's response to women, Hall concluded that the emergence of a distinctive, different minority cultural formation from the 1980s and 1990s is not recognized by the almost uniformly white advisors of the Labour party leadership: 'It is a blanked out space as far as the language of New Labour is concerned, written out of the imagined post-Millennium New Britain which the government is struggling to construct' (Hall, 1998a, p. 46). Huq (1998) also observed that while Asians were included in new Labour's election strategy, 'in government the indications show that, specific race relations legislation aside, ethnic minorities are to be largely treated as part of the British population per se. The colour blind approach does raise tensions' (Huq, 1998, p. 72).

Even if new Labour do not recognize it and we do not have the data to understand it, race and more specifically racism look set to increase as a locus of political activity. The most important event in the 1990s was the result of the 1998 Macpherson enquiry into the murder of the black teenager Stephen Lawrence in a racist attack four years earlier. The enquiry eventually (after much semantic dancing) supported the claim that the Metropolitan Police were 'institutionally racist'. As the story unravelled it seemed that somehow forces of good had pierced the maze of police obfuscation and popular prejudice against the media-worthiness of such stories, as the death of a perfectly innocent black youth from a perfectly respectable black family at the hands of five unequivocally racist thugs, who consistently escaped attempts to bring them to justice, attracted indignation from all quarters. The steadfast refusal of the family to give up until some kind of justice was obtained and the clear-cut elements of right and wrong somehow succeeded where more radical or politically motivated campaigns had failed. The Macpherson report 'raised the standard of racial debate in this country', charting 'a path from the crudest forms of racism to the most well-concealed; from Stephen's violent death to the Metropolitan Police's wilful negligence; from the failure of the Met to recruit ethnic minorities to the need for greater racial and cultural awareness in the national curriculum' (Younge, 1999, p. 330). The number of racist incidents recorded by police forces in 1998–9 rose by 75 per cent to almost 25 000 (having grown by only 6 per cent the previous year), suggesting that prior to the Macpherson enquiry there had been serious under-reporting and, according to the chief inspector of constabulary, 'improved police response and increased community confidence' (*Guardian*, 28 October 1999). Such statistics may substantiate the suggestion of some commentators that Britain's racial attitudes will never be the same again after the Lawrence inquiry, although Younge (1999) warned that similar sentiments were expressed by the (1970) Scarman report, with little result.

## Democratic innovations

Political participation is also changing in response to various democratic innovations. Citizen juries, used since the 1970s in America and Germany, are one form. In a citizens' jury, the face-to-face interaction and participation of a sample of individuals is considered to provide some information as to how the rest of the citizenry would behave if they participated or interacted. A group of 12–16 members of the public are selected at random to represent a broad cross-section of the local community and are asked to consider a specific issue, with aid from expert witnesses who give evidence and fine tune the agenda. Jurors question them and discuss issues amongst themselves; they are then expected to arrive at a set of concrete recommendations. Advocates of the idea argue that they provide a new mechanism for citizen participation in an increasingly specialist and professionalized policy process, allowing citizens the same chance to develop opinions as policy-makers. A government-sponsored initiative of this type, the Agenda for the Age, was held in 1998–9 and the Institute of Public Policy Research, the King's Fund, the Women's Unit of the Labour government and the Local Government Management Board (LGMB) have all sponsored a series of pilot projects during the 1990s. Smith and Wales (1999) argue that citizens' juries fulfil the aims of theories of deliberative democracy: 'the strength and power of the citizens' jury process lies in its potential for *informed* political deliberations between citizens based on the principles of mutual respect and mutual understanding' (Smith and Wales, 1999, p. 305, emphasis is in the original). However, such juries present a methodological challenge. It is very difficult to construct a sample that is both representative and of a feasible size for reasoned discussion. All the normal problems with the idea of social representation result: are women jurors expected to represent all women in the wider community, or black jurors the entire mixture of ethnic groups in British society? In the UK, the problem appears to be dealt with by the use of the word 'symbolic representation', which admits to rather than overcomes the problem.

Innovations like citizens' juries are a 'top-down' form of participation – that is, they tend to be initiated by government or policy-making organizations rather than by citizens themselves. Another such innovation in the late 1990s was the introduction of 'People's Panels'. During 1998, the Modernizing Public Services Group in the Cabinet Office commissioned MORI and Birmingham University to set up a People's Panel, consisting of 5000 randomly selected members of the public, designed to be a representative cross-section of the population by gender, age, background and region (ethnic group is not mentioned in the Cabinet Office's description of the project). Panel members are consulted on how public services are delivered and 'how that delivery can be improved from the point of view of the user, rather than the system' (Cabinet Office, 1999). The idea was heralded as 'a world first at national level' (Cabinet Office, 1999). The two 'waves' of results were announced in October 1998 and January 1999, the intention being that 'the results from each wave of research will inform decisions on the delivery of public services' (MORI, 1999). Among many other policy initiatives, responses from the People's Panel were claimed to have provoked a review of the way biotechnology and genetic modification is monitored and plans to speed up action to reduce main air pollutants.

The People's Panel involves the feeding of public opinion into policy-making and as such is a positive move in democratic terms, but the initiative is, in spite of the name, basically an opinion poll, the public sector equivalent of market research. Such initiatives are part of a wider move by central government to increase the incorporation of public opinion into policy-making. The draft local government bill states that 'every council is . . . to be required to consult its local community – local electors and other interested parties . . . about how that community is to be governed' (DETR, 1999b) and the Modern Local Government White Paper placed a new statutory duty on local authorities 'to consult and engage with their local communities' (DETR, 1998c, p. 39). However, in November 1999 the Audit Commission published a report entitled *Listen Up! Effective Community Consultation* (Audit Commission, 1999) based on research which found that while authorities face growing statutory duties to consult and some 'innovative authorities' were already using consultation to improve the quality and cost-effectiveness of services, many others needed to catch up with best practice. The Commission found that the quality of individual consultation exercises was patchy, and that many local authorities failed in practice to use the results of consultation to inform decisions about services; that some authorities used consultation techniques that allowed unrepresentative but articulate groups to dominate; and that few authorities evaluated their work. Such findings echoed Sanderson's (1999, p. 343) observation that as yet, 'there is actually little evidence found of real citizen empowerment' in such initiatives.

## Electronic participation

Forms of political participation are changing more dramatically with electronic means of communication, with the Internet proving a major new forum for political participation. By 1999, around 20 per cent of the British population (over 10 million) had Internet access and this figure was rising quickly (up from 7.4 million in 1998). Percentages of Internet penetration were radically higher for some groups; for example, around 40 per cent for 18–25 year olds; virtually 100 per cent for all students as universities automatically provide access with registration; and is very high amongst the disabled. Future usage figures were given a boost in October 1999, when the Chancellor announced that families on unemployment benefit or the New Deal work scheme would be able to lease reconditioned personal computers for £5 a month, intended to increase by 10 per cent the number of people with access to the Internet.

The Internet and e-mail open new windows for political participation of all kinds. Campaigning organizations are already creating systems that construct emails to appropriate policy-makers for people on the basis of responses to certain political questions. Illegal protest groups, such as the far-right group Combat 18, find the Internet particularly useful for communication and radical religious groups use the Internet as the prime means of recruitment – by targeting universities, for example. The Green party provides a 'webkit' on its national web site, to facilitate local Green groups to start up their own web sites and campaigning machinery. The June 1999 march of Reclaim the Streets was largely organized on the Internet, and before the second march in November the police were monitoring the web for details of the planned demonstration. At the same time, the organization Euro-Hippies were jamming the WTO's web server with repeated email questions, in a virtual joining of protests. A representative claimed that the environmental movement had been revolutionized by the Internet, as activists from different countries who had never met protested together in virtual forums.

Technological developments also enable citizens to participate in governmental activity, as well as to rail against it. There are new possibilities for 'open-book' governance (Dunleavy and Weir, 1998) as processes of government become increasingly visible while public consultation becomes easier and more diverse. The Internet allows organizations to give far more detailed information more cheaply and conveniently, respond to people's questions and ideas and encourage the public to submit proposals for action. The public is certainly ready to use electronic means to gain information; for example, the BBC's Election 97 Web site on election night itself recorded more than 1.5 million hits, allowing users to email queries and get answers. When the US bombed Iraq, the US television network CNN received 300 000 hits within two hours of the bombing. The BSE inquiry transferred daily transcripts of its proceedings to the web within hours of witnesses having spoken and there is no reason why other public enquiries, parliamentary select committees, Royal Commissions and other central bodies should not do the same. There are also major possibilities for a more discursive form of local democracy, whereby local councils and other public bodies can make clear how they shape their policies and invite interested citizens and specialists to participate directly in determining them. Interactive question and answer sessions, policy forums, panels and discussion groups, planning consultations, chat lines, even electronic voting can all generate a lot of information that policy-makers might consider (Dunleavy and Weir, 1998).

Most examples of this kind of participation in local government facilitated through electronic communication are as yet outside Britain, where a range of pilot projects have been designed to demonstrate the practical feasibility and democratic potential of community networks providing near universal civic access to the superhighway for some localities. A famous example is provided by the Amsterdam Digital City, first developed in 1994 < http://www.dds.nl >. Within months, it had attracted over 15 000 participants who accessed the city over 3000 times a day, dialling up from private computers or public access terminals. Since then, digital cities have been established in over 25 Dutch cities, with Amsterdam providing a platform for a number of well-supported public discussion groups on a wide range of issues – the extension of Schipol airport, the relationship between technology and democracy and racism. The evidence is that the British public might be ready to participate in such an experiment. In 1998, the first survey carried out for the 'People's Panel' asked the question: 'If you were able to use these devices to deal with government which, if any, do you think you would use?' Across the UK, support for new technology in dealing with government came from the younger age groups – 65 per cent in the 16–34 age group agreed that new technology would make dealing with government easier, compared to only 25 per cent of people over the age of 65 – the overall percentage was 35 per cent. Over 50 per cent of all respondents thought that new technology would make it easier for them to deal with government.

However, demand may outstrip supply. In 1997, the Prime Minister promised that by 2002, 25 per cent of central government's transactions with citizens would be able to take place electronically, and in the white paper *Modernizing Government* published in 1999, the promise was extended to 100 per cent of government's transactions with citizens being able to take place electronically by the year 2008 (Cabinet Office, 1999c). But by 1999, government's progress in developing electronic communication methods with citizens had lagged behind that of organizations outside government (NAO, 1999). Citizen-to-government communication got off to a bad start in 1995 when then Minister for Public Services became the first Minister to publicly announce his email address, but a senior official admitted that all internal communications necessary to answer the first query took place by post (Margetts, 1998, p. 7). Even by 1999, it was still more difficult to send an email to most government departments than to other categories of organization. If this division deepens, then policy-makers may become more resistant – rather than more open – to 'virtual' pressure and input. And if government organizations have a low presence on the web, citizens will increasingly turn to other organizations with whom to interact.

## Social capital: rise or fall?

During the 1990s Britain was deemed to present cause for optimism in academic discussion of political participation, when compared with declining levels of political activity in the US. Conceptual discussion of the basis for political participation revolved around the notion of 'social capital', defined by Robert Putnam (1993) as features of social life – networks, norms and trust – that enable participants to act together to pursue shared objectives. Putnam found a decline in the phenomenon in the US in the 1990s (Putnam, 1995). Social capital is evidenced by regular contact between individuals beyond the family, participation in common endeavours and trust in social associations and networks. Higher levels of these phenomena are deemed to facilitate participation in politics (Hall, 1999, p. 418). Social capital is reminiscent of 'civic culture', the phenomenon observed by Almond and Verba (1963), characterized by high levels of social trust, civic organization and political participation.

In contrast to the US, an influential article by Hall found no erosion in Britain of social capital equivalent to that observed in the US. Since the 1950s there have been shifts between the type of voluntary associations to which people belong, for instance from traditional women's organizations, which tend to be oriented towards homemakers, to environmental organizations (Hall, 1999, p. 421). Men and women show differential trends: while community involvement by men increased slightly, by about 7 per cent, between 1959 and 1990, the community involvement of women more than doubled to converge with the rates of men: 'in short, social capital has been sustained in Britain largely by virtue of the increasing participation of women in the community' (Hall, 1999, p. 437). Meanwhile, the number of citizens making charitable donations or involved in voluntary work had increased in the period to 1992, leading to a 'extensive and vibrant' voluntary sector (Hall, 1999, p. 425). Hall found that while social capital might be considered to be most strongly sustained by the middle class (Hall, 1999, p. 439), the number of British citizens who engage in some form of political participation beyond voting has risen dramatically (Hall, 1999, p. 450). He uses this evidence to conclude that Putnam's perceived relationship between social capital and levels of political participation is supported by the British case.

The upward trend in political participation that Hall observed does not seem to have continued into the 1990s. Membership of environmental organizations may have quadrupled between 1971 and 1992 (Hall, 1999) but by 1999 Greenpeace's membership for example was 170 000, closer to its 1985 levels than its 411 000 members in 1993 (Evans, 1997). Many of the examples of political activity and protest noted above took place outside the type of organizations that Hall observes. The newer environmental groups rely on symbolic action rather than mass mobilization for their effectiveness – and of all political ideologies are closest to anarchism: 'they have no central organization and no centralized pool of resources and there is a strong ideological commitment to avoiding any institutionaliza- tion' (Doherty, 1999, p. 289). Although supported during the trial by a core of activists and lawyers, the Lawrence family had previously belonged to no sectional group: 'the key protagonists in this particular drama had nothing to do with the black community at all' (Younge, 1999, p. 332). Initiatives to increase participation in policy-making have come largely from central government. Increased voting for smaller political parties has come at least in part from constitutional change. The attendees of Countryside marches, for example, are probably accounted for in Hall's analysis as enthusiastic volunteers and charitable donors whose access to social networks of power (for example, through the Conservative Party) ensured their influence on the political system until 1997. Now that their traditional domain has been challenged by a change of government and a crisis in the sector with which they are most likely to be associated (agriculture), such networks are no longer viable channels for influencing policy and a change in participatory behaviour has emerged.

It would thus be hard to link either the increases or decreases in different kinds of political participation during the period to social capital. Citizens' reactions to political issues are honed by a succession of experiences. For example, significant numbers of citizens seem to be aligning themselves on the 'against' side of the issue of genetically modified (GM) food with political effect, after cumulative experience of govern- mental failures in food policy, without joining groups or entering into formal methods of political participation – the parameters which Hall (1999) investigates. By 1999, environmental activists were labelled as such in television interviews, rather than as belonging to any specific group. While social capital enthusiasts place great importance on the phenomenon of 'social trust' as a measure of participatory health, many of the break- throughs in protest and participation during the 1990s actually seem to stem from a thriving lack of trust in information from political institutions. The GM food debate is intertwined with the legacy of the BSE crisis in British politics – and the public seem completely oblivious to government assurances on the subject. Social capital is a two-way phenomenon, and just as high levels of social trust may encourage participation in govern- ment, government actions of the past may shape citizen's participatory behaviour. By 1999 Foley and Edwards were asking 'is it time to disinvest in social capital?', having reviewed 45 recent articles on the subject, and arguing for the 'irrelevance' of generalized social trust and that the social resources made available to individuals and groups should be the prime focus and central attraction of the social capital debate (Foley and Edwards, 1999). Certainly the changed participatory behaviour of the countryside movement seems linked to a redirection of social resources rather than any change in social trust.

Another trend absent from the social capital debate is the dramatically rising use of the Internet as a forum for political participation. In his conclusion, Hall (1999, p. 457) points out that 'there may be ways of operating an effective democracy in an age of new media that do not require as much face-to-face interaction among the citizenry'; this possibility was, by 1999, a reality. email has burgeoned as a form of communication; a 1999 survey by MSN Hotmail, Microsoft's email service, found that British people have on average around 33 regular contacts on email and that seven out of 10 Britons use email in both professional and personal lives, using them in ways that has virtually died out with the dominance of the telephone (*Observer*, 28 November 1999). It could be perhaps that the US example is not as pessimistic as Putnam suggests; his indicators do not track this new development in the US, where widespread communication via the Internet has been present far longer than the UK and the minimal cost of local telephone calls makes Internet access far more widely available. Even by May 1997, over 80 per cent of Internet users and networked computers were in North America (Hill and Hughes, 1998, p. 81). In general, 'social capitalists' are accustomed to see new media such as television as a threat rather than a boost to participatory democracy (Putnam, 1995) and even Hall (1999, p. 435) argues that 'it is hard to imagine that levels of social interaction outside the household would not be higher if television did not exist'. By the late 1990s, television itself was becoming more of an interactive medium, as the BBC encouraged viewers to online question-and-answer sessions on its web sites at the end of selected television programmes. Greenpeace's membership has fallen considerably, but by October 1999 its interactive Web site received 43 300 visits every week.

## Conclusion

Constitutional change emerges as the key driver for political participation at the beginning of the twenty-first century. Devolution brings the possibility of a new public profile for tiers of government below central government, in stark contrast to the complete obscurity of local government in Britain during the 1990s. In contrast, government initiatives aimed explicitly at increasing participation, such as the People's Panel and citizens' juries, have yet to overcome the paradox that it is hard to mandate participation from the top. Meanwhile, 'grassroots' bottom-up participation has taken the form of protest and demonstration, particularly focused on the environment. The Labour government seem to have responded to the combination of both grassroots activism and consistently oppositional public opinion on the issue of genetically engineered crops with at least partial policy change. But there are the signs that the government also appear keen to keep radical activism out of policy-making in the future. A new Prevention of Terrorism Bill introduced in the autumn of 1999 made a broad new definition of terrorism; instead of the existing narrow 'use of violence for political ends', the bill will use 'the use of serious violence against persons or property, or the threat to use such violence to intimidate or coerce the government, the public or any section of the public for political, religious or ideological ends' (*Guardian*, 15 November 1999). Such a definition would seem to include campaigning groups such as Greenpeace, whose activists have destroyed GM crops, as well as animal rights' groups. In areas where there has been less political protest, with respect to issues of women and race, for example, then governmental activity has been minimal and reactive. There is a strong contrast between a feminist influence on political processes inside the Labour party before the election of 1997 and the strange silence of the party on the subject while in government. And only the death of Stephen Lawrence and other victims of racial violence seem able to pierce new Labour's colour blindness. The Internet emerges as fertile ground for future participation of every kind. New technologies fit perfectly with the modernist enthusiasm of 'new Labour' and the government is keen to play a role. But so far the progress of government in using the web to create 'open-book' governance, to raise its profile in social and informational networks and to transform its interactions with citizens has been well behind that of private companies, citizens and pressure groups.

# Chapter 12

# Citizenship and Culture

ELIZABETH FRAZER[1]

When the Labour government took office many individuals and groups
had high hopes and expectations of a change of approach and legal reform
in the area of citizenship. There are competing notions of 'citizenship',
however, and one aim of this chapter is to analyze what ministers and their
supporters, interested groups and the general public mean by the concept.
A related issue is whether the government's policy innovations really
promise to deliver the hoped-for changes.

Many link citizenship reform to a need for change in British political
culture. 'Culture' refers to aspects of social life to do with aesthetics (or
judgements of what is beautiful), values (what is thought to be good) and
the way these relate to typical patterns of interaction and association
between individuals. These include distinctive ways of relating cuisine and
eating, art and religion, leisure and work, distributions of power and
authority and the biological basis of social life in a coherent way of life.
Different ethnic, religious, caste, social class, political, national and
occupational groups have distinct cultures that find expression in different
ways of organizing food, drink, music, work, religious observance, leisure
pursuits and aesthetic judgements. From the viewpoint of political studies,
the issue is to explore how these cultures are related to individuals' and
groups' political identities and practices. A second aim of the chapter is,
then, to analyze what aspects of British political culture critics hope to
change, and the likelihood that these changes will flow from the policy
innovations that are proposed and under way.

## The death and funeral of Diana, Princess of Wales

To understand how ideas of citizenship and culture have been approached
by the Blair government, it is instructive to examine the public debate
surrounding the death and funeral of Diana, Princess of Wales. (The
Princess died on 31 August 1997; her funeral took place on 6 September
1997.) The press coverage was extraordinary in a number of ways. For the

203

eight days following the death of the Princess, the London broadsheet dailies dedicated 33–50 per cent of all writing, and 50–100 per cent of all pictures and graphics, to this one story. Moreover, print journalism in particular and the mass media more generally were themselves a significant aspect of the story. The Princess' relationship with writers, photographers and broadcasters, and the implications of this relationship for the Monarch and the Royal Family, for public life and political culture, were much discussed, as was press culpability in the human tragedy of the death of the Princess, her companion and their driver. Most significantly for present purposes, the story generated a wide range of comment on a number of themes not usually much addressed in the British media. The nature of the constitution, the nature of public life, the question of citizenship and issues of personal and social identity in a society and polity marked by changing sex roles and cultural diversity were all debated.

The Prime Minister set a particular tone, and can be argued to have established this agenda, with his address to the media on the morning of the Princess's death when he referred to her as 'the people's princess'. The unprecedented numbers of people who visited central London to leave flowers at Kensington Palace, to sign books of condolence, and to camp along the funeral procession route were described in the press coverage in novel and characteristic ways. The *Guardian* reported that 'Thousands inscribed their words like citizens' (*Guardian*, 8 September 1997, p. S7). The *Sunday Times* wrote that 'these people at the shrines or on the Internet are claiming a place in the public realm . . . all of them see this as the moment when they can seize a definite public role for themselves' (*Sunday Times*, 7 September 1997, p. 2). Moreover, the Royal Family was criticized, by journalists and by members of the crowds, for remaining in Scotland rather than coming to London, for wanting a 'private' rather than a 'state' funeral, for planning a short funeral procession rather than a long one and for sticking to protocol in the matter of flag flying at the Royal residences. Paddy Ashdown, then Liberal Democrat leader, argued that it was a symbolic change in which people had started behaving like 'citizens rather than subjects' in their demands on the Royal Family (*Guardian*, 8 September 1997 p. S4). From a Conservative political viewpoint, however, such 'citizenship' looked more like 'mob rule' (*Daily Telegraph*, 5 September 1997, p. 1).

The Princess' appeal and commitment to cultural diversity were also much commented on. So, too, was the way she had been part of the movement to disrupt an established gender order, bringing the institutions of masculine heterosexuality, upper-class marriage and formal styles of parenting into disrepute (*Independent* 1 September 1997, pp. 1, 9; *Guardian* 1 September 1997, pp. 19, 20). Among her best friends were many gay people. She was acknowledged as an important figure in the propulsion of 'feminine' rather than 'masculine' values into public life. Her determination to encounter, at a truly human level, people on the margins of society – the sick, the homeless, the poor – was much remarked on (*Guardian*, 1 September 1997, pp. 18, 19; *The Times*, 1 September 1997, pp. 1, 25).

Commentators agreed that Diana's life and death had modelled important political themes, including the intertwining of personal and domestic life with public matters and politics and the integration of marginal people into public life. The role of the Royal Family as the model family was energetically questioned, and the convention (or, more strongly, constitutional requirement) that those close to the monarch should be studiously neutral on policy matters also. The mass participation in grief, and the role of the crowds on the streets of London in influencing the style and organization of the funeral, were widely interpreted as a direct response, by the people and their tribunes, to the life and death of Diana and all she stood for, in a way that by-passed or even subverted established political culture and the constitution.

It was also widely commented that the Labour government, and especially the Prime Minister, were implicated in Diana's politics and in her political legacy. On the one hand, the key motif here was populism. The Labour government's landslide general election victory, followed so quickly by the unprecedented crowds in London after the Princess's death, and the largest television audience in history watching the funeral, were striking simply because of their scale, and because of the suggestion of 'people power' and mass presence in public spaces. But the language of citizenship, was also prominent, as was discussion of the shift in political culture that seemed to be marked by these events.

The response to and comment on the death of the Princess of Wales were, then, very significant:

- Ideals of and hopes for change in political culture were articulated very clearly by newspaper editors and leading commentators
- The role of the press and other mass media in modern democratic societies was questioned
- The idea that ordinary people should participate in public life was acted out
- The facts and values of cultural diversity, femininity, and humanity itself (all understood as values that were embodied in the Princess's life and in her death) came to the forefront of political discussion
- Theories and arguments about citizenship and democratic political culture that had been made in academic and policy circles for some years were discussed in a concentrated and extensive fashion, in a supremely practical and concrete context, in the pages of newspapers.

## Models of citizenship

What citizenship means, whether it is a 'good thing', and what social, economic and legal conditions have to be in place if people are truly to be citizens, are all controversial questions.

### Vague ideas of citizenship

In fact, citizenship is somewhat anomalous in mainstream British political culture, and in the context of the British political system and constitution. Research during the 1980s (Conover, Crewe and Searing, 1991) and 1990s (Hahn, 1998; Wilkins, 1999) found British respondents to be vague about the meaning of 'citizenship' compared to their counterparts in other European countries and the US. Some respondents thought of it as a vaguely foreign idea. As one respondent said, 'I [don't want] to be a citizen, I [want] to be a subject' (Citizenship Foundation, 1997, p. 4). Others thought of it as linked with a variety of Britishness they found repellent: 'disgusted of Tunbridge Wells', 'stiff upper lip and bowler hat' (Wilkins, 1999, p. 225). For most people, though, insofar as citizenship has any meaning, it is not to be distinguished from nationality. This of course signals a set of rights (to residence, most notably) and to protections by the state, that are available to some but not all people. In connection with migration and settlement, and requests for asylum, this aspect of citizenship has long been politically highly sensitive.

### Conservative citizenship

The Conservative governments and their supporters promoted the idea of citizenship from time to time in the 1980s and 1990s, (Harris, 1989; Hurd, 1989; Taylor, 1992; Cabinet Office, 1991) but associated it with a specific and limited range of social roles and institutions:

- *The identity of 'consumer'*: this was explicit in the 'Citizen's Charter' promulgated in 1991, which emphasized people's rights vis-à-vis public agencies that supplied goods and services to them
- *Individual self-reliance*: the language of citizenship was used by some Conservative politicians to promote the ideals of self-sufficiency in the provision of health, social insurance, education and housing
- *Kinship and family responsibilities*: and, to a lesser extent, responsibilities to neighbours and other members of 'the community'
- *British nationality*: the right to hold a British passport and to reside within the UK, and the concomitant obligation to be patriotic.

## New democratic citizenship

In explicit opposition to these ideas a range of political thinkers and organizations developed a new view of politics and citizenship. Theoretically, this grew out of the large body of academic literature on the ideals of civil society (Keane, 1988), multi-cultural society, (Young, 1990; Kymlicka (ed.), 1995, Kymlika 1995) and participatory democracy (Barber, 1984; Cohen, 1989, 1998). The main features of this alternative model of citizenship are as follows:

- *Civil associations and their members,* as well as individual voters and consumers, and established governmental institutions, are proper participants in government – that is, their needs must be taken into account and their voices must play a part in decision-making.
- Therefore, *communities* are an important focus for policy development and administration. There are two aspects to this. First is the important ethical and political principle that people are fundamentally related to each other, and that the persons so related constitute a whole, an 'us', to which each is committed. This idea became politically significant as a criticism of the individualism that was widely understood to be the defining characteristic of Conservative ideology in the 1980s and 1990s. Second is the more pragmatic idea that the realization of such social policy aims as the improvement of neighbourhoods, reduction of crime, delivery of welfare services and provision of leisure, housing and education, necessitates the involvement of members of the relevant communities, in both policy development and policy implementation (Tam, 1998).
- A *multi-cultural society* encompassing and incorporating many different ways of life and social identities is possible and desirable (Kymlicka, 1995; Young, 1990). This kind of pluralism has, in some traditions of political thought and practice, been thought to be inconsistent with stability. Such theories, of course, underpin racism and ideals of ethnic purity. By contrast, multi-culturalists argue for the ideals of 'difference within unity', and 'identity in difference'. Social, cultural and personal differences are consistent with political unity and with social cohesion. This unity and cohesion gets its strength from the vigour and values that proceed from a multi-cultural and tolerant society. An important value that has been introduced in normative political theory is 'recognition'. Individuals should not only enjoy rights and freedoms and the respect for their person that have long been cornerstones of a rights-based society. Their social identity – their religion, sexuality, ethnicity, cultural membership – should also be recognized by other social and political actors (Taylor, 1992). This extends the idea of respect for persons.

- The ideal of community also is connected with the proposal that *political power should be devolved*: to regions, cities and neighbourhoods where possible and appropriate. This is the other side of the principle that social stability and flourishing rely on the commitment and participation of people at the level as near as possible to the relevant ground.

## Debates about citizenship

We should note two distinct dimensions to these ideas of citizenship. First, there are the questions what citizenship ought to mean, and what norms should govern how citizens behave. Second, there are the questions who should be included in the category 'citizen', how widely the citizenship net should be cast and what conditions should govern entry into it.

## Culture and political culture

For analytical purposes, 'culture' can be considered a distinct realm of life, distinguished both from biological and physical constraints, and from pure economic interactions and motivations, even though all of these factors interact. Hence the understanding and status of business and market exchange can vary from one cultural group to another. Crucially, ideas about how governance should be done, and about the proper authority relations between persons, are also culturally variable.

A central concern of recent years has been the cultural, and therefore political, implications of the kind of market-oriented society associated with right-wing governments in the 1980s and 1990s. If individuals think of themselves above all as consumers, the argument goes, their cultural lives will be centred on commodity consumption, and the particular patterns of accumulation, spending and envy that this entails. Like all good market actors they will both rely on the maintenance of the legal and institutional framework that guarantees their freedom of contract, and will leave maintenance of this to others, such as politicians and judges. That is, they will not take on political responsibility. Democratic theorists are also concerned about other cultural traits that might be connected with political disengagement. If people's cultural lives emphasize and underscore their difference from those who typically have political power, that can reinforce any disinclination to participate politically. Hence, the cultural aspects of class and stratification are more politically relevant than some political theorists and scientists have thought. If people have broadly fatalistic beliefs about the social world, again this will have political consequences. Democratic theorists argue that citizens must take responsibility for political decision-making, as well as for their personal economic choices, and for other aspects of their ways of life. Otherwise the way is open to authoritarian and unjust rule, for democracy is a fragile good. But robust democracy will involve changes in the way people spend their time, the kinds of associations and relationships they participate in, what they value and prefer and how they relate to others.

It is difficult to talk straightforwardly about British political culture. On the one hand, the British constitution has some clear features that have been identified by many critics and policy-makers as constraints on energy and vitality in political life. These include the fact that, as critics tirelessly point out, traditionally 'we are not citizens, but subjects' (Barnett, 1997). The uncodified nature of the British constitution means that when people assert their rights they tend to be on much shakier ground than their counterparts in, say, the US. Many critics are concerned about the centralization of political power that seemed to accelerate during the Conservative administrations, and about the shift of governmental power to individuals and bodies that were not democratically accountable.

These constitutional characteristics can be connected with a tendency evident from interview research for British people to be vague about political ideas, and to express broadly antipathetic sentiments and views about politics as a process (Frazer, 2000b). They have also been connected with declining turnouts in local and national elections, and with declining memberships of political parties. A number of concerned organizations point above all to what appears to be increasing apathy and cynicism on the part of young people (Hansard Society, n.d.), and declining levels of trust in government and in others (Hall, 1999, p. 453). In contrast, increased signs of organization and increased levels of activity among fascist and racist groups, which seem disproportionately to attract members from younger age groups, have also contributed to anxiety (Hansard Society, n.d.).

It must be said that evidence for a decline in democratic political engagement is questionable. Undoubtedly there have been changes. But declining membership of parties is offset by increased membership of and allegiance to other political organizations, such as pressure and campaigning groups (Hall, 1999, p. 421; Roker, Player and Coleman, 1999, pp. 186–9). Decline in voting might not indicate a decline in other forms of activism (such as letter-writing, attending meetings, participating in campaigns, and so on). For many people, voting is the only political activity they engage in (Parry, Moyser and Day, 1992, p. 229). So if these 'only-voters' do not turn out at elections that might not impact at all on forms of participation that are more significant from a political culture point of view. And in comparative perspective, UK election turnouts are quite respectable.

Arguments about 'the youth of today' are, as they are in every decade, highly dubious. Some influential individuals argued before the Labour government took office that there is a genuine cohort effect at work, that the politically apathetic, cynical and amoral young people of today are going to age into the politically apathetic, cynical and amoral middle-aged and old people of tomorrow (Wilkinson and Mulgan, 1995). However, no evidence was offered in support of this contention. More importantly, recent analysis indicates that membership of associations, and activity outside the home, has not declined in the UK as it has in the US (Hall, 1999). While all democrats should be uneasy about the organizational success of a number of fascist and racist groups, it does seem that their culture and campaigns are at least counterbalanced by organizational capacity on the part of more democratically and just minded individuals.

Notwithstanding these empirical and interpretative grounds for caution, there was a widespread idea, voiced by academics, members of campaigning groups and politicians, that apathy, cynicism, disengagement and anti-democratic activity were signs that British political culture needed to be transformed or at least rejuvenated. Certainly, from the viewpoint of ideal democratic theory, British political culture leaves a lot to be desired. References to the need for a change of culture are ubiquitous in government documents and speeches on constitutional reform, the criminal law, education, welfare, housing and even transport.

Of course, Britain is a complex society, with diverse regions and localities incorporating the distinct national groups of Irish, English, Welsh and Scots people, and with variation in patterns of participation between social classes, between age groups and birth cohorts, and between ethnic and religious groups. Patterns of political culture are not uniform. Most obviously, antipathy to rule from Westminster is more pronounced in some regions than others. The 1997 general election results from Scotland and Wales were widely interpreted not only as evidence of geographical unevenness in dislike of the Conservative governments, but more strongly as evidence of Scotland's and Wales's claim to distinctiveness, culturally and politically. The Labour government was ready from the outset to respond to this claim with referendums and plans to devolve political power to the national assemblies.

As we have seen, the view that young people in particular are worryingly apolitical attracts wide assent. Education for citizenship and teaching democracy in schools were an aspect of the government's earliest policy proposals. The social, political and legal reactions to the murder of black teenager Stephen Lawrence were, by his own account, prominent in the Home Secretary's consciousness when he took office. An enquiry into the murder and its legal, political and social aftermath was set up (Home Office, 1999a, 1999b) and the Home Secretary published an action plan and committed himself to chairing a steering group to oversee the various policy changes involved in moving towards a racially just society and polity (Home Office, 1999c). The government's agenda also includes measures to emphasize the citizenship of gay men and lesbians by addressing inequalities in civil rights, and by tackling harassment and exclusion. The citizenship rights and powers of women as a group have been mentioned in connection with proposals and policies on childcare and employment. The government recognizes what political theorists and sociologists have found: for women, to a greater extent than for men, domestic life is a barrier to participation in public life.

## Citizenship and political culture in Labour government policy

Obviously, it is too early to say whether this normative model of citizenship, culture and politics will be genuinely realized in practice. In addition to gaps between what is said and what is done, legislative and administrative processes can have perverse effects and unintended consequences. Undoubtedly, within dominant formations such as capitalist business and the bureaucracy there are vested interests opposed to the kind of citizenship participation visioned in these ideas.

However, the government itself seems to be echoing a message that has become ubiquitous in critical political and social theory. Issues of citizenship and diversity cannot be addressed simply through formal legal rights and administrative reform. Changes in culture require non-legislative levers, and also what has come to be known ubiquitously, in one of new Labour's watchwords, as 'joined-up government'. At the level of documentation, at least, it is notable that there are numerous cross-references. The discussion document on the national curriculum mentions the Stephen Lawrence Inquiry. The education White Paper mentions the work of the Cabinet Office Social Exclusion Unit. Crime and Disorder Partnerships rely on developments in local government, and on gay men and lesbians being recognized and having their rights fully defended. (See, for instance, Cabinet Office, Better Regulation Task Force, 1999a.) However, limitations and obstacles have arisen.

In any case, use of the language of citizenship and democratic political culture is notable in its own right for at least two reasons. First, the language used in current policy debate shapes future policy debate: some people will be opposed to these ideas of citizenship, some will think they do not go far enough, some will be prompted to develop new ideas about the realisation of citizenship. Second, of course, the ideals of citizenship and democratic political culture can then be used as yardsticks against which to judge government performance, and as the basis for critical opposition to government and other power holders.

## Rights, freedoms and diversity

The documents and discussion surrounding many areas of reform emphasize the importance of multi-cultural values, racism awareness, valuing cultural diversity and promoting racial harmony. These themes can be understood as attempts discursively both to change the meaning and to extend the net of citizenship so as to include as full citizens individuals and groups who in the past have been either excluded altogether or marginalized.

One result of government reaction to Stephen Lawrence's murder is that the Crime and Disorder Act 1998 introduced new assault, harassment and public order offences. Where it can be shown that the offence is 'racially aggravated' significantly higher maximum penalties apply. This measure followed consultation via a document *Racial Violence and Harassment* (Home Office, 1997b) in which a number of issues were canvassed including concern 'whether the public order law was adequate in scope to tackle low level racial harassment'.

The Sexual Orientation Discrimination Bill sought to extend the scope of the Sex Discrimination Act to make discrimination in employment of, and in certain aspects of the provision of goods and services to, gay people illegal. This House of Lords Bill in the event ran out of parliamentary time. Subsequently a Liberal Democratic Party amendment to the Employment Relations Bill to address discrimination against gay men and lesbians, was not accepted by the government. Equalizing the age of consent for homosexual men has also been a difficult issue. Police forces are extremely reluctant to prosecute individuals for homosexual relations between the ages of 16 and 18, so a legislative change can be seen as ironing out an obvious anachronism. Yet the Sexual Offences (Amendment) Bill was defeated in the House of Lords on this issue. The clause was subsequently dropped by the government so that the rest of the Bill (which contained important legislation in connection with the protection of vulnerable young people) could pass. Reform of the Lords means that a new Bill should become law in 2000.

Some problems in the pursuit of rights, freedoms and diversity have been revealed. First, the symbolic power of laws is every bit as important as their substance; laws are crucial for their power to recognize certain kinds of people as worthy of protection, and to articulate the worth of certain kinds of relations between persons. And symbols attract as much passion as actual exercises of coercive power. Just because a legal change, on the face of it, brings the letter of the law into line with established practice (as with the age of consent for gay men), does not mean that it will not be fought tooth and nail by opponents. Second, harassment and intolerance are pervasive social phenomena which are, as the Home Secretary observes, most significant in their 'low level' manifestations. Yet attempts to address their 'low level pervasiveness' by targeting racial harassment together with harassment on the grounds of religious intolerance or homophobia, were specifically excluded in order not to dilute the message about racism (Cabinet Office, Better Regulation Think Tank, 1999a). Third, the attempt to incorporate the proscription of discrimination on the grounds of sexual orientation into the Employment Relations Bill was rejected because, while the Trade and Industry Minister acknowledged the need for legislation he said it was rightfully the responsibility of the Department of Education and Employment. So much for 'joined-up government'.

Soon after the government took office, the Cabinet Office Freedom of Information Unit published the White Paper *Your Right to Know* (Cabinet office, 1997), which associated hitherto excessive secrecy in British government with the public's decline of confidence in politics and government, and envisioned more open government as more accountable and in keeping with the aims of a revitalised citizenship. The White Paper announced that a draft bill would be published in the following year. However this did not happen, seemingly because of disagreement within government circles about the advisability and scope of freedom of information legislation. Critics believe that even the most progressive governments have a vested interest in protecting themselves from scrutiny and interference. A consultation paper on draft legislation was published, by the Home Office, in May 1999 (Home office, 1999d), which was said by critics to be more conservative overall, with a wider range of exempted institutions, and the power given to the Home Secretary to create additional exemptions.

Perhaps the single most significant piece of legislation, from the point of view of changing British political culture, is the Human Rights Bill which effectively incorporated the European Convention for the Protection of Human Rights and Fundamental Freedoms (EHCR) into British law. The Government's White Paper emphasized that the very ideas of 'rights and freedoms' have a British pedigree: 'It is language which echoes right down the corridors of history. It goes deep into our history and as far back as Magna Carta' (Home Office, 1997a). The idea that the Bill was 'bringing rights back home' was ubiquitous in the debates in the House of Lords and the House of Commons. Another prominent theme articulated by supporters of the Bill in these debates was that the legislation would 'create a culture of rights'.

However, it was notable that the journalists who reported and commented on this Bill and the relevant debates were preoccupied above all with potential clashes between citizens' rights to privacy and the press's right to freedom of speech and expression. Other rights – to marry, to be free of discrimination on grounds such as sex and race, to education – attracted little interest in the press. The view that the government wished to promote about the relationship between rights and citizenship was not, on this occasion, developed by journalists and commentators, because journalists and commentators were interested, above all, in the implications of the Bill for their own profession.

## Citizenship and migration

The government's approach to race relations and its commitment to valuing a diverse society have been explicitly connected with its approach to immigration and asylum by ministers. In the Preface to the relevant White Paper (Home Office, 1998b), the Home Secretary made reference to the Human Rights Bill in an effort to emphasize the government's commitment to anti-racism and human rights. One chapter was dedicated to a discussion of citizenship. Here it was spelled out that citizenship means not only nationality but also 'encompasses elements of involvement and participation, and sharing of rights and responsibilities'. Rights are not dependent upon citizenship in the sense of British nationality; migrants and temporary inhabitants also enjoy civil rights. But citizenship in this sense is declared to be 'a mark of [people's] integration into British society'. The White Paper emphasized that individuals can have multiple citizenships: 'we recognize that in the modern world, as well as owing an allegiance to the country in which they live, people also retain an affinity to the country of their roots. It is therefore possible to be a citizen of two countries and a good citizen of both' (Home Office, 1998b, p. 45). The Home Office also granted another significant concession. Where a couple have been living together for two years, including where they are 'legally unable to marry', the Home Office now grants residence rights to foreign partners. Thus implicitly the Home Office declares that it is possible to be a lesbian or gay [foreign] 'good citizen'.

The issue of asylum and immigration, though, raises in a very acute form the question not so much whether foreigners can be good citizens, but what 'good citizenship' entails in the way of attitudes to migrants. Conflict between existing residents and incoming asylum seekers in the summer of 1999 made some discursive facts abundantly clear. Evidently it makes perfect sense to many English and British citizens that the presence of 'too many' people who have a distinctive appearance, or speak languages other than English, living in a city or town justifies violence.

## Community

The language of community is peculiarly prominent within Labour government discourse. The Blairite notion of the 'Third Way' emphasizes collective group power, a theme that is ubiquitous in government consultation documents, White Papers and Bills. The Cabinet Office Social Exclusion Unit's report on how to 'develop integrated and sustainable approaches to the problems of the worst housing estates, including crime, drugs, unemployment, community breakdown and bad schools' is entitled *Bringing Britain Together* (Cabinet Office, 1998). It is focused on communities, meaning locales and the people in them: estates and neighbourhoods. This general issue – of poor neighbourhoods, or communities where 'problem families' are allegedly concentrated – has preoccupied governments throughout the twentieth century, and since the 1960s there has been programme after programme designed to target resources, tackle social problems with multi-agency approaches, and regenerate areas. *Bringing Britain Together* identifies a number of weaknesses in past programmes. They have been resourced for too short a time, undermined by some departments of state as they are supported by others ('joined-up government', again), and above all have failed to involve communities, although the need to do this is something of a commonplace and lip service has been paid to the principle.

The 'New Deal for Communities' is a programme to support locally organized projects by networks of voluntary organizations, public agencies, local authorities, businesses and local people to tackle issues like the coordination of management of an area and its public service, crime, employment, and environmental damage and degradation. It has been funded over three years (which hardly seems an improvement on previous short-term projects). A recurrent problem with state–voluntary sector arrangements has been that short-term funding for projects sets in train a perverse process whereby project workers have to spend significant amounts of resources on fundraising and securing the project, so that survival of the organization becomes the major mark of its 'success'.

'Sure Start' is a programme to support young children in deprived neighbourhoods, with programmes for 0–3 year olds aimed at having long-term effects on truancy levels, health awareness and educational attainment. The government has also implemented a series of 'action zones' – Employment Action Zones, Education Action Zones and Health Action Zones – which target needy areas with the relevant resources. In addition, the Single Regeneration Budget, introduced by the Conservative government, has been 'revamped to concentrate on areas of severe need, to give greater support to community development and involvement', and to complement the zones and the New Deal for Communities (Cabinet

Office, 1998, pp. 54–6). In addition, 18 teams cutting across 10 Whitehall departments have been instituted to report on a range of issues relevant to poor neighbourhoods, such as jobs, skills, business, neighbourhood and housing management, anti-social behaviour, leisure and educational provision.

Community involvement is also a stated aim, and a means of achieving aims, in other areas of government policy. The Crime and Disorder Act 1998 places a statutory duty on chief police officers and local authorities to work together to develop and implement strategies to reduce crime and disorder; gives the Secretary of State power to order the cooperation of bodies such as police authorities, health authorities and others, and gives her or him the power also to specify particular bodies or agencies which the responsible authorities must invite to participate in the process. It is envisaged that a range of community organizations and agencies, such as Drugs Action Teams, Drugs Reference Groups, Neighbourhood Watch Groups, Tenants' and Residents' groups and associations, Victim Support, ethnic minority and religious organizations, Councils for Voluntary Service, Racial Equality Councils and others will be involved in the formulation and implementation of crime and disorder strategies. It is hoped that these will coordinate the strategies and efforts of these organizations. At the local level, this policy has resulted in the formulation of 'crime and disorder strategies', which on paper reinforce the themes of community, citizenship and culture. For example, the Oxford strategy document sets out 'six priority areas for action, with an overriding theme of citizenship' (Atmosphere, 1999).

The *Guidance on Local Transport Plans* issued by the Department of the Environment, Transport and the Regions (DETR, 1998e) holds that measures must be acceptable to 'the local community' and suggests that local authorities should 'join with parish councils, community groups and other voluntary organizations in rural transport partnerships'. The DETR has also produced a series of discussion documents and consultation papers on the future of local government, all of which argue that government must be 'brought back to the people'.

The Department for Education and Employment also puts the themes of community and citizenship at the centre of its discussion. The White Paper *Excellence in Schools* (1997a) included commitments to promote schools' relationships and ties with the 'wider community': their neighbourhood, local businesses and civic associations as well as the families of pupils. It also includes a commitment to promote 'mentoring': the establishment of relationships between school children and adults who are not kin, but who will take an interest in and a measure of responsibility for a young person's educational progress and career. *Excellence in Schools* insists that it is proposing nothing short of 'creating a new culture in this country' (p. 3).

Most importantly, the White Paper makes a commitment to promoting and developing education for citizenship and the teaching of democracy, topics that are said to have been 'neglected' by schools (p. 63). Following the White Paper, the Secretary of State for Education established an Advisory Group on Citizenship to make a statement of the 'aims and purposes of citizenship education in schools' and to establish 'a broad framework of what good citizenship education in schools might look like, and how it can be successfully delivered' (Advisory Group on Citizenship, 1998). The recommendations of the working party have been accepted, and a discussion document on reform of the national curriculum, and subsequently the curriculum document, have been published (Department for Education and Employment, 1999, DfEE and Qualifications and Curriculum Authority, 1999). The media response to this provided an interesting example of the lack of salience in mainstream political culture of the concept of 'citizenship'. Broadcast journalists seemed unable to make much of the idea of citizenship education: discussion of the Secretary of State's announcement vaguely featured issues such as 'relationships', 'voluntary work', and 'spirituality'. By contrast, the Secretary of State himself, David Blunkett, seems to be committed to a robustly political model of citizenship, arguing that young people must be educated about democracy to understand how government works, and to participate in social and political organisations.

## Summary

A remarkable feature of the output of policy documentation from government departments since 1997 is the pervasiveness of a number of distinctive themes:

- *Culture*: It is acknowledged that 'cultural change' is required, and stated that this will be promoted in government policy regarding rights, education, poverty, local government and environment. The government wants to promote a 'culture of learning', a 'culture of rights', a 'change of culture within the public sector' in connection with freedom of information.
- *Community*: The government declares itself to be committed to promoting formal and informal links between the associations and organizations that are part of the different sectors of civil society – cultural, religious, educational, local, political, commercial; to promoting the ideal of community; and above all to involving communities at every stage in policy development and policy execution and administration.

- *Citizenship*: This is held to be an identity involving political rights and political participation: the right to vote but also the right to participate more fully in governance in and through a range of local and civil organizations such as schools, neighbourhoods, ethnic associations and voluntary bodies. Citizens, then, need to be educated in the ways of democracy, and to understand the constitution, institutions and laws of the polity in which they live.
- *Diversity*: Valuing cultural diversity, combating racism, promoting racism awareness and racial harmony are mentioned again and again in documents concerned with domestic policy. Citizenship is consistent with cultural, ethnic and religious diversity among citizens; and British citizenship is consistent with also being a national or a citizen of another country.

## Conclusion

The language of citizenship, and the proposal that revitalized citizenship requires changes in political culture, have been prominent in government policy discussions and proposals since May 1997. However, a number of problems with the realization of this aspiration to citizenship and revitalized political culture have been identified:

- government departmental barriers to 'joined-up government'
- vested social interests opposed to the inclusion of hitherto excluded, marginalized and otherwise weak groups
- continuing vagueness about the concept of 'citizenship' in such forums as the press and broadcast media
- continuing short-termism in funding 'community projects'.

Changing culture means changing individuals' patterns of relationships, their perception of their interests, as well as governmental administration. Whether these transformations can be realized remains to be seen.

## Note

I would like to thank Robert Kaye for assistance with collecting documents. I am particularly indebted to Debbie Gupta who read a draft of this chapter, and offered valuable critical comments on my interpretation of the material and suggested further sources. I have incorporated a number of her suggestions in the final version; responsibility for the selection and interpretation of material is, of course, my own.

# Chapter 13

# Economic Policy

COLIN THAIN

At the heart of new Labour's economic policy are four paradoxes. The first concerns the freedom of manoeuvre available to a Labour administration. Despite having an unassailable majority in the House of Commons and with it the capacity to adopt a more activist macroeconomic policy, the Chancellor, Gordon Brown, has removed from the Treasury's control a key instrument of economic policy management – monetary policy – and handed it to a reconstituted Bank of England. Brown has also gone further by creating a series of fiscal policy rules designed to restrict the room for manoeuvre in the remaining area of policy. He is the perfect model of an orthodox Minister of Finance – prudent and cautious. Such orthodoxy has extended into a domain previously reserved for the Conservative Party – commitment to liberating markets and an active competition policy. Yet this orthodoxy hides the start of a process of modest wealth and income redistribution by stealth, and the return of the goal of full employment as a cornerstone of economic strategy.

The second paradox involves Labour's traditional commitment to the welfare state (see Chapter 14). Despite its majority, the possibility of increasing public expenditure in areas crucial to the welfare state has been replaced by the tightest control mechanism imposed on Whitehall departments since the 1970s. At the same time the Comprehensive Spending Review (CSR) produced headline-grabbing stories of unprecedented plans to increase investment in schools and hospitals over the lifetime of the Parliament.

The third paradox is that an administration committed in some policy areas to decentralization and devolution has presided over a growth of Treasury power and influence quite unprecedented in the post-war era. Brown has wrought a quiet revolution in economic policy and in the role of the Treasury in UK central government. He has been given free rein to transform the Treasury as a Ministry of Finance *and* engine of economic and social policy reform. Giving power resources to the Bank of England has freed the Treasury to focus on other policy areas, and here Brown has shaped the Treasury in his image, to perform roles suited to his agenda for reform across the range of government policies.

The final paradox involves external economic policy-making. Under Brown, the Treasury has been a leading advocate of increased labour market flexibility and deregulation in an EU dominated by Social Democrat-led governments still committed to the Rhine Social Market model. A practical and ideological battle has been joined between the Blairite/Brown version of the Third Way (Blair, 1998b; Giddens, 1998), a transatlantic concept (Blumenthal, 1997) attempting to square social democracy and liberalism, and the rearguard defence of the Social Market model championed in Europe by the French (see Chapter 2). At the same time, Blair and Brown have tentatively moved the UK closer to joining the single European currency by stating a commitment in principle to joining, outlining a set of policy tests, and formulating a national changeover plan. The same Treasury has led an emerging international consensus to give debt relief to the world's poorest developing nations.

## Policy rules: limiting the room for manoeuvre

There are large elements of continuity between the macroeconomic policies of the Major and Blair administrations. What is different now is that the Treasury under Brown has moved to codify and consolidate an economic framework that seeks deliberately to limit the room for manoeuvre in large areas of policy. Rules have replaced discretion in ways not seen since the early years of the medium-term financial strategy (MTFS) in 1980. The MTFS was an attempt to impose a monetarist framework on Whitehall policy-making through money supply targets, reductions in public borrowing and public expenditure. Policy learning has taken place, with the Chancellor determined to remove policy-makers' responsibility for accentuating economic cycles. His policy statements have stressed the need for long-termism, avoiding 'stop–go' policies and providing stability and predictability. Technocratic solutions to policy problems are preferred. Brown's version of medium-term financial planning involves three elements: creating a new permanent monetary policy framework; setting out fiscal policy rules; and a new medium-term public expenditure planning regime. The core rationale for this is to promote policy stability and transparency so as to regain financial market confidence that UK policy-makers are locked into a long-term anti-inflation strategy. It represents a further move of Labour to accept the economic orthodoxy previously championed by governments of the right. Policy goals for reducing unemployment, redistributing income and investing in public services have to be achieved within the constraints imposed by this, or by using microeconomic tools.

## Ceding control of monetary policy

The new government's period in office began with the most radical and unexpected revolution in the way in which UK economic policy is managed. Within four days of moving into the Treasury, the Chancellor announced he was ceding operational control of setting interest rates to the Bank of England. For the first time in its history, the Bank would be given responsibility for achieving an inflation target set by the Chancellor and would be free to adjust interest rates in order to achieve this. Other changes in the division of responsibility between the major economic policy institutions of the UK state were also announced.

The decision to change the balance of power between the two institutions had a long gestation period. The Chancellor's economic team had discussed it during the previous three years (Pym and Kochan, 1998). The intellectual guiding light was the Chancellor's economics adviser and former *Financial Times* journalist, Ed Balls. The then Shadow Chancellor had a seminal meeting with the Chairman of the US Federal Reserve in March 1997, at which Brown was 'impressed again by the arguments for an independent central bank on the American model' (Pym and Kochan, 1998, p. 8). Blair agreed in principle and left the timing and details to Brown. The decision to institute the changes was conveyed in a letter from the Chancellor to the Governor of the Bank of England (Bank of England, 1997). These were subsequently enshrined in legislation amending the Bank of England Act 1946 (Treasury, 1999b). The arrangements involved changing the framework within which monetary policy would be set and changes in the Bank's objectives and structure.

The Bank of England was given the objective of ensuring price stability as defined by an inflation target set by the Chancellor, currently 2.5 per cent. This is as defined by RPIX (retail price change *less* the impact of mortgage interest payments). The target is symmetric, meaning that the Bank is required to act as robustly if inflation is likely to under-shoot, as it is if inflation is rising. Without prejudicing this overall objective, the Bank is expected to support the government's other economic objectives for growth and employment. This makes the arrangements closer to the US model than that of the German Bundesbank. The Bank has been given operational control of interest rates in order to achieve the inflation target, and is expected to publish a quarterly report outlining its analysis and justifying its policy actions. Only in extreme emergencies can the Treasury reimpose control over interest rates, and to do so it will have to obtain legislative approval from Parliament.

In order to discharge this new responsibility, the Bank was reconstituted. A new Monetary Policy Committee (MPC) was created. The Governor, two Deputy Governors and six additional members now take decisions on interest rate policy. The Treasury has the right to send an observer with non-voting rights. The Chancellor appoints the non-Bank members of the committee. The MPC meets on a regular monthly basis. In a further move to ensure that the new arrangements would be transparent, the Chancellor announced that the Bank would be accountable to the House of Commons through regular reporting to the Treasury Committee. In addition, minutes of the meetings of the MPC would be released no more than six weeks after each meeting.

Most of the anomalies of UK economic policy-making have revolved around the way in which the Bank of England's historic role has left it as the government's banker, responsible for managing borrowing and debt, regulating the financial system, ensuring the stability of the financial system and acting as the Treasury's agent in adjusting interest rates and intervening in the foreign exchange markets. Many of these roles are seen as potentially in conflict, especially regulating the financial system while being the guarantor of its stability. Brown's reforms dealt with these anomalies, too. The Bank's responsibility for supervising the banking system was transferred to a new Securities and Investment Board (SIB), and the Treasury took over responsibility for managing the government's debt, selling gilts and managing cash in the economy. Determining the exchange rate regime remains one of the Treasury's roles, although the Bank is allowed to keep some foreign exchange reserves for use in pursuit of its monetary objectives, and the Treasury continues to use the Bank as its agent in intervening on the foreign exchange markets.

Taken together, these changes represent a major shift in UK economic policy-making. Simultaneously the Chancellor took monetary policy out of party-political control and moved the UK closer to the stipulation of the Maastricht Treaty that the central bank be independent. The rationale was that by removing the control of interest rates from the Treasury, economic policy would be transparent, open and consistent. This would provide a stable background for business to plan and invest. The Chancellor was by implication accepting the prevailing wisdom that independent central banks are trusted by financial markets and therefore likely to produce lower rates of interest than would prevail if political control remained with the Treasury.

## The policy record

In its early years the MPC did not have an easy ride from either financial analysts or manufacturing industry. Ultimately, its success will be measured by whether inflation has remained at the target level. The Treasury asserts that average inflation has been 2.6 per cent since the Bank was given operational control (Figure 13.1). Methodologically it is difficult to ascertain whether this is due to the monetary policy framework, previous government policies, or benign conditions reducing inflationary pressures. A second measure of success is equally problematic to assess – whether inflationary expectations have been changed, and whether financial markets have enough confidence in the new regime to remove the so-called 'premium' of requiring higher interest payments on sterling investments. The view from one of the most influential members of the MPC is that there is evidence that there has been an effect (King, 1999). A proxy measure for falling inflationary expectations is financial markets' assessment of future rates of inflation through the expected yield on government bonds. Since 1997 inflationary expectations have fallen on long-term bond yields and the consensus forecast for inflation of major economic analysts.

One of the most significant developments in the operational policy regime announced by the Chancellor is the setting of a symmetrical inflation target of 2.5 per cent. Under the previous Conservative administration a target of 2.5 per cent inflation *or less* meant acquiescing in inflation well below this; the MPC is charged with acting to ensure inflation does not fall too low. This is in part a defence against anti-inflationary policy becoming so tight that it affects output and jobs, and a means by which the psychological value of prices and wages rising at a

**Figure 13.1** *Inflation performance since the MPC*

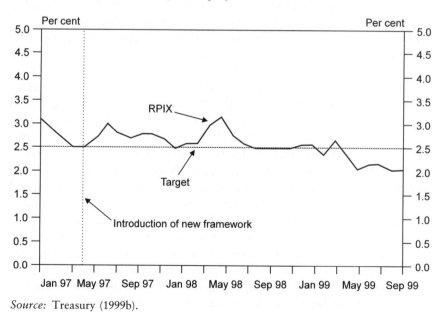

*Source:* Treasury (1999b).

reasonable pace is maintained. The commitment of the government is to stability and predictability.

## Policy debates: accountability, representativeness and transparency

Equally important has been the emergence of debates about the way in which the MPC operates. The British model has more in common with the US Federal Reserve than with the dominant EU model of the Bundesbank. The MPC as a whole is accountable for the achievement of the inflation target, and failure to achieve this triggers a letter from the Governor of the Bank to the Chancellor. In addition, the Bank is required to report to the House of Commons Treasury Select Committee. Minutes of the MPC are published, as are the voting records of the nine members of the committee at the monthly meetings. Such openness has been criticized by the ECB as liable to unsettle the financial markets. Criticisms have also been levied that the MPC is too analytical and 'academic'. However, it is arguable that in order to create credibility in UK anti-inflationary policy, noted for its long-term failure, it is necessary to be transparent and risk too many debates about the individual actions of members of the committee. There is also a tension built into the system, in that although the committee as a whole is accountable for decisions, so are individual members of the committee. This makes the UK 'experiment' unique. The cultural differences between the ECB/Bundesbank model, with its relative secrecy and lack of formal mechanisms of accountability, and the emerging UK approach suggests further problems for the UK in joining the euro.

The MPC has also been criticized for its lack of representativeness. This is code for the degree to which manufacturing industry regards the new system as being biased in favour of the interests of finance capital. This is a charge with a long pedigree. The specific criticism is that the MPC has no 'representative' from industry; of the 10 individuals who have served on the MPC (Edmonds, 1999), four are from outside the Bank of England. Two are academics (Charles Goodhart a former Chief Adviser to the Governor; and Willem Buiter), one is a former Chief Economic adviser to the Treasury (Alan Budd) and only one (DeAnne Julius) has experience in commerce, being a former chief economist at British Airways and Royal Dutch Shell. The bias is also seen as geographical, with the London metropolis over-represented. Behind this concern is the fundamental issue of the degree to which the exchange rate has been higher against the euro in part because interest rates have been higher. In unravelling the threads of these criticisms, it is clear that although the membership of the MPC and its rules of engagement can be justified as performing the single role of containing inflation, there remains an element of conflict over the protection of City interests over those of manufacturing capital. Moreover, the new monetary regime may have set anti-inflation policy on a more rational footing, but the 'problem' of sterling's volatility is not going to be resolved until it joins the single currency, and only then with potential costs in terms of other policy objectives. Conflicting policy objectives have not been removed by the new rules introduced by Brown, only reshaped and taken out of party political debate.

## Fiscal policy rules

Without the exigencies of a financial crisis or a collapse of economic strategy, the Chancellor announced a *Code for Fiscal Stability* in 1998 (Treasury, 1998c). This was a further example of embedding into policy-making the emergent Anglo–Saxon consensus on economic orthodoxy. The code set out five principles governing the conduct of fiscal policy: transparency in the setting of objectives and the reporting of progress; stability in policy processes and in the degree to which fiscal policy impacted on the real economy; responsibility in the management of public finances; fairness between generations (that is, not allowing current borrowing to be paid for by future generations); and efficiency in the design and implementation of fiscal policy. The code committed the Treasury to producing a pre-budget report and an Economic and Fiscal Strategy Report (EFSR) in addition to the usual budget documents. The EFSR crucially was intended to set out long-term strategy, assess short-term developments, determine the extent to which these were consistent with EU commitments and produce long-term economic projections. For the first time the National Audit Office (NAO) was charged with auditing the assumptions and conventions underlying the projections made.

In practical terms, this represented an incremental development of the approach adopted by Chancellor Kenneth Clarke, being a codification of previously implicit rules. Substantively, the Treasury committed itself to abiding by the 'golden rule' (Treasury, 1998a) that current expenditure is covered by taxation and any borrowing is only to fund investment. Two qualifications further constrain policy: that investment is sustainable over the economic cycle through public debt as a proportion of GDP being held stable and 'prudent'; and that the policies are consistent with the EU growth and stability pact (the component of EMU which stresses the importance of Finance Ministries containing their borrowing).

## Fiscal policy issues: stealth taxes, war chest and redistribution

The political and economic debates which have surrounded the Treasury's fiscal policy have focused on three elements. Has the tax burden increased as a result of taxing by stealth as income tax rates have been targeted for reductions? Does the Treasury have a 'war chest' of possible surpluses which can be 'spent' in a pre-election spree while still maintaining the rectitude implied by the code for fiscal stability? Is the Chancellor quietly redistributing income partly through the tax system but also through other social policies?

One of the 'ideas in good currency' which dominates the thinking of the Prime Minister, the Chancellor and their advisers is that Labour loses elections if it is ambivalent about levels of direct taxation. The mantra of 'responsible' economic management now includes a commitment to reducing the levels of direct taxation. The 1999 Budget (Treasury, 1999a) was the clearest example of this. The Chancellor announced a new starting tax rate of 10 per cent, effective from April 1999 for the first £1500 of taxable income, and a reduction in the basic rate of income tax from 23 per cent to 22 per cent from April 2000. The medium-term commitment is to increase the coverage of the 10 per cent band. These changes have been balanced by the abolition of the tax allowance on mortgage interest payments from April 2000.

These politically useful headline-grabbing reductions hide an underlying rise in the proportion of GDP taken in taxation as a whole. Figure 13.2 shows that following a dip in 2000–1, taxes as a proportion of GDP are set to rise to 37 per cent of GDP in 2002–3, a level last reached in 1988–9 under the Chancellorship of Nigel Lawson. This rise reflects higher indirect taxation such as VAT and excise duties, and higher social security payments in the form of National Insurance contributions. The Treasury under Brown is following a long-term departmental rule – to ensure that tax revenues are protected even during periods of reduction in income tax levels. There has never been a US-type policy of reducing total tax burden as measured by the proportion of GDP. The crises in public finances have been the result of higher public expenditure (mainly on social security) and reductions in revenue owing to economic recession. The Labour administration is continuing incrementally the previous government's approach of changing the balance in fiscal policy away from taxes on income to taxes on expenditure.

This approach also leads to a potential 'golden' political scenario of the Treasury being able to increase expenditure or reduce income taxes or both through the creation of a so-called 'war chest' – public finance surpluses in excess of what is required by fiscal policy 'rules'. The calculation of the amount available to the Chancellor for a pre-election fiscal boost is fraught with difficulties. Given the Chancellor's self-imposed fiscal rules, any 'surplus' would have to be in excess of the budget surpluses already built into the fiscal projections in Budget documents. The 1999 Budget outlined plans which implied surpluses on the current

**Figure 13.2**   *Tax as a proportion of GDP*

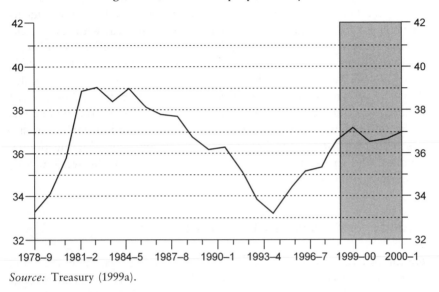

*Source:* Treasury (1999a).

budget (difference between current expenditure and tax receipts) of £4 billion in 2000–1 rising to £8 billion in the election year of 2001–2. (Treasury, 1999a). These figures imply that the UK will be comfortably inside the Maastricht criteria for joining the single currency with a *surplus* on the budget of 0.3 per cent and 0.2 per cent of GDP for each of the years 1999–2000 to 2001–2, instead of an allowed *deficit* of 3 per cent of GDP. The calculation of what is in the 'war chest' rests primarily on the degree to which Treasury has under-estimated in these plans the amount of economic growth likely over the two-year period. Higher growth increases revenues from corporation taxes and indirect taxes, tends to increase employment levels and hence income tax receipts and reduces expenditure on unemployment benefit. Surpluses depend upon high levels of growth being maintained. By this means the Chancellor will be able to fill a war chest, generating additional monies to increase expenditure or reduce taxes in any subsequent budget, something always helpful to any government keen to use the economy to help engineer its re-election.

Is the Chancellor presiding over a modest programme of redistribution? Is this a further paradox, that despite gaining a reputation for fiscal rectitude, the Chancellor has driven through Whitehall a number of initiatives that put redistribution of income back on the political agenda? Research on poverty and measures of social exclusion (Howarth *et al.*, 1999) show authoritatively that the number of people with 'very low incomes' (40 per cent of average income) increased by more than a million to 8 million in the two years to 1998; and health inequalities have worsened. The two main policy initiatives which would provide evidence that the government has a redistributive agenda to deal with these issues are the National Minimum Wage, in operation from April 1999 and set at £3.60 per hour as the minimum wage for adult workers over the age of 22 and £3.00 per hour for those between 18 and 21, and the Working Families Tax Credit which guarantees a minimum income for a family with children to £200 per week. It is difficult to assess whether this will reverse the trend to higher levels of income inequality. The Chancellor's approach has been to prioritize the importance of securing work for the poorest families, and to use the tax and benefits system to make work pay by guaranteeing income levels.

## Public spending control and targeting

On the face of it, there was not much difference between the new Labour government's Comprehensive Spending Review (CSR), unveiled through departmental letters by the then Chief Secretary, Alistair Darling, in June 1997, and the 'fundamental expenditure review' which began during Michael Portillo's stint as Chief Secretary in February 1993. Treasury officials had to consult their lexicons closely and choose an appropriately robust word, far enough away from a previous exercise, while using the same coded language. Portillo had stressed that the aim was that by the end of the Parliament all public expenditure would be subject to 'a long-term exercise involving in-depth reviews of the public spending programmes of each Department of State' and that 'it is a very important part of the fundamental reviews that they should ask the question: Is what the State is doing something which needs to be done, and, if it is something which needs to be done, is it something which needs to be done by the State?' Darling stated that the CSR 'will be focused on the long term', and will 'consider whether [spending] meets the public interest'.

The CSR appeared to be a further example of governance by policy review and a subterfuge to cover the failure to introduce a more radical spending programme than Labour had inherited. The Treasury was faced with a hard circle to square. By committing the government to Clarke's last spending plans, the Treasury team was locked into a tight envelope of overall spending whilst at the same time creating expectations that expenditure would be prioritized differently to allow scope for more spending on education and health. Both reviews carried messages from the Treasury to a wider audience. The Portillo review was a signal that post-ERM fiscal policy would be tight even though the public expenditure survey was opened up through the creation of EDX (a Cabinet Committee on public expenditure). Darling sent a signal to spending departments that the Chancellor was serious about finding scope for spending cuts. It was no accident that the CSR included the commitment to a 'thorough look at whether the best use is being made of public assets, with a view to disposing of those which are surplus'. Unlike Portillo's review, Darling's was intended to deliver quick results, inside a year. This points up the political urgency of squaring the spending circle in time for a second-term victory platform. Labour had shackled itself to the previous government's tight spending plans for next two years; yet it had pledged to increase the share of GDP going to areas such as education and health. The question was one of reshaping priorities without raising overall spending. Departments were being told to make savings from low-priority areas, to switch resources to front-line services.

There were interesting dimensions to the review. First, it represented a further flowering of the Treasury's more strategic 'hands-off' approach to spending management following the fundamental review of running costs and the creation of the Cabinet committee EDX. Essentially the reviews were undertaken by the departments, with terms of reference for each agreed in conjunction with the Treasury. A parallel exercise was conducted within the Treasury's expenditure divisions. The aim was to sign each Secretary of State up to the concept and incorporate the review into a new ordering of priorities determined by the new government's manifesto (hence far more party-political in its focus than previous Treasury exercises).

Second, the review had three components – individual departmental reviews, cross-departmental reviews and a review of the government's spending as a whole. The cross-departmental component represents an earnest attempt by a new administration to find the holy grail of inter-departmental coordination and policy cohesion. This has become part of the Prime Minister's quest for 'joined-up government'. The review of the criminal justice system, for example, envisaged cooperation between the Home Secretary, Lord Chancellor and Attorney General. Its remit called for greater partnerships between agencies and a more strategic approach towards the funding of the criminal justice system. Other reviews which cut across departmental boundaries included the review of the local government finance system (always a cause of mayhem in departmental battles), the countryside and rural policy and housing.

## Continuity and change

When the CSR (Treasury, 1998b) was published, it was notable for four reasons. First, the Treasury was reinstituting medium-term planning. The totals for expenditure for the three years of the cycle, 1999–2000 to 2001–2, were intended to be firm, unlike the incremental drift which had characterized the system to 1997 (Thain and Wright, 1995). Second, departments were to be closely monitored to see that any increases in expenditure were linked to the achievement of modernizing programmes. A new 'public service agreement' was set out between departments and the Treasury, overseen by a Cabinet committee (PSX). This represented a significant shift in power from departmental discretion to greater centralized control. There was yet another paradox here. The review itself showed the Treasury continuing with a less intrusive, more strategic role begun under Clarke. However, the spending plans which resulted would be used to ensure that the Treasury could attach more strings to resources assigned than at any time since the fiscal crisis of control in 1976. Third, the review talked the language of targeting. The Treasury was more concerned than ever with the *outputs of expenditure* – what was bought in terms of improved services – than the *inputs of resources*. Fourth, there were headline figures of increased spending in priority areas. Here the Treasury continued a long-standing approach of producing politically clever statistical tricks to show the agreed plans in the best light. In the past this had been used as subterfuge for increases which were supposed to be decreases under the mantra of Thatcherite 'public expenditure is bad'; now the process was reversed. Cash figures were used to give the appearance of a massive increase in expenditure. The White Paper talked of £19 billion for education over three years and £20 billion for the health service. In real terms, expenditure on the health service is growing by less than the average rate of growth under the Conservatives. Overall spending levels are planned to rise by the trend rate of growth of the economy as a whole, at 2.25 per cent a year. This effectively was the aim of Conservative policy-makers from the late 1980s onwards.

The challenge facing the Chancellor and Chief Secretary Andrew Smith is to cope with rising demands for increased expenditure at a time when the perception is of a significant 'war chest' available for use. Public perceptions tend to match the realities that although spending has risen on social policy priorities, these do not match the demands or accumulated pressures for increased investment in health, education and transport. Public expenditure is projected to remain under 40 per cent of GDP for the remaining years of the current Parliament, compared to nearly 42 per cent in the last full year of the Major administration. The rhetoric of higher cash figures cannot hide the reality that real levels of spending are little changed from the trends during 18 years of Conservative governments. Demographic pressures, increased costs of technology and rising public expectations of improved services, represent a public spending time bomb. Fiscal rectitude and a reputation for giving priority to the welfare state cannot forever be squared without some trade-off.

## The Treasury under Brown

### The Blair–Brown axis

The relationship between the Prime Minister and the Chancellor of the Exchequer is one of the most vital in any administration (Jenkins, 1998). There is no better example than the Blair administration. Blair's relationship with Brown cannot be described as a conventional power battle, nor as an ideological struggle, but neither can it be seen as dual-executive power. It can best be described as *managed competition*. It is unique in post-war political administration. The Blair–Brown axis has a pedigree of a close personal friendship (Routledge, 1998), and close political views from the period when both were chosen by John Smith to spearhead the further modernization of the Labour Party after he succeeded Neil Kinnock as leader in 1992. At one level this has been a singular driving force behind the rise of new Labour: Blair the popularizer of the 'Third Way', acceptable to middle-class 'middle England', Brown the engine of economic and social policy reforms giving substance to the claim to philosophical cohesion. Nevertheless, behind this coincidence of view and symbiosis, there is a personal battle built on some bitterness on the part of Brown from having given way to Blair in the leadership election to replace John Smith (Routledge, 1998; Pym and Kochan, 1998). The power battle has been by stealth and much of it by proxy, focusing on the role and position of Peter Mandelson, as a key figure in Blair's circle. What has resulted is a fascinating mix of personal rivalries, battles for control of key elements of the core executive – at the same time as considerable cooperation and coordination. Brown was given unprecedented dominance in economic policy-making by Blair, in opposition and then in government.

### Power resources, policy and control

On taking office, Brown was given enormous amounts of constitutional and political power resources as part of this deal. The Chancellor chairs the key economic committees of the Cabinet (see Chapter 6). The importance of his dominance in this sphere is underlined by the fact that two of those committees – Productivity and Welfare-to-Work – deal with policy business at the heart of the new government's domestic agenda. In total the Chancellor is a member of nine Cabinet committees, and sits on a tenth on occasion – the JCC with the Liberal Democrats.

The second element in growing Treasury power has been in the realm of public spending. Brown has continued the trend begun under Lamont and Clarke of turning the Treasury into more of a strategic controller of spending – less interested in in-year control, cheese parings and more concerned about the contribution of spending to wider objectives. Brown's particular contribution has been to shift the emphasis still further to a concern about policy outputs – what is bought with the additional expenditure – and policy outcomes – does it produce, say, better health or education? Departments now sign a *public service agreement* with the Treasury. Increases in spending are dependent on departments delivering value for money and policy improvements aimed at modernizing the public sector. The PSX committee, chaired by Brown, is charged with monitoring progress. This represents an unprecedented increase in Treasury involvement in departmental policy-making.

Third, the Treasury drives the core domestic policy-making agenda of the new Labour government, rather than playing its more traditional participant and veto roles. Welfare-to-work is a Brown initiative. Social security reform has been shaped by the Treasury and not the DSS. The 'new deal' for the young unemployed is seen as representing the Chancellor's brand of radicalism. The drive to increase productivity and competitiveness comes not from the DTI but the Treasury. This does not stop at domestic policy-making. The Treasury has been instrumental in shaping the UK's positions on third world debt relief, reform of international financial institutions and, crucially, policy toward the euro. The Treasury's *National Changeover Plan* (Treasury, 1998d), brings it into the role of advising business and the public sector on preparations for the euro, which was traditionally the job of the DTI. More broadly still, the Chancellor has made the running on setting out the criteria for joining the euro, and has been ahead of a more cautious Prime Minister in acting as an advocate for UK membership.

The sheer breadth of Treasury involvement in almost every aspect of government ironically gives substance to the charge of 'Treasury power' that in the past was claimed amid great fanfare but was in fact more rhetorical than real. The changes to Treasury responsibilities and role that have occurred since 1997 raise a number of important issues. Historically the Treasury has always been a typically British institution, evolving and adapting. The core role of protecting the public purse has been expanded and augmented by broader macroeconomic responsibilities. It is a highly political beast, adapting to the personalities of its Chancellors. In some respects, the changes under Brown are no more than a continuation of this evolutionary trend.

However, what is different now is the expansion of the Treasury into direct policy-making and agenda control in a way that does not reflect accepted structural responsibilities but the interests of its Chancellor. There are dangers in this. Practically, does the official Treasury have the capacity to monitor the range of policy tasks now set, after nearly a decade of reductions in senior staff numbers? Can the Chancellor, despite his legendary work rate (fast approximating Gladstone's reputation in what was a quieter age), keep up the pace? The enormous increase in power resources is predicated on the assumption that prudence and long-termism will pay economic and political dividends. What if economic conditions worsen? What if policy delivery is not in line with the modernization plans? The Thatcher and Major governments began the process whereby central government departments have to justify their existence. Brown's expansion of the Treasury's role can be seen as part of the turf wars of Whitehall. Is there a need for the DSS as a policy department if the Treasury performs that role? What of the value of the DETR in this new configuration? This presupposes that the changes outlive the Chancellor. Is the Treasury being turned into an instrument of Brown's concerns – a sort of bespoke departmental tailoring – that could not be sustained by another Chancellor? If that is the case then there is a real danger of the over-politicization of the most important of the central departments, too dependent on its master. The agenda may be laudable and pursued by a committed minister on top of his brief, but the means chosen for its delivery represent double centralization and control: of a powerful individual and of a powerful institution.

Why have the Chancellor and the Treasury as his instrument become so powerful? Any explanation has to focus on the trauma of four successive electoral defeats for Labour from 1979 to 1992. Discipline and rectitude in economic policy-making are seen as essential prerequisites for gaining and keeping power. Both Blair and Brown want to capture the traditionally Conservative sobriquet of being 'competent' managers of the economy. The decision to maintain Conservative spending plans for the first two years of government and then increase spending only in targeted ways is a clear example of this approach. Similarly, the commitment to being a low income tax government is seen as politically expedient. This fiscal 'conservatism' gives crucial political power resources to the Treasury, which remains at heart a traditional Ministry of Finance.

The Treasury has gained from the centralization of control in government with ministers disciplined by collective responsibility to the Blair 'project' despite ideological misgivings among 'traditional Labour' ministers. This has enabled the Chancellor to impose changes in the public spending regime. However, it does not explain why the Chancellor has been able to move into policy-making areas traditionally the preserve of the departments. In part this is explained by the solidity of the Blair–Brown axis on policy issues. The other explanation is that the Treasury has been liberated from its post-war role of managing monetary policy and the intellectual and organizational resources released have enabled it to 'meddle' in departmental business. The absence of real politico–administrative antagonism to this remains a surprise. The network of Brown or Blair supporters in key ministries does not fully explain the absence of bureaucratic unease at the rebalancing of Whitehall relations in favour of the Treasury.

However, this is by no means a 'cosy' story of Brown–Blair partnership. Blair has continued a trend which began under Major of making the Cabinet Office into an explicit engine room for coordination and centralization. The difficult task of combining the role of servicing the Cabinet as a whole (and hence acting neutrally) and yet also acting as a means by which Prime Ministerial authority is strengthened has been achieved by the combination of personnel changes and administrative initiatives. For the first time the Prime Minister has explicitly linked his role, that of his Office and that of the Cabinet Secretary, to the other previously disparate elements of the Lord Privy Seal's office and the rest of the Cabinet Office. The network of offices, advisers and ministers combines the roles of parliamentary management, civil service management, servicing the Cabinet and specific cross-Whitehall initiatives (see Chapter 6).

## The euro: continuity and change

Whether or not to join the European single currency has been a central dilemma for British policy-makers since the Maastricht Treaty (see Chapter 4). Major's 'opt-out', which allows the UK to choose if and when it wants to join the euro, has not reduced the controversy. At first sight the Blair administration has adopted a far more positive attitude; the Cabinet is not bitterly divided on the issue and European policy in its rhetoric is more *communautaire*. Yet the detail of the policy statement by the Chancellor in October 1997 could have been made by his predecessor. Essentially the government is committed in principle to join providing five economic tests are applied and found satisfactory. Then a recommendation will be made and a referendum will decide the issue. This effectively means that the UK will not be ready to join until 2002 at the earliest.

The 'five tests' (Box 13.1) show the remarkable consistency in the UK policy elite's attitude to the euro. The debacle of 'black Wednesday' in September 1992, when sterling was forced out of the ERM by speculative pressure, has had a profound effect on the 'assumptive worlds' of policy-makers. The fear is that the UK economy is on a different economic cycle to the continental European economy, and that interest rates prevailing in the euro-zone will thus be inappropriate for economic conditions in the

UK. However, such economic considerations appear less pressing than the fundamental fear of Blair and Brown that a referendum on membership might be lost in the face of a campaign based on the loss of national identity and sovereignty wrapped in the concept of an 'independent' currency. The Prime Minister began as a more cautious advocate of membership; the Chancellor a more committed one. Those roles have reversed with the Treasury concerned at the initial poor performance of the euro and the sluggishness of the European economy. The fourth criterion appears the one most exercising the Treasury: will the City's role as a leading financial centre be damaged by non-participation in the euro? After the 2001 General Election Gordon Brown described policy toward the euro as 'considered and cautious' and one of 'pro-euro realism', a statement widely interpreted as a move to cool speculation that early British entry was likely and seemingly ruling out an early referendum.

---

## Box 13.1 The five economic tests for UK membership of the ECU

The Chancellor's five tests which have to be satisfied before a recommendation for the UK to join the single currency would be made:

(1) Are business cycles and economic structures compatible so that the UK and others could live with euro interest rates on a permanent basis?
(2) If problems emerge, is there sufficient flexibility to deal with them?
(3) Would joining EMU create better conditions for firms making long-term decisions to invest in Britain?
(4) What impact would entry into EMU have on the competitive position of the UK's financial services industry, particularly the City's wholesale markets?
(5) Would joining EMU promote higher growth, stability and a lasting increase in jobs?

These tests were placed within the context of a need for 'sustainable and durable' convergence between the UK and European economy. In particular the Treasury emphasises that the British economy:

- has to have converged with Europe
- can demonstrably be shown to have converged, and
- that this convergence is capable of being sustained, and
- that there is sufficient flexibility to adapt to change and unexpected economic events.

What is different about the Blair administration's approach is the active planning for UK membership. In 1998 the Treasury published an *Outline National Changeover Plan* (Treasury, 1998d). The document was a combination of a draft timetable for joining, a report on central government preparations and an *aide memoire* to a number of sectors on what was required for them to prepare for membership.

The changeover plan envisages a 40-month period from the point at which the government might recommend joining, followed by the EU Commission and ECB's report on whether the UK has converged with the euro-zone, through to the point at which the euro would become the currency of the UK and sterling would be withdrawn. The Treasury anticipates a period of two to two-and-a-half years for businesses and the public sector to prepare for the introduction of euro cash and for the conversion of accounting systems and cash machines.

More generally, the Treasury's commitment under Brown to neo-liberal ideas in economic policy is given concrete expression in statements on competition policy. This has effectively been taken out of the control of the DTI and has been driven by the Treasury. The Chancellor has identified relatively poor productivity, lack of competitiveness and lack of innovation as major structural weaknesses in the UK economy. The prescription is for government to seek partnership with business and for a tightening of competition policy. The stress has been on creating flexible, open markets. The Competitiveness White Paper commits the government to strengthening legislation dealing with unfair and anti-competitive behaviour. A new Competition Commission has replaced the Monopolies and Mergers Commission (MMC), and merger policy is to be reviewed. There is a European dimension to this, with an explicit commitment to press for the liberalization of markets in the EU.

## Conclusion

Three clear themes emerge from this review of economic policy under new Labour. There has been an attempt to build a coherent philosophy of governance based on an emerging Anglo–Saxon 'Third Way', attempting to modernize social democracy and incorporate liberal values (see the debate between Hall, 1998a, Hobsbawn, 1998 and Mulgan, 1998). This involves a whole-hearted commitment to neo-liberal ideas – the creation of a stable anti-inflation policy built on technocratic control by the Bank of England, prudence in fiscal policy, tight control of public expenditure, commitment to liberalising markets and an active competition policy. Coupled with this there is an attempt to target increases in public expenditure to modernize public services. The social democratic element of the Third Way is further bolstered by policies signalling a commitment to full employment and by modest measures to deal with social exclusion.

Secondly, there has been a rebalancing of power between the institutions of the central state. The Treasury has ceded control of monetary policy, divesting itself of a role which marked it out as a unique Ministry of Finance in the industrialized world. It has, however, augmented its role in being a central department directing and controlling large parts of the domestic policy agenda. This is via the Chancellor's control of key elements of the government's reform programme and as a result of changes in the way the public expenditure regime has been calibrated to enhance central control. What is remarkable is the lack of overt opposition to this paradoxical increase in Treasury power.

Thirdly, there has been a juxtaposition of continuity and change in large elements of economic policy. Despite the rhetoric, public spending plans are not radically different from those of the Conservatives. The control regime is different. There appears to be a greater commitment to joining the euro, yet the cautious language and 'wait and see approach' of the five economic tests would not have rested uneasily if articulated by Major and Clarke. Monetary policy has been changed, but with the significant qualification of the granting of operational independence for the Bank, the framework of policy is an incremental development from that evolving under Lamont and Clarke. What is different is the degree to which Brown has locked in so many constraints on discretionary policy action in monetary and fiscal policy.

# Chapter 14

# Welfare Policy

PETE ALCOCK

The election of the new Labour government in 1997 was welcomed by commentators and pundits as heralding a new era of welfare, involving in particular a departure from the Thatcherite policies of the 1980s and their concerns with 'rolling back' the boundaries of the welfare state. Labour's manifesto in 1997 had promised that 'things could only get better' and had made much of promises to improve services, for example by cutting class sizes in schools and reducing national health service (NHS) waiting lists. Change and improvement could therefore be expected.

In fact it took the new government longer to cut class sizes and waiting lists than some might have hoped. It also became increasingly clear that short-term promises on welfare were being subsumed within a wider, and more significant, debate about the future direction for social policy within the UK, and beyond. New Labour, it was claimed, had not only rejected the anti-state individualism of Thatcherism, but had also cast off the old Labour commitment to redistribution and monopoly public services. Both the state and the market were replaced at the centre of policy planning by a new 'Third Way' for welfare, championed directly by Blair himself (Blair, 1998b). The appeal of such a new direction for welfare at the beginning of a new century was indeed an attractive one, and to some extent, as we shall see, it did draw upon a rethinking of policy priorities and ideological commitments within the Labour party. However, it also involved the importation of many of the past Thatcherite reforms into a new policy planning framework. Such accommodations are perhaps an inevitable consequence of pragmatic policy developments – new directions for welfare are not realized overnight. However, as the government developed its welfare policy it seemed that it was increasingly pragmatism, rather than principle, that characterized the policy mix being developed within the Third Way.

## The policy planning framework

Tracing the context for Labour's new direction for welfare policy is a complex matter and needs to be set briefly within a broader historical and geographical context. The need for rethinking was begun in earnest after the 1992 election by the Social Justice Commission set up by the late John Smith (Borrie, 1994). By this time it was also clear that the pressures on welfare policy were affecting all developed capitalist societies. Esping Andersen's (1996) analysis revealed that by the beginning of the 1990s all welfare states were 'in transition', with all welfare commitments under review. In this wider international context Britain in fact emerged as a low-welfare country in European terms, although not when compared to North America and the Far East (see Table 14.1).

On coming to power, however, Labour inevitably inherited the legacy of past reforms. These included in particular the introduction of competition and marketization into health, education and social services and the stricter benefits code for the unemployed, all of which had only just begun to mature in the late 1990s. If there was one common lesson implicit in the development of these changes it was the time which it had taken the previous four Conservative regimes to bring about such fundamental reform – 18 years is a long time in politics but it is a relatively short time in which to alter the direction of welfare institutions like the NHS or the social security system. The new government knew it could not, and perhaps should not, seek to reverse such changes overnight, even if a reversal was itself desirable, which was not necessarily the case.

Rather than apologising for inaction therefore, Labour made a virtue out of the need for a period of financial stability and policy reflection, leading to an agenda for reform which would extend into the early decades of the twenty-first century – and into the second, or third, terms of government. The earliest evidence of this was the commitment to remaining within the overall public spending limits of the previous administration for the first two years of office (see Chapter 13). This meant no immediate increase in taxes to finance new public expenditure – reversing a promise which was felt to have cost Labour dear in their past election defeats. It

Table 14.1    *Public social security and health expenditure as a percentage of gross GDP, 1990*

| Sweden | 33.1 | Canada | 18.8 |
|---|---|---|---|
| Denmark | 27.8 | New Zealand[1] | 17.9 |
| France | 26.5 | United States | 14.6 |
| Germany | 23.5 | Japan[1] | 12.2 |
| United Kingdom | 22.3 | Australia[1] | 9.2 |

*Note:* [1] 1986.
*Source:* Adapted from Esping Andersen (1996), Table 1.1.

also meant no early rises in benefits or other social services – a feature of the 1970s' Labour administrations which was felt to have restricted policy options in the later years of office. However, it did not mean *no* change in public spending priorities. Within overall constraints spending could be switched around to meet particular policy priorities. Thus savings in defence and social security expenditure were used to finance additional spending on health (£500 million in the 1998 budget and a further £250 in November of that year), education (£250 million in 1998) and transport (£500 million).

Furthermore the windfall tax of £3.5 billion on the new utilities, promised in the manifesto to pay for a new initiative to get 16–24 year olds into work, was exempt from the two-year moratorium, and provided scope for some high-profile new spending. The new government also developed a subtle strategy of making early announcements of expenditure commitments which would not in fact come into effect until after April 1999. These were a particularly important feature of the 1998 budget and included increases to Child Benefit and Income Support benefits for children from April 1999 and a new, more generous, Working Families Tax Credit (WFTC) to replace Family Credit in October 1999. Prefiguring policy changes which in any event would require bureaucratic reform to implement, such as the WFTC, was in one sense merely practical policy planning. However, it could also have the benefit of providing a double political impact, once when first announced and then again when the additional support was actually received – and in the case of the WFTC this was milked further by several later 'announcements', including a promise in 1999 to increase the basic level of support even before the initial scheme had come into operation.

Forward planning such as this was not restricted to early announcements of future policy change, however. The new government also wanted to promote political debate about the long-term development of welfare policy into the early decades of the next century. This was particularly the case in the social security area, where such debate took on human form with the appointment of Labour maverick, and one-time director of the Child Poverty Action Group (CPAG), Frank Field, as a new Minister for Welfare Reform. Field's brief was characterized as an opportunity to 'think the unthinkable', including the production of an early Green Paper on welfare reform. A separate review of pensions was also commissioned, and a Royal Commission established to examine support for long-term care. The message in all cases was that policy change was required, but that this should be planned over the *longue durée,* following extensive review and consultation – neatly captured in the welfare reform paper by the phrase *Welfare 2020.* In fact Field's appointment turned out to be something of a non-event and he resigned in the summer of 1998 after failing to get promotion in a reshuffle. The paper on welfare reform eventually appeared only after the 1998 budget (DSS, 1998a) and did not owe much to Field's own thinking. The report on pensions followed in December of that year (DSS, 1998b), and the Royal Commission the subsequent March (Sutherland, 1999).

Review of policy planning and spending priorities in other areas of welfare was taken up by Labour as part of a Comprehensive Spending Review (CSR) announced in July 1997 and intended to set the scene for public expenditure commitments for the final three years of the first term of office, once the two-year moratorium had come to an end. In fact the CSR was not a comprehensive review. Defence spending was excluded from scrutiny and social security spending was assumed to be covered by the Green Papers commissioned above. What is more, although in theory the review was intended as a policy planning process, in which all departments would reassess their budgets from a zero base, identifying inefficiencies and new priorities in practice what emerged in the summer of 1998 were those commitments to additional spending which the government felt could be accommodated within predictable economic and fiscal trends (Treasury, 1998c). The main commitments here were an extra £21 billion for health and £19 billion for education over the three years from 1990/2000 to 2001/2 – although the real value of these figures was hotly disputed because they were based upon a cumulative calculation of increased spending which in effect meant that the first year's increase when rolled forward would be counted three times. Other new spending commitments included over £2 billion for transport and for local authority services, and money for new initiatives to tackle drugs and support pre-school care. Despite their exclusion from the review, however, savings were also anticipated from defence and agriculture, and from some aspects of social security. The overall result was therefore a significant shift in spending priorities, as Table 14.2 demonstrates.

The CSR did not attract political attention to welfare policy planning in the way which might have been expected of such a potentially wide-ranging reappraisal of spending priorities. Inevitably, perhaps, it was the final spending decisions that emerged from the annual budget statements that provided evidence of real policy priorities. In 1999 only cautious moves were made to increase spending in line with CSR commitments. However, by the autumn of that year it was clear that growth within the wider economy was likely to boost tax returns and leave the Chancellor with a surplus of around £3.5 billion on the public expenditure account at the end of the financial year. This provoked debate about whether scope could be found for increased expenditure commitments in the later years of

Table 14.2   *Growth in public spending and spending plans, 1993/4 – 2001/2*

|  | Real annual growth rate | | | |
|  | 1993/4 to 1996/7 | 1996/7 to 1998/9 | 1998/9 to 2001/2 | 1996/7 to 2001/2 |
|---|---|---|---|---|
| NHS (England) | 2.1 | 2.3 | 4.7 | 3.7 |
| Education (GB) | 0.7 | −0.2 | 5.1 | 2.9 |
| Total Managed Exp. | 1.3 | 0.1 | 2.7 | 1.7 |
| Social Security (inc. new deal) | 1.6 | 0.5 | 2.0 | 1.4 |
| Defence | −4.3 | −0.9 | −1.4 | −1.2 |
| GDP | 3.1 | 2.4 | 2.2 | 2.3 |

*Source:* Burchardt and Hills (1999), Table 2.2; adapted from HM Treasury.

the first term (see Chapter 13). But by this time debate about the scale of public policy commitments had been subsumed within a broader consideration of the shape of welfare services – encapsulated in promotion of the Third Way.

## The Third Way

The idea that Labour policy on welfare was based on a Third Way, between the alternatives of state socialism and the free market which dominated policy development over the past century, was one associated directly with the Prime Minister himself (Blair, 1998). It was also a notion which could be found within many of the new policy documents produced by the government (DSS, 1998a, p. 2). However, it is far from clear what exactly was meant by, or implied within, a Third Way for policy development (see Chapter 2) – and in practice differing perceptions and differing perspectives have been employed by different protagonists (Driver and Martell, 1998; Jones and MacGregor, 1998; Levitas, 1998; Powell, 1999).

In part, at least, the notion of the Third Way is a direct descendant of the Social Justice Commission's review of social policy after the 1992 election (Borrie, 1994). In their report, the Commission sought to characterize approaches under three broad groupings:

- *Levellers*: the old Labour left, concerned to use public services and benefits to redistribute from rich to poor
- *Deregulators*: the new right protagonists of the free market and private protection

- *Investors*: using public resources to invest in opportunities for all in order to improve economic competitiveness.

The Commission endorsed the third approach, and it is a broadly similar distinction which new Labour has since sought to capture in distancing itself from the welfare statism of old Labour and the free marketeering of the Thatcherite Conservatives. To some extent this is an endorsement of the need for social policy and social spending to be developed within the context of an economic policy geared to ensure economic growth within the new competitive global market – summed in one word, *prudence*, by the Chancellor, Gordon Brown (see Chapter 13). However, it is also informed by a new, and perhaps distinctive, ideology of welfare – 'prudence for a purpose'.

Labour's purpose in welfare reform, and the Third Way which it is claimed this represents, can be identified by both positive and negative characteristics. The positive characteristics of the Third Way are the endorsement of a mixed economy of welfare services and the partnership in policy planning and delivery that is implicit in this, the active promotion of equality of opportunity and the belief in the broader values of welfare spending as an investment in 'social capital'. The negative characteristics are to do with what the Third Way is not. It is not a return to old Labour policies of tax and spend, redistribution to achieve (spurious) equality and producer dominated monopoly public services; and it is not the new right credo of free market deregulation, privatization, contracting-out and individual self-protection.

Endorsement of a mixed economy of welfare providers is at one level merely recognition of the real diversity in social provision which exists within Britain's 'welfare state'. Public services were developed and have always coexisted alongside the private, voluntary and informal sectors. Thatcherism may have altered the balance slightly between these but it was a shifting balance in any case, which Labour is merely adjusting more openly. An important feature of the new balance which Labour is seeking to achieve can be found in their promotion of partnership. What is being promoted here is a revitalization of the old notion of 'civil society', within which all partners, and all citizens, have mutual interests and obligations in securing local social and economic progress.

Linked to this is Labour's approach to the problem of inequality. They eschew the egalitarian ideals of redistributive policies aimed at equality of outcome, in favour of a more dynamic model of equality of opportunity. However, the dynamism in the model recognizes the barriers which some may face in competing equally for the opportunities on offer, especially where these operate cumulatively over time to reduce individual, or whole community, life chances. Such a dynamic model of inequality and poverty was contained most significantly in a Treasury paper on poverty and opportunity published in March 1999 (Treasury, 1999c). It is model of equal opportunity based upon 'the equal start rather than the open road', to paraphrase Tawney, quoted in Powell (1999, p. 18).

Investment in social capital is also, of course, not a new idea. Welfare spending on areas such as education, health and social security to support economic growth has been a central feature of recent analysis of the role of welfare spending in buttressing competitiveness in welfare capitalist economies (Pfaller, Gough and Therborn, 1991; Esping Andersen, 1996). What Labour have now done is incorporate these dual values of welfare – individual protection and collective growth – into a virtuous circle, which contrasts starkly with the contradictory tension exemplified by the new right fears of public welfare crowding out private initiative.

There are, however, in reality an extensive range of alternatives to both old Labour statism and new right neo-liberalism. Partnership, social investment, equality of opportunity, mixed economies and so on can be pursued in different forms and with different investment and outcome priorities. To lump all of these together as a Third Way can disguise as much as it reveals. Thus Labour's new Third Way for welfare is really the beginning of a process of policy analysis and development, rather than the culmination of one.

## The ideological framework

In their first two years of office Labour produced a wide range of policy reviews and official statements. These included a plethora of Green and White Papers on social security, pensions, education, health, childcare, families, local government and more; a Royal Commission report on long-term care; and the work of a new unit to tackle social exclusion. Much has also been written by journalists, think tank specialists and academics about the new Labour project and its policy implications (Oppenheim, 1998; Powell, 1999). There have also been the commentaries on the Third Way by Blair himself (1998), and by one of his leading policy gurus (Giddens, 1998). In all of this writing a number of new (or revitalized) concepts appear and re-appear; and these provide a guide to the ideological framework behind the government's new welfare policies.

For a start there is the use of the term *welfare* itself to describe social – and, in particular, social security – policy. 'Welfare' is an ambiguous term. It has positive connotations of meeting people's basic human needs – providing for their welfare. However, it also has negative connotations inherited especially from American concerns with welfare dependence and the growing cost of public expenditure. The Blair government's close association with the Clinton programme of reform and renewal in the US (Jordan, 1998a) has resulted in an increasing tendency to use the term in this narrower, more pejorative, sense – although its dual meaning also reveals a potential contradiction at the heart of the new Labour project between the commitment to provide for welfare for all and the determination to promote self-improvement and self-protection through the labour market.

This duality can be found in another key element of the Third Way, the link between rights and responsibilities. The right to welfare was a core principle of the post-war welfare state in Britain, captured famously by Marshall (1950) in his claim that such rights were the defining feature of twentieth-century social citizenship. Such a paternalistic approach is challenged by Labour, however, in favour of a more contractual model within which citizens have duties to fulfil in order to secure their rights to social protection. This can be seen most clearly in the policy initiatives surrounding Labour's key concept of 'welfare-to-work', within which welfare provision is set against the obligation to seek self-protection within through paid employment.

This contractual model is also exemplified in the notion of stakeholding. The stakeholder society was promoted by the Commission on Social Justice. It has also been taken up by another of Blair's gurus, Hutton (1995), for whom it implied the promotion of an economic order in which both individuals and corporate capital had obligations to the wider society from which they drew benefits. This can be contrasted with the approach of Field (1995, 1996), who based stakeholding more upon the investment model of social insurance in which protection would be 'purchased' through the contribution of a stake within a fund for mutual security. However, the notions of mutuality and investment ran through both; and these are captured, too, in an even broader, and more significant, concept – that of *citizenship*.

The link between citizenship and welfare has always been a central feature of welfare provision in modern societies – it was Marshall's (1950) key concept in the 1940s. It is therefore not a new idea. Nor indeed is its re-emergence owed entirely to new Labour thinking. Many scholars have been writing about citizenship in the 1990s (Andrews, 1991; Roche, 1992; Lister, 1998), and its role in a revitalization of public welfare was promoted in the 1980s by Plant (1988). Nevertheless Labour has embraced this new concern and linked it to their contractual model of welfare.

This model is quite distinct, however, from new right notions of private contracting within a free market. Labour see a continuing role for the public provision of welfare and have moved away from the privatization agenda of the 1980s. This is most clearly revealed in their promotion of a new approach to the improvement of services, symbolized by the notion of *Best Value*, and discussed as a project of *modernization* of public services. Labour see themselves as the modernizers of welfare services; and they included the term in their early papers on reform of local government (DETR, 1998b) and social services (DoH, 1998a). The claim to modernity might appear to be a curious one, at a time when so many pundits are writing about the Western world having entered the 'post-modern' era, although the quest for modernization addresses rather similar issues to those raised in many debates about post-modernity – and 'post-modernizers' is not such a catchy buzzword.

In general modernization is simply a plea for recognition that the world has changed since the post-war period, as noted by Esping Andersen (1996) and others. Giddens' (1998) analysis of the Third Way situates this in the context of the different risks and uncertainties which citizens now face in planning for their lives. These new risks require a new relationship between citizens and service providers.

Finally, what is particularly interesting about the modernization project upon which the new government has embarked is the extent to which it embodies a new 'consensus' over welfare reform at the beginning of the twenty-first century. Certainly many of the government's core concepts are shared by the Liberal Democrats, who have now joined them in government in the devolved Parliament in Scotland. More importantly perhaps they receive little challenge from a much-weakened Conservative opposition. This may in part be due to the devastating rejection the Conservatives experienced in 1997. However, it may also be the result of their recognition that a Third Way between the state and the market is the only practical foundation for welfare in the 'post-modern' world.

## Rebuilding public services

### Health

Ever since its creation in 1948 the NHS has been a central feature of public service provision; and, despite some veiled threats, even the Conservatives of the 1980s and 1990s never challenged this public base. What they did do, of course, was introduce significant internal reform of the NHS to institute a 'quasi-market' in health provision in which purchasers (GPs) would secure services from separate providers (hospitals) (Klein, 1995). Whatever the merits of these quasi-markets in improving (or not) the efficiency of health services and responding to the needs of consumers, they did result in major organizational and managerial change. They had taken many years to plan and to implement; and an incoming government was not going to find it easy to overturn them, even if it felt minded to do so. Labour did not promise to repeal the internal market in health care therefore; rather they directed their initial concerns to making the NHS work better within existing managerial constraints, by focusing upon practical issues such as cutting waiting lists and securing additional spending.

In December 1997, however, the government published a White Paper on the NHS with the subtitle 'modern, dependable', suggesting some compromise between the established values of public service and the new approaches of the third way (DoH, 1997). In part, this implied an abandonment of the internal market, and in particular it included the abolition of GP fund-holding. But in part it contained a reformation of this, with the retention of the purchaser/provider split and the establishment of Primary Care Groups (replacing health authorities and GP fund-holders) as the new purchasers for populations of around 100 000 – more of a continuation and development of past reforms than a retreat from them.

Organizational change is not all, however; and in practice the size of the budget has always been the main factor determining the scale and scope of health policy. New Labour were concerned to expand this budget as much as possible. Within the first two years some extra money was found for health; and in the CSR the £21 billion additional spending earmarked for the NHS was a top priority. How much additional provision will flow from the additional funding is disputed, however, with some at least likely to go on improved salaries to underpaid health workers.

More generally, too, the new government's partnership approach to welfare has had some impact in the health care field. For a start the problem of health inequalities was openly recognized by government, notably by the publication of the Acheson Inquiry in 1998. This was followed by a Green Paper (DoH, 1998b) on health promotion set very much in the context of the Third Way and talking of the importance of social policy in determining health outcomes and the need for partnership activity to combat inequalities. From this flowed the Health Action Zones (HAZs) as local sites for coordinated partnership activity to promote improved health – an example of locally-based action also extended to education, employment and broader regeneration activity. Of course, such local projects are small beer compared to the overall scale of NHS expenditure, and their impact on health outcomes will inevitably work only over a long timescale. They are evidence of a Third Way that is therefore very much at the margins of broader service delivery – or at least at the margins of current policy planning.

## Education

The most abiding memory of Labour's 1997 election campaign was their outspoken support for education – 'education, education, education', as the campaign slogan put it. Central to this was a renewed commitment to the notion of education as investment in social capital, as well as a belief that it was through the opportunity afforded by improved education that individuals would be able to escape social exclusion and rejoin economic activity. Education was good for individuals and it was good for society, too; and Labour was acutely aware that the numbers of people participating in education at various levels of society, was lower in Britain than in many competitor countries. This commitment was translated into practical promises to cut class sizes, increase investment in building repair, reward successful teachers and extend access; as a result, education was also a key priority in the CSR.

As in the health field, however, Labour inherited organizational reforms introduced by the Conservatives. These included local management of schools (LMS) and parental choice, which would be particularly difficult for the new government to overthrow since Blair himself had taken advantage of open access to send one of his children to a school outside of the local area. In any event, Labour claimed that open access to schools (in theory at least) fitted well with the Third Way emphasis upon consumer accountability and best value. The league tables of results published by schools and the use of OFSTED inspections to assure quality of provision were welcomed as means of maintaining public control over standards of service, although the plan to reflect such concerns in differential pay rewards for high-performing teachers met with resolute resistance from the unions and professional bodies.

Labour also welcomed past commitments to the reform and expansion of further and higher education. Further expansion was also planned; and, in the case of higher education, was to be paid for by student loans and contributions to fees, going beyond what Tories had delivered here. This involved the development, too, of what was now called 'lifelong learning' – the idea that education was an opportunity which could, and should, be available not just in childhood but throughout adult life. The growth of mature students in higher education from the 1970s had begun this process; but now it was to be extended as a principle to all post-school education, linked to retraining and skill development, and incorporated into the packages offered to those participating in employment initiatives like the New Deal.

In education in particular, therefore, it seemed that there was a close link between Labour's third way and the policies of the past Conservative administrations. That a new consensus on the values of public education was emerging was confirmed by the tacit support of the opposition for most of the government's new or continuing initiatives in the area. The Liberal Democrats also strongly backed the government's support for education, arguing only that more public resources should be directed towards it. If the Third Way could characterized as the replacement of old divisions with support for a new role for accountable public services, then education might well be seen as an early example of this.

## Social services

In the social services field, too, Labour inherited major organizational reforms, and in large part sought to build on, rather than to dismantle, these. Most significant here was the mixed economy of care introduced by the community care reforms of the early 1990s, shifting the role of local social service departments from one of providers to one of enablers, working to provide appropriate packages of support for consumers (Baldock and Ungerson, 1994; Means and Smith, 1998). Far from challenging this, the new government aimed to enhance it. A White Paper was published in November 1998 extolling the values of partnerships between local authorities and health authorities and links with voluntary organisations and community groups (DoH, 1998a); and with this came promises of £3 billion additional local spending over three years, plus £1.3 billion for modernization.

Long-term care needs were dealt with by the Royal Commission report (Sutherland, 1999). This was a wide-ranging, and forward-looking, document which openly dismissed the fears of a 'demographic time bomb' and recommended the establishment of a permanent Commission to oversee policy development. However, its main theme was the need for public support for the future care needs of all, funded from general taxation at a cost of around £1 billion a year, and mixed with individual provision for living and housing costs.

## Housing

Housing had been one of the early priorities for reform by the Conservative governments of the 1980s. The introduction of the 'right to buy' for council tenants was a swift confirmation of the privatization and individualism that were to underlie many later reforms. It was also hotly contested by the then Labour opposition. Two decades later, however, the new Labour government has not repealed the right to buy, nor indeed any of the later Conservative reforms to permit whole estates to transfer into private hands and to replace local authorities with housing associations

(HAs) as the main providers of newly built rented housing. Here, too, the Third Way appears to embrace a large measure of the Thatcherite agenda for shifting the balance of public responsibility in welfare services.

Labour have also inherited the changing focus of public spending in the housing field, with public subsidies for building and maintenance (bricks and mortar) largely replaced by public support for individual housing costs through Housing Benefit. However, local authorities have been permitted to use the 'receipts' from council house sales to finance new capital projects – or, more accurately, to use these as a basis for borrowing for investment. Mortgage interest tax relief has also been much reduced in scope and value, and Housing Benefit put under review. But Labour is as strongly committed to owner-occupation as the preferred housing tenure for the majority as were the Conservatives, and is unlikely to engineer any change to the continuing decline of the public sector.

At the start of the new century, therefore, public housing has become a residual form of tenure (Murie, 1997); and this in itself has created a new policy agenda for government. There is concern that the run-down and unpopular council estates that now constitute much of public housing are in themselves a cause of social exclusion and social unrest (Power, 1997). Policy development has therefore moved towards strategies to combat such problems through investment in packages of measures to renew or regenerate deprived urban neighbourhoods, such as the Social Regeneration Budget (SRB) and the recommendations of the Social Exclusion Unit, discussed below.

## Social security

Social security is by far the largest item of public expenditure, totalling over £100 billion a year at the end of the century. Not surprisingly, therefore, it has been one of the most significant areas for policy development during the early years of the new Labour government, leading to a wide-ranging Green Paper (DSS, 1998a), a number of new legislative measures, and the most high-profile Cabinet sackings – Harriet Harman and Frank Field. In fact, however, the sheer scale and complexity of social security policy make it an unlikely candidate for rapid or radical reform. What is more the existing expectations of millions of claimants, many very poor, are built into current benefit schemes. Reducing or removing entitlement can be unpopular, as the new government quickly found out with back bench revolts over cuts in lone parent support and public demonstrations against proposed reductions in protection for disabled people. Backing the reforming zeal of Field was therefore always a risky commitment for the government, and the steadier approach of Darling is in practice a more accurate reflection of Labour's benefit strategy.

The Green Paper on welfare reform (DSS, 1998a), was followed by much more detailed proposals on the major area of current and future social security spending – pensions (DSS, 1998b). This provided an important example of Third Way thinking. Conscious of the potentially spiralling costs of state support as pensioners come to comprise a larger and larger proportion of the population, the government have withdrawn from any commitment to restore basic pension levels to those enjoyed in the 1970s or to maintain current levels against increasing wage inflation, marking a significant break from 'old Labour' priorities. Instead they are planning a means-tested minimum income guarantee to protect basic standards for all pensioners, and promoting a new partnership between state and private (or occupational) protection for the majority of future pensioners, replacing SERPS with a new state pension for the low paid and expecting the rest to take out personal ('stakeholder') protection.

Legislation introduced in 1999 also reformed other aspects of social security provision. The major target for change was Incapacity Benefit (ICB), which had seen a massive growth in claimants in the 1990s. For new claimants, this will be subject to an 'affluence test', reducing entitlement where other income is received and contribution criteria will be tightened. All new claimants, including those on ICB, will also be subject to a 'gateway' interview with claimant advisors to establish their availability for work and to discuss their plans for securing independence. Implicit in both of these reforms is a renewed commitment to targeting in welfare provision, described as making sure money goes to 'those who need it most', and to ensuring that receipt of benefits is seen as platform from which to jump rather than a state into which to fall.

This, too, provoked mutiny within the Labour ranks, with over 50 MPs voting against the proposal to 'means-test' ICB, despite minor amendments conceded by Darling; and it suggested that there was some dissension within the party over the adoption of further targeting within social security policy. It is indeed debatable whether extended means-testing is an element of the Conservative legacy which can be reconciled within a Third Way commitment to 'contractual welfare'. More generally, however, the government expect their approach to combating poverty and social exclusion to be judged on their higher-profile commitments to welfare-to-work and social cohesion.

## Welfare-to-work and social exclusion

One of the government's most prominent manifesto promises was the 'New Deal' for the young unemployed, financed by the windfall levy. The

New Deal included many of the key features of Labour welfare thinking, but in many ways it echoed also the supply-side approach to employment policy developed by the Conservatives. It offered training and work experience for up to 250 000 young unemployed people, financed by state subsidies provided to employers or other providers, who might include voluntary sector organisations; and was later extended too to lone parents and the long-term unemployed. The belief was that such opportunities would help people to establish connections with the labour market and so escape continued poverty and dependence upon benefits – from welfare to work.

Making work the most attractive and viable pathway out of dependence is central to such a strategy and it was supported by a range of other measures introduced during the first two years of office. These included the minimum wage and the Working Families Tax Credit (WFTC). The WFTC is in practice little more than an extension of Family Credit, first introduced by the Conservatives in 1971, although it will be paid primarily as a tax rebate rather than a benefit. Nevertheless, together with the minimum wage, it should make work a more attractive option than unemployment for most claimants. Work has also been made more attractive by Labour's embracing of more progressive EU policies on employment rights. These include the early endorsement of the Social Chapter of the Maastricht Treaty and the implementation of the Working Time Directive on hours and conditions at work.

Renewed intervention in the labour market has been summarized as, 'work for those who can, security for those who cannot'; and, as critics have pointed out, this mantra includes two of the most problematic features of the welfare-to-work strategy. First, work must be available for 'those who can', and yet in many parts of the country this has continued to be far from the case. As with the Conservative initiatives of the 1980s, welfare-to-work is a supply-side approach to labour market support. Without commensurate measures to stimulate labour demand, especially in areas experiencing the most dramatic declines in local employment, its ability over time to provide permanent routes out of poverty and exclusion must seriously be questioned. Secondly, such a strategy still requires support to be provided for those who cannot work (or rather cannot enter the paid labour market). Yet, as 54 academics writing to the *Financial Times* in 1998 pointed out, in their early years of office there was little evidence that the government was taking any measures to ensure that such support would be guaranteed; and the proposed cuts in benefit for ICB claimants appeared to compound this. For those outside, or on the margins of, the labour market, finding a place in Labour's new social order may prove to be an elusive goal; and in such circumstances problems of poverty and social exclusion will remain.

The problem of social exclusion is a complex one, in particular because it is sometimes used interchangeably with poverty. There is not the space here to enter into the complexities of the poverty and social exclusion debate (Room, 1995; Alcock, 1997, Ch. 6; Oppenheim, 1998) – suffice it to say, however, that social exclusion is taken to include problems of participation and access to services as well as lack of money, and is viewed by the Treasury and others as a dynamic phenomenon spreading deprivation across the life cycle. Most importantly social exclusion has been identified as a key target for government action with the establishment in December 1997 of a new Social Exclusion Unit (SEU), reporting directly to No. 10 (see Chapter 6), and publication in 1999 of a first annual report on the government's record in tackling poverty and social exclusion, which outlined 32 indicators against which policy progress was in future to be assessed (DSS, 1999).

The SEU was to include seconded civil servants and external members, and its work was overseen by a ministerial network. In both cases the aim was to ensure a wide range of departmental involvement in order to ensure coordination of government activity – described by Blair as 'joined-up solutions to joined-up problems'. And joining-up the actions of others was a necessary feature of the unit's work as it was not itself given a significant budget. It has, however, had clear targets for action, including in particular the 'problem estates' identified by housing policy specialists. From this flowed an important new policy initiative, the £800 million 'New Deal for Communities', to finance neighbourhood projects in (initially 17) districts experiencing high levels of deprivation and exclusion.

Combating poverty and social exclusion through neighbourhood action is a key element in Labour's welfare policy, recognizing that where more general policies of employment promotion and economic growth do not initially work, then additional targeted assistance may be necessary. The Health and Education Action Zones adopt a similar philosophy and practice. They are not, however, a particularly new idea, and have been tried before by both Labour and Conservative governments, with mixed success (Loney, 1983). They also intersect with other important political and policy issues, most notably crime, which is generally identified as a major problem in most areas of high deprivation. However, Labour's 'get tough' policies on crime may come into conflict with the community focus of their neighbourhood initiatives, where the price for supporting some members of communities may be the exclusion of others.

That there may be contradictory pressures in pursuing new policy initiatives which aim both to promote participation and responsibility and to target exclusion and deprivation, is perhaps an inevitable feature of Labour's Third Way thinking on welfare. And it raises important questions about the extent to which the various measures being pursued in different spheres can be conceived – or, more importantly, delivered – as a consistent approach to welfare reform.

## Conclusion: a new social policy?

Challenging social exclusion and promoting welfare-to-work are key elements in the development of a new social policy under Labour at the end of the twentieth century. Both draw on policy initiatives begun under the Conservatives, and have echoes of some of the ideas supported by past Labour administrations. But then this is the government's point: the Third Way is about taking the best of the state and the market, and about building on the past while restructuring for the future – 'modern and dependable', as the NHS White Paper (DoH, 1997) put it. As we pointed out earlier, however, the Third Way is a slippery concept, to which many shades of political opinion could in practice happily subscribe; and it is debatable whether the rhetoric of modernization has indeed been followed through by Labour with the development of a genuinely new direction for social policy. Most early commentators claim that the jury is still out on Labour's new welfare state (Powell, 1999), and it far from clear that behind the rhetoric of rethinking lies a realistic alternative model of welfare practice.

Of course there have been significant new ideas and policy changes; and the broader policy debates and political structures which Labour have created are likely to continue the pressure for policy implementation. For a start there is the likely impact of the major constitutional changes which the government has now put in place. A devolved parliament in Scotland has produced a Labour/Liberal Democrat coalition, with a Scottish Nationalist opposition. Real powers to determine social policy planning have been devolved to the Scottish parliament in the fields of health, home affairs, housing, agriculture, education, social services and implementation of EU directives. And this has immediately created pressure for changes, such as the abolition of university tuition fees. Devolution to Northern Ireland and Wales has also taken place; and within England regional planning has been given a renewed prominence through the establishment of the Regional Development Agencies (RDAs). Further political initiative and policy development are also likely to flow from the establishment of new democratic bases for city mayors in London and other major centres. These political pressures are evidence of new alignments in British politics, which inevitably will influence the policy debate; and they are likely to be accentuated by further constitutional reform.

In addition to these internal political and policy changes is the influence which will continue to be brought to bear by Britain's membership of the

EU. Labour have tried hard to shake of the mantle of 'reluctant Europeans' inherited from the Conservatives, and have embraced many EU social policy initiatives. If, as seems likely, they eventually take the country into the EU monetary union, then economic and social pressures for policy convergence will grow ever stronger. The EU has always been primarily an economic and trading union; but, at the end of the century, it is dominated by new Social Democratic governments concerned to marry economic with social development. Such a context could strengthen the case for Third Way policies in all member nations.

Finally there is the government's own policy agenda. Whatever the weight of the Thatcher legacy, Labour are not simply the new right in another guise. For Blair the securing of genuine equality of opportunity is an over-riding moral imperative; and for his Chancellor, Gordon Brown, achieving some measure of social justice is an economic, as well as a social, policy objective. Both are strong supporters of social markets and welfare capitalism. These require changes in the direction of political debate and policy development, and to some extent the government has succeeded in bringing this about. In 1999 the minimum wage and the WFTC began to take effect; there were also increases in benefits and tax relief for children, for maternity and for pensioners; an extension of the provisions to support welfare to work; and changes in NI contributions and tax allowances to claw back some income from the better-off. These may not have been the shifts in priorities hoped for by some old Labour critics, but they were nevertheless a change in the direction of tax and benefit policy – described by some pundits as 'redistribution by stealth'.

Redistribution by stealth is not in itself evidence of a new social policy, however; and the relatively minor changes introduced after 1997 go only a small way in reversing the massive shift of resources from poor to rich engineered by the Conservatives in the previous two decades. If the predicted budget surplus permits the Chancellor to make more extensive changes to benefits and public expenditure in future years then such a reversal may be more possible. Yet there is little evidence that the government is committed to such a return to past Labour preoccupations with financial inequality and fiscal redistribution – for instance, the targets listed in the government commitments to tackling poverty and social exclusion (DSS, 1999) do not refer directly levels of taxation or benefit.

At the beginning of the twenty-first century Labour's policy agenda is inevitably moving from its initial focus upon policy review and long-term planning to a more pragmatic concern with deliverable policy goals. And it is certainly the case that the new government have made rapid moves to implement a wide range of policy measures across the welfare state. These draw to some extent upon the need to redistribute resources and tackle poverty and exclusion; but they also encompass an embracement and rolling forward of many Conservative measures for marketization, targeting and the promotion of employability. New Labour may not be the new right, but it practice they have adopted many of the reforms championed by members of the previous Conservative administrations. Such a 'pick-'n-mix' pragmatism may allow the government to move within and between the state and market in their pursuit of a Third Way for welfare reform, but it is far from clear that it provides a consistent base for a new vision for social policy in the new millennium.

# Chapter 15

# Environmental Policy

ANDREW JORDAN

Within weeks of assuming power, Tony Blair was busy doing something no previous British Prime Minister had done before: touring the world preaching the merits of environmental protection to fellow world leaders. At his first G7 summit in June 1997, he rebuked the US government for seeking to stall a global deal on climate-altering gases. Then, flanked by no fewer than three Cabinet colleagues, including his Deputy Prime Minister, John Prescott, he moved on to address a UN meeting in New York on progress made in implementing the accords brokered at the 1992 Earth Summit in Rio (Jordan and Voisey, 1998). There he implored world leaders 'to make the process of government green. The environment must,' he warned: 'be integrated into all our decisions, regardless of sector. They must be in at the start, not bolted on later.' The tone of these remarks was an order of magnitude greener than anything uttered by a serving Labour Prime Minister or Blair's predecessor, John Major, who viewed environmental issues with studied indifference.

The key question addressed by this chapter is whether Blair's warm words of support have succeeded in ushering in a genuinely *new* era of environmental politics in Britain, one in which protecting the environment is fully and sympathetically integrated into the mainstream process of making the economy strong. In the past Labour has always viewed environmentalism as a threat to growth, blue-collar jobs and economic prosperity, and never warmly embraced its core message. Under the Conservatives Britain was often derided as the 'Dirty Man' of Europe. But here was Blair arguing for green concerns to be at the very centre of government thinking, and a more proactive environmental stance in Europe. Why? This chapter asks whether his new found commitment to greening the machinery of central government has borne fruit or whether new Labour has found it just as difficult to advance a genuinely progressive environmental agenda as did the Conservatives.

Nowadays, environmental policy integration – that is, ensuring that environmental considerations are factored into the 'core' areas of policy-making such as foreign affairs, transport, energy production, agriculture and so on – is regarded as a vital prerequisite of *sustainable development*.

Sustainable development, or 'sustainability', for short, is now the dominant *leitmotif* of environmental policy in Britain, the EU and much of the world. Significantly, sustainable development is not simply economic development as conventionally understood 'greened' by bolting on cleaner technologies and reducing waste, but an enduring *process* of human development which simultaneously satisfies social, economic and environmental goals, within and between different generations both North and South of the world.

Politically, achieving sustainable development is a policy project of the utmost complexity. A succession of Conservative governments pledged themselves to developing sustainably, but none really grappled with the tendency for policies in 'non'-environmental sectors to undermine the pursuit of environmental imperatives. Labour has signalled its determination to make Whitehall more receptive 'to new ideas that take the long-term view and cut across organizational boundaries to get to the root of the problem' (Cabinet Office, 1999c, p. 49). It is difficult to think of a better test of this new line of thinking than sustainable development. In this chapter we ask whether Labour has delivered the 'joined-up' policy making (Cabinet Office, 1999c) demanded by sustainability. It focuses on two key policy areas – namely, transport and energy supply – in which Blair has tried to seize the initiative, both nationally and internationally.

## Environmentalism metamorphoses into sustainability

Environmental policy has now reached a critical stage in its relatively short life. In the 1970s governments across the world responded to environmentalism by putting in place measures to address specific problems such as oil pollution, acid rain and ozone depletion as and when they arose. These and other problems were regarded as essentially technical in nature, requiring the application of scientific expertise. The policies adopted tended to be reactive rather than proactive, and sectoral rather than integrated across policy domains. The 'old' politics of pollution control (Weale, 1992) were also extremely cyclical in nature. Environmental standards were ratcheted up when an unforeseen disaster such as the sinking of an oil tanker surprised the political system. But the commitment to protect the environment was only ever ephemeral and the political machine soon returned to its preoccupation with 'quantity of life' issues such as the economy, jobs and defence.

The 'greening' of central government in Britain really began only in the late 1980s. Departments normally opposed to green initiatives such as the Ministry of Agriculture (MAFF) and the then Department of Trade and Industry (DTI), established their own environment units and assessment procedures to cope with the tide of domestic and European environmental legislation. But the onset of recession in the early 1990s and various government-led deregulatory initiatives dampened Whitehall's appetite for more radical change (Hill and Jordan, 1994).

This episodic pattern, which Anthony Downs (1972) characterizes as an 'issue–attention cycle', is now coming under unprecedented challenge from those, like Blair, who claim that the time has come for the environment to be integrated more systematically into *every* aspect of decision-making. But standing in their way are huge obstacles, built into the very structure of the British political system. It is clear, for example, that environmentalism has achieved huge strides since the early 1970s in terms of getting governments, local and national, international organizations and businesses to adopt environmental policies, environmental assessment procedures, environmental standards and awards. And yet, 30 years on, the environment continues to under-achieve politically, occupying a restricted zone at the margins of British politics. Periodically, environmental 'crises' such as Brent Spar, BSE and roads protesting, capture media attention. But 'the environment' as an issue is simply too amorphous, touching as it does almost every aspect of life, to be neatly captured in simple, sound-bite politics. Consequently, it tends to be ignored by most mainstream politicians. Unless and until political reform in the UK delivers green parties a proportional share of the popular vote, it seems extremely unlikely that the environment will break into the realms of day-to-day-party political competition in the foreseeable future.

Therefore, at the start of a new millennium environmental policy finds itself in the rather paradoxical situation of being both an established part of British politics (insofar as there is mainstream acceptance of the environmental case for change) and marginalized in the sense that few politicians champion it with passion. For instance, it is now almost universally accepted that problems such as climate change require fundamental, long-term solutions – a view which achieved little purchase when it was first aired in the 1970s. Critically, the solutions rely less on 'end-of-pipe' technical measures such as pollution abatement and more on transforming the whole of society and the economy. In the 'new' politics of the environment (Weale, 1992), the solutions are inter-connected, scientifically highly complex, international in their scope and deeply radical in the sense that they openly and fundamentally challenge the existing order of things. Politicians finds themselves drawn to environmental problems but for a variety of reasons find the solutions uncomfortable and hence politically unpalatable. One of the main reasons is that public opinion in Britain is far from united on environmental issues, being strongest among the affluent, well-educated middle classes and weakest among poorer social groups (see Norris, 1997b). Across Europe, public support for the environment is slightly weaker than in the 1990s. However, a survey of nearly 16 000 people from the different EU member states commissioned by the European Commission in 1999 revealed that two-thirds were in fact *more* worried about environmental problems than in 1994 (ENDS Daily, 1999).

## Environmental policy integration

The emerging orthodoxy in Europe and beyond is that environmental thinking must be *permanently* integrated into all areas of policy. It reflects a dawning realization that the key driving forces of pollution and habitat loss reside in 'non'-environmental sectors. Unless they are addressed at root, environmental protection will always be a reactive, piecemeal and ad hoc activity, prone to the vagaries of the issue–attention cycle. The key question is how? Government environmental bodies have done their best to object to or ameliorate the most damaging effects of policies decided elsewhere in the policy system using tools such as environmental impact assessment (EIA). But more often than not, the environment is ignored or introduced when the die of policy has already been cast. Rarely is the need for the over-arching policy – whether it is providing greater social mobility by building more roads or increasing the output of energy by constructing new power stations – fundamentally questioned, or the possibility of alternative course of action considered. The location, scale and detailed character of a given project may shift, but somewhere, somehow, the original formulation essentially gets its way and the environment is trimmed to fit.

The Blair government did not, of course, start with a blank canvas. It inherited a number of mechanisms from the Tories, including:

- A *Cabinet Committee* on the environment chaired by the Deputy Prime Minister: the Committee (ENV) is the principal decision-making body for government policy on sustainable development
- A *Committee of Green Ministers* from each government department to consider and report on the environmental impact of their own department's policies and to implement green 'housekeeping' issues such as energy efficiency and recycling
- A cross-departmental *Sustainable Development Unit* (SDU) to promote the sustainable development agenda across government
- An *appraisal system* for assessing the environmental impact of departmental policies, backed up by guidance, training and external reporting.

To these Labour added a Green Globe task force to inform the Foreign Office's 'ethical' foreign policy, a parliamentary select committee on sustainable development to chase progress across government departments and a special cross-departmental sustainable development unit located in the Department of Environment, Transport and the Regions (DETR), now renamed the Department of Transport, Local Government and the Regions (DTLGR), to update the Conservatives' sustainability strategy (DETR, 1999b). This was warmly received by greens because it addressed a major discontinuity in central government, re-uniting the separate functions performed by the Departments of the Environment (DoE) and Transport (DoT). Comprehensive policy reviews were ordered in the energy and transport sectors – two key drivers of environmental change – and spending was earmarked for an environmental task force to help the young unemployed back into work. Finally, the Labour government introduced a set of key sustainability indicators to sit alongside the headline inflation and GDP figures. These are meant to show whether or not the UK is on a sustainable growth path, and to flag the need for appropriate policy interventions (DETR, 1998c). Labour has labelled these initiatives 'Greening Government'. In bureaucratic terms, they represent the most profound evidence yet that environmentalism is beginning to permeate the heart of UK government.

However, there are growing pressures on the Blair administration to build still further on these initiatives to ensure that the environment permeates the central nervous system of central government – the processes and procedures of policy making. These include:

## Sustainability: a new paradigm of environmental policy

The 1990s have seen the emergence of sustainable development as the main organizing principle of modern environmental policy the world over. Nowadays, no corporate environmental brochure is complete without some reference to sustainability, sustainable growth or sustainable lifestyle. But what does it actually mean? The concept emerged in the early 1980s but it gained much wider political currency after the publication of the 1987 Brundtland Report, named after the former Prime Minister of Norway, Gro Harlem Brundtland, who chaired the UN committee that wrote it. The Brundtland Report defined sustainable development as 'development that meets the needs of the present without compromising the ability of future generations to meet their own needs' (WCED, 1987, p. 43). Simply put, Brundtland insists that social *and* economic development must operate within the limits set by the earth's ecosystems and material resources. It implies that the current generation should live within its environmental means by learning not to pass on uncompensated costs such as pollution, habitat loss and excessive resource exploitation, to future generations. Sustainable policies are therefore those polices which minimize pollution, reduce non-renewable resource use (oil, gas, etc.), close product loops, use renewable resources carefully and care for the environment so it can continue to supply these services now and forever.

Not surprisingly, sustainability has received a much warmer reception than the gloomy environmental prognoses of the 1970s, which pitted environmental protection and economic growth against one another. Sustainability is so politically palatable precisely because it carries the comforting message that the world *can* grow its way out of ecological and geopolitical crisis. Although easily understood in this broad sense, experience has shown that sustainable development is not easy to define in detail or to apply in day-to-day decision-making situations. Politicians find this ambiguity comforting. As Lélé (1991, p. 613) wryly remarks, it is a political '"metafix" which unites everybody from the profit-minded industrialist and risk minimising subsistence farmer to the equity seeking social worker, the pollution-concerned or wildlife loving First Worder [*sic*], the growth maximising policy maker, the goal orientated bureaucrat, and, therefore, the vote counting politician'. UK experience neatly illustrates this ambiguity. The Conservatives always played down the social and equity dimensions of sustainability (see Box 15.1), but Labour has reintroduced them as a tangible illustration of the need for 'Third Way' politics which reconcile the rights of the individual with those of society.

## International and European environmental commitments

Although sustainability has emerged as the new paradigm of environmental policy, international obligations continue to provide the main impetus to British environmental policy. They also function as a powerful backstop preventing the UK government from disavowing its commitments. Currently, over 80 per cent of British environmental policy originates in the EU, which began to develop an environmental dimension only as recently as the early 1970s (Jordan, 1999a; Lowe and Ward, 1998). Across many issues, the EU has forced the UK to adopt much higher environmental standards than would otherwise have been the case, and introduced a more formal, source-based and precautionary approach to standard-setting (Jordan, 1998a). One of Blair's first acts as Prime Minister was to sign the Amsterdam Treaty which makes integration in pursuit of sustainable development a formal objective of the EU (Jordan, 1998b).

Membership of the EU has undoubtedly increased the need for cross-departmental coordination, in terms of developing national negotiating positions prior to the development of policy and during the implementation of whatever commitments are eventually entered into. When policy-making is purely domestic, governments have the 'luxury' of leaving the resolution of coordination problems to the implementation phase (Peters, 1998, p. 306). However, the privatization of the water industry in the 1980s powerfully revealed the extent to which the government's hands had become progressively tied through its membership of the EU, forcing greater inter-departmental collaboration (Jordan, 1999b). The impact of Europe on Whitehall has been far from uniform but, over time, the DETR and its antecedents have slowly learned to use the EU to gain leverage over other departments in Whitehall, particularly Energy, Agriculture and Industry. Labour has also used the EU to try to get other states to take the idea of environmental policy integration more seriously. For instance, a highlight of the British EU Presidency in the first half of 1998 was an unprecedented joint meeting of Environment and Energy Ministers, and joint policy initiatives on environment and transport.

---

## Box 15.1 New Labour and sustainability: 'a better quality of life'?

Tony Blair believes that sustainable development means 'delivering the best possible quality of life for all of us' (DETR, 1999b, p. 1). The government divides the concept into four key policy objectives:

- Social progress which recognizes the needs of everyone: 'everyone [must] live in a clean and safe environment'
- Effective protection of the environment: 'protect[ing] things which people need or value'
- Prudent use of natural resources: 'using resources efficiently and recycling waste where appropriate'
- Maintenance of high and stable levels of economic growth and employment 'so that everyone in Britain can share in high living standards and greater job opportunities'.

This definition is considerably wider than that adopted by the Tories who were always chary of embracing the 'anti-growth' message which is implicit in sustainability discourse. However their own neo-liberal interpretation came close to having one's cake and eating it: '[s]ustainable development does not mean having less economic development: on the contrary, a healthy economy is better able to generate the resources to meet people's needs, and new investment and environmental improvement go hand in hand' (HM Government, 1994, p. 7). By widening the term, the government hopes to engage as many departments as it can, so they feel they have a stake in the issue.

The other important source of external pressure on the UK government is transmitted through the international convention process overseen by the UN. The three main environmental agreements on climate change, biodiversity conservation and sustainable development signed at Rio, have intensified the need for inter-departmental coordination. However, the externally imposed and audited discipline of accounting for and reducing greenhouse gas emissions has laid bare the contradictions between environment, energy and transport, differences which in an earlier period could have been more easily overcome via inter-departmental bargaining (O'Riordan and Jäger, 1996). The EU's involvement in the so-called UN Kyoto Protocol process of reducing emissions has undoubtedly lent further urgency and credibility to the UK's mitigation efforts. One of the most pressing issues in the early part of the new millennium will be precisely how to achieve the reduction targets demanded by the EU. British industry has developed a plan to allow trading in carbon emission credits but if this fails to deliver the necessary reductions the government will find itself under enormous pressure either to legislate or to introduce a politically unpopular tax on the use of energy.

## Domestic political pressure

Until relatively recently, the environment was regarded by most politicians as an unimportant and largely self-contained area of political activity. In the past 'non'-environmental departments interpreted any escape of environmental issues from the 'environmental ghetto' (HC 517-I, session 1997–8, p. xvii) as unwarranted interference to be resisted wherever possible. However, the growing scale and scope of environmental legislation, and the steady politicization of the environment, have made it harder for them to stand aloof. In this respect, the greening government initiative is pressing against a slowly opening door in Britain. For instance, virtually all departments have had to learn, often painfully, how to justify their 'non'-environmental policies in environmental terms to a more environmentally astute public.

When the Conservatives were in power the 1995 Brent Spar crisis brilliantly revealed how poorly prepared the then Department of Trade and Industry (DTI) was to meet the political demands posed by the sustainability agenda (Bennie, 1998). However, Labour, too, has shown itself to be unprepared to deal with precisely the sort of issues that greening government was supposed to prevent. In particular, the rapid escalation of at least one issue, the commercialization of genetically modified organisms (GMOs), caught the new Labour government completely flat-footed and, more worryingly, revealed deep splits within the heart of the new, supposedly more 'joined-up' administration. Environmental pressure groups in Britain had warned of the potential threat posed by GMOs to wildlife as long ago as the early 1980s, but they were largely dismissed as doomsayers. Throughout the 1980s and 1990s the commercialization of genetically modified (GM) crops in the US continued apace, driven by large multi-national companies like Monsanto with huge marketing and advertizing budgets. Today, tens of millions of acres of GM crops are grown each year in the US.

In 1990, the EU created a regulatory system to oversee the commercialization process in Europe and to ensure a unified market in GM crops. However, three developments in 1998 virtually stopped the commercialization of GM crops dead in its tracks. The first, in 1996, was Monsanto's decision to cease sorting supplies of genetically manipulated soya beans from normal stocks. This delivered a huge campaigning opportunity to the environmental groups in Europe, which quickly pointed out that the genetically modified soya, a basic component of many foodstuffs, would quickly find its way into the entire food system, leaving consumers practically no choice as to whether they wanted to consume it or not. Public opinion became much more resistant to what was perceived to be an enforced denial of consumer choice. Second, dissident scientists in the UK began to publish findings suggesting that GM foods could adversely affect health. The Royal Societies of London and Edinburgh, the chief scientific institutes in Britain, issued a damning condemnation of the underlying science, but they secured huge media coverage nonetheless. Quickly, the public, whose trust in science and policy-making had been badly dented by the BSE crisis, withdrew its support from the new technology. The major high street supermarkets picked up on this and removed food containing GM ingredients from their shelves. Finally, stung by similar levels of domestic criticism, other EU member states began to block or hold back the commercialization of GM food, which completely logjammed the EU's regulatory system and threatened to provoke a damaging trade war with the US.

For all Blair's commitment to a new, integrated form of environmental politics, the GMO debate quickly took on all the hallmarks of an old-style environmental crisis: institutional failure, contested science, determined pressure group campaigning and public unease. The government's initial response to the media storm that broke in 1998 was to seek refuge in the argument that it was proceeding on the basis of 'sound science'. But this proved inadequate in the face of deep-seated public unease about the scientific, moral and ethical issues raised by GM technology. As public resistance hardened in 1998–9, the government responded by overhauling the body which advises the DETR on trials of GM crops, ACRE. Previously eight of ACRE's 13-member committee had had ties with the biotechnology industry; only one represented a middle-ground environmental group. Realizing it had completely under-estimated the strength of public unease, in 1999 the biotechnology industry announced a voluntary moratorium on the commercialization of new crops until 2002. However, this succeeded only in shifting the front line of the dispute to the very fields where the biotech companies hoped to undertake a series of crop trials. 1999 witnessed running battles between direct action campaigners intent on uprooting the crops, the police and local farmers backed by the crop companies.

The politics of the dispute cry out for joined-up policy solutions. The UK is a world leader in biotechnology and, understandably, Blair, backed by powerful Whitehall departments keen to encourage this success, is fearful of surrendering the competitive edge, not to mention jobs and future investment, simply to appease 'irrational' public opinion. Until the crisis broke, the biotech companies were openly advocating deregulation but now this seems a very distant prospect. The DETR in particular proved itself to be more sympathetic to public fears and made efforts to achieve a stronger and more transparent regulatory system. Overall, though, the government has shown itself to be incapable of steering events, and there has been precious little evidence of joined-up policy-making for sustainability. Symptomatic of this was Labour's belated decision to establish a new cabinet committee on biotechnology 'to establish clear and firm policies in a number of complex areas which cut across Departmental boundaries and which are also of great concern to the public' (ENDS, 1998a, 34).

## Barriers to 'joined-up' policy-making

Although conceptually sustainability is very different to environmentalism, the dispute over GMOs powerfully reveals just how little political purchase or profile it had outside the environmental policy networks centred on the DETR. Here, in a way, lies the rub of the problem, neatly summarized by Brundtland thus: 'Those responsible for managing natural resources and protecting the environment are institutionally separated from those responsible for managing the economy. The real world of interlocked economic and ecological systems will not change; the policies and institutions concerned must' (WCED, 1987, p. 9). In simple bureaucratic terms, greening government required colonization of the key centres of power in the political system, by winning over the more powerful departments of state to its way of thinking. Both at home and in European fora, Prescott campaigned during his time at the helm of the DETR for greater coordination. The paradox is that joined-up policy-making can be delivered only via the very institutionalized system of inter-departmental bargaining that leads to fragmented and sectorized thinking. The political difficulty of overcoming this deep-seated paradox of government should not be under-estimated. Whitehall has its own, highly effective ways of thwarting new cross-sectoral initiatives (Peters, 1998, p. 295).

Of all the barriers to 'joined-up thinking', one of the most fundamental is the basic organizational structure of government. Many influential accounts stress the extent to which it is deeply fragmented into competing departments of state. Richardson and Jordan (1979, pp. 26, 28) coined the phrase 'departmental pluralism' to describe the tendency for different parts to compete with one another. The segmentation of government works into independent, functionally discrete departments, insulated from external pressure by policy networks of special interests, thwarts cross-cutting initiatives such as sustainability. According to a Minister in the DTI, the 'danger' of these divisions, is that Ministers find themselves 'locked into silos ... one department does one thing, another does another, and they actually undermine each other and never talk to each other' (HC 517-II, Session 1997–8, p. 145). Potentially 'over-riding issues' such as the environment tend to fall between the cracks between departments, or are simply dissipated unless there is strong leadership from the centre (Peters, 1998, p. 306).

Typically, each department defends its own position while resisting a line that, while it might be beneficial to society as a whole, could work against its 'own' interests. Those interests are often related to an ideology or philosophy of working which pre-exists any 'rational' assessment of a particular policy problem or its solution. This aspect of policy-making is captured by the popular aphorism 'the departmental view', but it is also closely connected to the concept of policy paradigms. The best example is probably agricultural policy, which under the MAFF has been almost exclusively concerned with intensifying production and protecting farmers' incomes regardless of the environmental cost. Similarly, in the transport sector the former Department of Transport always favoured building more roads to meet a predicted level of demand over the provision of better public transport facilities or demand management. Conceived of in these terms, sustainability is the DETR's policy paradigm.

So how well have the coordinating mechanisms fared? The performance to date underlines how far the DETR has to go to win other departments round to its way of thinking. The Audit Committee (HC 517-I, session 1997–8) detected 'some failure to grasp the overarching nature of sustainable development' – diplomatic code for 'thwarted by departmental resistance and weak central leadership'. Apparently, the Cabinet Committee (ENV) hardly ever meets and its activities are in any case secret. It emerged that ENV's main task is to resolve contentious inter-departmental conflicts, not systematically integrate environmental concerns into all areas of policy formulation and implementation. When he appeared before the Environmental Audit Committee, the Environment Minister admitted that other parts of Whitehall were opposed to what the DETR was trying to achieve. The Committee was, for example, told that ENV did not consider the environmental implications of the 1997 Budget before it was announced (HC 517-II, Session 1997–8, p. 272) – surely an important acid test of how well greening government is performing. It also discovered that the 1998 Comprehensive Spending Review, which determines the shape of public spending well into the next century and whose environmental implications are obviously enormous, was undertaken separate from the DETR's sustainability initiative. In fact, the DETR was the only department to include sustainability in its terms of reference for the Review. Under questioning from MPs, Michael Meacher conceded that there was simply too much at stake for the whole process to be held up by greening government: economic 'necessities' can all too easily trump environmental desiderata. The overall impression given by the Committee was that there was no systematic environmental policy integration beyond that dictated by EU Directives and political expediency generated by controversial political events and electoral considerations. Attempts to create cross-departmental coordinating machinery has been left to fairly low-level working groups of well-intentioned officials. The Green Ministers, who met just seven times in five years under the Tories and twice in the first year of the Blair government, have not been visible, and seem to deal mainly with 'housekeeping' issues such as departmental purchasing policy. An independent review of the policy appraisal process commissioned by the DETR revealed that most appraisals were undertaken very poorly – when they were carried out at all (ENDS, 1997, pp. 3–4). Environmental groups claim that most departments pay only lip service to the DETR's advice when appraising their own policies (HC 517-II, pp. 101–8). The fact that the SDU is located in the DETR rather than in the Cabinet Office where, in opposition, Labour had promised to put it (Labour Party, 1994, p. 43), suggests that greening government is not one of the Blair administration's political priorities. So, is integration progressing any faster in particular policy areas?

## Transport: a policy mess?

There is no better example of the need for better inter-departmental coordination than transport policy. The rising costs of congestion coupled to health fears about smog in urban areas (childhood asthma rates have doubled in the last 20 years) and a rising wave of protest about plans to run new roads through greenfield sites in affluent parts of the South and

South East (Doherty, 1998), have greatly politicized the issue of transport in the last five years. With road traffic currently growing at around 2 per cent per year, large parts of the existing road network are racing towards permanent gridlock by the early part of the next century. John Prescott is the first Transport Secretary openly to admit that '[d]oing nothing is not an option' (ENDS, 1998b, p. 21), but the painful truth is that solving the crisis requires the reconciliation of policies that for the last 40 years have run in opposite directions. Transport is an example *par excellence* of a 'policy mess' which typically arises 'when policy problems do not correspond to the structure of government' (Rhodes, 1986, p. 28).

## Conflicting policy paradigms

For the past 40 years, transport policy has worked on the 'predict and provide' principle that forecasted levels of growth should be catered for a continuous programme of building new roads. The policy paradigm suited the interests of a tightly integrated policy community of engineers, haulage firms, car producers and road builders that surrounded the DoT, insulating it from external political pressure (Finer, 1958; Rawcliffe, 1998). Realizing that the situation was both socially and environmentally unsustainable, the DoE fought to impose a ceiling on future traffic growth but found itself blocked by the DoT (ENDS, 1994, p. 19; *New Scientist*, 1993). The DoT tried to circumvent political protest by subdividing key routes into separate sections. This meant that by the time each individual road was assessed the decision to proceed was effectively a foregone conclusion. The DoT even resisted the DoE's attempts to include the cost of environmental damage in formal cost-benefit assessments of new roads (Pearce, 1998). During the 1990s, the DoE announced new planning guidelines to curb new out-of-town developments that stimulate and sustain car use, but this did not deflect the main thrust of the road-building programme. Worse still for the DoE, its attempts to reduce car dependency were challenged by the privatisation–deregulation agenda pursued by the DoT under the Conservatives, which saw British Rail and local authority bus services broken up into competing units.

### A 'new deal' for transport?

The 1990s have witnessed a paradigm shift in transport policy (Dudley and Richardson, 1996; 1998) (see Box 15.2). Here, at least in theory, Labour is on firm ground because the transport conundrum is highly amenable to Third Way thinking, bound up as it is with balancing rights with responsibilities. Overdependence on the car socially excludes the poor who also suffer the most from poor air quality. However, transport is tightly bound to patterns of development and housing, and to popular social activities such as recreation. Despite growing public unease over vehicle congestion, asthma, noise and photochemical smog, the public's well-established love affair with the car shows no sign of abating. The creation of the DETR has helped address the mismatch of institutions to problems, but Prescott's determined efforts to craft a sustainable policy have been stymied by the Treasury and what he termed the 'teeny boppers' in Blair's inner circle. Much to his annoyance, Blair has intervened on more than one occasion to pacify the anxious car drivers of Middle England, personified by the archetypal 'Mondeo Man' who bore him to power in 1997.

---

## Box 15.2    A new paradigm of transport policy?

In the 1990s transport policy underwent a deep-seated change, brought about by a combination of different factors:

- *Paradigm failure*: the 'predict and provide' philosophy of building roads to cater for a predicted level of demand became discredited when politicians realized they had neither the money nor sufficient popular support to build their way out of the problems of congestion, pollution and urban sprawl. The turning point was a report from the Royal Commission on Environmental Pollution (RCEP) which stated that building new roads simply leads to more traffic, more congestion and more accidents. Current transport policy, it concluded, constitutes 'one of the greatest obstacles to achieving sustainable development' (RCEP, 1994, p. 1)
- *Environmental protest*: direct action protests in the heartlands of Middle England made the construction of new trunk roads a political nightmare for John Major's government (Doherty, 1998). The DoT learnt that it was politically more acceptable to concentrate on extending and maintaining existing routes, and building by-passes to reduce congestion in particular towns, than driving new roads through virgin countryside, but even this failed to win popular support
- *International pressure*: the European Commission has jousted with the DoT over the adequacy of the environmental assessment of new road schemes. The transport sector is also the fastest growing source of carbon dioxide, the main greenhouse gas, and poses a serious threat to the UK's long-term compliance with the UN Climate Convention
- *Treasury pressure*: road building is regarded as a relatively soft option for Treasury cuts in order to fund Labour's flagship education and health policies. Labour's transport review made the politically easy decision of trimming many large and unpopular projects from the road-building programme, saving the Treasury a small fortune and sparing 41 Sites of Special Scientific Interest (SSSIs) from damage (*Financial Times*, 1 August 1998)

The centrepiece of Prescott's strategy was a White Paper entitled 'A New Deal for Transport' (DETR, 1998f). Although it undoubtedly represented a sea change in thinking, with new money for public transport, stronger local authority powers and provision for charging on parking and congestion, many of the most difficult issues were dropped, devolved to local authorities or required enabling legislation (ENDS, 1998b). Prescott did well out of the Comprehensive Spending Review (CSR) but plans for a strategic rail authority and other innovative measures lost out in the competition for parliamentary time and will not appear until late in Blair's term in office. Significantly, the Commons environment committee bemoaned the absence of national road traffic reduction targets to steer the new policy (HC 32-I, session 1997–8). It also identified a lack of coordination within government, chiding the DTI for proposing to relax planning consents to enable science parks to be built on greenfield sites: in the past, greenfield developments have served only to fuel the demand for travel.

Labour is tackling the long-standing transport policy mess with much greater determination than the Tories, but even with a huge parliamentary majority it remains remarkably wary of proceeding too rapidly. As a leader writer in The *Daily Telegraph* (21 July 1998, p. 20) succinctly put it:

Life in rural areas ... would be unbearable without cars ... For many businesses ... cars are obligatory. Our roads are economic arteries: the prosperity of a modern nation depends on the velocity of exchange. And the car has liberated women ... To be anti-car is therefore, in varying degrees, to be anti-countryside, anti-business, anti-women and anti-children.

Since *no* government can possibly afford to be any of these if it wants to secure re-election, the DETR was forced, in the words of Michael Meacher, to introduce 'the minimum changes that people don't like, but are nonetheless effective' (*New Statesman*, 25 October 1998, special supplement, p. v).

## Energy: the dangers of serendipitous policy-making?

Labour's energy policy is to provide secure and diverse supplies of energy at competitive prices. Then there is the commitment to sustainable development. Unfortunately, these objectives do not necessarily pull in the same direction. So which one is winning out? The government has environmental commitments to reduce greenhouse and acid emission to attend to. The DTI, which absorbed the Department of Energy in 1992, is primarily concerned with supply-side issues, chiefly securing fuel diversity and lower prices in order to achieve economic growth. Then there are a variety of non-departmental government bodies with diverse goals. The Environment Agency's task is to regulate emissions from power stations; the electricity regulator, OFFER, oversees the pricing of electricity and has responsibilities for protecting the interests of consumers. The result is not a 'policy mess', but nor is it integrated long-term planning.

In order to achieve a genuinely sustainable energy policy Labour has to reconcile three conflicting goals:

- *Affordable energy prices*: privatization of the energy industry and liberalization of the domestic energy market, two flagship policies of the Conservative government, combined with changes in the world-wide energy market, have led to a steady decline in the electricity price paid by consumers. The DTI regards this as a vindication of its policies and, with OFFER, is promoting further liberalization. However, as prices have fallen, the amount of energy consumed per unit of GDP has increased. In relative terms, the UK is using its energy reserves more and more inefficiently, and generating large amounts of pollution in the process.
- *Jobs*: privatization and fiercer competition dealt a savage blow to the coal industry. As recently as 1990, coal generated two-thirds of the UK's electricity. By 2000, the figure is likely to be less than 20 per cent, compared to over 40 per cent for gas. The 'dash' for cheap, relatively clean but finite supplies of gas decimated the domestic coal industry. The Tories allowed market forces to prevail but Labour has intervened. Faced with the imminent collapse of the domestic coal industry in old Labour heartlands, in December 1997 Blair stepped in and declared a moratorium on new gas-fired power stations in order to save jobs. Nuclear power sits in the political and economic doldrums. By 2015 there are likely to be only a handful of stations still in service.
- *Environmental goals*: like transport, energy generates large amounts of the climate-altering gas $CO_2$, as well as other gases which contribute to acid rain. As an EU member state, the UK has a binding commitment to make long-term reductions in both these areas. Currently greenhouse gases present the key policy problem. In all probability, the UK and Germany will be the only EU states to attain the climate change targets agreed at Rio in 1992, and the UK will do this only because of the windfall saving produced by the collapse of the relatively 'dirty' coal industry. However, at Kyoto, Prescott agreed to tighten emission targets substantially. According to latest estimates, UK emissions of the six gases covered by the Kyoto Protocol are projected to fall by 10 per cent from 1990 to 2010 under policies and actions already planned – 2.5 percentage points short of the UK's commitment. However, $CO_2$

emissions will fall by only 3 per cent by 2010, compared to the goal that Labour committed itself to in opposition of 'at least' 20 per cent (Labour Party, 1994, p. 41).

Currently, there are three pressure points at which these different priorities collide headlong. As in the transport sector, international commitments greatly reduce the government's ability to fudge a compromise.

## The energy 'mix'

The DTI published the results of a year-long Energy Review of fuel sources in October 1998. It tries to square the circle of propping up the coal industry and maintaining competition in energy supply by restricting new gas power stations and removing distortions in the energy market which have made coal so unattractive. However, the White Paper predicts that even with these adjustments, coal could end up with just 10 per cent of the electricity market by 2003, with gas taking 50–60 per cent. In sustainability terms, the outcome of the Review is decidedly mixed. This may reflect the allegedly low priority that the DTI gave to the government's environmental commitments during the course of the review (ENDS, 1998c). Gas is a non-renewable resource and at the current rate of extraction the UK will become a net importer sometime early in the next century. But in environmental terms, any increase in coal burn would push up greenhouse gas emissions, jeopardizing the UK's Kyoto commitment. It would also spell problems on acid rain because it is unlikely that generators would voluntary fit expensive cleaning equipment when the market is becoming increasingly competitive and fragmented. The UK should reach its short-term climate target but problems remain in the period after 2010. By then, the windfall effect will have dried up as the nuclear industry, a relatively greenhouse-friendly fuel source, and the gas sector both decline, while road traffic and energy use are both expected to rise.

## Domestic energy consumption

Given the difficulties of reducing emissions from the transport sector, the DETR decided to focus on the domestic sector in the hunt for the extra cuts in greenhouse gases needed to fulfil the UK's Kyoto target. The main barrier here is the deep contradiction between the DTI's drive to reduce energy prices and promote competition (through which energy suppliers compete to supply as much electricity as possible), and the DETR's campaign to boost energy efficiency and reduce polluting emissions. The fear is that lower prices will produce a 'rebound effect', prompting consumers to consume more energy. So far, the windfall saving has deflected attention from the poor performance of existing government policies to promote energy efficiency. Chief among them is the Energy Saving Trust. Created in 1992 by the DoE to encourage the uptake of energy efficient devices in the domestic and industrial sector, it was supposed to be funded from a levy on domestic energy bills but the strategy was hobbled when the head of OFGAS, who is appointed by the DTI, withheld her support and funding had to be dramatically scaled back (O'Riordan and Rowbotham, 1996).

## Renewable energy production

The gap left by gas and nuclear could be filled by renewables. In theory, renewable energy sources (solar, wind, hydroelectric power, etc.) provide the most sustainable solution to Britain's energy needs, with minimal air pollution. However, renewables have traditionally been the Cinderella of British energy policy, consistently elbowed aside by the politically more powerful coal and nuclear lobbies. Consequently they currently account for just 2 per cent of the UK's electricity needs. In opposition, Labour promised to supply 10 per cent of electricity from renewable sources by 2010 (Labour Party, 1994, p. 25). The main delivery mechanism is likely to be the Non-Fossil Fuel Obligation (NFFO) Orders, although the scheme, which helps commercialize promising new technologies by placing a levy on domestic electricity bills, is due to expire very soon.

In the meantime the policy of achieving the 10 per cent target is proceeding at a snail's pace. Renewables are generally more costly than conventional sources and, given the background of declining prices and tough competition, the big generators are wary of taking up new and uncertain technologies. By 2003, renewables are expected to generate only 5 per cent of UK needs (c.1000 MW) (HC Written Answers, 19 October 1998). Any attempt to increase the NFFO will almost certainly be resisted by the electricity regulator, who has warned that the economic cost, some £11–15 billion (equivalent to a 6–7 per cent levy on fuel bills), does not justify the environmental benefits (ENDS, 1998d, p. 7). Again sustainability is being thwarted by bureaucratic squabbles and the short-term demand for unsustainable consumption.

## Conclusion

In opposition, Tony Blair openly courted the green movement, embracing sustainability with all the zeal of the recently converted. In a keynote speech he 'welcome[d] the fact that so many environmentalists now recognize that for lasting change to come about we need to explore the common ground between 'social justice' and the environmental' (Blair, 1996b). But after a promising start, Labour has found it increasingly difficult to coordinate policy across the many strands of social, environmental and economic activity in pursuit of sustainability. Ambitious objectives on renewable energy, climate change and integrated transport are proving harder to deliver than expected. The simmering political dispute over whether or not to commercialize GMOs powerfully revealed Blair's deep-seated political determination not to forsake the potentially huge commercial benefits of developing new foodstuffs in order simply to placate the environmental lobby.

Labour is publicly committed to greening government, but so far sustainable development has made headway only when political and economic circumstances have permitted. The delayed responses to the GMO crisis and Prescott's failure to cut the Gordian knot of transport policy are two good cases in point. The cynic might well conclude that achieving re-election was the dominant lodestar of the Labour government, not sustainability. There is probably more than a grain of truth in that claim: in spite of its huge parliamentary majorities, a Middle England agenda does appear to be driving Labour's environmental policy. Spin doctors seem too fearful of alienating 'Mondeo man' to countenance a progressive environmental agenda encompassing eco-taxes, policy assessments and green indicators of economic growth. More worryingly for the environmental movement is the lack of a truly championing Minister effective in Whitehall and the Cabinet Office. For all his ebullience and connections with old Labour, Prescott had many other distractions and found himself reshuffled out of post following the 2001 election. In spite of the obvious synergies with its environmental concerns, Labour's political antennae remain firmly fixed on health, education and sound financial management. Labour shows a stronger commitment to the environment than the Conservatives, but large parts of the government are 'off message' as far as the DETR's vision of an environmentally sustainable society is concerned.

## Note

Andrea Lenschow, Steve Crooks, Neil Adger, Tim O'Riordan, Ian Holliday and the other editors of *Developments 6* made extremely useful comments on earlier drafts of this chapter. Responsibility for remaining errors of fact and interpretation rests entirely with the author.

# Chapter 16

# Foreign and Defence Policy

JOANNA SPEAR

The post-Cold War period presents both opportunities and challenges for British foreign policy-makers. The bipolar system that structured international relations for more than four decades has given way to a situation of flux and multi-polarity. Like her allies, Britain is seeking to steer a course through this period of uncertainty. For Britain, the issue of a European versus an Atlanticist identity is one key challenge (Peterson, 1999). It is not new, but it has taken on new potency in the post-Cold War period. With the Soviet Union gone, the US is engaged in an internal debate over the future scope and direction of its foreign policy. After a period of intense activism and intervention in the immediate post-Cold War period, the US has become more reticent about international involvement – particularly where core issues are not involved – and isolationism has once more gained some currency. In Europe, the changed international environment has spurred discussion of greater foreign policy cooperation. British foreign policy-makers therefore face the question of which alliance to prioritize. Political leaders, from the prime minister and foreign secretary down, all claim that there is actually no need to make a choice here: being a good European reinforces the UK's appeal for Washington. Whilst this may be true, the balancing act is difficult to maintain.

In addition to challenges, the current international environment generates opportunities. In particular, in a rather more benign environment policy-makers can take a wider range of values into account when choosing a foreign policy course. For this reason, it has been possible for the Blair government to introduce 'ethical' concerns into foreign policy – concerns which would have been considered a security liability in the Cold War years. Nevertheless, to cover themselves from charges of going 'soft' on foreign policy, Tony Blair and Robin Cook deny that there is a dichotomy between an 'ethical' foreign policy and a 'realist' one, a claim which tends to be treated sceptically by their critics. Although the government's policies may be realistic in terms of security, they can be regarded as unrealistic in terms of trade – one of the key foreign policy tools of the post-Cold War era. In this chapter, the difficult issues that confront UK foreign policy in the new century are analyzed.

## Labour's foreign policy intentions

Labour's 1997 manifesto promised a fundamental review of British defence policy for the post-Cold War period. There was also a pledge to increase the commitment to development by, among other things, creating a department devoted to international development issues. In addition, campaign rhetoric raised expectations that a Labour government would institute greater controls over British arms exports. In contrast to previous manifestos, however, there were no references to countries which would be denied access to British arms. These initiatives sat very well with the Labour Party's internationalist tradition which placed emphasis on introducing morality into foreign policy. However, despite indicating some changes of direction, they did not really form a foreign policy agenda.

Are there, then, any clues in the emerging political philosophy of 'Third Way' politics? According to Blair (1999a), 'The driving force behind the Third Way is globalization. No country is immune from the massive change that globalization brings' (see Chapter 2). 'Globalization' can be defined as 'the intensification of economic, political, social and cultural relations across borders' (Kegley and Wittkopf, 1997, p. 249). An important dimension is the way in which different national economies are becoming part of a global network and consequently having to change the way they operate. The concept is therefore intimately linked to economic competitiveness issues. 'Third Way' politics are regarded as the best way for a political economy to function in a globalized market. Globalization brings states into much closer contact and means that events and policies initiated in one place can have effects elsewhere. The 'sensitivity' of societies and markets to what is going on elsewhere gives every state a stake in solving common problems, be they the environment, poverty, drugs or civil war. Consequently, according to Blair, 'Our task is to build a new doctrine of international community, defined by common rights and shared responsibilities' (Blair, 1999a). It is clear that before entering office the Labour Party did not see foreign policy as having any intrinsic value. Rather, the international system was merely viewed as the source of important trends in political economy which would impact on the government's ability to fulfil its domestic policy agenda. The lack of a clear foreign policy agenda meant that Labour's foreign policy would be 'reactive diplomacy', responding to events in the international system rather than implementing a clearly articulated policy.

Nevertheless, only two weeks after entering office Foreign Secretary Robin Cook launched a 'mission statement' for his department consisting of four goals. Three were both vague and uncontroversial: the Foreign Office would promote security and prosperity for Britain while seeking to enhance the quality of life. The fourth caused more of a stir: 'we shall work through our international forums and bilateral relationships to spread the values of human rights, civil liberties and democracy which we demand for ourselves' (Cook, 1997, p. 2). This was presented in the media as a declaration of an 'ethical' foreign policy, although Cook preferred the more modest idea of an 'ethical dimension' to foreign policy. The second major issue facing Labour – the question of a European or an Atlanticist identity (or both) – was not addressed so explicitly early on. Instead, ministers sought to project a clear willingness to be more 'European' whilst at the same time maintaining the strong Atlantic ties developed by Thatcher and Major (notably during the Reagan and Bush presidencies).

## Multiple actors in foreign policy

There are many makers of UK foreign policy. The three lead departments are the Foreign and Commonwealth Office (FCO), the Ministry of Defence (MoD) and the new Department for International Development (DFID). However, foreign policy is now made by, and its implementation affected by, a multiplicity of actors, governmental, non-governmental and international.

Alongside the three main departments are other parts of government. As Chancellor in the late 1980s, John Major launched a Treasury campaign to significantly decrease the debt burden on the world's poorest countries. This initiative was continued by subsequent post-holders, and expanded by Gordon Brown, who was responsible for negotiating with finance ministers from the Group of Seven major economies (G7), members of the Organization for Economic Cooperation and Development (OECD), officials from the International Monetary Fund (IMF) and World Bank, and Commonwealth finance ministers. Alongside this initiative, the DFID has sought to re-orient EU aid policies towards the world's poorest countries. The policy began to bear fruit when, in April 1999, the IMF agreed to finance debt relief by selling some of its gold supplies. Britain has also led by example in pledging $100 million extra in debt relief. In June 1999, G7 ministers meeting in Cologne announced a $100 billion (£63 billion) package of debt relief. This financial initiative, although spearheaded by the Treasury, has important foreign policy implications: for Britain's position within the Commonwealth, for bilateral relations with third world countries, and for relations with other major economies.

In addition to a wide range of government departments, there are also occasions when Parliament and the courts can play a key role. A good example is the decision of the Law Lords to deny ex-President Pinochet of

Chile sovereign immunity from an extradition request lodged by Spain to stand charge for allegedly orchestrating the murder of Spanish citizens in Chile between 1973 and 1983. Home Secretary Jack Straw had the ultimate decision of allowing Pinochet's extradition to go ahead, another instance of an ostensibly domestic political decision having foreign policy implications.

Non-governmental actors can also have a profound impact on foreign policy making or its implementation. The Labour government's intentions to create a unified European defence industry have been undermined, for instance, by decisions taken by a major British defence company, British Aerospace (BAe). The Blair government is much more sympathetic to the idea of a European defence identity than previous British governments, and ministers encouraged the consolidation of national defence industries into a single European aerospace and defence company ('Euroco'). However, these hopes were dashed by the merger plans of BAe, which in late 1998 summarily rejected a merger offer from the German firm Dasa (the Daimler Chrysler aerospace division), opting instead to launch a £7 billion takeover of British firm Marconi Electronic Systems. BAe is also looking to the US for future consolidation and teaming. Although not ruling out further European consolidation, BAe's clear preference is for transatlantic alliances – seeing this as the route to enhancing shareholder value. Although initially in sympathy with Blair's preferences, the interests of the defence firm ultimately led it in a direction which undermined government initiatives for Euroco.

In addition, several elements of what was traditionally British foreign policy are now made and implemented by EU institutions. Although at times the Blair government has become directly engaged in trade disputes, for example, trade is no longer a unilateral concern. Foreign policy in this area is often negotiated and implemented by the European Commission. Thus, it was the EU which was in dispute with the US in the so-called 'banana war' and later involved in a dispute over US beef imports to the EU. In the banana dispute, the EU sought to block market access for Central American bananas in order to protect Caribbean producers. However, the World Trade Organization (WTO) ruled in favour of the US, and awarded $191 million in damages. The dispute illustrates a further entanglement. Justice for Caribbean farmers is difficult to achieve because under the terms of the WTO agreement that the EU signed up to, any obstacles to free trade are unacceptable. This is a foreign policy problem with a clear 'ethical' dimension (preserving the livelihoods of farmers in the former British and French colonies of the Caribbean) which the government and the EU can do little about, tied as the issue is to the greater importance of the WTO as a whole. The real losers are the Caribbean banana growers, who will lose favourable access to the EU market and be faced with competition from very rich and more efficient US-based multinationals.

The complexity of the foreign policy process and the multiplicity of actors who can play a role constrain the ability of the executive to control policy in a complex world. Moreover, there is greater potential for disjunction between different policy initiatives and for institutional conflict between departments. During the war in Kosovo in 1999, there was conflict in government between an offer of hospitality to Kosovan refugees and a proposed Asylum and Immigration Bill – under the terms of which the Kosovans would not have been eligible to come to Britain. This also led to unequal treatment of refugees who fled the region prior to Straw's extension of hospitality, and those who subsequently took advantage of it.

## Policy dilemmas: arms trade issues

For many, the arms trade is a key test of the 'ethical dimension' to foreign policy. Labour faces a tension between the desire for arms transfer restraint and the best interests of the British defence industrial base (DIB), including domestic issues such as employment. In the run-up to the 1997 election, Labour produced eight policy pledges for a responsible arms trade:

1.  No licences for arms to regimes that might use them for internal repression or international aggression
2.  Increased transparency and tighter controls on defence equipment as advocated in the Scott Report on arms to Iraq in the Thatcher–Major years; publication of an Annual Report on UK Strategic Exports, listing equipment transferred, country, total values and details of export licences granted and denied
3.  Pressure for a European Register of Arms Exports
4.  Work to strengthen the UN Register, including extending the categories to include weapons such as small arms
5.  Work for the introduction of a European Code of Conduct
6.  No British manufacture, sale or procurement of equipment designed primarily for torture, plus pressure for a global ban
7.  Total bans on anti-personnel land mines and parts and a moratorium on use; pressure for quicker activity on demining
8.  Strengthened monitoring of end-use certificates to prevent diversion to third parties or misuse; work for a common approach to end-use within the EU and the Wassenaar Arrangement (a forum for agreeing export controls on weapons of mass destruction, technologies and conventional weapons).

These have become the policy touchstones for Labour in office, but are balanced by a clear and oft-repeated commitment to maintain the British DIB. The pledges actually demand little of the Labour government. Four (3, 4, 5, 8) rely on multi-lateral action and cannot be instituted by Britain alone. The pledges on landmines and torture equipment (6, 7) were both expected, and are not out of line with public opinion. The pledge concerning end-user controls (8) merely extends existing British policy. The rest are modest advances on previous government policies.

The tension between sales and restrictions has led to institutional conflict within the government over policy implementation. The Defence Export Services Organization (DESO) in the MD and the Department of Trade and Industry (DTI) have been involved in several wrangles with the FCO and 10 Downing Street over individual decisions, the degree of transparency which could be achieved (given the requirements of 'commercial confidentiality') and interpretation of the eight points. In terms of overall arms transfer levels, there has been no decrease in British arms sales since Labour came to office. In fact, exports increased by 10 per cent in 1997: orders worth $8.8 billion kept Britain in second position (behind the US) in world defence exports (*Jane's Defence Weekly*, 1998). Do individual arms deals show evidence of restraint? It is hard to tell as the government does not name states it has refused to sell to. We know only about sales which are made, including those to Indonesia, a country long banned from purchasing weapons from the US and Belgium because of its human rights record, but a valued customer for British arms exports. Before its shift to a more democratic regime in 1999, Indonesia was regarded as the 'acid test' of the new arms transfer policy and commitment to human rights. The Labour government's decision to honour its predecessor's arms sales commitments led to criticisms that its 'ethical foreign policy' was a sham.

The first annual report on arms transfers was released in 1999, somewhat later than had been anticipated because of a wrangle between the FCO and the MD over its contents. As Wheeler and Dunne noted when considering the general openness of the new government, 'At a conceptual level, it is a bold move since it furnishes journalists, activists and intellectuals with the information necessary to hold the government accountable for its actions' (Wheeler and Dunne, 1998, p. 853). A major achievement of the British Presidency of the EU in 1998 was getting the EU to adopt a code of conduct, though it was weaker than the government wanted because of pressure from the French.

One of the most vaunted achievements of the new arms transfer policy was a speedy move to ban anti-personnel (AP) landmines. The new Labour government reversed its predecessor's stance and signed the Ottawa Convention banning the production, stockpiling and deployment of AP landmines. It was amongst the first to begin to destroy stocks of AP landmines when the Treaty came into force in March 1999. However, this policy was not an entirely dramatic change, being more of a qualitative improvement on a pre-existing ban on the export of AP landmines and commitment to deploy only landmines containing a self-destruct mechanism.

## The Strategic Defence Review

In fulfilment of a long-standing policy commitment, Labour launched a strategic review of defence policy – the first in 17 years, and thus the first to consider Britain's defence priorities in the post-Cold War world. The result, the Strategic Defence Review (SDR) entitled *Modern Forces for a Modern World* (Ministry of defence, 1998), sought to provide a coherent defence policy for Britain until 2015. One innovation was a commitment to consult different groups with an interest in British foreign and defence policy, an approach designed to bring new ideas and greater openness into the policy-making process. However, as Bruce George, chair of the Parliamentary Defence Committee remarked at the launch of its report on the SDR, the nearer to decisions the government got, the less democratic and open the process became.

The SDR recognizes that the threats Britain now faces are fundamentally different and include crises (environmental, drugs, ethnic conflict, resource issues, etc.) around the world which threaten international stability and national interests (McInnes, 1998, pp. 833–4). In a world of more varied threats, British forces may be called upon to play a number of roles in military, peacekeeping and relief operations. They therefore need to be rapidly deployable and to be flexible enough to be combined into a 'package' geared to the scenario they are confronting. The SDR created a Joint Rapid Reaction Force (JRRF) to pool resources and units from all three services to fulfil this requirement for flexibility and speed. In November 1999 the government supported an EU initiative to create a flexible rapid deployment force of some 50–60,000 troops.

The SDR was welcomed by the armed services both because it gave them a strong basis for future planning and because the associated cuts were much smaller than had been feared. At the outset of the review only one new programme was ring-fenced, the Eurofighter programme (for a next-generation fighter), because of its importance to British defence industries and jobs in the UK. There were therefore fears that other programmes would be cut. However, in the event only one major programme was cancelled. The SDR also confirmed Labour's commitment to a nuclear deterrent, despite opposition from the grassroots of the party. In response to criticism from its own backbenchers, the government stressed that only one nuclear submarine would be on patrol at any one time, and would carry only 48 missiles (half the amount planned by the last Major government), with missiles 'de-targeted' and requiring several days notice before firing. Thus, Labour sought to reassure critics by stressing that it had moved to a minimal deterrent posture and remained committed to multilateral arms control.

The House of Commons Select Committee on Defence was generally supportive of the SDR but identified two 'critical weaknesses' and one issue avoided. They were concerned about the decision to cut the size of the Territorial Army (TA) and the consequences for 'home defence'. They were also concerned that the SDR did not deal effectively with the issue of 'asymmetric threats' (for example, terrorism, chemical and biological weapons threats, hostage-taking, etc.). The issue that was avoided was a possible European defence identity. In the House of Commons the plan to decrease the TA attracted most attention; this criticism led to a rethink, which resulted in a reduction in the planned cut and a promise that none of the existing 'badges' would be lost. Through the SDR Labour pulled off a difficult task, producing a future vision for British defence with which the armed services, the defence industries and the majority of Labour supporters were content.

## Continuing crises with Iraq

A recurring problem for the Blair Government has been Iraqi challenges to the UNSCOM (United Nations Special Commission) inspection regime imposed after Iraq's defeat in the Gulf Conflict. UN Resolution 687 of April 1991 stipulated that Iraq must permit the destruction or removal of its Weapons of Mass Destruction (WMD) and ballistic missiles with a range of over 150 kilometres. Once the disarmament was certified by UNSCOM inspectors, economic sanctions could be lifted. Since the first inspection in June 1991, Iraq has pursued a policy of obstruction. Its challenges to the UNSCOM inspection teams have been designed to undermine the unanimity of the UN Security Council and are particularly aimed at the 'waverers' – France and Russia – both of which have economic interests in Iraq. If unanimity broke, it would mean the end of sanctions.

Two periods of heightened tension – February 1998 and November–December 1998 – are particularly noteworthy, and show a hardening attitude. Throughout 1997 Iraq increased its opposition to UNSCOM, in January 1998 preventing inspectors from carrying out their work and denying UNSCOM access to eight so-called 'Presidential' sites, which it declared were 'sensitive'. UNSCOM feared that these sites held SCUD-type missiles with chemical and biological warheads, and 4000 tonnes of unaccounted for chemical and biological agents. The response was a further build-up of US and British forces in the Gulf. There were also warnings from President Clinton that if it continued to defy the UN, Iraq would face military action on a large scale. This led to frantic diplomatic activity from Russia, France and the Arab League designed to persuade Saddam Hussein to cooperate. The situation was resolved by UN Secretary General Kofi Annan, who persuaded Iraq to accept an agreement allowing UNSCOM unfettered access to all sites, with a special team composed of diplomats and UNSCOM inspectors to visit the eight 'Presidential' sites – as a sign of respect for Iraqi sovereignty. This 'inspectors plus suits' deal ended the immediate crisis. However, British and American forces were to remain in the region until it was clear that UNSCOM was back on track. The February crisis occurred during Britain's EU Presidency. Blair unhesitatingly acted to support the US in the crisis without even consulting his European allies – whom he was supposed to be representing.

Over the summer of 1998 it looked as though the unresolved issues about Iraqi WMD could be handled quickly. In June, UNSCOM Executive Chairman Richard Butler agreed a schedule of work which would allow all remaining issues to be dealt with in six weeks. However, at the end of the six weeks when Iraq demanded that Butler certify that they had met all the conditions of Resolution 687 he refused, as important issues were still outstanding. Iraq therefore ended all cooperation with the UNSCOM inspectors, demanding that the oil embargo be lifted, Butler be removed and UNSCOM headquarters be transferred from New York to Geneva or Vienna. The response was swift. America and Britain described Iraqi defiance as an 'act of war'. Even allies in the region blamed Iraq for the latest problems, and Russia and France were silenced as Baghdad had so clearly broken the 'inspectors plus suits' agreement. Reflecting this consensus, UN Resolution 1137 condemned Iraqi violation of the UN-SCOM agreements. There was a sharp build-up of allied forces in the Gulf and by November 1998 military action looked imminent. Saddam Hussein played the situation right to the brink, agreeing to climb down only when he was (secretly, but strategically) informed by the French that US bombers and cruise missiles were in the air. On 15 November 1998, hearing of Saddam Hussein's retreat – and against the advice of many of his military advisers – Clinton called his military forces back. It was decided that UNSCOM should resume its work and report back in one month on the progress made.

The resultant report made it clear that again the Iraqis had been uncooperative. The response from the US and Britain was immediate, but enjoyed little international support. Operation Desert Fox – four nights of military action which ceased as the holy month of Ramadan began – was launched. Its military success was debatable. Moreover, it brought an effective end to the UNSCOM inspection regime and as yet a formula for new inspections has not been agreed, although Britain is playing a diplomatic role here. Conflict is not at crisis level, but there are constant confrontations with Iraqi forces in the two 'no-fly zones' policed by Britain and the US.

## Kosovo

The 1999 conflict in Kosovo has a long lineage (Caplan, 1999; Judah, 1999). The immediate precursor to bombing Serbia was the failure of February 1999 talks at Rambouillet, designed to ensure the safety of the majority ethnic Albanian population in the Serb region of Kosovo. Serbian President Slobodan Milosevic refused to countenance the presence of armed NATO peacekeepers in Kosovo, being determined to deal with the problem of the Kosovo Liberation Army (KLA) whom he deemed terrorists and drug runners. With the failure of the Rambouillet talks and the evidence of increased Serb 'ethnic cleansing' activity against Kosovan Albanians, the NATO alliance acted. A campaign of strategic bombing was launched against transport, communications and militarily significant targets. The bombing lasted for 78 days before Serbia gave into allied demands.

The war in Kosovo is interesting on a number of levels. First, there seems to have been little serious planning for what should happen if bombing did not work. This was in part a consequence of Clinton's preoccupation with saving his presidency during the Lewinsky scandal, which meant that little critical attention was paid to CIA estimates that Milosevic would swiftly capitulate. It also reflects the fact that American public opinion would need to be persuaded of the importance of further military action in Kosovo (that is, the deployment of ground troops) and on this issue Clinton was led by the people, rather than leading them.

Second, European unity held throughout the conflict, with many neutral member states supportive of the military action. That said, however, strains did begin to show, with Greece, Italy and Germany anxious for a termination of military action (primarily owing to domestic political pressures). Also, European unity was not tested to its limits, and might not have held if a ground invasion had been necessary. Third, stemming from Clinton's failure to lead, Blair had a high international profile as the leader most committed to acting over Kosovo, being willing to put ground troops in before a full settlement had been reached. Nevertheless, Yugoslavia's capitulation could not have been more timely for Blair. In advocating a ground intervention he was looking increasingly isolated from other leaders and out of touch with public opinion in the majority of NATO countries (excluding Britain).

Fourth, the conflict in Kosovo has led many to call for a substantive EU defence force. American prevarication over Kosovo was a source of extreme irritation for many. Indeed, it is thought that Blair's new enthusiasm for a European Security and Defence Identity (ESDI), made public in October 1998 in Austria (and in contrast to his stance at the previous Amsterdam summit), was in part motivated by his frustration with US foot-dragging over Kosovo. The issue of ESDI had been stymied for a number of years, and the fact that it was Britain – traditionally a brake on the process – which seemed to be producing the new momentum for action was particularly novel.

Fifth, the Kosovo conflict shows the extent to which the traditional notions of left and right are challenged by events in the post-Cold War international system. The conflict saw significant shifts from Cold War stances, with Ken Livingstone backing the war and Lord Healey against it. The case of Clare Short is also revealing. In contrast to her previous stances, and to the advantage of the Labour leadership, she turned her withering scorn on those who opposed the conflict, particularly her old allies on the left of the Labour party. Sixth, and significantly for the Labour government, one effect of the intervention in Kosovo was to banish the old perception that Labour was unwilling to use military power effectively. This perception had been a thorn in the Labour side since the days of unilateralism in the 1980s, and an electoral weakness. Since Kosovo, this ghost has been effectively laid to rest.

## Conclusion: ethical issues and measures of success

Wheeler and Dunne (1998) identify five factors that suggest there has been a real shift in British foreign policy under Labour:

● the projection of a new, more positive identity for Britain ('cool Britannia')
● the use of a new language of international relations (moving away from a purely realist interpretation of the world)
● the addition of an 'ethical dimension' to foreign policy
● putting human rights concerns at the centre of foreign policy
● widening and opening the policy process.

Of these, the latter three have the greatest substance.

The aspects of the 'ethical dimension' and human rights that have gained most attention are Labour's arms transfer policies and practices. The arms trade aims were a lot more modest than most assumed. Many elements of that modest agenda have been fulfilled: an EU code of conduct exists; there is a total British landmine ban; the process has become more transparent, and so on. However, British arms sales totals have continued to rise (although that in itself does not indicate unethical activity) and, to take just one instance, British-made Hawk jets were used to intimidate East Timorese voters, in contravention of Indonesian promises. The definition of 'ethics' is, then, narrowly drawn here, referring only to human rights' abusers and states that are internationally aggressive, rather than acknowledging the more pervasive connections between arms purchases and under-development. Even on this more limited basis, the Labour government is open to criticism about how the policy has been implemented.

What is important, though, is the way in which ethical concerns have informed British 'reactive diplomacy', particularly during the Kosovo crisis. Blair's single-minded commitment to protecting Kosovan Albanians took both policy analysts and some of his government colleagues by surprise. He called the military action a 'just war', regarding it as a moral issue and leading some to describe him as a 'post-Gladstone leader', a comparison which Blair himself has alluded to (Blair, 1999c). Moreover, it has become clear that for Blair this was an 'ethical' foreign policy in practice. His moral certainty that the military action was right enabled him to stand firm when other leaders were backing away from the option of intervening on the ground. What we have in practice is a foreign policy with a perhaps surprising moral streak to it. However, the 'ethical dimension' does not come at the place where it might be expected, in restraint (for example, in the arms trade), but in activism. As Blair explains:

> Countries have a right to live free from the threat of force. But they also have a responsibility to maintain peace, and not to threaten or attack their neighbours. Otherwise the international community has a responsibility to act . . . People say you can't be self-appointed guardians of what's right and wrong. True, but when the international community agrees certain objectives and then fails to implement them, those who can act, must. (Blair, 1999a)

British foreign and defence policy under Blair is showing that the government is prepared to use traditional tools of foreign policy (military power and diplomacy) to fulfil a progressive agenda which takes seriously issues such as human rights.

Other elements of Labour's foreign policy can be seen as progressive. The commitment to real development, concerns about a wider range of security threats and the desire to use 'defence diplomacy' (in the words of the SDR) to tackle these issues in a pre-emptive manner are all very positive. However, none can be achieved unilaterally and part of the government's diplomacy has been directed towards getting other states to follow a similar agenda. In this, the US (despite the political compatibility between the two governments) has been a disappointment, particularly over the crucial issue of Kosovo. For Britain this was an 'ethical' issue which demanded action (even possibly a ground campaign). For the US it was an issue of concern and worthy of a (safe) air campaign, but not important enough to demand the commitment of American lives.

Attempts to institute openness in the foreign and defence policy process have certainly been seen – though as Bruce George noted 'openness remains a relative term when applied to the MoD' (George, 1998, p. 28). Alongside this, though, we have seen the increasing use of sophisticated public relations management, or 'spin', in foreign and defence policy. In November 1998, for example, during the crisis with Iraq, the government formed an 'Iraq Media Group' within Whitehall to coordinate the government's message. The group was composed of officials from the FCO, MoD and Downing Street, including on one occasion Blair's chief press spokesman Alistair Campbell. Similarly, just before the public release of the SDR the BBC showed a remarkedly anodyne 'fly on the wall' documentary about its preparation, setting the stage for the release of the document. In the Kosovo crisis, one of the decisive early interventions of the Blair team was to 'professionalize' the NATO public relations department fronted by Jamie Shea. At British insistence the Department was beefed up, including the transfer of government public relations personnel to NATO for the duration of the crisis. Thus, at the same time as the government has attempted to create a more open foreign policy process, it has sought to keep a tighter rein on the flow of information, how policy is presented and therefore how it is perceived.

Finally, on the key issue of balancing relations with Europe and the US, Blair has sought to deny that there is a problem: 'We have deluded ourselves for too long with the false choice between the US and Europe' (Blair, 1998b). Britain under Labour can have the best of both worlds. To some extent, this seems to have happened, at least on the level of personal diplomacy. Blair has good relations with Clinton and is well received in Europe. However, both these responses are to Blair the centrist politician with an interesting domestic programme, rather than to his foreign policy. As noted above, on the issue of Iraq he upset the Europeans, and on the issue of Kosovo he aggravated the Americans.

Traditionally, Britain has tilted more towards the US than Europe, but with the end of the Cold War, the development of the EU into an effective political and economic bloc and the costs of maintaining independent military forces, there are structural and economic pressures for Britain to become more involved in a European defence identity. The policy of the Labour government is to respond to these pressures. The Kosovo conflict provided fresh impetus for closer defence cooperation within Europe, and the SDR generated a means by which to continue to pursue a Europeanization of defence production (albeit in a piecemeal fashion). In practice, these issues, combined with the structural pressures, are leading to an increasing interest in a European defence identity. To the list of distinctive elements of foreign policy under Labour cited above we should add the fact that Blair has a more positive attitude to a European defence identity than any of his predecessors.

# Chapter 17

# Policy Agendas in a Multi-Level Polity

## ANDREW GAMBLE

A revolution in government is taking place. Government in the UK may not be disappearing, but the policy process is certainly being transformed as governments grapple with profound challenges arising from globalization, European integration, devolution and administrative reform. The state is becoming much more fragmented and diversified. There is a tendency for it to lose both unity and coherence, making the policy process harder to understand both for politicians and for citizens. Nobody seems to be in control any more, and it is increasingly hard to pinpoint where policies come from and how policy agendas become established, because decisions are taken at so many different levels, and by so many different bodies. Lines of accountability and responsibility have become blurred, and many of the old levers of power no longer work in the way they used to, so that ways of shaping policy have become less obvious. In some respects governments have never been more intrusive, yet at the same time never so lacking in capacity actually to formulate and implement coherent policies.

The extent of change should not be exaggerated, nor its unity. The changes have different logics, they operate at different speeds, and often they conflict. But there is little doubt that together they are forcing a reassessment of the way in which government is perceived. The policy process in the UK can no longer be analyzed in terms of the older narratives of British government which treated the UK as a single-level polity and a self-contained sovereign nation-state. No state now has the resources or the capacities to control the policy process across all areas of public policy (Wallace, W., 1996).

What is emerging in place of the old narratives is the idea of a multi-level polity, which stresses the variety of institutions and processes through which societies are governed, so talks of *governance,* rather than *government* (see Chapter 3 and Pierre, 2000). But two different approaches are evident. In the first a multi-level polity often means no more than a particular form of *national or regional governance,* at the centre of which is a state, whether national like the UK or regional like the EU. The policy process is largely within states or between states (there is a lively dispute as to whether the EU is an example of an inter-state or intra-state policy process) (Hix, 1994). The second conception is to think of the multi-level polity in global terms, as an emerging framework for *transnational governance*, a development which grows out of an increasingly inter-connected global economy and transnational civil society (Rosenau, 1995). It recognizes that the international system is both an inter-state system which has national governments at its core, and a transnational system, which permits many kinds of connections between organizations and networks beyond the control of national governments.

The national governance approach applies to the UK state insights drawn from the analysis of policy processes in other kinds of multi-level polities, notably those found in federal systems such as the US. The UK state now has policy-making systems at three different levels: the national level organized through the executive and legislative institutions of Westminster; the regional level, organized through the devolved institutions for Wales, Scotland and Northern Ireland; and the supranational level, organized through the institutions of the EU, which according to one estimate is the level at which up to 60 per cent of what used to be regarded as domestic policy-making now takes place (Richardson, 1996). The sovereignty of the old Westminster state has been shared with these other bodies, with many of its former functions and policy competences being transferred to them. This trend may develop further in the future if more powers are devolved to the English regions and to city mayors, or transferred to the EU. In this conception of a multi-level polity, the UK government is still the key source of legitimacy and authoritative decision-making. It decides which powers and competences to share with other bodies or to transfer to them. The policy process is more complex and more differentiated with several sites and levels, and a bewildering variety of public and private actors, but the nation-state remains at its core (see Chapter 3).

Transnational governance, drawing on perspectives in international political economy, approaches the problem from the other end. It starts with the global economy and transnational civil society, and understands the policy process in the UK as part of the system of transnational governance. There are continual tensions between the increasingly con-nected character of the global economy and transnational society, and the fragmented and territorial nature of political authority in the inter-state system. An increasingly connected global economy creates many global public goods, including energy, water, the protection of the biosphere, security and human rights (Kaul, Grunberg and Stern, 1999). National governments cannot deliver these on their own; international cooperation is therefore required to create international regimes and agencies at the global level which can formulate and implement policy solutions. But despite some successes the extent of cooperation remains inadequate to the problems. In the global polity, much less even than at the EU level, there is far from being a global government with the capacity and resources to impose solutions or broker compromises, as national governments are used to doing. What exists is an embryonic state operating in a multi-level polity; the policy process is organized at many different levels and sites, and with many different authorities, from key supranational agencies like the WTO, the IMF and the World Bank, to regional governments without statehood like the EU (Wallace, W., 1996), nation-states, as well as many non-state actors, such as transnational companies and transnational social movements. In this highly complex and fragmented world, many policies are still decided at the national level through the policy process focused on national political institutions, and nation-states remain key brokers between institutions at different levels of the international system. But few policy issues can be dealt with any longer within a domestic policy process alone. Solutions to policy problems increasingly require forms of international cooperation and agreement, which inevitably means that sovereignty is pooled and shared (Cerny, 1990; Held, 1995).

The policy process is conventionally divided up into stages: agenda-setting, formulation, decision, implementation. In a single-level polity all these stages take place at the same site and level. But in a multi-level polity, there are several policy processes taking place at different levels, as well as disputes as to the appropriate level at which a policy should be decided. Monetary policy is a good example. There is a lively debate as to the merits of Britain holding on to its own currency or joining the euro, and thereby transferring responsibility to the European level. Even if formal control of a policy remains at one level, real control may reside at another. In a global economy how much autonomy does a national government like the British have in operating monetary policy independently of the monetary policies of Britain's leading trading partners, particularly the US and EU? The advantage of the transnational governance perspective is that it constantly asks such questions: where and by whom are policy agendas really being shaped?

In any policy process some interests and ideas will be privileged; they set the agenda, they shape the process of implementation, they determine outcomes. Other interests and ideas are marginalized. How these choices are made and how they become formalized in institutions, the rules and conventions that shape decisions and behaviour, are some of the most important aspects of any political system. They go to the heart of the relationships of power and authority which define it and which result in unequal outcomes for different groups and societies (Schattschneider,

1960). The strength of the transnational governance perspective on the policy process is that it directs attention to the question of how agendas are often set by forces outside the British state and British civil society, utilizing theoretical approaches which emphasize the strategic calculations of individual actors, as well as those which emphasize the historically evolved structures of the polity and the economy (Hall and Taylor, 1996). Any complete analysis of the policy process has to understand both agency and structure, the calculations, intentions and strategic interactions of agents, in combination with the constraints, identities and preferences which cultural, ideological, economic, legal, and political structures impose (Hay, 1996).

## Setting agendas: agency

In thinking about policy agendas it is important to distinguish between the policy agenda of civil society and the policy agenda of government (Peters, 1986, 1996). The first is a broad concept that includes all those issues put forward to the decision-making authorities with recommendation for some form of public action. Such issues are raised and discussed within civil society through political parties, pressure groups, churches, universities, think tanks, trade unions, companies, public and private organizations, social movements and media of all kinds. The second is a narrower definition that refers to those issues that form part of the agenda of specific government departments or agencies, and thereby become part of the policy process and policy implementation. This is the world of elites, professional bodies, experts, think tanks and policy communities, which often seek to define the government agenda in their own way, and resist the issues and still more the solutions put forward in the more open forum of civil society.

This distinction was developed to analyze the formation of policy agendas, and how issues on the broader agenda of civil society move, or are prevented from moving, to the narrower agenda of government. There are many examples from the history of policy in Britain. Some issues, for example unilateral nuclear disarmament, never do make the transition. Others, like the abolition of capital punishment, take a very long time to reach the agenda of government, and after they have been implemented remain controversial and the subject of attempts to reverse them. But the distinction can also be applied to agenda formation under conditions of transnational governance; transnational civil society includes many transnational agents and organizations as well as purely national ones, while in the multi-level polity there are many different agencies with decision-making powers. An issue like GM food is a transnational issue, involving matters of public health and biodiversity, and efforts have been made by the coalition of interests supporting and opposing its introduction to put it on the agenda of many different agencies – the World Trade Organiszation (WTO), the World Health Organization (WHO), national governments and their various agencies, and the EU Commission. The battle is fought across transnational civil society (see Chapter 11).

Agency-centred explanations tend to focus on the role of parties, think tanks and pressure groups, and specifically on the role of policy entrepreneurs within these. Policy entrepreneurs act as catalysts for moving issues on to the policy agenda of government, by drawing on ideas and interests in civil society to create advocacy coalitions or interest coalitions which gain such support and momentum that public agencies have to take account of them. Such accounts see policy agendas very much as the expression of opinion in civil society which has to be formed and mobilized, but which is ultimately determinant.

## Setting agendas: structure

Structure-centred explanations put much less weight on the role of individual or collective actors in influencing agendas, and instead focus on the institutional constraints which determine how state elites select some policies and exclude others. The sources of these constraints are various; they can derive from the power of particular interests, or from particular conceptions of the world, or from structural biases inherent in the way in which the society and economy are organized and reproduced (Dunleavy, 1991). In historical institutionalist accounts they impart huge inertia to the policy process because they have been formed over a long period and are very hard to adjust. The Conservative governments in power in Britain for 18 years set as one of their major goals a substantial reduction in the share of national resources spent by the state. But despite having clear ideological objectives, substantial Parliamentary majorities and strong leaders, these governments failed to reduce the state's share of GDP: at best, it was kept from rising.

Another kind of structuralist argument emphasizes the role of a process like globalization in setting constraints on the policy process within nation-states. Hyperglobalist arguments envisaging the sweeping away of nation-states and national decision making have been rightly criticized (Hirst and Thompson, 1996; Held *et al.*, 1999), and the continuing importance of the nation-state as a site of regulation has been recognized. But Held and his colleagues make a convincing case that the international system cannot be understood just as an inter-state system. Globalization is one of the chief causes of the rise of a multi-level polity and transnational governance because it creates new forms of connection and dependence, and new problems (such as global warming) which nation-states are incapable of tackling on their own.

National governments, like the British Labour government, often claim that globalization imposes particular policy choices (see Chapter 2). The need to keep the confidence of the financial markets and the international economic agencies dictates a set of policies which includes open trading arrangements, free movement of capital, flexible labour markets, privatization of public sector assets and enterprises, deregulation of the business sector, prudent fiscal policies and tight monetary discipline. The scope for deviating from such policies is argued to be limited, and likely to result in the kind of financial crisis visited on France in 1981 or Sweden in 1994.

What national governments have chiefly lost by these changes is the ability to conduct a national economic policy aimed at reflating the domestic economy, and promoting full employment. But except in closed economies such policies were always subject to external constraints. The domestic policies of British governments from the 1940s to the 1970s were severely hampered by balance of payments constraints and the need to keep within the terms of the fixed exchange rate system established at Bretton Woods in 1944. The new factor since the 1970s has been the existence of floating exchange rates and the increasing size and volatility of the financial markets. Policies which result in large persistent trade or fiscal deficits may trigger a collapse of the currency, which because of the way in which contemporary financial markets operate can have a devastating and sudden impact, as Britain has several times discovered, most recently in the financial crisis which led to the suspension of Britain's membership of the ERM in 1992 (Stephens, 1996).

If globalization were all-powerful, there would be a convergence of institutions and policies in all states across the world. The variation of institutions and policies, size of public sectors and types of intervention in the economy remain, however, extremely varied, and there are no signs of this changing. But as at other times in the history of the global economy there are some dominant ideas as to what constitutes 'best practice' in economic and social policies, which is actively promoted by various transnational and national actors within the international system. Among the interesting questions are how far there is room for variation within this global economic architecture, what kinds of social democracy are still viable (Krieger, 1999) and how far different institutional arrangements and policy agendas can flourish at local and regional levels if states are decentralized in ways which allow this.

## Policy competences

Once we think of the contemporary UK state as a multi-level polity in a system of transnational governance it is no longer possible to discuss the UK policy process as though it were taking place at a single site (see Chapter 3). There are several different sites and levels, which raises questions of how functions and authority are distributed between them. Britain, in common with other states, is no longer involved in one master policy process and policy agenda, but in many. This reflects the increasingly complex organization of the state and the different levels of the polity which are now emerging, accelerated in part by the far-reaching programme of constitutional change to which Labour is committed. However piecemeal and disjointed it sometimes appears, this programme is introducing some radical changes in the way in which the policy process operates in Britain. Apart from the constitutional reforms there have also been important changes to the way in which macroeconomic policy and European policy are conducted. A multi-level polity was already developing before Labour was elected, but the Conservatives under both Margaret Thatcher and John Major were in general hostile to such trends, particularly devolution and a closer EU, and sought to resist them whenever they could. Labour has proceeded at times with great caution, as over electoral reform for Westminster, but the cumulative effect of its constitutional changes seem set to change British government permanently.

If the nation-state is no longer the exclusive focus either of legitimacy or of policy capacity, how are the different policy competences, which in a single-level polity are all concentrated in one place, to be shared out between the different levels? One way of thinking about this problem is to use the framework developed by Theodore Lowi for understanding the US federal policy process and adopted by William Wallace for understanding the policy process in the EU (Lowi, 1972; Wallace, W., 1996). Lowi distinguishes four major types of policy: constituent policies which determine the fundamental rules and priorities of the political system; redistributive policies which challenge the structural distribution of costs and benefits between citizens and regions; distributive policies which allocate resources through government-funded programmes; and regulatory policies, which provide rules governing particular sectors. The first two are the focus of most political argument and struggle, since they are about the fundamentals of the social and economic order, while the second two are the heart of the contemporary extended state.

For Britain most constituent issues are now decided at supranational levels in the various treaties and agreements on security, trade, currency and the environment, which British governments have signed. These treaties have created a number of international regimes and international agencies.

The major constituent issues at the level of the British polity itself centre on questions of the internal constitution of the British state, particularly devolution, electoral reform and freedom of information, as well as whether Britain should sign any more treaties ceding further sovereign powers to the EU (for example, by signing up to the euro). Many of the constituent issues of the past, such as whether the economy should be organized on capitalist or socialist principles, are no longer live ones.

Redistributive issues are important at the EU level – for example, over the budget, and regional aid. They are also increasingly important at the global level, in debates on world poverty and the impact of world trade rules, as the 1999 WTO meeting in Seattle demonstrated, when there was a sharp conflict between delegates representing poor and rich states and between the US and the EU. The problem for groups in transnational civil society seeking to put such issues on transnational government agendas is finding arenas where they can do so, and getting access to agencies which have either the capacity or the will to act. At the national level redistributive issues have declined greatly in importance, and some argue that redistributive policies have disappeared from British politics, but this judgement is probably premature.

Distributive issues remain very important at the national level, because the British government is still responsible for many major spending programmes. The scope for distributive politics at the EU is extremely limited because the budget remains so small (only just above 1 per cent of EU GDP), so is confined to programmes such as agriculture and regional aid. Devolution within the UK transfers responsibility for many distributive issues and programmes to the new regional institutions. In all cases distributive policies are associated with policy networks and policy communities, and the creation of strong links between them and relevant government departments in order to facilitate both formulation and implementation of policy.

Regulatory issues have assumed increasing importance at global and EU levels, but also at the national level, as British governments have sought to move away from the politics of distribution and redistribution. The rise of a regulatory state has been a strong trend in recent decades, related to the doctrines of the new public management, which has changed the scope and instruments of government through outright privatization, as well as the use of specialist agencies, outsourcing and public–private partnerships for the delivery of government-funded public services. As the number of service providers has increased, so the need for regulation and new forms of accountability has grown. In the EU, the process is complicated by the need to harmonize different national regulatory styles.

From the standpoint of the policy process what is important is that different policy issues increasingly relate to different levels, and this is not a static picture but one that is constantly evolving. Trade issues, for example, are now handled by the EU, which negotiates on behalf of all its members with the WTO. What drives transnational policy agendas are the requirements of an open liberal economic order, and this agenda is promoted both by the international agencies themselves and by transnationally oriented companies, trade unions, media and think tanks as well as political parties.

Nation-states remain the pivot of this system, but recognizing the gains from cooperation in an interdependent world national governments have been prepared to give up sovereignty or to pool it, and accept the jurisdiction of international and regional bodies. In the case of the UK the most striking instance of this has been its membership of the EU, and its acceptance (reluctant at times) of the various treaties which have deepened the process of European integration. The British courts have acknowledged that the Treaties give the European Court of Justice (ECJ) jurisdiction over Britain, and in appropriate cases can over-rule British judicial decisions. On many questions now policy agendas have to be formed at the European level, and lobbying to influence that agenda has to take place in Brussels.

The EU is not developing into a 'United States of Europe' organized on federal lines, rather it consists of a set of supranational institutions created to fulfil particular purposes and functions. The policy agendas of the EU revolve around questions such as agriculture, competition policy and regional aid, and increasingly the question of enlargement, the single market, foreign and defence policy, social policy and economic and monetary union. The policy process in the EU has different characteristics from the policy process in Britain. It is more open, there are many more points of access and it makes much greater use of regulation and law. It is also much more fragmented, prone to deadlock and therefore much less able to provide binding decisions. The policy agendas of the EU are heavily influenced by the interests of the European states through the Council of Ministers, but they are also driven by the policy entrepreneurship of the Commission. The European Parliament is gradually assuming a larger role, but European public opinion is not yet effectively organized. Business interests and trade unions are, however, well organized at the European level and lobbying organizations have sprung up to service them. In addition, there are many networks of experts and professionals who seek to influence the agendas that are formed.

The national level remains the most developed in the UK polity and the most important for understanding policy agendas. The UK polity has been in many respects highly centralized, although with numerous anomalies. The battle to shape policy agendas is overwhelmingly concentrated on London. The centralization of British media, political parties, the civil service, transnational companies, finance and trade unions has always been striking, and has produced the strong sense of unity of the British state. This state, however, was always a superimposition over the original nations of the British Isles, which the move to devolve power from Westminster has acknowledged. The new emerging pattern of regional bodies makes possible the emergence of a distinctive policy process at this level.

The trends towards the creation of a multi-level polity are clear both at the regional and at the global and European levels. How far are these trends likely to result in policy differentiation in the UK? There has always been some because of the special arrangements within the British constitution that were developed to take account of the special needs of Scotland, Wales and Northern Ireland. When there was still some genuine local democracy, before the Thatcher era, there was also some policy differentiation at the local level as well – South Yorkshire's cheap bus fare policy was a famous example. In Scotland the persistence of a different educational system and legal system from England helped sustain policy difference as well, but the uniform policies of the welfare state have tended to harmonize conditions throughout the UK. The devolved bodies in Scotland and Wales (and eventually in Northern Ireland) will have an opportunity to reverse those trends, although many policy areas remain reserved for Westminster (including foreign policy, defence, monetary and fiscal policy and social security) while for others which are devolved (including health, education, housing, transport, economic development, prisons, agriculture, arts and the environment) the scope for independent initiative appears low, particularly since the tax-varying powers are so small (see Chapter 7). Nevertheless a start has been made, and a number of issues, notably tuition fees and land ownership in Scotland, and agricultural subsidies in Wales, have already come to the fore. How much this policy differentiation will develop in the future will depend on how much Westminster still tries to control what happens in the devolved bodies, and how much a civil society in Wales and Scotland generates pressure for further changes. The more powers the devolved bodies acquire, the more they will become the focus of lobbyists and think tanks and the more policy differentiation can be expected. But there remains a doubt as to how far Labour is pleased with the genie it has let out of the bottle, and how far it will keep trying to shove it back in.

## Parties and governments

In a multi-level polity how effective are parties, interests and ideas in setting policy agendas? One view of political parties is that they are above all policy entrepreneurs, aggregating interests in civil society, assembling coalitions and drawing up manifestos on which they appeal for support. They act as a transmission mechanism, offering to translate demands from particular interests and groups into policies for government to deliver. Party manifestos define the main elements of the policy agenda for government. The role of the civil service is to provide advice and support to ministers to help them implement their manifesto commitments. In this model, political parties have a big role to play in shaping policy agendas. Every change of government becomes potentially significant, a new beginning. Political parties naturally in their rhetoric do everything possible to sustain this view of how the political system works, since it makes them central to it. While the role of parties is important, however, it can easily be exaggerated. In a multi-level polity political parties seem certain to become less significant in setting agendas so long as they remain focused on the nation-state. Unless they become transnational actors themselves they are unlikely to be the vehicles that mobilize opinion within transnational society.

A second view of the role of parties also ties them to particular nation-states. Political parties are often the instruments for defending and sustaining the existing policy consensus within government rather than acting to break up that policy consensus and forge a new policy agenda. Sometimes a change of government does signal a major alteration of the policy agenda, but when policy agendas do change, the change is often not related to changes of government. The most important changes in policy agendas and in the direction of policy often occur in the middle of parliaments rather than at the end when governments change hands (Rose, 1984). This appears true in many areas of policy since Labour was elected in 1997, and there is already a considerable literature arguing that this Labour government is working within the parameters established by its Conservative predecessor (Hay, 1999; Heffernan, 2000; Kerr, 2000).

The centralization of power in the British system and the unchecked nature of the 'dictatorship' which the possession of a parliamentary majority confers on the executive have been reinforced by the strong drive for central control by the Labour leadership over their own party and then over the government's programme, and also by the downgrading within the Government of the Cabinet, and the increasing desire of Downing Street to control all aspects of the Government's programme (see Chapter 6). This drive for greater central control contrasts with Labour's wish to encourage pluralism, decentralisation and cooperation with other parties and political forces, expressed through its constitutional reform pro-gramme, which recognizes that the UK is now a multi-level polity. Labour seems to be running with two very different policy styles, and very different approaches to the construction of policy agendas. The first is adversarial and centralist, the second is consensual and pluralist. Both have their advocates and detractors, and the argument is often associated with positions for and against electoral reform for Westminster. The first-past-the-post system is credited both by its supporters and its critics with providing firm and decisive government, clear choices and bold initiatives, even when the government commands only minority support, while forms of proportional representation (PR) move parties away from adversarial and winner-take-all politics towards consensus-building and coalition-forming politics. There is not much doubt which is better suited to a multi-level polity.

By introducing PR for elections to the Scottish Parliament, Welsh Assembly and European Parliament, the Labour government is committing itself to a new style of politics and negotiation over policy, and has formed a coalition with the Liberal Democrats to govern Scotland. But at Westminster Labour has been reluctant to sanction reforms to the electoral system or to Parliament which would undermine executive control. It has continued to use all the centralized powers which the British Constitution bestows on governments. However at the same time the government has acted in most fields with extreme caution – sticking to inherited Conservative spending levels for the first two years of the Parliament was one example – and has also made a virtue of consulting other parties on proposed changes even including the Liberal Democrats on one Cabinet Committee. This 'Big Tent' approach to policy-making has also extended to making use of prominent Conservatives whenever possible on Government bodies and Committees (e.g. Wakeham, Patten, Heseltine and Clarke). In some important respects the government has been restrained, certainly in comparison with some previous Labour and Conservative governments, in using its majority to push through major policy changes. This highlights the problem which all parties now face in a multi-level polity; the gap between what the electorate expects them to do and what they can deliver is growing. The number of different agencies and levels which have to be coordinated make the desire for joined-up government ever more necessary, but at the same time ever more difficult. A centralist and adversarial political style increases expectations of what governments can do, but does not increase their capacity to deliver.

Some of the complexities of contemporary policy-making can be seen in two issues that have been very high profile for the government: genetically modified (GM) food and the welfare of the countryside. Each has generated a major campaign within civil society (see Chapter 11). Fears about GM food centred both on the issue of food in the shops which had been genetically modified and on plant trials which might carry risks for biodiversity. The government tried to stick to its preferred policy agenda – which was strongly supported by the policy community of business interests and scientific experts, as well as by the rules of the WTO – that the existing foods were entirely safe, and that the trials were necessary to gather knowledge about whether GM crops would be safe in the future. Its stance, however, commanded very little public support because of the success of groups like Greenpeace in putting the issue of the safety of GM crops firmly on the policy agenda. What followed was determined government resistance by Ministers to prevent their policy agenda from being highjacked, including ill-advised statements from the Prime Minister that he was perfectly happy eating GM foods. Other ministers, notably Environment Minister Michael Meacher, began to explore ways to diffuse the issue and to reassure the public that proper safety checks would be applied, while not conceding the principle of allowing GM foods to be sold and plant trials to continue. The issue was complicated because of the potential involvement of both the WTO, as guardian of the principle of the free movement of goods (most of the GM foods and the biotech companies involved were American) and the EU, which began discussing whether there should be a European-wide ban imposed on the development of these foods. The British government attitude was dictated by the importance which the Office of Science and Technology (OST) and DTI placed on the British biotech companies as one of Britain's potentially few leading edge industries.

The welfare of the countryside became a major issue orchestrated by the Countryside Alliance, which attacked the government for neglecting the interests of those who lived in rural areas and representing only urban interests. Targets of the campaign included the proposals to ban hunting with dogs, putative threats to other field sports, price hikes on petrol, the commitment to introduce rights of access to moorlands and heaths, the EU ban on export of British beef and the increased regulation which had been introduced in its wake and the collapse of farm prices particularly for livestock on hill farms. Some of these issues, such as the beef ban, could be tackled only at the European level, while others were best focused on the new devolved bodies. The Welsh Assembly, for example, was determined to introduce its own rescue plan for hill farmers. The proposal to ban hunting with dogs was not originally a government measure, and at first failed to gain sufficient parliamentary time, but it was then rescued in 1999 by Tony Blair reaffirming his own personal support. The government, however, in general trimmed to the demands of the Countryside Alliance and in 1999 promised additional funding to meet their grievances.

On many matters, however, which the alliance wished to place on the agenda, it was powerless to assist. Reform of the CAP was something much desired by ministers, but impossible to secure without a fundamental reorganization of the EU. The ban on British beef was at last lifted by the EU in 1999, but the British government could do little to restore the beef markets which had been lost. The heavy burden of rising petrol prices on those living in rural areas was noted, but at the same time the government wished to affirm its support for its green agenda on fuel emissions. In its dealings with the Countryside Alliance the government showed both strength and weakness. On a matter like banning hunting with dogs, which was supported by large majorities of MPs and the electorate, the government acted cautiously at first, but ultimately did decide to support a Private Members' Bill, although compromises were still being discussed in the early months of 2000. On other questions the government was prepared to offer subsidies, of a kind which were no longer so readily available for failing industries, showing the effectiveness of the Countryside Alliance and their media allies in raising the issue of the countryside and forcing it on to the government's agenda.

## Interests

The effectiveness of interests in shaping policy agendas in a multi-level polity depends on their ability to organize, either through campaigns and movements in civil society or through 'insider' strategies. The interest group universe in the UK polity was traditionally centred on the central state, but in the last 20 years it has undergone significant changes partly as a result of internal domestic changes and partly as a result of the emergence of a multi-level polity. Labour in 1997 inherited the unbalanced interest group universe established during the long period of Conservative hegemony in British politics after 1979. Apart from the structural bias in favour of business that is inherent in a capitalist market economy (Lindblom, 1977), the active influence of organized capital relative to that of organized labour was greatly increased under the Conservatives as a result of legislation which removed trade union legal immunities and freedoms. The weakening of trade unions occurred at the same time as long-term occupational and technological changes which led to a sharp decline in trade union membership.

This imbalance between labour and capital in terms of political influence is not something which Labour has tried to reverse in any serious way. The trade unions have not been reinstated as an insider group in the way in which they were in previous Labour and some Conservative administrations. The dominant influences in the contemporary policy process in the UK are business and the numerous lobbyists and organizations which represent it. Business is central to the numerous policy networks attached to the central spending programmes and regulatory regimes established by the UK and the EU. The countervailing power which labour exercised between 1945 and 1979 has been largely removed.

This situation at the same time frees and constrains governments. There is no longer any need for the attempt made by many post-war governments to establish elaborate tripartite arrangements to discuss policy on economic growth or prices and incomes. What governments now need to do is make sure that their policy agenda is aligned with that of the leading business interests if they wish to avoid serious conflict over the implementation of their policies as well as keeping the confidence of the financial markets. Occasionally, as with the euro, business opinion is divided; on other issues, such as GM food public opposition can cause business interests to diverge as well as making it difficult for government to stick to the policy agenda which has been agreed. The big supermarket chains removed all GM foods from their shelves as soon as public disquiet became apparent, increasing the isolation of the government and the biotech industry. But in general the weakening of the labour interest in contemporary Britain has meant that since the early 1980s British governments have been free to align their policies with those of the business interest, and have mostly done so. What is good for business is good for the country.

Business groups have as a result become very prominent in setting policy agendas in Britain, and this in itself has posed problems for British governments, because of the appearance that successful business lobbying, and still more business donations to political parties, has payoffs in terms of the policies which are adopted. The Labour government in its first year in office was embroiled in controversy over its acceptance of a £1 million donation from Bernie Ecclestone, the head of Formula 1, which was followed by a postponement of the government's decision to outlaw sports sponsorship by tobacco companies. Direct links between donations and policy decisions can never be proved, and some may be coincidences, but what these cases as well as the various scandals around the lobbyists illustrate is the contemporary culture of British government, which is one of easy access by business interests to ministers, and the key facilitating role played by the lobbying firms which have sprung up in recent years. A climate has been created in which attention to the needs of business and the views of business has become the principal determinant of policy agendas. It always was an important determinant, but in the last 20 years it has acquired a new dominance which Labour has been keen to affirm. Whether the issue is the *Fairness at Work* White Paper, the New Deal, transport policy, stakeholder pensions, or the search for more effective delivery of public services, the views of business are extensively canvassed. There has not been a major policy introduced since 1997 to which business has seriously objected, not even the minimum wage which was set at a level which business found acceptable. This is a measure of the structural power which business now enjoys in British politics, and its effects can be seen in the policy agendas in every area of British government.

The impact of the trend towards a multi-level polity has been to fragment the former rather closed interest-group world of British politics. Particular interest groups such as the farmers have particularly suffered because their closed policy community with the Department of Agriculture (MAFF) has been shattered by the powers transferred to the European level over agricultural pricing and subsidies. The existence of the EU has forced British trade unions and British companies as well as many other private organizations and public bodies such as local authorities and universities to organize at the European level also. A similar effect, although not so marked, is observable with the creation of the Welsh Assembly and the Scottish Parliament. These provide a new focus for lobbying activity, although they remain dwarfed by London. Interests, particularly those of the big producer groups, have always been seen as important for the determination of what gets on policy agendas, in part because they have such influence over what can be implemented. Their cooperation in the past was deemed vital. In a multi-level polity this may not always be so. There is more scope for a skilful government to play off different interests against one another, since some interests will be more focused on one level of the polity than another, and can more easily be bypassed or neutralized by shifting the focus of the issue to another level.

## Ideas

Ideas also have a major role in shaping policy agendas. Assumptions and organizing concepts play an important part in how agendas and issues are constructed and defined. In this way, orthodoxies and paradigms are established, and policy change often comes about through challenges to the dominant paradigm. Ideas are also much more transnational than interests or political parties, and the networks which promote ideas, such as epistemic communities based on particular forms of knowledge and expertise, are an important element of transnational civil society.

Ideas are used in many different ways in the policy process. Public intellectuals like Hayek or Keynes articulate broad principles for the conduct of public policy, and identify issues which should be part of the policy agenda. Public intellectuals range all the way from professors of philosophy to tabloid commentators. Forms of media, and particularly television, have become increasingly important in shaping the way in which ideas are disseminated and issues are framed. Managing the media has become one of the essential skills of politics (see Chapter 10).

Ideas are also employed in framing agendas for government. Here the concern is not with general issues and principles, but with how policies might be designed which would actually work in practice and be implemented successfully. The complexity of modern government and the long links in the policy process from agenda-setting to implementation mean that there is an increasing need for policy specialists. A new breed of policy advisers and researchers has been created, much of it separate from universities, and increasingly organized through think tanks. Governments in the past always had need of this kind of specialist, technical advice. Sometimes it came from outside government – Keynes was unusual because he combined the roles of public intellectual and technical adviser. But mostly it was provided by the civil service. Today the civil service retains an important role in policy design, but it is increasingly supplemented by the think tanks and the army of special advisers and freelancers which modern governments employ.

The marketplace of ideas, especially with the aid of the Internet, has become international, and successful policy ideas are copied and transferred quickly between states. Think tanks again play an important role in this. The close links between the new right think tanks of Britain and the US have been well documented (Cockett, 1994; Denham, 1996; Stone, Denham and Garnett, 1998). Think tanks are increasingly flexible. Although some are aligned with one particular political party, such as the Centre for Policy Studies (CPS) with the Conservatives and the Fabian Society and the Institute for Public Policy Research (IPPR) with Labour, others including the IEA, Demos and the Adam Smith Institute have looser alignments, and increasingly position themselves to offer advice to whichever party is in government.

Think tanks fly kites for governments, as well as drawing in a range of experts and opinion to think through new policy options. They are judged not just by the quality of the original ideas which they put forward but by the detailed plans they offer for how they might be implemented. Providing a grand narrative and a vision goes only so far. It may be useful for a party in opposition, but in government what is urgently required are ideas which work and which can make some impact on the complex long-term problems which the government faces. The argument that in Britain there is an estrangement between Labour's public intellectuals and the Labour government (Lloyd, 1999) is hardly surprising: it has been true of every government, particularly Labour ones. What is distinctive about the current situation, however, is that the professionalization of policy advice has gone further than ever before, and the roles of public intellectual and policy adviser have become more distinct so that it is much rarer to find the same individual occupying both roles as Keynes once did. These are different functions in the generation of policy agendas, and increasingly so.

Some of the most challenging tasks which think tanks attempt is when they try and forge a new consensus on the way ahead on a major area of policy. Examples include the Adam Smith Institute's Omega project on the reform of the welfare state and public services; the IPPR's Social Justice Commission which laid the foundations for Labour's new ideas on welfare and redistribution; the Fabian Society's Commission on Tax and Citizenship, and the IPPR's Commission on Private/Public Partnerships. All of these combine thinking about principles and values, with clear specification of policy objectives and detailed policy design.

Many think tanks still tend to be mainly focused on national decision-making centres, although this is beginning to change with the development of a multi-level polity. The establishment of the new Scottish Parliament has provided a focus for think tanks in Scotland such as the Scottish Council Foundation, and this pattern can be expected to spread if there is more regional devolution in the future. The growth of European and transnational think tanks are also likely to develop in the future as these levels of decision-making grow in importance. There are earlier examples of networks of experts and knowledge (epistemic communities) forming around particular ideas, such as the idea of European integration. Such networks can be a crucial factor in advancing a particular policy agenda. In an increasingly diversified, complex and uncertain policy process in the multi-level polity which transnational governance is creating, the importance of the role of ideas and the networks associated with them is likely to grow; that of organizations such as political parties which remain tied to one level of the multi-level polity will diminish. New forms of organization are needed for political effectiveness in the new world of multi-level politics and transnational governance.

# Guide to Further Reading

## Chapter 2 A new politics?

Demos is the think tank most associated with the 'new politics'; Geoff Mulgan, its former Director, now works in the Number 10 Policy Unit. See Mulgan (1994) and the Demos Web site < http://www.demos.co.uk > for a better insight into the sometimes bizarre world of this organization.

The most interesting analysis of Labour since the advent of Tony Blair is contained in Driver and Martell (1998), which advances the idea that new Labour is 'post-Thatcherite'. Recent developments are placed in a wider historical context in Fielding (1999). The Prime Minister's own thoughts about the 'Third Way' are expressed in Blair (1998), which sets out how he presently defines this rather troublesome concept. To keep up to date with Blair's views, regular visits to Number 10's Web site < www.number-10.gov.uk > are useful as it archives speeches that are never properly reported in the press. Labour's own Web site < www.labour.org.uk > may eventually be worth inspection.

An accessible account of Conservatism which includes events up to John Major's leadership can be found in Evans and Taylor (1996). On the debate about the direction of the party after 1997, see Gray and Willetts (1997) and the special edition of *Political Quarterly*, 69(2) (1998). The Conservative Web site < www.conservative-party.org.uk > is pretty dull, but contains recent speeches by prominent figures.

Those who wish to think about party ideology in a wider intellectual context should consult Freeden (1996), the best and most recent work on the subject.

## Chapter 3 Towards multi-level governance

Books that remind readers that the world of multi-level governance is not simply a creation of new Labour's constitutional innovations are Rhodes (1988), Nairn (1977), Bulpitt (1983) and George (1998). In terms of the new Labour experience of multi-level governance it is difficult to identify many books based on research rather than informed speculation. The key sources for the next few years are likely to be journal articles, magazines and newspaper material for, at least, giving some feel of the unfolding agenda. There are a number of books that provide useful accounts of the world of governance as it emerged under the Conservatives during the 1980s and 1990s. See Stoker (1999a), Stoker (1999b), Peterson and Bomberg (1998). For discussion of the concept of governance see Rhodes (1997a), Stoker (1998), Jessop (1999), Pierre (2000) and Pierre and Peters

(2000). Useful Web site addresses include the Scottish Executive Parliament < www.scottish-devolution.org.uk >, the CCTA Government Information Service, which gives access to all government departments and all other public sector bodies < www.open.gov.uk > and 10 Downing Street, which includes the mission statements of all government departments and outlines the remit of cabinet committees < www.number-10.gov.uk/index.html >. The EU's server is < europa.eu.int > (includes the European Commission, Court of Justice, etc.); < www.europarl.eu.int > is the European Parliament's site; < www.cec.org.uk > is the European Commission Office in London's site (very informative, containing information more specific to the UK than the Europa server); < www.worldbank.org > is the World Bank site; < www.imf.org > is the International Monetary Fund's (IMF) site; < www.g7.utoronto.ca > is the University of Toronto G8 Information Centre (contains reports and analysis of summits, documents, etc.).

## Chapter 4   Britain, the EU and the euro

For a comprehensive survey of the historical relationship between Britain and Europe see George (1998). For a more controversial view see Denman (1996). For introductory texts on the EU see McCormick (1999), Dinan (1999) or Nugent (1999). For more advanced books, which analyze the EU using general political science theories, see Hix (1999b) and Richardson (1996). On the EU institutions, see Edwards and Spence (1997); on the Commission, Hayes-Renshaw and Wallace (1998); on the Council, Corbett, Jacobs and Shackleton (1995) on the European Parliament, Delhousse (1998); on the Court of Justice. On the inputs side of EU politics, see Gabel (1998a) on public opinion, Hix and Lord (1997) on political parties, Greenwood (1997) on interest representation and Eijk and Franklin (1996) or Blondel, Sinnott and Svensson (1998) on European elections. On the policy outputs of the EU, see Wallace and Wallace (1996) for a general survey, Laffan (1997) on budgetary and redistributive policies, Majone (1996) on regulatory policies, De Grauwe (1997) on economic and monetary union and Piening (1997) on external trade and security policies.

The main EU Web site is < europa.eu.int/index-en.htm >. The sites of the EU institutions are: < europa.eu.int/comm/index_en.htm > (Commission), < http:// ue.eu.int/en/summ.htm > (Council), < www.europarl.eu.int/sg/tree/en > (Parliament), < www.curia.eu.int/en/index.htm > (Court of Justice) and < www.ecb.int > (European Central Bank). The Eurobarometer polls and other EU opinion surveys are available at < europa.eu.int/en/comm/dg10/infcom/epo/ polls.html >. The Commission office in the UK is at < www.cec.org.uk >, and the European Parliament office in the UK is at < www.europarl.eu.int/uk/ index.html >.

On the European policies of the British parties, see the 1999 European election manifestos at: < www.pes.org/english/frames4.htm > (Labour), < www.conservative-party.org.uk/ee/manifesto.html > (Conservative), < www.libdemseuro99.cix.co.uk/manifesto.htm > (Liberal Democrats),

< www.greenparty.org.uk/homepage/elections/1999european/manifesto/
manifesto.htm > (Green), < www.independenceuk.org.uk/manifesto/ > (UK
Independence Party), < www. snp.org.uk/ep99.pdf > (Scottish Nationalists) and
< www.plaidcymru.org/ > (Plaid Cymru).

## Chapter 5    The law and the constitution

There is now a rich literature on constitutional reform. For a useful overview see
Hazell (1999) which should be supplemented with specialist studies from the
Constitution Unit. Himsworth and Munro (1998) is a good guide to the Scotland
Act 1998. Lazorowicz (1998) explores the relationship between Scotland a
changing Europe. Less has been produced on Wales but Davies (1999) and Gray
(1997) are all insightful. Legal studies of the impact of the Human Rights Act are
Baker (1999) and Outhwaite and Wheeler (1999). Richard (1999) raises many of
the issues involved in the contemporary debate about House of Lords reform.
There are still relatively few up-to-date and accessible studies of the British
judiciary and legal system from a political science perspective but Malleson (1999)
is extremely useful. Egan (1999) offers some insight into the role of the Lord
Chancellor but is very partisan. Robertson (1998) is an excellent study of judicial
decision-making. Delhousse (1998) offers a concise overview of the European
Court of Justice.

   Web sites are extremely useful sources of information in this area. Especially
good are the Lord Chancellor's Department < www.open.gov.uk/lcd > and the
Home Office < www.homeoffice.gov.uk > The Scottish Parliament also has an
excellent site < www.scottish.parliament.uk >.

## Chapter 6    Executives and administrations

On the UK core executive, full analyses are Burch and Holliday (1996) and James
(1999). A good set of essays is Rhodes and Dunleavy (1995). A recent textbook is
Smith (1999). Lee, Jones and Burnham (1998) is also worth consulting. A great
mass of information on all aspects of the UK state can be found at the Government
Information Service (GIS) Web site, < www.open.gov.uk/ >. This is an essential
resource for any student. On the EU, good textbooks are Nugent (1999) and
Geddes (1999). The EU's site < europa.eu.int/ > is also worth a visit. For
obvious reasons, little has yet been published on the devolved assemblies. The
relevant sites can be reached through the GIS site. For keeping abreast of
constitutional developments, the Constitution Unit's Web site < www.ucl.ac.uk/
constitution-unit/ > is good.

## Chapter 7    Legislatures and assemblies

Norton (1990) is a useful introduction to legislatures as a species. For the two
existing UK legislatures, Silk and Walters (1998) is a good on the procedure of the

UK Parliament; Norton (1993) is more useful on the Parliament's non-legislative roles, as is Judge (1993); Westlake (1994) and Smith (1999) are the best introductions to the European Parliament. Each parliament has its own Web site: www.parliament.uk and < www.europarl.eu.int > .

Most writing on devolution covers the structure and functions of the new bodies only briefly, concentrating predominantly on the history. Perhaps the best single work is Bogdanor (1999), which does both, and is excellent on the powers of the Scottish and Welsh legislatures. More specialist works include the collection of essays in both Hassan (1999) on the Scottish Parliament and Osmond (1999) on the National Assembly. These tend to be somewhat *parti pris*. Rallings and Thrasher (1999) is a more neutral introduction to the topic – covering the three new legislatures, London, Europe *and* local councils –but at £35 in paperback it is not one for every shelf. The new legislatures also have their own Web sites that are invaluable: < www.scottish.parliament.uk > ; < www.ni-assembly.gov.uk > .

## Chapter 8   Elections and party politics

British election studies have been stuck in the doldrums for nearly 20 years now, repetitively mulling over a set of issues first defined by Butler and Stokes (1970) and largely unchanged since. Many of the intellectual problems here are explored well in Catt (1996). Sanders (1997) provides a useful introduction to the aggregate-data-analysis approach to analyzing government popularity in terms of influences from economic performance. The approach has run into severe credibility problems since 1992 when the Conservative government fared pretty well despite recession, and then went on to be comprehensively defeated despite economic prosperity in 1997. Essential updates on the 1997 general election are given in compilations by Norris (1997) and Denver et al. (1998). The annual series of books published by Frank Cass under the title *British Elections and Parties Review* contains valuable updates on electoral and party statistics and political events, as well as useful papers. Among journals *Electoral Studies* and *Party Politics* are the most clear and helpful. The comparative analysis of electoral systems is well introduced by Farrell (2001), while the references in Chapter 8 explore British electoral system change in detail.

## Chapter 9   Political parties: adapting to the electoral market

For an extended discussion of all of the themes covered in this chapter, plus a wide-ranging review of party politics in Britain, see Webb (2000). A recent 'cutting-edge' review of the electoral changes of the past 35 years is provided in Evans and Norris (1999). The classic models of party development are outlined in Duverger (1954), Kirchheimer (1966), Panebianco (1988) and Katz and Mair (1995). The subject of political marketing has received considerable attention in recent years, and an excellent review of this literature can be found in Scammell (1999). More detailed studies are available in Franklin (1994), Scammell (1995),

Kavanagh (1995) and Rosenbaum (1997). Useful overviews of party organizational change between 1980 and the early 1990s are provided by Kelly (1994) and Webb (1994), while the detail of recent reforms affecting intra-party democracy are to be found in Labour Party (1997) and Conservative Party (1998). The Neill Commission's report on party funding (1998) is not only essential reading for the recommendations it proposes, but constitutes a very good and readable overview of the subject in its own right. The main party Web sites are Labour < www.labour.org.uk >, Conservative < www.conservative-party. org.uk >, Liberal Democrat < www.libdems.org.uk >, Scottish Nationalist < www.snp.org.uk >, Plaid Cymru < www.plaidcymru.org >, Ulster Unionists < www.uup.org >, Democratic Ulster Unionists < www.dup.org.uk >, Alliance Party of Northern Ireland < www.allianceparty.org >, Sinn Fein < www.sinnfein.ie >, SDLP < www.sdlp.ie >. An excellent general gateway to party Web sites can be found at Richard Kimber's Keele University Web page < http://www.psr.keele.ac.uk/parties.htm >.

## Chapter 10   New media, new politics

Seaton (1998) provides overviews of how market changes in Britain affect the way media covers political life. Norris *et al.* (1999) examines the effects of political communications at the 1997 general election, and campaigning and media roles are discussed in Crewe and Thomson (1999) and Butler and Kavanagh (1997). Gould (1998), Jones (1999) and Routledge (1999) provide insider accounts of Labour's communications and spin doctoring. For historical developments in British political marketing see Kavanagh (1995), Scammell (1995) and Franklin (1994). General introductions to media in Britain are found in Seymour-Ure (1998) and Curran and Seaton (1997). The best general introduction to media and political campaigning in an international comparative context is Swanson and Mancini (1996). Schudson (1995) is also an excellent introduction to the major contemporary debates, politics and media, their mainly US focus notwithstanding.

## Chapter 11   Political participation and protest

The paucity of systematic study of British political participation is highlighted by the extent to which Parry, Moyser and Day (1992) –an innovative study for its time, but based on a small sample in restricted localities –is still cited in virtually all writing on political participation in Britain. A special issue of *Policy and Politics*, 27 3 (July 1999) contains several articles on citizenship and locality and participation and renewal. Doherty (1999) is a good article on environmental activity and contains many useful references. Verba, Lehman Schlozman and Brady (1995) is a seminal work on participation in the US. Key works on social capital include Putnam (1993, 1995a, 1995b) and Hall (1999).

   The use of the Internet as a forum for political participation means that Web sites are an excellent source of evidence of political behaviour. MORI polls and surveys are held at < http://www.mori.com/polls/ >. The bookshop Politico's sponsors the British Politics Web Pages at < http://www.ukpol.co.uk >, which contains over 2500 sites on British politics. You can email your MP while you are there. Beware, however, of a lack of updating, and note that some useful sites are not listed. Media sites are good sources of election results, stories of political protest and opinion polls – the *Financial Times* at < http://www.ft.com >, the Guardian at < http://www.guardian.co.uk > and the BBC at < www.bbc.co.uk > all have searchable archives and the *Guardian* provides news round ups and links to related sites for key issues and links to related sites. The *Local Government Chronicle* provides a subscription service at < http://www.lgcnet.com > but provides a lot of useful information on local government for free, including local elections data provided by the Local Elections Centre at the University of Plymouth. Virtually all political parties, voluntary organizations and pressure groups have Web sites and a good place to find any not listed on any of the above is < http://www.askjeeves.com >. Government sites are listed on the UK government site at < http://www.open.gov.uk >. The Cabinet Office maintains a site at < http://www.servicefirst.gov.uk > which gives information of participatory initiatives such as the People's Panel.

## Chapter 12   Citizenship and culture

This chapter touches on many issues each with their own extensive academic literature. The concept and theories of 'citizenship' are thoroughly covered in Heater (1990), while more recent developments in normative ideals of citizenship are covered in a collection edited by Beiner (1995), and with particular reference to the UK by Clarke (1997). For a good discussion of gender and citizenship see Lister (1998) and for nationality race and citizenship and the prospects under the Labour government see Dummett (1999). Good studies and analyses of race and ethnicity with reference to government and politics in Britain are presented by Kellas (1998) and Mac an Ghaill (1999). British immigration policy and its implications are covered by Spender (1997). Levitas (1998) is a book-length study of new Labour social policy, including analyses of discourses of social exclusion. Finally, Gilbert *et al.* (1999) contains some respectable analyses of the political impact of Diana, Princess of Wales. Frazer (1999) is an extended analysis of the ideal of community and its relation to practical politics.

## Chapter 13   Economic policy

For coverage of the debate about the economic and political philosophy of new Labour, see Driver and Martell (1998) and Giddens (1998). Biographies of Gordon Brown provide insights into debates about power and personality. See Routledge (1998) and Pym and Kochan (1998). A combination of data and independent commentary on UK economic policy-making can be found in a number of Web sites: the influential National Institute of Economic and Social Research,

< http://www.niesr.ac.uk/ > and the Institute for Fiscal Studies, < http://www.ifs.org.uk >. Outside the UK see the OECD at < http://www.oecd.org/ >; and the IMF < http://www.imf.org >. Of the official Governmental sites see the Treasury at < http://www.hm-treasury.gov.uk > and the Cabinet Office < http://www.cabinet-office.gov.uk >. The Bank of England's site is of increasing value and importance: < http://www.bankofengland.co.uk >, as are European institutions such as the EU Council of Ministers for economic policy coordination, < http://ue.eu.int/emu/en/index.htm; >, the Commission itself, < http://www.europa.eu.int/comm/index_en.htm; >, and the European Central Bank < http://www.ecb.int/index.html >. Think tanks offer radical commentaries from left and right. See the Institute of Public Policy Research < http://www.ippr.org.uk/; >, the Fabian Society < http://www.fabian-society.org.uk/; >, the Institute of Economic Affairs < http://www.iea.org.uk/; >, and the Adam Smith Institute < http://www.adamsmith.org.uk/ >.

## Chapter 14    Welfare policy

Most early books on Labour's welfare policy are edited collections, comprising chapters on different aspects of policy. Driver and Martell (1998) set new Labour in the context of the Thatcher legacy. Jones and MacGregor (1998) look specifically at the 1997 election promises. Powell (1999) estimates the extent to which Labour's policy agenda constitutes a new future for welfare policy. Ellison and Pierson (1998) sets current policy debates in a broader context of social policy analysis. The Borrie Commission report (1994) is still worth examining as the precursor of much more recent new Labour policy development.

Government Web sites now provide an extensive and up-to-date source of information on policy development, and many government departments now place information on the Web. < http://www.open.gov.uk > is a general information service. Departmental sites are < http://www.doh.gov.uk >, < http://www.dfee.gov.uk >, < http://www.dss.gov.uk >, < http://www.detr.gov.uk >, < www.hm-treasury.gov.uk >. The Social Exclusion Unit can be found at < http://www.cabinet-office.gov.uk/seu/ . Local government information can be accessed through < http://www.lga.gov.uk >. Some useful research sites are < http://www.ifs.org.uk >, < http://www.iea.org.uk >, < http://www.ippr.org.uk >, < http://www.jrf.org.uk >, < http://www.psi.org.uk > and < http://www.essex.ac.uk >.

## Chapter 15    Environmental policy

Most introductory textbooks on British politics include a general chapter on the environment and there is an academic journal, *Environmental Politics*, dedicated to exploring the theory and *praxis* of modern environmentalism. There are, however, still surprisingly few good introductory texts on environmental policy and politics (but see Doyle and McEachern, 1998). O'Riordan (1999) is strong on the role of science in policy-making, while Carley and Christie (1992) provide a crisp introduction to sustainable development. Weale (1992), Gray (1995) and McCormick (1991) describe British environmental policy but are now somewhat dated. Lowe and Ward (1998) investigate the continuing Europeanization of British environmental policy, but currently the single most important international driver is UN climate change policy (O'Riordan and Jäger, 1996). The main government departments with environmental responsibilities have informative Web sites which allow you to access press releases and consultation documents: DETR < http://www.detr.gov.uk >; Treasury < http://www. hm-treasury.gov.uk >; DTI < http://www.dti.gov.uk >. The main environmental pressure groups also have extensive Web pages: Friends of the Earth < http:// www.foe.uk >; Greenpeace < http://www.greenpeace.uk >. There are numerous Web sites run by the EU institutions which can be accessed through the *Europa* gateway < http://europa.eu.int >. It is also worth checking out the UK Environment Agency for the latest developments in environmental regulation < http://www.environment-agency.gov.uk >.

## Chapter 16    Foreign and defence policy

A comprehensive source for contemporary British foreign policy documents is the Royal United Services Institute's, *Documents on British Foreign and Security Policy* (RUSI, 1998). A valuable online source of speeches and policy initiatives in the Foreign and Commonwealth Office Web site < http://www.fco.gov.uk >. A good treatment of the ethical issues in the Labour Government's foreign policy is Wheeler and Dunne (1998). For further information on Britain's defence and security relations with the US and Europe, see Schake, Bloch-Lainé and Grant (1999), Grant (1997) and Grant (1998). McInnes (1998) provides a useful overview of the SDR. The SDR document is online at < www.army.mod.uk >.

In terms of the issues discussed in the chapter, on the issue of poverty, the Government's Development White Paper *Elimination of World Poverty* (1997) is a good source. The UN Web site also has interesting information and links < http:// www.un.org/ >. For more on the *Jubilee 2000* campaign for debt relief and on the issue of debt relief see < http://www.newsunlimited.co.uk >. For more details on the Pinochet case, see Lagos and Muñoz, (1999) and Weller (1999). Most broadsheet newspaper Web sites will carry the latest news on the case. On the issue of landmines there are several good sources including an article by UN Secretary-General Boutros Boutros-Ghali (1994), and a ground-breaking book from Human Rights Watch (1993). A useful Web site on this is < http://www.oneworld.org/ guides/landmines/index.html >. For more on Iraq see the UNSCOM Web site < http://www.un.org/Depts/unscom/index.html >. On the background to the Kosovo crisis both Caplan (1999) and Judah (1999) are recommended.

## Chapter 17   Policy agendas in a multi-level polity

Different perspectives on governance are presented in Pierre (2000). See also Rosenau (1995) and Cerny (1991). For the impact of globalization on the viability of social democracy in British politics see Krieger (1999). For globalization, more generally see Held *et al.* (1999). Policy-making in the EU is covered extensively in Richardson (1996) and Wallace and Wallace (1996). Agency–structure issues are discussed by Hall and Taylor (1996) and Hay (1996). A good introduction to think tanks is Stone, Renham and Garnett (1998).

# Bibliography

Acheson, D. (1998) *Independent Inquiry into Inequalities in Health*, London, The Stationery Office.

Addison, P. (1994) *The Road to 1945*, London, Pimlico.

Advisory Group on Citizenship (1998) *Education for Citizenship and the Teaching of Democracy in Schools*. London, Qualifications and Curriculum Authority, September.

Alcock, P. (1997) *Understanding Poverty*, 2nd edn, London, Macmillan.

Almond, G. and Verba, S. (1963) *The Civic Culture: Political attitudes and democracy in five nations*, Princeton, Princeton University Press.

Anderson, C. and Kalthenthaler, K. (1996) 'The Dynamics of Public Opinion Toward European Integration, 1973–93', *European Journal of International Relations*, 2(2), pp. 175–99.

Andrews, G. (ed.) (1991) *Citizenship*, London, Lawrence & Wishart.

Andrews, L. (1999) *Wales Says Yes: The inside story of the Yes for the Wales referendum campaign*, Bridgend, Seren.

Atmosphere (Alliance to Make Oxford a Safer Place) (1999) *Crime and Disorder Strategy for Oxford 1999–2002*, Oxford, Oxford City Council.

Attwood, F. (1999) 'The Politics of Mourning', *New Formations*, 36, pp. 158–60.

Audit Commission (1999) *Listen Up! Effective Community Consultation*, London, Audit Commission.

Axelrod, R. (1970) *Conflict of Interest*, Chicago, Markham.

Bagehot, W. (1963) *The English Constitution*, London, C. A. Watt.

Baker, C. (1999) *The Human Rights Act: A practitioner's guide*, London, Sweet & Maxwell.

Baker, D., Gamble, A. and Seawright, D. (1998) 'Preliminary Report of the 1998 ESRC – Members of Parliament Project Survey of Westminster MPs on Europe', Manchester, Manchester Business School, unpublished mimeo.

Baldock, J. and Ungerson, C. (1994) *Becoming Consumers of Community Care: Households within the Mixed Economy of Welfare*, York, J. R. Foundation.

Bale, T. (1999) 'The Logic of No Alternative? Political scientists, historians and the politics of Labour's past', *British Journal of Politics and International Relations*, 1(2), pp. 192–204.

Bank of England (1997) 'Changes at the Bank of England', *Bank of England Quarterly Bulletin*, 37(3), pp. 241–7.

Barber, B. (1984) *Strong Democracy*, Berkeley, University of California Press.

Barker, A. (1998) 'The Labour Government's Policy "Reviews" and "Task Forces": An initial listing and analysis', *Essex Papers in Politics and Government*, 126.

Barnett, A. (Charter 88) (1997) 'Britain Needs a Written Constitution', < http://www.charter88.org.uk/pubs/ > .

Barnett, S. and Curry, A. (1994) *The Battle for the BBC*, London, Aurum.

317

Barnett, S. and Seymour, E. (1999) *A Shrinking Iceberg Travelling South: Changing trends in British television*, London, Campaign for Quality Television.

Bates, T. St J. (1997) *Devolution to Scotland: The Legal Aspects: Contemplating the imponderable*, Strathclyde, Centre for Policy and Legal Studies.

BBC (1999) *The BBC Beyond 2000* < www.bbc.co.uk/info/news/2000 > .

Beiner, R. (ed.) (1995) *Theorizing Citizenship*, Albany, State University of New York Press.

Bennie, L. (1998) 'Brent Spar, Atlantic Oil and Greenpeace', *Parliamentary Affairs*, 51(3), pp. 397–410.

Betts, C. (1999) 'Balanced on the Scales of Power', in *Assembly Handbook 1999*, Cardiff, *Western Mail*.

Birkinshaw, P. and Parry, N. (1999) 'Every Trick in the Book: The Freedom of Information Bill 1999', *European Human Rights Law Review*,4, pp. 373–90.

Blackburn, R. and Plant, R. (eds) (1998) *Constitutional Reform: The Labour Government's agenda*, London, Longman.

Blair, T. (1996a) *New Britain: My vision of a young country*, London, Fourth Estate.

Blair, T. (1996b) *Speech to the Green Alliance/ERM Seminar Series, Royal Society of Arts, London, 27 February 1996*, London, Labour Party.

Blair, T. (1998a) *Leading the Way: A new vision for local government*, London, Institute for Public Policy Research.

Blair, T. (1998b) *The Third Way: New politics for the new century, Fabian Pamphlet*, 588, London, Fabian Society.

Blair T. (1998c) 'Britain's Role in the EU and the Transatlantic Alliance', speech by Prime Minister Mr Tony Blair, to mark the 150th Anniversary of the Associated Press, London, 15 December, FCO Web site < http://www.fco.gov.uk > .

Blair T. (1999a) 'Facing the Modern Challenge: The Third Way in Britain and South Africa', Speech by Prime Minister Mr Tony Blair, The Parliament Building, Cape Town, South Africa. 8 January, FCO Web site < http://www.fco.gov.uk > .

Blair T. (1999b) 'Doctrine of the International Community', Speech by Prime Minister Mr Tony Blair, Economic Club of Chicago, 22 April, FCO Web site < http://www.fco.gov.uk > .

Blair T. (1999c) 'The Kosovo Conflict: A turning point for South Eastern Europe', Speech by Prime Minister Mr Tony Blair.

Blair, T. and Schröder, G. (1999) 'Europe: The Third Way/die Neue Mitte', Labour Party website < www.labour.org.uk > .

Blondel, J. (1968) 'Party Systems and Patterns of Government in Western Democracies', *Canadian Journal of Political Science*, 1, pp. 180–203.

Blondel, J., Sinnott, R. and Svensson, P. (1998) *People and Parliament in the European Union: Participation, democracy, and legitimacy*, Oxford, Oxford University Press.

Blumenthal, S. (1997) 'Along the Clinton–Blair Axis', *The Times*, 5 May.

Bobbio, N. (1996) *Left and Right. The significance of a political distinction*, Cambridge, Polity.

Bogdanor, V. (1999) *Devolution*, Oxford, Oxford University Press.

Bonham-Carter, J. (1997) 'The Liberal Democrats' Media Strategy', paper presented to conference assessing the 1997 election, University of Essex, September.

Borrie, Sir G. (1994) *Social Justice: Strategies for national renewal, The Report of the Commission on Social Justice*, London, Vintage.

Boutros Boutros-Ghali (1994) 'The Landmine Crisis', *Foreign Affairs*, September–October, pp. 8–13.

Bowers, P. and Dodd, T. (1998) 'Anti-Personnel Mines and the Policies of Two British Governments', Royal United Services Institute, *RUSI Journal*, 15, February.

Boyd, C. (1997) 'Parliament and the Courts: Powers and dispute resolution', in Bates, T. St J., *Devolution in Scotland*, pp. 21–35.

Braggins, J., McDonagh, M. and Barnard, A. (1993) *The American Presidential Election 1992 – What can Labour learn?*, London, Labour Party.

Brown, G. (1995) 'Foreword', in Crouch, C. and Marquand, D. (eds), *Reinventing Collective Action: From the global to the local*, Oxford, Blackwell.

Brown, G. (1999) 'Equality – Then and Now', in Leonard, D. (ed.), *Crosland and New Labour*, London, Macmillan.

Bruce G., MP (1998) 'Political Perspectives on the Outcomes of SDR: The House of Commons Defence Select Committee Report', *RUSI Journal*, October, pp. 26–30.

Bulpitt, J. (1983) *Territory and Power in the United Kingdom*, Manchester, Manchester University Press.

Burch, M. and Holliday, I. (1996) *The British Cabinet System*, Hemel Hempstead, Prentice Hall/Harvester Wheatsheaf.

Burch, M. and Holliday, I. (1999) 'An Executive Office in All But Name: The Prime Minister's and Cabinet offices in the UK', *Parliamentary Affairs*, 52, pp. 32–45.

Burchardt, T. and Hills, J. (1999) 'Public Expenditure and the Public/Private Mix', in Powell, M. (ed.), *New Labour, New Welfare State?*, Bristol, Policy Press, pp. 29–51.

Burchill, J. (1998) *Diana*, London, Weidenfeld & Nicolson.

Burns, A. (1999a) 'The Powers of the Parliament', in Hassan, G. (ed.), *A Guide to the Scottish Parliament*, Edinburgh, The Stationery Office.

Burns, A. (1999b) 'How the Parliament will Work', in Hassan, G. (ed.), *A Guide to the Scottish Parliament*, Edinburgh, The Stationery Office.

Burrows, N. (1999) 'Unfinished Business: The Scotland Act 1998', *Modern Law Review*, 62(2).

Butler, D. and Kavanagh, D. (1997) *The British General Election of 1997*, London, Macmillan.

Butler, D. and Stokes, D. (1970) *Political Change in Britain*, Harmondsworth, Penguin.

Butler, N. (1998) 'Disarmament Issues in the UK Parliament', *Disarmament Diplomacy*, October, pp. 15–17.

Bynoe, I. (1999) *Mainstreaming Human Rights in Whitehall and Westminster*, London, IPPR.

Cabinet Office (1987, 1995) *The Judge Over Your Shoulder*, London HMSO.

Cabinet Office (1991) *The Citizen's Charter: Raising the standard*. Cm 1599, London, HMSO.

Cabinet Office (1997) Freedom of Information Unit, *Your Right to Know: The Government's proposals for a Freedom of Information Act*, Cm 3818, London, The Stationery Office.

Cabinet Office (1998) Social Exclusion Unit, *Bringing Britain Together: A national strategy for neighbourhood renewal*, Cm 4045, London, The Stationery Office.

Cabinet Office (1999a) Better Regulation Task Force, *Anti-Discrimination Legislation Review*, London, Central Office of Information.

Cabinet Office, (1999b) *Modernizing Government*, Cmnd. 4310, London, The Stationery Office.

Campbell, B. (1998) *Diana Princess of Wales: How sexual politics shook the monarchy*, London, The Women's Press.

Campbell, C. (1999) 'The International Arms Trade', *Bulletin of Arms Control*, 33, March, pp. 1–8.

Caplan, R. (1998) 'International Diplomacy and the Crisis in Kosovo', *International Affairs*, 74(4), 745–61.

Cappella, J. and Jamieson, K. (1997) *The Spiral of Cynicism: The press and the public good*, Oxford, Oxford University Press.

Carley, M. and Christie, I. (1992) *Managing Sustainable Development*, London, Earthscan.

Catt, H. (1996) *Voting Behaviour: A radical critique*, London, Leicester University Press.

Cerny, P. (1991) *The Changing Architecture of Politics: Structure, agency, and the future of the state*, London, Sage.

Chalmers, M. (1999) 'Kosovo: The crisis and beyond', *Saferworld Report*, London, Saferworld, May.

Christopherson, R. (1999) 'Off Message but on Record', *The Guardian*, August 20.

Citizenship Foundation (1997) *Citizenship and Civic Education: Colloquium on Education and Citizenship – A presentation of the findings of a comparative research programme into aspects of citizenship in Britain and the United States carried out by Professors Ivor Crewe, Donald Searing and Pamela Conover*, London, Citizenship Foundation.

Clarke, M. (1997) *Renewing Citizenship and Democracy*, Birmingham, Institute for Citizenship Studies and School of Public Policy.

Cm 4183 (1999) *Modernising Parliament: Reforming the House of Lords*, London, The Stationery Office.

Cm.4413 (1999) *The Funding of Political Parties in the UK: The Government's proposals for legislation in response to the Fifth Report of the Committee on Standards in Public Life*, London, The Stationery Office.

Cockett, R. (1994a) 'The Party, Publicity and the Media', in Seldon, A. and Ball, S. (eds), *Conservative Century: The Conservative Party since 1900*, Oxford, Oxford University Press, pp. 547–77.

Cockett, R. (1994b) *Thinking the Unthinkable*, London, HarperCollins.

Cohen, J. (1989) 'Deliberation and Democratic Legitimacy', in Hamlin, A. and Pettit, P. (eds), *The Good Polity* Oxford, Blackwell.

Cohen, J. (1999) 'Democracy and Liberty', in Elster, J. (ed.), *Deliberative Democracy*, Cambridge, Cambridge University Press.

Colomer, J. (2001) *Political Institutions: Democracy and Social Choice*, Oxford, Oxford University Press.

Committee on Standards in Public Life (1995), *First Report of the Committee on Standards in Public Life*, 2 vols [Nolan Report], Cm 2850, London, HMSO.

Conover, P. J., Crewe, I. and Searing, D. (1991) 'The Nature of Citizenship in the United States and Great Britain: Empirical comments on theoretical themes', *Journal of Politics*, 53, pp. 800–32.

Conservative Party (1998) *Fresh Future*, London, Conservative Party.

Conservative Party (1999) *Listening to Britain*, London, Conservative Party.

Cook, R. (1997) 'British Foreign Policy', 12 May 1997, FCO Web site.

Coote, A. (1999) 'Labour's Love's Lost on Worcester Woman', *Fabian Review*, Summer.

Corbett, R., Jacobs, F. and Shackleton, M. (1995) *The European Parliament*, 3rd edn, London, Catermill.

Cowley, P. (1999) 'The Absence of War? New Labour in Parliament', in Fisher, J., Cowley, P., Denver, D. and Russell, A., (eds), *British Elections and Parties Review*, 9, London, Frank Cass.

Cowley, P. (2000) 'The Marginalisation of Parliament?', *Talking Politics*, forthcoming.

Cowley, P. and Norton, P. (1996) *Are Conservative MPs Revolting?*, Hull, Centre for Legislative Studies.

Cowley, P. and Stuart, M. (2000) 'Daleks or Deviants? The Parliamentary Labour Party', *Politics Review*, forthcoming.

Craig, P. and Walters, M. (1999) 'The Courts, Devolution and Judicial Review', *Public Law*, pp. 274–303.

Crewe, I. and Thomson, K. (1999) 'Party Loyalties: Realignment or dealignment?', in Evans, G. and Norris, P. (eds), *Critical Elections*, pp. 64–85.

Crewe, I., Sarlvik, B. and Alt, J. (1977) 'Partisan dealignment in Britain 1964–74', *British Journal of Political Science*, 7, pp. 129–90.

Crick, B. and Millar, D. (1995) 'To Make the Parliament of Scotland a Model for Democracy', Edinburgh, John Wheatley Centre.

CSG (1999) *Report of the Consultative Steering Group on the Scottish Parliament*, Edinburgh, The Stationery Office.

Curran, J. and Seaton, J. (1997) *Power without Responsibility: The press and broadcasting in Britain*, Washington, DC, Congressional Quarterly.

Currie, D. (1997) *The Pros and Cons of EMU*, London, HM Treasury.

Curtice, J. and Semetko, H. (1994) 'Does it Matter what the Papers Say?', in Heath, A., Curtice, J. and Jowell, R. (eds), *Labour's Last Chance?. The 1992 election and beyond*, Aldershot, Darmouth.

Dalyell, T. (1977) *Devolution: The end of Britain?*, London, Jonathan Cape.

Daniel, C. (1997) 'May the Taskforce be with you', *New Statesman*, 1 August, pp. 27–31.

Davies, J. (1999) 'Princess: Diana, Femininity and the Royal', *New Formations*, 36.

Davies, R. (1999) *Devolution: A process not an event*, Cardiff, Institute of Welsh Affairs.

Davis, D. (1999) 'Blair's Brave New Britain is a Catastrophe', *The Times*, 5 August.

De Grauwe, P. (1997) *The Economics of Monetary Integration*, 3rd edn, Oxford, Oxford University Press.

de Smith, S. A. and Brazier, R. (1994) *Constitutional and Adminstrative Law*, 7th edn, Harmondsworth, Penguin.

Delhousse, R. (1998) *The European Court of Justice: The politics of judicial integration*, London, Macmillan.

Denham, A. (1996) *Think-Tanks of the New Right*, Aldershot, Dartmouth.

Denman, R. (1996) *Missed Chances: Britain and Europe in the twentieth century*, London, Cassell.

Denver, D., Fisher, J., Cowley, P. and Pattie, C. (eds) (1998) *British Elections and Parties Review 9: The 1997 General Election*, London, Frank Cass.

Department for Education and Employment (DfEE) (1997a) *Excellence in Schools*, Cm 3681, London, The Stationery Office, July.

Department for Education and Employment (1997b) *Millennium Volunteers Consultation Document* < http://www.dfee.gov.uk/millen/ > , October.

Department for Media, Culture and Sport (DCMS) (1999) 'Building a Global Audience: British television in overseas markets', A Report by David Graham and Associates, London, DCMS.

Department of Health (DoH) (1997) *The New National Health Service: Modern, dependable*, London, The Stationery Office.

Department of Health (DoH) (1998a) *Modernizing Social Services: Promoting independence, improving protection, raising standards*, Cm 4169, London, The Stationery Office.

Department of Health (DoH) (1998b) *Our Healthier Nation*, London, The Stationery Office.

Department of Social Security (DSS) (1998a) *A New Contract for Welfare: New ambitions for our country*, Cm 3805, London, The Stationery Office.

Department of Social Security (DSS) (1998b) *A New Contract for Welfare: Partnership in pensions*, Cm 4179, London, The Stationery Office.

Department of Social Security (DSS) (1999) *Opportunity for All: Tackling poverty and social exclusion*, London, The Stationery Office.

Department of the Environment, Transport and the Regions (DETR) (1998a) *Modernizing Local Government: Improving local services through best value*, London, The Stationery Office.

Department of the Environment, Transport and the Regions (DETR) (1998a): *Modernising Local Government: A new ethical framework*. consultation paper < http://www.local.detr.gov.uk/sponsor/ethical.htm > .

Department of the Environment Transport and the Regions (DETR) (1998b) *Local Leadership, Local Choice*, London, DETR.

Department of the Environment, Transport and the Regions (DETR) (1998c) *Modern Local Government: In touch with the people*, Cm 4014, London, DETR.

Department of the Environment, Transport and the Regions (DETR) (1998e) *Guidance on Local Transport Plans*, < http://www.local-transport.detr.gov.uk/ltp9811/08.htm > , November.

Department of the Environment, Transport and the Regions (DETR) (1998f) *Sustainability Counts: Headline indicators*, London, DETR.

Department of the Environment, Transport and the Regions (DETR) (1998g) *A New Deal for Transport: Better for everyone*, London, The Stationery Office.

Department of the Environment, Transport and the Regions (DETR) (1999a) *Modernising Local Government: Local democracy and community leadership* consultation paper, March, London, DETR.

Department of the Environment, Transport and the Regions (DETR) (1999b) *Modern Local Government. In touch with the people*, London, HMSO.

Department of the Environment, Transport and the Regions (DETR) (1999c) *A Better Quality of Life: A strategy for sustainable development in the UK*, Cm 4345, London, The Stationery Office.

DfEE (1999) *Review of the National Curriculum in England: The Secretary of State's proposals and consultation materials*, London Qualifications and Curriculum Authority.

DfEE and Qualifications and Curriculum Authority (1999) *Citizenship: The National Curriculum for England*, London, HMSO.

DfID (1997) *The Elimination of World Poverty: A challenge for the twenty first century* (British Government Development White Paper, November).

Dinan, D. (1999) *Ever Closer Union? An introduction to the European Community*, 2nd edn, London, Macmillan.

Doherty, B. (1998) 'Opposition to Road Building', *Parliamentary Affairs*, 51(3), pp. 371–83.

Doherty, B. (1999) 'Paving the Way: The rise of direct action against road-building and the changing character of British environmentalism', *Political Studies*, 47, pp. 275–91.

Downs, A. (1957) *An Economic Theory of Democracy*, New York: Harper & Row.

Downs, A. (1972) 'Up and Down With Ecology: The issue–attention cycle', *The Public Interest*, 28, pp. 38–50.

Doyle, T. and McEachern, D. (1998) *Environment and Politics*, London, Routledge.

Draper, D. (1997) *Blair's Hundred Days*, London, Faber & Faber.

Driver, S. and Martell, L. (1998) *New Labour. Politics after Thatcherism*, Cambridge, Polity.

Dudley, G. and Richardson, J. (1996) 'Why Does Policy Change over Time? Adversarial policy communities, alternative policy arenas and British trunk roads policy, 1945–1995', *Journal of European Public Policy*, 3(1), pp. 63–83.

Dudley, G. and Richardson, J. (1998) 'Arenas without Rules and the Policy Change Process: Outsider groups and British roads policy', *Political Studies*, 46, pp. 727–47.

Dummett, A. (1999) 'Citizenship and National Identity', in Hazell, R. (ed.), *Constitutional Futures*, pp. 213–29.

Dunleavy, P. (1991) *Democracy, Bureaucracy, and Public Choice*, Hemel Hempstead, Harvester Wheatsheaf.

Dunleavy, P. (1996) 'Political Behaviour: Institutional and experiential approaches', in R. Goodin and H.D. Klingemann (eds), *A New Handbook of Political Science*, Oxford, Oxford University Press, pp. 276-93.

Dunleavy, P. and Jones, G.W. (1993) 'Leaders, Politics and Institutional Change: The decline of prime ministerial accountability to the House of Commons, 1968–1990', *British Journal of Political Science*, 23(3).

Dunleavy, P., Jones, G. W. and O'Leary, B. (1990) 'Prime Ministers and the Commons: Patterns of behaviour, 1868 to 1987', *Public Administration*, 68, pp. 123–40.

Dunleavy, P. and Margetts, H. (1998a) *Report to the Government Office for London, Electing the London Mayor and Assembly*, London, LSE Public Policy Group.

Dunleavy, P. and Margetts, H. (1998b) 'The Preference Structure of British Voters for Political Parties in the 1990s', paper presented to the UK Political Studies Association Conference, University of Keele, 7–9 April 1998.

Dunleavy, P. and Margetts, H. (1999a) 'Mixed Electoral Systems in Britain and the Jenkins Commission on Electoral Reform', *British Journal of Politics and International Relations*, 1(1), pp. 12–38

Dunleavy, P. and Margetts, H. (1999b) 'From Majoritarian to Pluralist Democracy? Electoral reform in Britain since 1997', paper presented to the American Political Science Association Conference, Atlanta.

Dunleavy, P., Margetts, H., O'Duffy, B. and Weir, S. (1997) *Making Votes Count: Replaying the 1990s General Election under Alternative Electoral Systems*, Colchester, Democratic Audit, University of Essex, *Democratic Audit Paper*, 12.

Dunleavy, P., Margetts, H. and Weir, S. (1998a) *Making Votes Count 2: Mixed electoral systems*, Colchester, Democratic Audit, University of Essex, April 1998, *Democratic Audit Paper*, 14.

Dunleavy, P., Margetts, H. and Weir, S. (1998b) *The Politico's Guide to Electoral Reform in Britain*, London, Politicos.

Dunleavy, P. and Rhodes, R. A. W. (1990) 'Core Executive Studies in Britain', *Public Administration* 68, pp. 3–28.

Dunleavy, P. and Weir, S. (1998) *New Statesman*.

Dunleavy, P. and Weir, S. with Subrahmanyam, G. (1995) 'Sleaze in Britain: Media influences, public responses and constitutional significance', *Parliamentary Affairs*, 48 (4), pp. 602–16.

Duverger, M. (1954) *Political Parties: Their organisation and activity in the modern state*, London, Methuen.

Dyke, G. (1999) 'My Vision for the BBC', *Spectator*, 20 November, pp. 22–4.

Easton, D. (1965) *A Framework for Political Analysis*, Englewood Cliffs, Prentice-Hall.

Easton, D. (1975) 'A Reassessment of the Concept of Political Support', *British Journal of Political Science*, 5, pp. 435–57.

*Economist* (1998a) 'Ex-dictators are not Immune', 28 November, pp. 15–16.

*Economist* (1998b) 'Chile and Pinochet – Indignant up to a point', 28 November 1998, p. 80.

*Economist* (1999a) 'A New Corporatism', 14 August, pp. 48–50.

*Economist* (1999b) 'The Cafetière Theory of Government', 21 August, pp. 47–9.

Edmonds, T. (1999) 'The Monetary Policy Committee: Theory and performance', *House of Commons Library Research Paper*, 99/17, London, House of Commons.

Edwards, G. and Spence, D. (eds) (1997) *The European Commission*, 2nd edn, London, Catermill.

Egan, D. (1999) *Irvine: Politically correct?*, London, Mainstream.

Eijk, C. van der and Franklin, M. (eds) (1996) *Choosing Europe? The European electorate and national politics in the face of union*, Ann Arbor, University of Michigan Press.

Ellison, N. (1994) *Egalitarian Thought and Labour Politics: Retreating visions*, London, Routledge.

Ellison, N. and Pierson, C. (eds) (1998) *Developments in British Social Policy*, London, Macmillan.

ENDS (Environmental Data Services) (1994) 'Advancing the Sustainable Development Agenda', *ENDS Report*, 228, London, ENDS, pp. 18–24.

ENDS (Environmental Data Services) (1997) 'Government's Fresh Attempt at Greening of Whitehall', *ENDS Report*, 271, London, ENDS, pp. 3–4.

ENDS (Environmental Data Services) (1998a) 'Ministers Unveil Plans to Dampen Unease Over GM Crops', *ENDS Report*, 285, London, ENDS, pp. 34–5.

ENDS (Environmental Data Services) (1998b) 'Shades of Grey in Prescott's "New Dawn" For Transport', *ENDS Report*, 282, London, ENDS, pp. 21–4.

ENDS (Environmental Data Services) (1998c) 'Environment Takes a Back Seat in Government's Energy Review', *ENDS Report*, 281, London, ENDS, pp. 30–32.

ENDS (Environmental Data Services) (1998d) 'Battle Backs Off-shore Wind as Row Brews on 10% Renewables Target', *ENDS Report*, 284, London, ENDS, pp. 7–8.

ENDS (Environmental Data Services) Daily (1998e) 'EU Presidency Push For More Policy Integration', *ENDS Daily*, 19 February, London, ENDS.

ENDS (Environmental Data Services) Daily (1999) 'Environmental Concerns "Less Immediate" – Poll', *ENDS Daily*, 22 October 1999, London, ENDS.

EOS Gallup (1998) *The European Union: "A View from the Top" – Top decision makers and the European Union*, Brussels, EOS Gallup Europe.

Esping Andersen, G. (ed.) (1996) *Welfare States in Transition: National adaptations in global economics*, London, Sage.

Evans, B. and Taylor, A. (1996) *From Salisbury to Major. Continuity and change in Conservative politics*, Manchester, Manchester University Press.

Evans, G and Norris, P. (eds) (1999) *Critical Elections: British parties and voters in long-term perspective*, London, Sage.

Evans, M. (1997) 'Political Participation', in Dunleavy, P., Gamble, A., Holliday, I. and Peele, G. (eds), *Developments in British Politics 5*, London, Macmillan.

Ewing, K. and Gearty, C. A. (1990) *Freedom Under Thatcher: Civil liberties in modern Britain*, Oxford, Oxford University Press.

Farrell, D. (1996) *Electoral Systems: A Comparative Introduction*, Basingstoke and New York, Palgrave.

Field, F. (1995) *Making Welfare Work: Reconstructing welfare for the millennium*, London, Institute of Community Studies.

Field, F. (1996) *Stakeholder Welfare*, London, Institute of Economic Affairs.

Fielding, S. (1993) '"White Heat" and White Collars: The impact of "Wilsonism"', in Coopey, R., Fielding, S. and Tiratsoo, N. (eds), *The Wilson Governments, 1964–1970*, London, Pinter.

Fielding, S. (1999) *Labour: Decline and Renewal*, 2nd, edn, Tisbury, Baseline.

Fielding, S. (2000) 'Labour and its Past', in Tanner, D., Thane, P. and Tiratsoo, N. (eds), *A Centenary History of the Labour Party*, Cambridge, Cambridge University Press.

Fielding, S. and Tonge, J. (1998) 'Economic and Industrial Policy', in Kelly, R. (ed.), *Changing Party Policy in Britain: An introduction*, Oxford, Blackwell.

Finer, S. (1958) 'Transport Interests and the Road Lobby', *Political Quarterly*, 1, pp. 47–58.

Finer, S. (1980) *The Changing British Party System, 1945–1979*, Washington, DC, American Enterprise Institute.

Finlay, A. (n.d.) 'The Human Rights Act: The LCD's preparations for implementation', *European Human Rights Law Review*, 5, pp. 512–18.

Finlayson, A. (1999) 'Third Way Theory', *Political Quarterly*, 70(3), pp. 271–9.

Fisher, J. (1996) *British Political Parties*, Hemel Hempstead, Prentice Hall.

Foley, M. (1998) *The Politics of the British Constitution*, Manchester, Manchester University Press.

Foley, M. and Edwards, B. (1999) 'Is it Time to Disinvest in Social Capital?', *Journal of Public Policy*, 19(2), pp. 141–73.

Foote, G. (1997) *The Labour Party's Political Thought*, London, Macmillan.

Franklin, B. (1994) *Packaging Politics*, London, Edward Arnold.

Franklin, M., Marsh, M. and McLaren, L. (1994) 'Uncorking the Bottle: Popular opposition to European unification in the wake of Maastricht', *Journal of Common Market Studies*, 32(4), pp. 101–17.

Frazer, E. J. (1999) *Problems of Communitarian Politics: Unity and conflict*, Oxford, Oxford University Press.

Frazer, E. J. (2000a) 'Probably the Most Public Occasion the World has ever Known': Public and private in press coverage of the death and funeral of Diana, Princess of Wales, *Journal of Political Ideologies*, forthcoming.

Frazer, E. J. (2000b) 'Citizenship Education: Anti-political culture and political education in Britain', *Political Studies*, 48.

Freeden, M. (1996) *Ideologies and Political Theory: A conceptual approach*, Oxford, Oxford University Press.

Fukuyama, F. (1992) *The End of History and the Last Man*, London, Hamish Hamilton.

Gabel, M. (1998a) *Interests and Integration: Market liberalization, public opinion, and European union*, Ann Arbor, University of Michigan Press.

Gabel, M. (1998b) 'Public Support for European Integration: An empirical test of five theories', *Journal of Politics*, 60(2), pp. 333–54.

Gabel, M. and Whitten, G. (1997) 'Economic Conditions, Economic Perceptions, and Public Support for European Integration', *Political Behaviour*, 19(1), pp. 81–96.

Galbraith, J. K. (1992) *The Culture of Contentment*, London, Sinclair Stevenson.

Gamble, A. (1990) 'Theories of British Politics', *Political Studies*, 30, pp. 404–20.

Garner, R. and Kelly, R. (1998) *British Political Parties Today*, 2nd edn, Manchester, Manchester University Press.

Gay, O. (1998) *The Scotland Bill: Devolution and Scotland's Parliament*, London, House of Commons.

Geddes, A. (1999) *Britain in the European Union*, 2nd edn, Tisbury, Baseline.

George, S. (1998) *An Awkward Partner: Britain in the European Community*, 3rd edn, Oxford, Oxford University Press.

Gibb, F. (1999a) 'Judges Fight Back against Challenges by Lawyers', *The Times* 6 September.

Gibb, F. (1999b) 'Top Judge Says US-style Vetting Will Harm Bench', *The Times*, 18 October.

Giddens, A. (1994) *Beyond Left and Right. The future of radical politics*, Cambridge, Polity.

Giddens, A. (1998) *The Third Way. The renewal of social democracy*, Cambridge, Polity.

Gilbert, J., Glover, D., Kaplan, C., Bournal Taylor, J. and Wheeler, W. (eds) (1999) *Diana and Democracy*, London, Lawrence & Wishart.

Goddard, P., Scammell, M. and Semetko, H. (1998) 'Too Much of a Good Thing? Television in the 1997 election campaign', in Crewe, I., Gosschalk, B. and Bartle, J. (eds), *Why Labour Won the General Election of 1997*, London, Frank Cass, pp. 149–75.

Gould, P. (1998) *The Unfinished Revolution: How the modernisers saved the Labour Party*, London, Little, Brown.

Grant, C. (1998) *Can Britain Lead in Europe?* London, Centre for European Reform.

Grant, R.P. (1997) 'Transatlantic Armament Relations under Strain', *Survival*, 39(1).

Gray, J. (1997) *Endgames: Questions in late modern political thought*, Cambridge, Polity.

Gray, J. and John Osmond, J. (1997) *Wales in Europe: The opportunity presented by a Welsh Assembly*, Cardiiff, Institute of Welsh Affairs.

Gray, J. and Willetts, D. (1997) *Is Conservatism Dead?*, London, Profile.

Gray, T. (ed.) (1995) *British Environmental Policy in the 1990s*, London, Macmillan.

Greenwood, J. (1997) *Representing Interests in the European Union*, London, Macmillan.

Griffiths, J.A.G. (1977) *The Politics of the Judiciary*, Manchester, Manchester University Press.

Hague, W. (1999) 'Strengthening the Union after Devolution', speech to the Centre for Policy Studies, 15 July.

Hahn, C. (1998) *Becoming Political: Comparative perspectives on citizenship education*, Albany, State of University of New York Press.

Hall, P. and Taylor, R. (1996) 'Political Science and the Three New Institutionalisms', *Political Studies*, 44(5), pp. 926–57.

Hall, P.A. (1999) 'Social Capital in Britain', *British Journal of Political Science*, 29(3), pp. 417–61.

Hall, S. (1998a) 'The Great Moving Nowhere Show', *Marxism Today*, November–December.

Hall, S. (1998b) 'Aspiration and Attitude . . . Reflections on Black Britain in the nineties', *New Formations*, 33, pp. 38–46.

Hall, S. and Jacques, M. (eds) (1990) *New Times. The changing face of politics in the 1990s*, London, Lawrence & Wishart.

Hansard Society (1993) *Making the Law*, London, The Hansard Society.

Hansard Society (n.d.) 'Education for Democratic Citizenship: A commission of enquiry into the causes, consequences and solutions to political disaffection amongst young people in the UK today', (proposal document), London, The Hansard Society.

Harris, R. (1989) *The Conservative Community: The roots of Thatcherism – and its future*, London, Centre for Policy Studies.

Harrison, B. (1996) *The Transformation of British Politics, 1860–1995*, Oxford, Oxford University Press.

Hart, R. (1994) *Seducing America*, New York: Oxford University Press.

Hassan, G. (ed.) (1998a) *A Guide to the Scottish Parliament*, Edinburgh, The Stationery Office.

Hawthorn, G. (1999) 'Pinochet: The Politics', *International Affairs*, 75(2), pp. 253–8.

Hay, C. (1996) *Restating Social and Political Change*, Buckingham, Open University.

Hay, C. (1999) *The Political Economy of New Labour*, Manchester, Manchester University Press.

Hayes-Renshaw, F. and Wallace, H. (1997) *The Council of Ministers*, London, Macmillan.

Hazell, R. (1999) 'Westminster: Squeezed from Above and Below', in Hazell, R. (ed.), *Constitutional Futures*, pp. 111–35.

Hazell, R. (ed.) (1999) *Constitutional Futures: A history of the next ten years*, Oxford, Oxford University Press for the Constitution Unit.

HC 185 (1999) *The Procedural Consequences of Devolution: Fourth Report from the Select Committee on Procedure.*

HC 190 (1997) *The Legislative Process: First Report from the Select Committee on the Modernization of the House of Commons.*

HC 194 (1999) *Sittings of the House in Westminster Hall: Second Report from the Select Committee on the Modernization of the House of Commons.*

HC 60 (1998) *The Parliamentary Calendar: Initial Proposals: First Report from the Select Committee on the Modernization of the House of Commons.*

HC 791 (1998) *The Scrutiny of European Business: Seventh Report from the Select Committee on the Modernization of the House of Commons.*

Heater, D. (1990) *Citizenship: The civic ideal in world history, politics and education*, London, Longman.

Heath, A. and McDonald, S. (1988) 'The Demise of Party Identification Theory?', *Electoral Studies*, 7 (2), pp. 95–107.

Heath, A., Jowell, R., Curtice, J., Evans, G., Field, J. and Witherspoon, S. (1991) *Understanding Political Change*, Oxford, Pergamon.

Heffernan, R. (2000) *New Labour and Thatcherism*, London, Macmillan.

Held, D. (1995) *Democracy and the Global Order: From the modern state to cosmopolitan governance*, Cambridge, Polity.

Held, D., McGrew, A., Goldblatt, D. and Perraton, J. (1999) *Global Transformations: Politics, economics and culture*, Cambridge, Polity.

Henley Centre (1999) *Media Futures*, London, Henley Centre.

Hennessy, P. (1986) *Cabinet*, Oxford, Blackwell.

Hennessy, P. (1998) 'The Blair Style of Government: An historical perspective and an interim audit', *Government and Opposition*, 33, pp. 3–20.

Herbst, S. (1998) *Reading Public Opinion: How political actors view the democratic process*, Chicago, University of Chicago Press.

Heywood, A. (1997) *Politics*, London, Macmillan, p. 247.

Hill, J. and Jordan, A. (1994) 'The Greening of Government: Lessons from the White Paper process', *ECOS*, 14(3–4), pp. 3–9.

Hill, K. and Hughes, J. (1998) *Cyberpolitics: Citizen activism in the age of the internet*, Baltimore, Rowman & Littlefield.

Himsworth, C. M. G and Munro, C. R. (1998) *Devolution and the Scotland Bill*, Edinburgh, W. Green.

Himsworth, C. M. G and Munro, C.R. (1999) *The Scotland Act 1998*, Edinburgh, W. Green/Sweet & Maxwell.

Hirst, P. and Thompson, G. (1996) *Globalization in Question*, Cambridge, Polity.

Hix, S. (1994) 'The Study of the European Community: The challenge to European Politics', *West European Politics*, 17(1), pp. 1–29.

Hix, S. (1999a) 'Dimensions and Alignments in European Union Politics: Cognitive constraints and partisan responses', *European Journal of Political Research*, 35(1), pp. 69–101.

Hix, S. (1999b) *The Political System of the European Union*, London, Macmillan.

Hix, S. and Lord, C. (1997) *Political Parties in the European Union*, London, Macmillan.

HM Government (1994) *Sustainable Development: The UK strategy*, Cm. 2426, London, HMSO.

Hobsbawm, E. (1995) *Age of Extremes: The short twentieth century, 1914–1991*, London, Abacus.

Hobsbawm, E. (1998) 'The Death of Neo-Liberalism', *Marxism Today*, November–December.

Holbrooke, R. (1999) 'No Media – No War', *Index on Censorship*, 3, pp. 20–1.

Holliday, I. (1999) 'Territorial Politics', in Holliday, I. Gamble, A. and Parry, G. (eds), *Fundamentals in British Politics*, London, Macmillan, pp. 119–41.

Holme, R. and Holmes, A. (1998) 'Sausages or Policeman? The role of the Liberal Democrats in the 1997 general election campaign', in Crewe, I., Bartle, J. and Gosschalk, B. (eds), *Political Communications: Why Labour won the general election of 1997*, London, Frank Cass.

Home Affairs Select Committee (1999) *The Working of the Lord Chancellors' Department*, HC882–I, 8 December.

Home Office (1997a) *Rights Brought Home: The Human Rights Bill*, Cm 3782 < http://www.official-documents.co.uk/document/hoffice/rights/ > , October.

Home Office (1997b) *Racial Violence and Harassment: A consultation document* < http://www.homeoffice.gov.uk/rvah.htm > , September.

Home Office (1998a) *The Crime and Disorder Act: Introductory guide.* < http:// www.homeoffice.gov.uk/cdact/cdainf25.htm > .

Home Office (1998b) *Fairer, Faster and Firmer – A modern approach to immigration and asylum*, Cm 4018, London, The Stationery Office, July.

Home Office (1999a) *The Stephen Lawrence Inquiry: Report of an Inquiry by Sir William Macpherson of Cluny*, Cm 4262–1, London, The Stationery Office, February.

Home Office (1999b) *Stephen Lawrence Inquiry: Home Secretary's action plan*, London, Home Office, March.

Home Office (1999c) *Freedom of Information: Consultation on draft legislation*, Cm 4355, London, Home Office, May.

Hood, C. (1998) *The Art of the State: Culture, rhetoric and public management*, Oxford, Oxford University Press.

Hood, C. and Scott, C. (1996) 'Bureaucratic Regulation and New Public Management in the UK: Mirror image developments?', *Journal of Law and Society* 23, pp. 332–45.

Hooghe, L. and Marks, G. (1998) 'The Making of a Polity: The struggle over European integration', in Kitschelt, H., Lange, P., Marks, G. and Stephens, J. (eds), *The Politics and Political Economy of Advanced Industrial Societies*, Cambridge, Cambridge University Press.

Hooton, E. R. (1998) 'Britain's Strategic Defence Review: Smiles all round', *Military Technology*, 22(6), pp. 32–6.

Hope, J. A. D. (1998) *Working with the Scottish Parliament: Judicial aspects of devolution*, Edinburgh, David Hume Institute.

Hornung, R. (1999) 'How Consensus Politics will be Structured', in *Assembly Handbook 1999*, Cardiff, *Western Mail*.

Horsman, M. (1999) 'Dyke's Dilemma', *Guardian* (Media), 28 June.

Hotelling, H. (1929) 'Stability in Competition', *The Economic Journal*, 39 (1), pp. 41–57.

House of Commons (1998) *The Scotland Bill: Some operational aspects of devolution*, Research Paper, 98/2.

House of Lords (1997) *Debates*, 3 November.

Howarth, H., Kenway, P., Palmer, G. and Miorelli, R. (1999) *Monitoring Poverty and Social Exclusion 1999* (New Policy Institute), London, Rowntree Foundation.

Hughes, C. and Wintour, P. (1990) *Labour Rebuilt: The new model party*, London, Fourth Estate.

Human Rights Watch and Physicians for Human Rights (1993) *Land Mines: A deadly legacy*, Washington, DC, Human Rights Watch.

Humphrys, J. (1999) 'What the Devil's Advocate Really Said', *Guardian* (Media), 30 August.

Huq, R. (1998) 'Currying Favour? Race and diaspora in a new Britain', in Coddington, A. and Perryman, M. (eds), *The Moderniser's Dilemma: The radical politics in the age of Blair*, London, Lawrence & Wishart.

Hurd, D. (1989) 'Freedom will Flourish where Citizens accept Responsibility', *Independent*, 13 September.

Hutton, W. (1995) *The State We're In*, London, Jonathon Cape.

Ingle, S. (1996) 'Party Organisation', in MacIver, D. (ed.), *The Liberal Democrats*, Hemel Hempstead, Prentice-Hall, pp. 113–33.

Inglehart, R. (1977) 'Long Term Trends in Mass Support for European Unification', *Government and Opposition*, 12(2), pp. 150–77.

Inglehart, R. (1991) 'Trust Between Nations: Primordial ties, societal learning and economic development', in Reif, K. and Inglehart, R. (eds), *Eurobarometer: The dynamics of European public opinion – Essays in honour of Jacques-René Rabier*, London, Macmillan.

International Institute of Strategic Studies (1998) *Strategic Survey 1997/98*, London, Oxford University Press.

Irvine, Lord (1999) 'Activism and Restraint: Human rights and the interpretative process', *European Human Rights Law Review*, Issue 4, pp. 350–72.

James, M. (1998) 'The Assembly at Work', in Osmond, J. (ed.), *The National Assembly Agenda*, Cardiff, Institute of Welsh Affairs.

James, S. (1999) *British Cabinet Government*, 2nd edn, London, Routledge.

*Jane's Defence Weekly* (1998) 'UK Boosts Defence Exports', 29(11), 18 March.

Jefferys, K. (1991) *The Churchill Coalition and Wartime Politics*, Manchester, Manchester University Press.

Jenkins, R. (1998) *The Chancellors*, London, Macmillan.

Jessop, R. (1995) 'The Regulation Approach and Governance Theory: Alternative perspectives on economic and political change', *Economy and Society*, 24(3), pp. 307–33.

Jessop, R. (1999) 'Governance Failure', in Stoker, G. (ed.), *The New Politics of British Local Governance*, London, Macmillan.

Johnston, R. *et al.* (1999) 'New Labour's Landslide and Electoral Bias: An exploration of the differences between the 1997 UK general election result and the previous thirteen', in Fisher, J., Cowley, P., Denver, D. and Russell, A. (eds), *British Elections and Parties Review 9*, London, Cass, pp. 20–45.

Johnston, R. J., Pattie, C. and Fieldhouse, E. (1994) 'The Geography of Voting and Representation: Regions and the declining importance of the cube law', in Heath, A., Jowell, R. and Curtice, R. (eds), *Labour's Last Chance? The 1992 election and beyond*, Aldershot, Dartmouth, pp. 255–74.

Jones, H. and MacGregor, S. (eds) (1998) *Social Issues and Party Politics*, London, Routledge.

Jones, J. B. (1998) 'The Committees', in Osmond, J. (ed.), *The National Assembly Agenda*, Cardiff, Institute of Welsh Affairs.

Jones, N. (1999) *Sultans of Spin: The media and the new Labour government*, London, Victor Gollancz.

Jordan, A. J. (1998a) 'The Impact on UK Environmental Administration', in Lowe, P. and Ward, S. (eds), *British Environmental Policy and Europe: Politics and policy in transition*, London, Routledge.

Jordan, A. J. (1998b) 'Step Change or Stasis? EC environmental policy after the Amsterdam Treaty', *Environmental Politics*, 7(1), pp. 227–36.

Jordan, A. J. (1999) 'EU Water Policy Standards: Locked in or watered down?', *Journal of Common Market Studies*, 37(1), pp. 13–37.

Jordan, A. J. (ed.) (1999) 'EU Environmental Policy at 25', *Environment and Planning C (Government and Policy)*, 17(1), pp. 1–112.

Jordan, A. J. and Voisey, H. (1998) 'The "Rio Process": The politics and substantive outcomes of "Earth Summit II"', *Global Environmental Change*, 8(1), pp. 93–7.

Jordan, W. (1998) *The New Politics of Welfare: Social justice in a global context*, London, Sage.

Judah, T. (1999) 'Kosovo's Road to War', *Survival*, 41(2), pp. 5–18.

Judge, D. (1993) *The Parliamentary State*, London, Sage.

Judge, D. (1999) 'Capital Punishment: Burke and Dicey meet the European Convention on Human Rights', *Public Law*, Spring.

Judge, D., Stoker, G. and Wolman, H. (1995) 'Urban Politics and Theory: An introduction', in Judge, D., Stoker, G. and Wolman, H., *Theories of Urban Politics*, London, Sage, pp. 1–13.

Katz, R. S. and Mair, P. (1995) 'Changing Models of Party Organization and Party Democracy: The emergence of the cartel party', *Party Politics*, 1, pp. 5–28.

Kaul, I., Grunberg, I. and Stern, M. (eds) (1999) *Global Public Goods: International cooperation in the twenty first century*, New York, Oxford University Press.

Kavanagh, D. (1987) *Thatcherism and British Politics. The end of consensus?* Oxford, Oxford University Press.

Kavanagh, D. (1995) *Election Campaigning: The new marketing of politics*, Oxford, Basil Blackwell.

Keane, J. (1988) *Democracy and Civil Society*, London, Verso.

Kegley, C. and Wittkopf, E. (1997) *World Politics: Trend and transformation*, New York, St Martins Press.

Kellas, J. G. (1998) *The Politics of Nationalism and Ethnicity*, revised edn, London, Macmillan.

Kelly, R. N. (1989) *Conservative Party Conferences: The hidden system*, Manchester, Manchester University Press.

Kelly, R. N. (1994) 'Power and Leadership in the Major Parties', in Robins, L., Blackmore, H. and Pyper, R. (eds), *Britain's Changing Party System*, Leicester, Leicester University Press, pp. 26–56.

Kerr, P. (2000) *From Conflict to Consensus: The evolution of post-war British politics 1945–1997*, London, Routledge.

King, A. (1998) 'Why Labour Won – At last', in King, A. (ed.), *New Labour Triumphs: Britain at the polls*, Chatham, NJ, Chatham House.

King, M. (1999) 'The MPC Two Years On', Lecture given at Queen's University, Belfast, May.

Kirchheimer, O. (1966) 'The Transformation of Western European Party Systems', in LaPalombara, J. and Weiner, M. (eds), *Political Parties and Political Development*, Princeton: Princeton University Press, pp. 177–200.

Klein, R. (1995) *The New Politics of the NHS*, 3rd edn, Harlow, Longman.

Kogan, M. and Kogan, D. (1982) *The Battle For The Labour Party*, London, Fontana.

Kohler C., Koch, B. and Knodt, M. (1997) 'Multi-Level Governance: The joy of theorizing and the anguish of empirical research', paper presented at the ECPR Joint Sessions of Workshops, Berne, 27 February–4 March.

Kooiman, J. (1993) 'Social–Political Governance: Introduction', in Kooiman, J. (ed.), *Modern Governance*, London, Sage, pp. 1–9.

Kooiman, J. and Van Vliet, M. (1993) 'Governance and Public Management', in Eliassen, K. and Kooiman, J. (eds), *Managing Public Organisations*, 2nd edn, London, Sage.

Krieger, J. (1999) *British Politics in the Global Age: Can social democracy survive?*, Cambridge, Polity.

Kymlicka, W. (1995) *Multicultural Citizenship: A liberal theory of minority rights*, Oxford, Clarendon Press.

Kymlicka, W. (ed.) (1995) *The Rights of Minority Cultures*, Oxford, Oxford University Press.

Labour Party (1994) *In Trust for Tomorrow*, London, Labour Party.

Labour Party (1997) *Labour into Power: A framework for partnership*, London, Labour Party.

Labour Research (1999) 'Judging the Judges', *Labour Research*, 88(6).

Laffan, B. (1997) *The Finances of the European Union*, London, Macmillan.

Lagos, R. and Muñoz, H. (1999) 'The Pinochet Dilemma', *Foreign Policy*, 114, pp. 26–39.

Laver, M. and Schofield, N. (1990) *Multiparty Government*, Oxford, Oxford University Press.

Laver, M., Rallings, C. and Thrasher, M. (1987) 'Coalition Theory and Local Government Coalition Payoffs in Britain', *British Journal of Political Science*, 17(4).

Lazorowicz, M. (1998) *New Scotland, New Europe: Working with the expanding European Union*, Edinburgh, Centre for Scottish Public Policy.

Leadbeater, C. (1999) *Living on Thin Air: The new economy*, Harmondsworth, Viking.

Lee, J.M., Jones, G.W. and Burnham, S. (1998) *At the Centre of Whitehall: Advising the Prime Minister and Cabinet*, London, Macmillan.

Lélé, S. (1991) 'Sustainable Development: A critical review', *World Development*, 19(6), pp. 610–23.

Letwin, O. and Marenbon, J. (1999) 'Conservative Debates', *Politeia Policy Debates*, 16.

Levitas, R. (1998) *The Inclusive Society? Social exclusion and New Labour*, London, Macmillan.

Lindberg, L. and Scheingold, S. (1970) *Europe's Would-Be Polity: Patterns of change in the European Community*, Cambridge, MA, Harvard University Press.

Lindblom, C. (1977) *Politics and Markets*, New York, Basic Books.

Lipow, A. and Seyd, P. (1996) 'The Politics of Anti-partyism', *Parliamentary Affairs*, 49, pp. 273–84.

Lister, R. (1998) *Citizenship: A feminist perspective* London, Macmillan.

Lloyd, J. (1999) 'Falling Out: Intellectuals and new Labour', *Prospect*, October.

Loney, M. (1983) *Community Against Government: The British community development project 1968–78*, London, Heinemann.

Longley, L.D. (1996) 'Parliaments as Changing Institutions and as Agents of Regime Change: Evolving perspectives and a new research framework', *Journal of Legislative Studies*, 2(2).

Lord Chancellor's Department (1996a) *Access to Justice: Final Report to the Lord Chancellor on the Civil Justice System in England and Wales* [Woolf report], London, HMSO.

Lord Chancellor's Department (1996b) *Striking the Balance: The future of legal aid in England and Wales*, Cm 3305, London, HMSO.

Lord Chancellor's Department (1999) *Departmental Report 1999–2002*, Cm 4206, London, HMSO.

Loveland, I. (1999) 'The Government of London', *Political Quarterly*, 70(1).

Lowe, P. and Ward, S. (eds) (1998) *British Environmental Policy and Europe: Politics and policy in transition*, London, Routledge.

Lowi, T. (1972) 'Four Systems of Policy, Politics and Choice', *Public Administration Review*, 32, pp. 298–310.

*Lustig-Prean and Becket* v. *UK* Judgment 27 September 1999.

*M.* v. *Home Office* (1992) QB.

Mac an Ghaill, M. (1999) *Contemporary Racisms and Ethnicities*, Milton Keynes, Open University Press.

MacArthur, B. (1999) 'I Know What the People Want', *The Times* (Media), 30 April.

MacLeod, J., Kosicki, G. and MacLeod, D. (1994) 'Expanding the Boundaries of Political Communication Effects', in Bryant, J. and Zillmann, D., *Media Effects: Advances in theory and research*, London, Lawrence Erlbaum, pp. 123–62.

Mair, P. (1994) Party Organizations: From civil society to state', in Katz, R. S. and Mair, P. (eds), *How Parties Organize: Change and adaptation in party organizations in western democracies*, London, Sage, pp. 1–2.

Mair, P. (1995) 'Political Parties, Popular Legitimacy and Public Privilege', *West European Politics*, 18, pp. 40–57.

Majone, G. (1996) *Regulating Europe*, London, Routledge.

Malleson, K. (1999) *The New Judiciary: The effects of expansionism and activism*, Aldershot, Dartmouth.

Margetts, H. (1998) *Information Technology in Government*, London, Routledge.

Marks, G., Hooghe, L. and Blank, K. (1995) 'European Integration since the 1980s: State-centric versus multi-level governance', paper presented at the American Political Science Association Meeting, Chicago, 31 August–3 September.

Marquand, D. (1998a) *Must Labour Win?*, London, Fabian Society.

Marquand, D. (1998b) 'The Blair Paradox', *Prospect*, May, pp. 19–24.

Marsh, D. and Rhodes, R. A. W. (eds) (1992) *Policy Networks in British Government*, Oxford, Clarendon Press.

Marsh, D., Buller, J., Hay, C., Johnston, J., Kerr, P., McAnulla, S. and Watson, M. (1999) *Postwar British Politics in Perspective*, Cambridge, Polity.

Marsh, M. and Norris, P. (eds) (1997) 'Special Issue: Political representation in the European Parliament', *European Journal of Political Research*, 32(2), pp. 153–289.

Marshall, T. H. (1950) *Citizenship and Social Class*, Cambridge, Cambridge University Press.

May, J. D. (1973) 'Opinion Structure of Political Parties: The special law of curvilinear disparity', *Political Studies*, 21, pp. 135–51.

Mazey, S. and Richardson, J. J. (eds) (1993) *Lobbying in the European Community*, Oxford, Oxford University Press.

McChesney, R. (1998) 'Media Convergence and Globalisation', in Thissu, D. (ed.), *Electronic Empires*, London, Arnold.

McCormick, J. (1991) *British Politics and the Environment*, London, Earthscan.

McCormick, J. (1999) *Understanding the European Union: A concise introduction*, London, Macmillan.

McInnes, C. (1998) 'Labour's Strategic Defence Review', *International Affairs*, 74(4), pp. 823–45.

McKenzie, R. T. (1955) *Political Parties*, London, Heinemann.

McLean, I. (1987) *Public Choice*, Oxford, Blackwell.

Means, R. and Smith, R. (1998) *Community Care*, 2nd edn, London, Macmillan.

Mellors, C. (1989) 'Non-majority British Local Authorities in a Majority Setting', in Mellors, C. and Pijenburg, B. (eds), *Political Parties and Coalitions in European Local Government*, London, Routledge.

Miller, W. (1991) *Media and Voters: The audience, content and influence of the press and television in the 1987 general election*, Oxford, Clarendon Press.

Miller, W. L. (1998) 'The Periphery and its Paradoxes', in Berrington, H. (ed.), *Britain in the Nineties*, London, Frank Cass.

Ministry of Defence (1998) *Modern Forces for a Modern World*, London, MOD.

Ministry of Defence (MoD) (1998) *The Strategic Defence Review: Modern forces for a modern world*, Cm 3999, London, (can be found at < www. army.mod.uk > .

MORI Polls and Surveys (1998) A poll on 15 September 1998 for Nat West and the Institute of Citizenship (at http://www.mori.co.uk).

MORI (1999) Press release for the People's Panel, 29 January.

Mulgan, G. (1994) *Politics in an Antipolitical Age*, Cambridge, Polity.

Mulgan, G. (1998) 'Whinge and a Prayer', *Marxism Today*, November–December, pp. 15–16.

Mulgan, G. (ed.) (1997) *Life After Politics. New thinking for the twenty-first century*, London, Fontana.

Murie, A. (1997) 'The Social Rented Sector, Housing and the Welfare State in the UK', *Housing Studies*, 12, pp. 437–61.

Nairn, T. (1977) *The Break-Up of Britain: Crisis and neo-nationalism*, London, New Left Books.

National Audit Office (NAO) (1999) *Government on the Web*, London, HMSO.

Neill, Lord (1998) *Report of the Committee on Standards in Public Life on the Funding of Political Parties in the UK*, 1, CM 4057–1, London, The Stationery Office.

Neill, P. (1995) *The European Court of Justice: A study in judicial activism*, London, European Policy Forum.

*New Scientist* (1993) 'Wheels Steer Green Policies', *New Scientist*, 31 July, p. 3.

Newton, K. (1999) 'Mass Media Effects: Mobilization or media malaise', *British Journal of Political Science*, 29, pp. 577–95.

Norris, P. (1995) 'May's Law of Curvilinear Disparity Revisited: Leaders, officers, members and voters in British political parties', *Party Politics*, 1, pp. 29–47.

Norris, P. (1997a) 'Anatomy of a Labour Landslide', in Norris, P. and Gavin, N. (eds), *Britain Votes 1997*, Oxford, Oxford University Press.

Norris, P. (1997b) 'Are We All Green Now?', *Government and Opposition*, 32(3), pp. 320–39.

Norris, P. (1998) 'New Politicians? Changes in party competition at Westminster', in Evans, G. and Norris, P. (eds), *British Parties and Voters in Long-term Perspective*, pp. 22–430.

Norris, P. (ed.) (1997) 'The 1997 General Election', Special Issue of *Parliamentary Affairs*, 50(4).

Norris, P., Curtice, J., Sanders, D., Scammell, M. and Semetko, H. (1999) *On Message: Communicating the campaign*, London, Sage.

Norton, P. (1980) *Dissension in the House of Commons 1974–1979*, Oxford, Oxford University Press.

Norton, P. (ed.) (1990) *Legislatures*, Oxford, Oxford University Press.

Norton, P. (1993) *Does Parliament Matter?*, Hemel Hempstead, Harvester Wheatsheaf.

Norton, P. (1996) 'Philosophy: The principles of Conservatism', in Norton, P. (ed.), *The Conservative Party*, London, Prentice Hall.

Norton, P. (1999) 'Parliament in Transition', in Pyper, R. (ed.), *British Government under Blair*, London, Macmillan.

Norton, P. and Wood, D. (1993) *Back from Westminster*, Lexington, KY, Kentucky University Press.

Nugent, N. (1999) *The Government and Politics of the European Union*, 4th edn, London, Macmillan.

O'Riordan, T. (1999) *Environmental Science for Environmental Management*, 2nd edn, London, Longman.

O'Riordan, T. and Jäger, J. (eds) (1996) *Politics of Climate Change*, London, Routledge.

O'Riordan, T. and Rowbotham, E. (1996) 'Struggling for Credibility: The UK's response', in O'Riordan, T. and Jäger, J. (eds), *Politics of Climate Change*, London, Routledge.

O'Shaughnessy, N. (1990) *The Phenomenon of Political Marketing*, London, Macmillan.

Oborne, P. (1999) *Alastair Campbell: New Labour and the rise of the media class*, London, Aurum.

Ohmae, K. (1995) *The End of the Nation State*, New York, Free Press.

Oliver, D. and Heater, D. (1994) *The Foundations of Citizenship*, Hemel Hempstead, Harvester Wheatsheaf.

Oppenheim, C. (ed.) (1998) *An Inclusive Society*, London, Institute for Public Policy Research.

Osmond, J. (ed.) (1998) *The National Assembly Agenda*, Cardiff, Institute of Welsh Affairs.

Outhwaite, W. and Wheeler, M. (1999) *The Civil Practitioners Guide to the Human Rights Act 1998*, Oxford, Oxford University Press.

Page, E. (2000) *Governing By Numbers*, forthcoming.

Panebianco, A. (1988) *Political Parties: Organisation and power* Cambridge, Cambridge University Press.

Parry, G., Moyser, G. and Day, N. (1992) *Political Participation and Democracy in Britain*, Cambridge, Cambridge University Press.

Patterson, T. (1993) *Out of Order*, New York: Vintage.

Peach, L. (1999) *Independent Scrutiny of the Appointment Processes of Judges and Queens Counsel*, London, HMSO.

Pearce, D. W. (1998) 'Cost-Benefit Analysis and Environmental Policy', *Oxford Review of Economic Policy*, 14(4), pp. 84–100.

*Pepper* v. *Hart* (1993) 1AER.

Peters, B. G. (1998) 'Managing Horizontal Government: The politics of co-ordination', *Public Administration*, 76, pp. 295–311.

Peters, B. G. (2000) 'Governance and Comparative Politics', in Pierre, J. (ed.), *Debating Governance*, Oxford, Oxford University Press.

Peters, G. (1986) *American Public Policy: Promise and performance*, Chatham, NJ, Chatham House.

Peters, G. (1996) 'Agenda Setting in the European Union', in Wallace, H. and Wallace, W., *Policy-Making in the European Union*, 3rd edn, Oxford, Oxford University Press.

Peterson, J. (1999) 'Sovereignty and Interdependence', in Holliday, I. Gamble, A. and Parry, G. (eds) *Fundamentals in British Politics*, London, Macmillan.

Peterson, J. and Bomberg, E. (1999) *Decision-Making in the European Union*, London, Macmillan.

Pfaller, A., Gough, I. and Therborn, G. (1991) *Can the Welfare State Compete?*, London, Macmillan.

Piening, C. (1997) *Global Europe: The European Union in world affairs*, Boulder, CO, Lynne Rienner.

Pierre, J. (ed.) (2000) *Debating Governance*, Oxford, Oxford University Press.

Pierre, J. and Peters, B. G. (2000) *Governance, Politics and the State*, London, Macmillan.

Pimlott, B. (1988) 'The Myth of Consensus', in Smith, L. (ed.), *The Making of Britain: Echoes of greatness*, London, Macmillan.

Plant, R. (1988) *Citizenship, Rights and Socialism*, London, Fabian Society.

Powell, M. (ed.) (1999) *New Labour, New Welfare State?*, Bristol, Policy Press.

Power, A. (1997) *Estates on the Edge*, London, Macmillan.

Przeworski, A. and Sprague, J. (1986) *Paper Stones: A history of electoral socialism*. Chicago, Chicago University Press.

Putnam, R. (1993) *Making Democracy Work: Civic traditions in modern Italy*, Princeton, Princeton University Press.

Putnam, R. (1995) 'Tuning In, Tuning Out: The strange disappearance of social capital in America', *PS: Political science and politics*, 28, pp. 664–83.

Puttnam, D. (1999) 'Time for Local Heroes', *Guardian* (Media), 28 June.

Pym, H. and Kochan, N. (1998) *Gordon Brown: The first year in power*, London.

*R.* v. *Bow Street Metropolitan Stipendiary Magistrates and others ex parte Pinochet Ugarte (No. 2)* (1999) 1 AER.

*R.* v. *Secretary of State for Transport ex parte Factortame* (1991) 1 AC 603.

Rae, D. W., Hanby, V. and Loosemore, J. (1971) 'Thresholds of Representation and Thresholds of Exclusion: An analytic note on electoral systems', *Comparative Political Studies*, 3, pp. 479–88.

Rallings, C. and Thrasher, M. (1998) 'Split-ticket Voting at the 1997 British General and Local Elections – An aggregate analysis', in D. Denver *et al.* (eds), *British Elections and Parties Review, 8: The 1997 General Election*, London, Cass, pp. 111–34.

Rallings, C. and Thrasher, M. (1999a) 'Jockeying for PR Position', *LGC*, 9 July.

Rallings, C. and Thrasher, M. (1999b) *New Britain: New elections*, London, Vacher Dod Publishing.

Rawcliffe, P. (1998) *Swimming with the Tide*, Manchester, Manchester University Press.

RCEP (Royal Commission on Environmental Pollution) (1994) *Transport and the Environment*, Cm 2674, London, HMSO.

Redwood, J. (1999) *The Death of Britain?*, London, Macmillan.

Reif, K. and Schmitt, H. (1980) 'Nine Second-Order National Elections: A conceptual framework for the analysis of European Election results', *European Journal of Political Research*, 8(1), pp. 3–45.

Rentoul, J. (1995) *Tony Blair*, London, Little, Brown.

Rhodes, R. A. W. (1986) *The National World of Local Government*, London, Allen & Unwin.

Rhodes, R. A. W. (1988) *Beyond Westminster and Whitehall: The sub-central government of Britain*, London, Allen & Unwin.

Rhodes, R. A. W. (1996) 'The New Governance: Governing without government', *Political Studies*, 44, pp. 652–67.

Rhodes, R. A. W. (1997) 'From Marketization to Diplomacy: It's the mix that matters', *Public Policy and Administration*, 12(2), pp. 31–50.

Rhodes, R. A. W. (1997a) *Understanding Governance*, Buckingham, Open University Press.

Rhodes, R. A. W. and Dunleavy, P. (eds) (1995) *Prime Minister, Cabinet and Core Executive*, London, Macmillan.

Richard, I. (1999) *Unfinished Business: Reforming the House of Lords*, London, Vintage.

Richardson, J. (ed.) (1996) *European Union: Power and policy-making*, London, Routledge.

Richardson, J. and Jordan, G. (1979) *Governing Under Pressure: The policy process in a post-parliamentary state*, Oxford, Martin Robinson.

Riddell, P. (1998) 'Members and Millbank: The media and parliament', in Seaton, J. (ed.), *Politics and the Media: Harlots and prerogatives at the turn of the millennium*, Oxford, Blackwell, pp. 8–18.

Riker, W. (1962) *The Theory of Political Coalitions*, New Haven, CT, Yale University Press.

Robertson, D. (1998) *Judicial Discretion in the House of Lords*, Oxford, Oxford University Press.

Robins, J. (1999) 'BBC: Barren, banal and confused', *Independent on Sunday*, 15 August.

Roche, M. (1992) *Rethinking Citizenship: Welfare, ideology and change in modern society*, Cambridge, Polity Press.

Roker, D., Player, K. and Coleman, J. (1999) 'Young People's Voluntary and Campaigning Activities as Sources of Political Education', *Oxford Review of Education*, 25, pp. 185–98.

Room, G. (ed.) (1995) *Beyond the Threshold: The measurement and analysis of social exclusion*, Bristol, Policy Press.

Rose, R. (1967) *Influencing Voters: A study of campaign rationality*, London, Faber & Faber.

Rose, R. (1984) *Do Parties Make a Difference?*, London, Macmillan.

Rose, R. and McAllister, I. (1986) *Voters Begin to Choose: From closed class to open elections in Britain*, London, Sage.

Rosenau, J. (1992) 'Governance, Order and Change in World Politics', in Rosenau, J. and Czempiel, E.-O. (eds), *Governance without Government: Order and change in world politics*, Cambridge, Cambridge University Press, pp. 1–30.

Rosenau, R. (1995) 'Governance in the Twenty-First Century', *Global Governance*, 1, pp. 13–43.

Rosenbaum, M. (1997) *From Soapbox to Soundbite: Party political campaigning in Britain since 1945*, London, Macmillan.

Routledge, P. (1998) *Gordon Brown: The biography*, London, Simon & Schuster.

Routledge, P. (1999) *Mandy: The unauthorised biography of Peter Mandelson*, London, Simon & Schuster.

Rowe, M. (2001) 'In focus', *Politics Review*, 11(2), p. 34.

Royal Commission on the Reform of the House of Lords (2000) *A House for the Future*, London, The Stationery Office, Cm 4534.

Royal United Services Institute (RUSI) (1998) *Documents on British Foreign and Security Policy, Volume 1: 1994–1997*, London, RUSI.

Rozenberg, J. (1995) *The Search for Justice*: An anatomy of the law, London, Spectre.

Sanders, D. (1997) 'Voting and the Electorate', in Dunleavy, P., Gamble, A., Holliday, I. and Peele, G. (eds), *Developments in British Politics 5*, London, Macmillan, pp. 45–74.

Sanderson, I. (1999) 'Participation and Democratic Renewal: From "instrumental" to "communicative" rationality?', *Policy and Politics*, 27(3), pp. 325–45.

Sarlvik, B. and Crewe, I. (1983) *Decade of Dealignment*, Cambridge, Cambridge University Press.

Sassoon, D. (1997) *One Hundred Years of Socialism. The West European left in the twentieth century*, London, Fontana.

Scammell, M. (1995) *Designer Politics: How elections are won*, London, Macmillan.

Scammell, M. (1999) 'Political Marketing: Lessons for political science', *Political Studies*, 47, pp. 718–39.

Scammell, M. and Harrop, M. (1997) 'The Press', in Butler, D. and Kavanagh, D. (eds), *The British General Election of 1997*, London, Macmillan, pp. 156–85.

Scarman, L. (1992) *Why Britain Needs a Written Constitution*, London, Charter 88.

Scarrow, S. E. (1996) *Parties and their Members*, Oxford, Oxford University Press.

Schake, K., Bloch-Lainé, A. and Grant, C. (1999) 'Building a European Defence Capability', *Survival*, 41(1), pp. 20–40.

Schattschneider, E. (1960) *The Semi-Sovereign People: A realist's view of democracy in America*, New York, Holt.

Schlesinger, P. (1998) 'Scottish Devolution and the Media', in Seaton, J. (ed.), *Politics and the Media: Harlots and prerogatives at the turn of the millennium*, Oxford, Blackwell, pp. 55–74.

Scott, R. (1996) *Inquiry into the Export of Defence Equipment and Dual Use Goods to Iraq and Related Prosecutions*, London, HMSO.

Scully, R. (1997) 'The European Parliament and the Co-Decision Procedure: A reassessment', *Journal of Legislative Studies*, 3(3).

Searle, G. (1995) *Country Before Party*, London, Longman.

Seaton, J. (ed.) (1998) *Politics and the Media: Harlots and prerogatives at the turn of the millennium*, Oxford, Blackwell.

Seyd, P. (1998) 'Tony Blair and New Labour', in King, A. (ed.), *New Labour Triumphs: Britain at the polls*, Chatham, NJ: Chatham House, pp. 49–73.

Seyd, P. (1999) 'New Parties/New Politics? A Case Study of the British Labour Party', devaluing the activists', *Party Politics 5*, pp. 383–405.

Seyd, P. and Whiteley, P. (1992) *Labour's Grassroots: The politics of party membership*, Oxford, Clarendon Press.

Seymour-Ure, C. (1998) *Harlots Revisited: Media barons and the new politics*, Iain Walker Memorial Lecture, Green College, University of Oxford.

Sharp, J. (1999) 'Anglo–American Relations and Crisis in Yugoslavia', Institut Français des Relations Internationales, *Les Notes de l'IFRI*, 9, Paris, IFRI.

Shaw, E. (1994) *The Labour Party since 1979: Crisis and transformation*, London, Routledge.

Shaw, M. (1998) 'Legislative Committees', in Kurian, G. T. (ed.), *World Encyclopedia of Parliaments and Legislatures*, Washington, DC, Congressional Quarterly, 2.

Shephard, M. (1998) 'The European Parliament: Crawling, walking, and running', in Norton, P. (ed.), *Parliaments and Governments in Western Europe*, London, Frank Cass.

Shephard, M. (1999) 'The European Parliament: Getting the house in order', in Norton, P. (ed.), *Parliaments and Pressure Groups in Western Europe*, London, Frank Cass.

Silk, P. (1998) 'The Assembly as a Legislature', in Osmond, J. (ed.), *The National Assembly Agenda*.

Silk, P. and Walters, R. (1998) *How Parliament Works*, 4th edn, London, Longman.

Slynn, G. (1992) *Introducing a European Legal Order*, London, Stevens, Sweet & Maxwell.

*Smith and Grady* v. UK Judgment 27 September 1999.

Smith, A. (1997) 'Studying Multi-Level Governance: Examples from French translations of the structural funds', *Public Administration*, 75 pp. 711–29.

Smith, G. and Wales, C. (1999) 'The Theory and Practice of Citzens' Juries', *Policy and Politics*, 27(3), pp. 295–308.

Smith, J. (1999) *Europe's Elected Parliament*, Sheffield, Sheffield Academic Press.

Smith, M. (1999) *The Core Executive in Britain*, London, Macmillan.

Smith, T. (1998) *Re-casting Citizenship: From apathy and alienation to active participation*, Thirteenth T. H. Marshall Memorial Lecture, University of Southampton, 23 February.

Spear, J. (1992) 'The Labour Party and Foreign Policy', in Smith, M. J. and Spear, J. (eds), *The Changing Labour Party*, London, Routledge, pp. 185–200.

Spender, I. R. G. (1997) *British Immigration Policy since 1939: The making of multiracial Britain*, London, Routledge.

*Spending Review: New Public Spending Plans 1999–2002*, Cm 4011, London, The Stationery Office.

Stephens, P. (1996) *Politics and the Pound*, London, Macmillan.

Stewart, J. (1996a) 'A Dogma of our Times – the separation of policy-making and implementation', *Public Policy and Management*, July–September, pp. 1–8.

Stewart, J. (1996b) 'Democracy and Local Government', in Hirst, P. and Khilnani, S. (eds) (1996) *Reinventing Democracy*, Oxford, Blackwell.

Stoker, G. (1998) 'Governance as Theory: Five propositions', *International Social Science Journal*.

Stoker, G. (2000) 'The Urban Political Science and the Challenge of Governance', in Pierre, J. (ed.), *Debating Governance*, Oxford, Oxford University Press.

Stoker, G. (ed.) (1999a) *The New Management of British Local Governance*, London, Macmillan.

Stoker, G. (ed.) (1999b) *The New Politics of British Local Governance*, London, Macmillan.

Stone, D., Denham, A. and Garnett, M. (1998) *Think Tanks across Nations: A strategy report 1998*, Cm 3978, London, The Stationery Office, June.

Sutherland, Sir S. (1999) *With Respect to Old Age: Long-term care – rights and responsibilities*, Cm 4192, London, The Stationery Office.

Svennevig, M. (1999) *Television Across the Years: The British public's view*, London, ITC.

Swanson, D. and Mancini, P. (eds) (1996) *Politics, Media and Modern Democracy*, Westport, Connecticut, Praeger.

Tam, H. (1998) *Communitarianism: A new agenda for politics and citizenship*, London, Macmillan.

Taylor, C. (1992) in Guttman, A. (ed.), *Multiculturalism and the Politics of Recognition*, Princeton, Princeton University Press.

Taylor, I. MP (1999) *Releasing the Community Spirit: A framework for the active citizen*, Cambridge, Tory Reform Group.

Taylor, M. and Cruddas, J. (1999) *New Labour, New Links*, London, Unions 21.

Taylor, M. and Laver, M. (1973) 'Government Coalitions in Western Europe', *European Journal of Political Research*, 1(3).

Thain, C. and Wright, M. (1995) *The Treasury and Whitehall: The planning and control of public expenditure, 1976–1993*, Oxford, Clarendon Press.

Theakston, K. (1997) 'New Labour, New Whitehall?', *Public Policy and Administration*, 13, pp. 13–34.

Travers, A. (1998) 'The Freedom to be more Unequal', *New Statesman* 26 June, xii–xiii.

Treasury (1997) *UK Membership of the Single Currency: An assessment of five economic tests*, London, HM Treasury.

Treasury (1998a) *Stability and Investment for the Long Term: Economic and fiscal*.

Treasury (1998b) *Modern Public Services for Britain: Investing in reform*.

Treasury (1998c) *Code for Fiscal Stability*, London, HM Treasury.

Treasury (1998d) *Outline National Changeover Plan*, London, HM Treasury.

Treasury (1998e) *Modern Public Services for Britain: Investing in reform (Comprehensive Spending Review)*, Cm 4011, London, The Stationery Office.

Treasury (1999a) *Building a Stronger Economic Future for Britain: Economic and fiscal strategy report and financial statement and budget report March 1999*, HC 298, London, The Stationery Office.

Treasury (1999b) *The New Monetary Policy Framework*, London, HM Treasury.

Treasury (1999c) *The Modernisation of Britain's Tax and Benefit System, Number Four: Tackling poverty and extending opportunity*, London, HM Treasury.

Tsebelis, G. and Garrett, G. (1997) 'Agenda Setting, Vetoes and the European Union's Co-Decision Procedure', *The Journal of Legislative Studies*, 3(3).

Turner, B. S. (1990) 'Outline of a Theory of Citizenship', *Sociology*, 24, pp. 189–217.

Verba, S., Lehman Schlozman, K. and Brady, H. E. (1995) *Voice and Equality: Civic voluntarism in American politics*, Cambridge, MA, Harvard University Press.

Vibert, F. (1999) 'British Constitutional Reform and the Relationship with Europe', in Hazell, R. (ed.), *Constitutional Futures*.

von Neumann, J. and Morgenstern, O. (1947) *Theories of Games and Economic Behavior*, 2nd edn, Princeton, Princeton University Press.

Wallace, H. (1996) 'Politics and Policy in the EU: The challenge of governance', in Wallace, H. and Wallace, H. (eds), *Policy-Making*.

Wallace, H. and Wallace, W. (eds) (1996) *Policy-Making in the European Union*, 3rd edn, Oxford, Oxford University Press.

Wallace, W. (1996) 'Government without Statehood', in Wallace, H. and Wallace, W. (eds), *Policy-Making*.

Wallace, W. and Smith, J. (1995) 'Democracy or Technocracy: European integration and the problem of popular consent', in J. Hayward (ed.), *The Crisis of Representation in Europe*, London, Frank Cass.

Ward S. and Gibson R. (1998) 'The First Internet Election', in Crewe, I., Gosschalk, B. and Bartle, J. (eds), *Political Communications: Why Labour won the general election of 1997*, London, Frank Cass.

Watts, C. (1999) 'Unworkable Feeling: Diana, death and feminisation', *New Formations*, 36, pp. 34–46.

WCED (World Commission on Environment and Development) (1987) *Our Common Future*, Oxford, Oxford University Press.

Weale, A. (1992) *The New Politics of Pollution*, Manchester, Manchester University Press.

Webb, P. D. (1992a) *Trade Unions and the British Electorate*, Aldershot: Dartmouth.

Webb, P. D. (1992b) 'Election Campaigning, Organisational Transformation and the Professionalisation of the British Labour Party', *European Journal of Political Research*, 21, pp. 267–88.

Webb, P. D. (1994) 'Party Organizational Change in Britain: The iron law of centralization?', in Katz, R. S. and Mair, P. (eds), *How Parties Organize: Change and adaptation in Western democracies*, London, Sage, pp. 109–33.

Webb, P. D. (1995) 'Are British Parties in Decline?', *Party Politics*, 1(3), pp. 299–322.

Webb, P. D. (2000) *The Modern British Party System*, London, Sage.

Weiss, L. (1998) *The Myth of the Powerless State: Governing the economy in a global era*, Cambridge, Polity.

Weller, M. (1999) 'On the Hazards of Foreign Travel for Dictators and Other International Criminals', *International Affairs*, 75(3), pp. 599–617.

Westlake, M. (1994) *A Modern Guide to the European Parliament*, London, Pinter.

Westlake, M. (1998) 'The European Parliament', in Kurian, G. T. (ed.), *World Encyclopedia of Parliaments and Legislatures*, 2 Washington, DC, *Congressional Quarterly*.

Wheeler, N. J. and Dunne, T. (1998) 'Good International Citizenship: A third way for British foreign policy', *International Affairs*, 74, 847–70.

Whiteley, P., Seyd, P. and Richardson, J. (1994) *True Blues: The politics of Conservative party membership*, Oxford, Clarendon Press.

Wilkins, C. (1999) 'Making "Good Citizens": The social and political attitudes of PGCE students', *Oxford Review of Education*, 25, pp. 217–30.

Wilkinson, H. and Mulgan, G. (1995) *Freedom's Children*, London, Demos.

Willetts, D. (1992) *Modern Conservatism*, Harmondsworth, Penguin.

Willetts, D. (1997) 'Conservative Renewal', *Political Quarterly*, 69(2), pp. 110–17.

Wolstenholme, I. (1999) 'Watching over Whitehall: Is the Public Accounts Committee successful?', unpublished undergraduate dissertation, Hull, University of Hull.

Wring, D. (1996a) 'From Mass Propaganda to Political Marketing', in Rallings, C., Farrell, D., Denver, D. and Broughton D. (eds), *British Elections and Parties Yearbook 1995*, London, Frank Cass, pp. 105–24.

Wring, D. (1996b) 'Political Marketing and Party Development in Britain', *European Journal of Marketing*, 30, pp. 100–11.

Young, I. M. (1990) *Justice and the Politics of Difference*, Princeton, Princeton University Press.

Younge, G. (1999) 'The Death of Stephen Lawrence: The Macpherson Report', *Political Quarterly*, 70, pp. 329–34.

# Index

344